GIANT BASIC SKILLS™
K-1 WORKBOOK

Modern Publishing
A Division of Unisystems, Inc.
New York, NY 10022

Cover art by Michelle Hill
Illustrated by Arthur Friedman
Educational Consultant, Shereen Gertel Rutman, M.S.

Copyright © 1991, 1993, 1996 by Modern Publishing, a division of Unisystems, Inc. Previously published as ™ Early Learner Math Workbook, ™ Early Learner Spelling Workbook, and ™ Early Learner II Grades K-1 Workbook

™ Giant Basic Skills K-1 Workbook is a trademark of Modern Publishing, a division of Unisystems, Inc.

® Honey Bear Books is a trademark owned by Honey Bear Productions, Inc., and is registered in the U.S. Patent and Trademark Office. No part of this book may be reproduced or copied without written permission from the publisher. All Rights Reserved.

Printed in the U.S.A.

TO THE PARENTS

Dear Parents,

As your child's first and most important teacher, you can encourage your child's love of learning by participating in educational activities at home. Working together on the activities in this workbook will help your child build confidence, learn to reason, and develop skills necessary for early childhood education.

The following are some suggestions to help make your time together both enjoyable and rewarding.

- Choose a time when you and your child are relaxed.

- Provide a writing utensil that your child is familiar with.

- Don't attempt to do too many pages at one time or expect that every page be completed. Move on if your child is frustrated or loses interest.

- Praise your child's efforts.

- Discuss each page. Help your child relate the concepts in this book to everyday experiences.

ESSENTIAL SKILLS

The repetitive activities within each chapter have been designed to help children learn to sort, separate, put together, and figure out—the organizational skills so necessary for learning and thinking.

CHAPTER 1 Handwriting Skills
Learning to control the small muscles of the hand (**fine motor skill development**) allows the child to make the precise movements necessary for forming letters, while activitiies such as **writing from left to right, tracing,** and **forming lines** help to refine **eye/hand** coordination. Making **associations**—recognizing what things "go together" (for example, a dog and a bone)—enables a child to recognize that an upper case "A" and a lower case "a" go together.

CHAPTER 2 Colors, Shapes, and Numbers
Looking at familiar shapes helps children notice similarities and differences. Activities in which the child reproduces shapes and/or matches shapes to words encourage **sight vocabulary recognition** and the ability to make **associations between words** and **objects**. Grouping things according to common attributes such as color, size, shape, etc. (**classification activities**), encourages development of a child's ability to reason and make **logical connections. Recognizing number words**, writing numerals, and **forming sets of objects** all prepare a child for basic math skills.

CHAPTER 3 Counting and Math Skills
Becoming familiar with the **order of numbers from 1-10, learning to write those numbers,** and **understanding the connection between a set of objects and its corresponding numeral**, all prepare a child to understand the concepts of addition and subtraction.

CHAPTER 4 Measuring
Children develop logical reasoning skills as they **compare the size and length** of objects. They use a variety of measurement systems to learn **basic measurement skills**. Children estimate the **weight and capacity** of various containers.

CHAPTER 5 Time and Money
In this chapter children learn about the **numbers on the clock,** and how to **tell time to the hour and half hour**. Children also explore money concepts and use **pennies, nickels and dimes**.

CHAPTER 6 Reading Readiness
Determining which items in a group "go together" (**making associations**), and learning to group things according to common attributes (**classification skills**), prepare a child to **notice details**. These skills are necessary for learning to recognize and reproduce the letters of the alphabet.

CHAPTER 7 Phonics Skills I
This chapter focuses on teaching a child **to recognize the initial and final consonant sounds, to learn to write letters and words using these sounds,** and **to understand the association between sounds, symbols, and words.**

CHAPTER 8 Phonics Skills II
Phonics II focuses on training a child to **hear and reproduce the long and short vowel sounds**, as well as the sounds made by combining two letters to make **consonant blends** and **consonant digraphs**.

CHAPTER 9 Putting Words Together
The activities in this chapter help children learn commonly used words. Children **read, spell and write** words that form a basic **sight vocabulary**. The words learned in previous chapters are used to **form sentences**. Children **spell and write words in complete sentences**.

TABLE OF CONTENTS

Handwriting Skills 6

Colors, Shapes, and Numbers 49

Counting and Math Skills 94

Measuring 156

Time and Money 175

Reading Readiness 196

Phonics Skills I 239

Phonics Skills II 271

Putting Words Together 294

HANDWRITING SKILLS

Start at the dots. Trace the broken lines. Then finish the page.

Skills: Fine motor skill development; Eye/hand coordination; Forming vertical lines

HANDWRITING SKILLS

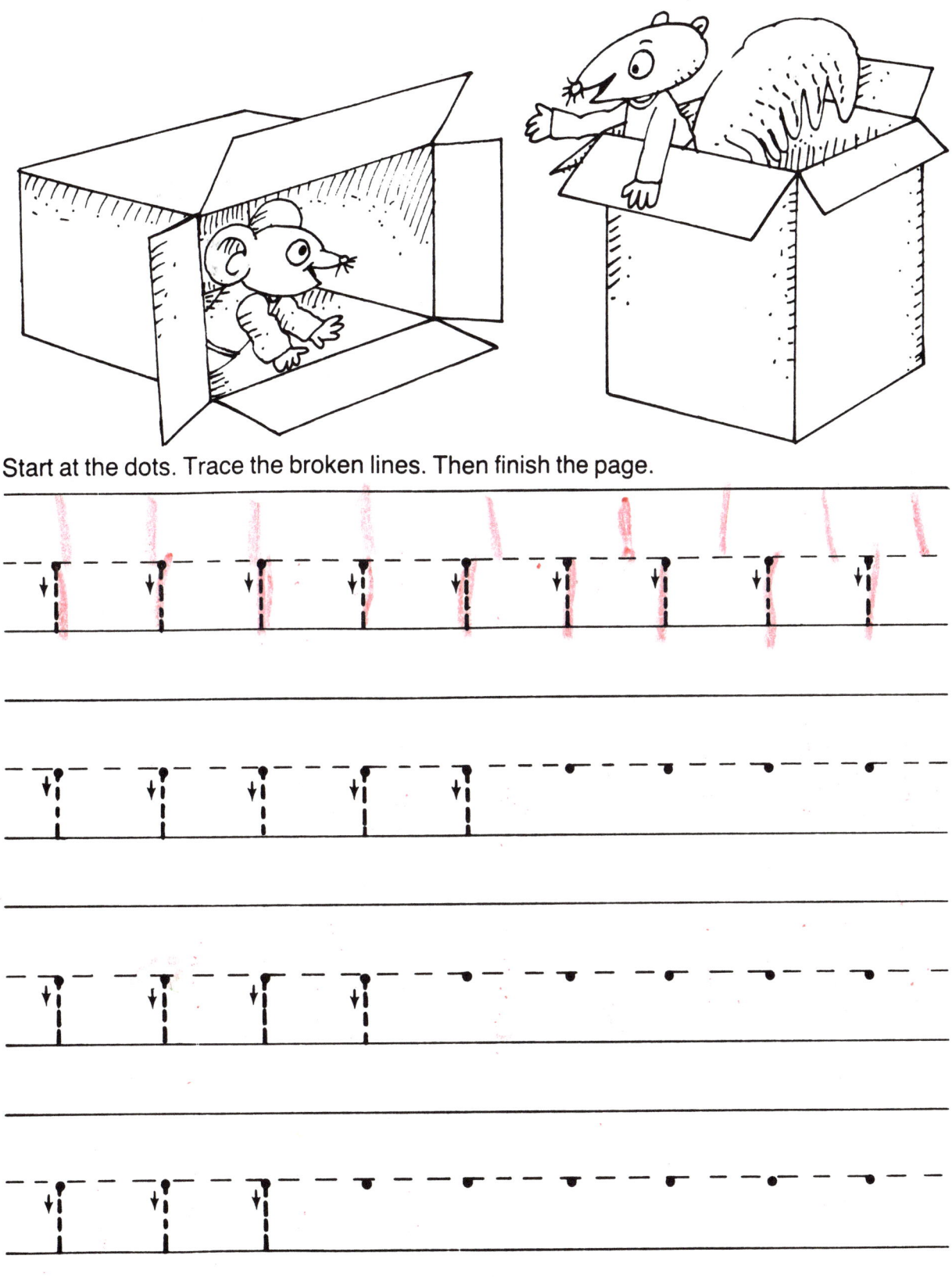

Start at the dots. Trace the broken lines. Then finish the page.

Skills: Fine motor skill development; Eye/hand coordination; Forming vertical lines

HANDWRITING SKILLS

Start at the dots. Trace the broken lines. Then finish the page.

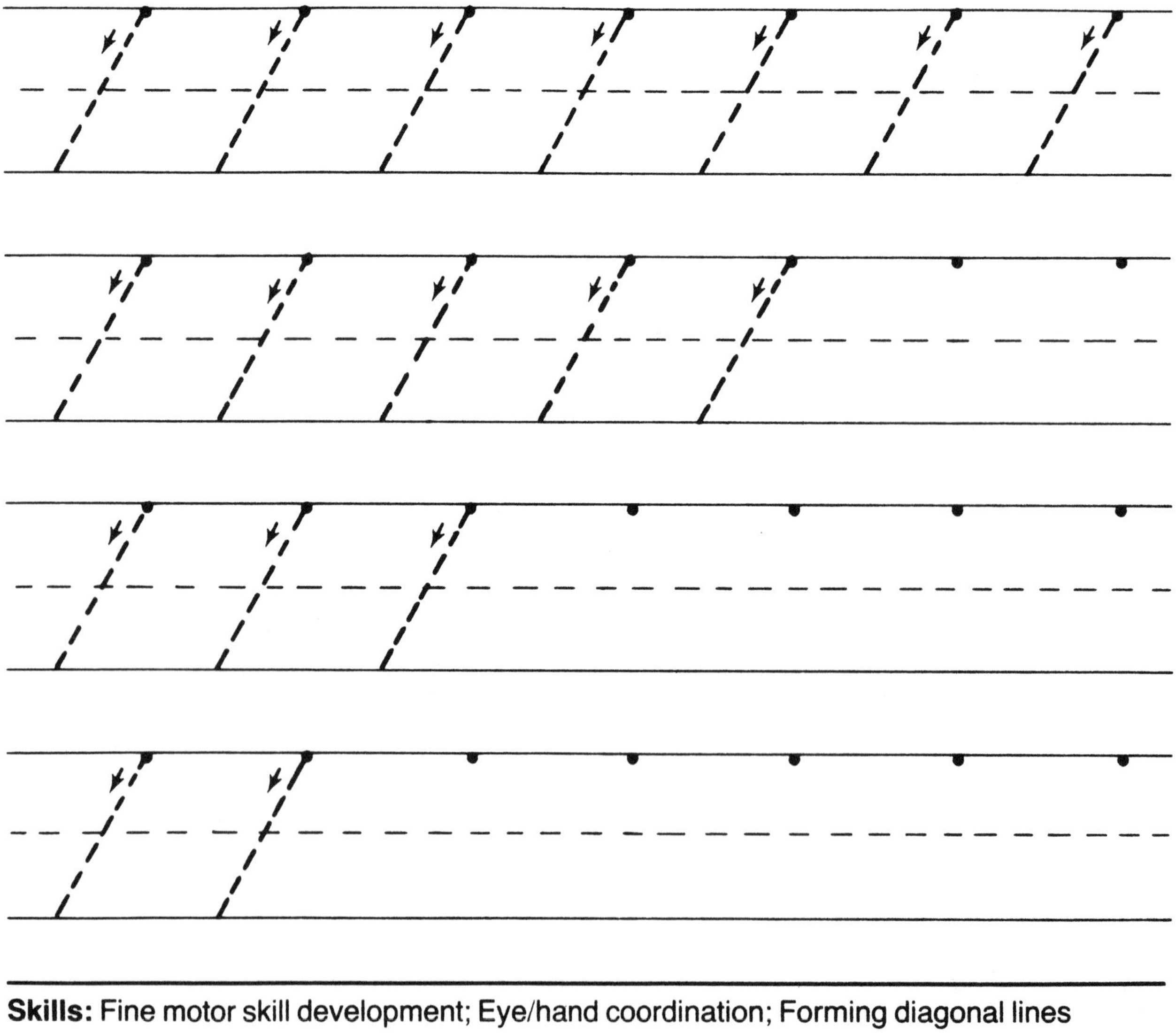

Skills: Fine motor skill development; Eye/hand coordination; Forming diagonal lines

HANDWRITING SKILLS

Start at the dots. Trace the broken lines. Then finish the page.

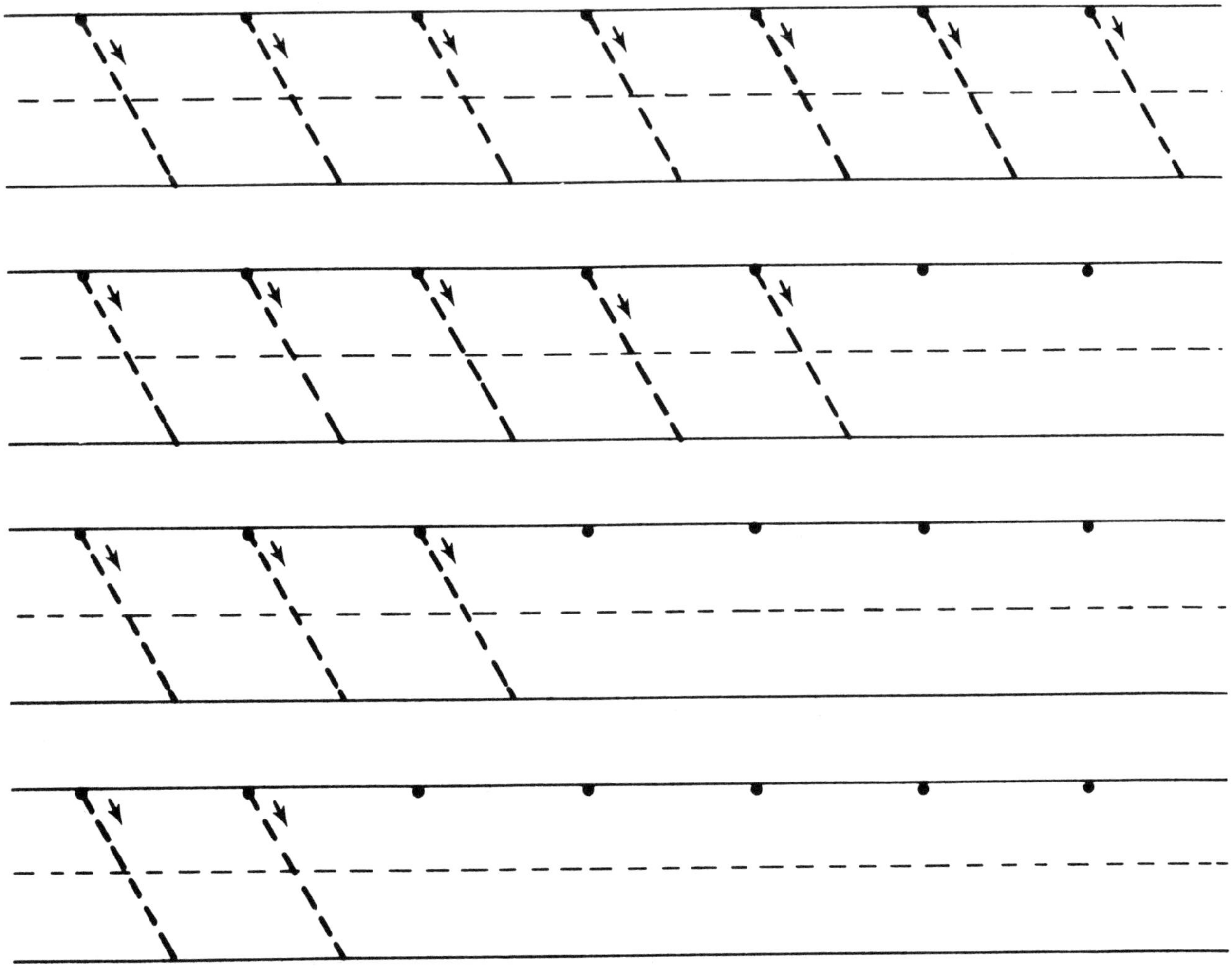

Skills: Fine motor skill development; Eye/hand coordination; Forming diagonal lines

HANDWRITING SKILLS

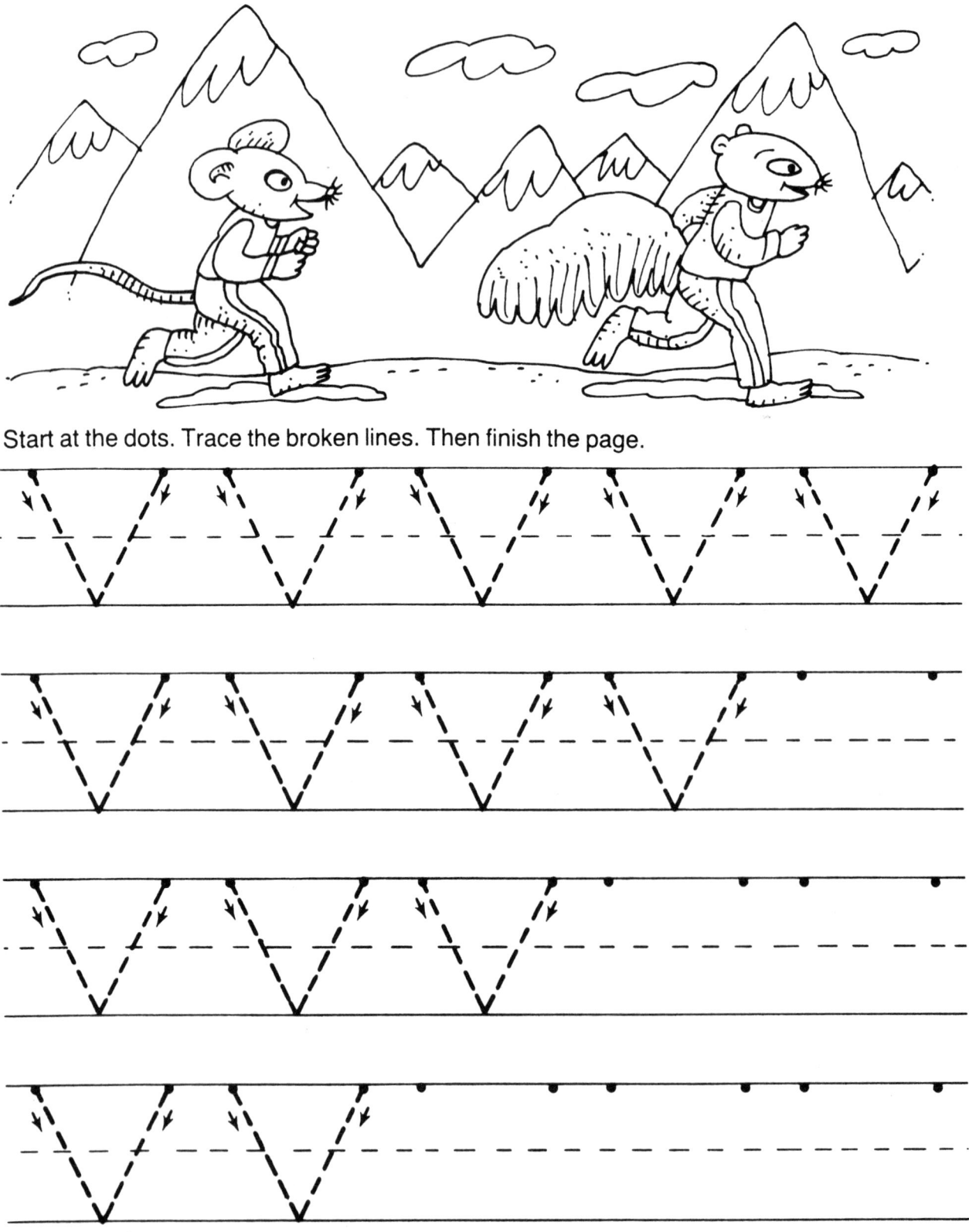

Start at the dots. Trace the broken lines. Then finish the page.

Skills: Fine motor skill development; Eye/hand coordination; Forming diagonal lines

HANDWRITING SKILLS

Start at the dots. Trace the broken lines.

Skills: Fine motor skill development; Eye/hand coordination; Forming open curves

HANDWRITING SKILLS

Start at the dots. Trace the broken lines.

Skills: Fine motor skill development; Eye/hand coordination; Forming open curves

HANDWRITING SKILLS

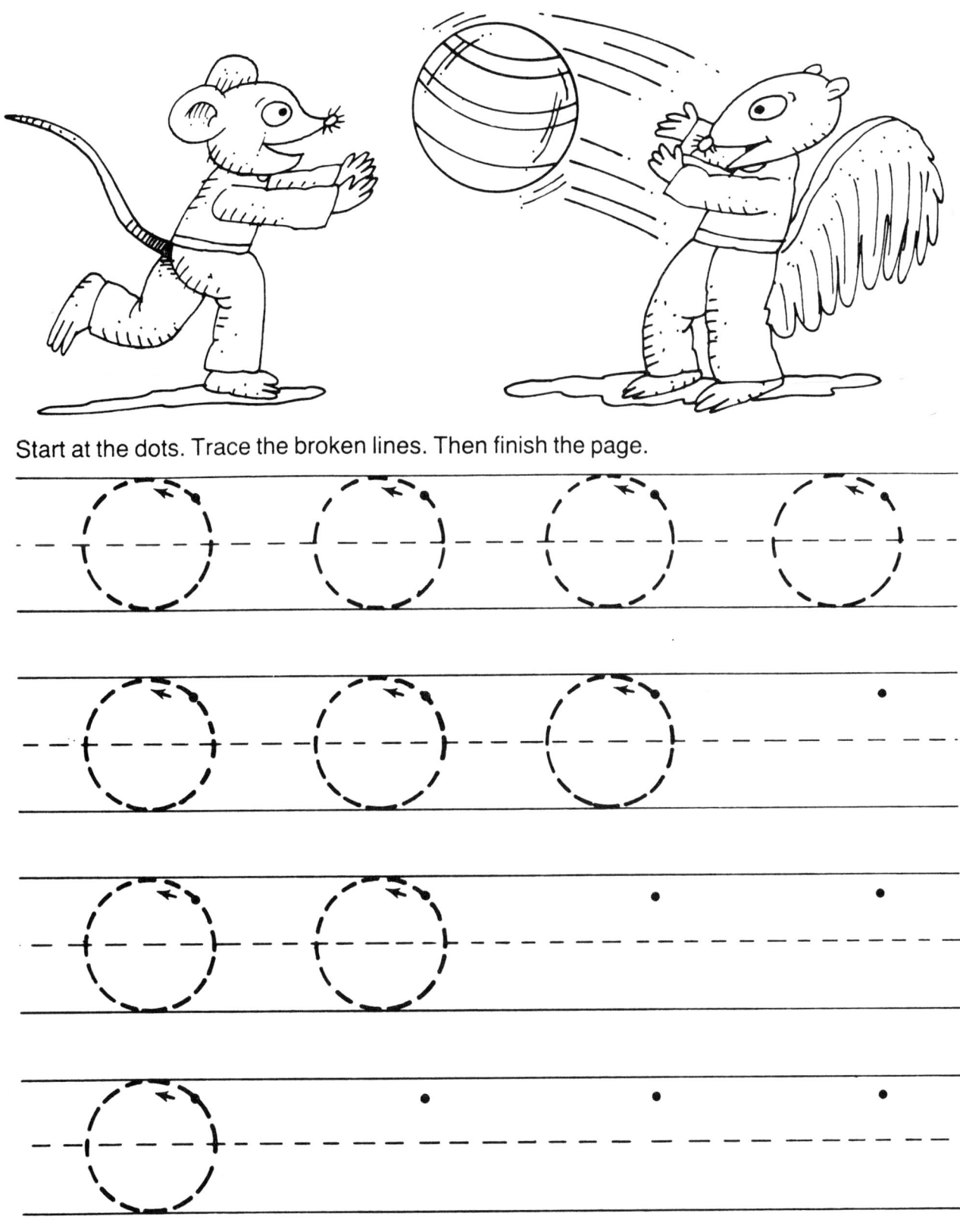

Start at the dots. Trace the broken lines. Then finish the page.

Skills: Fine motor skill development; Eye/hand coordination; Forming closed curves

HANDWRITING SKILLS

Start at the dots. Trace the broken lines. Then finish the page.

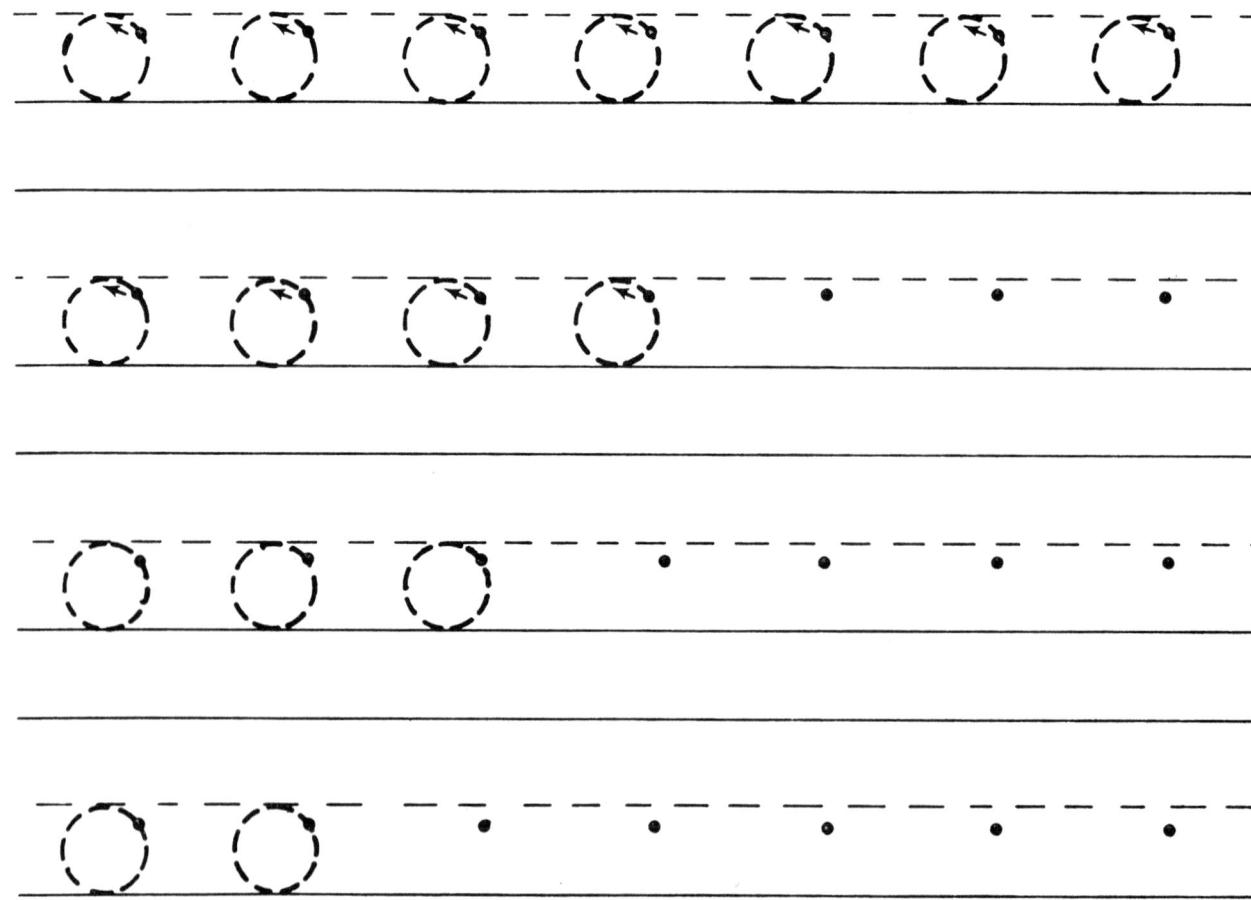

Skills: Fine motor skill development; Eye/hand coordination; Forming closed curves

HANDWRITING SKILLS

Start at the dots. Trace the broken lines.

Skills: Fine motor skill development; Eye/hand coordination; Forming open curves

HANDWRITING SKILLS

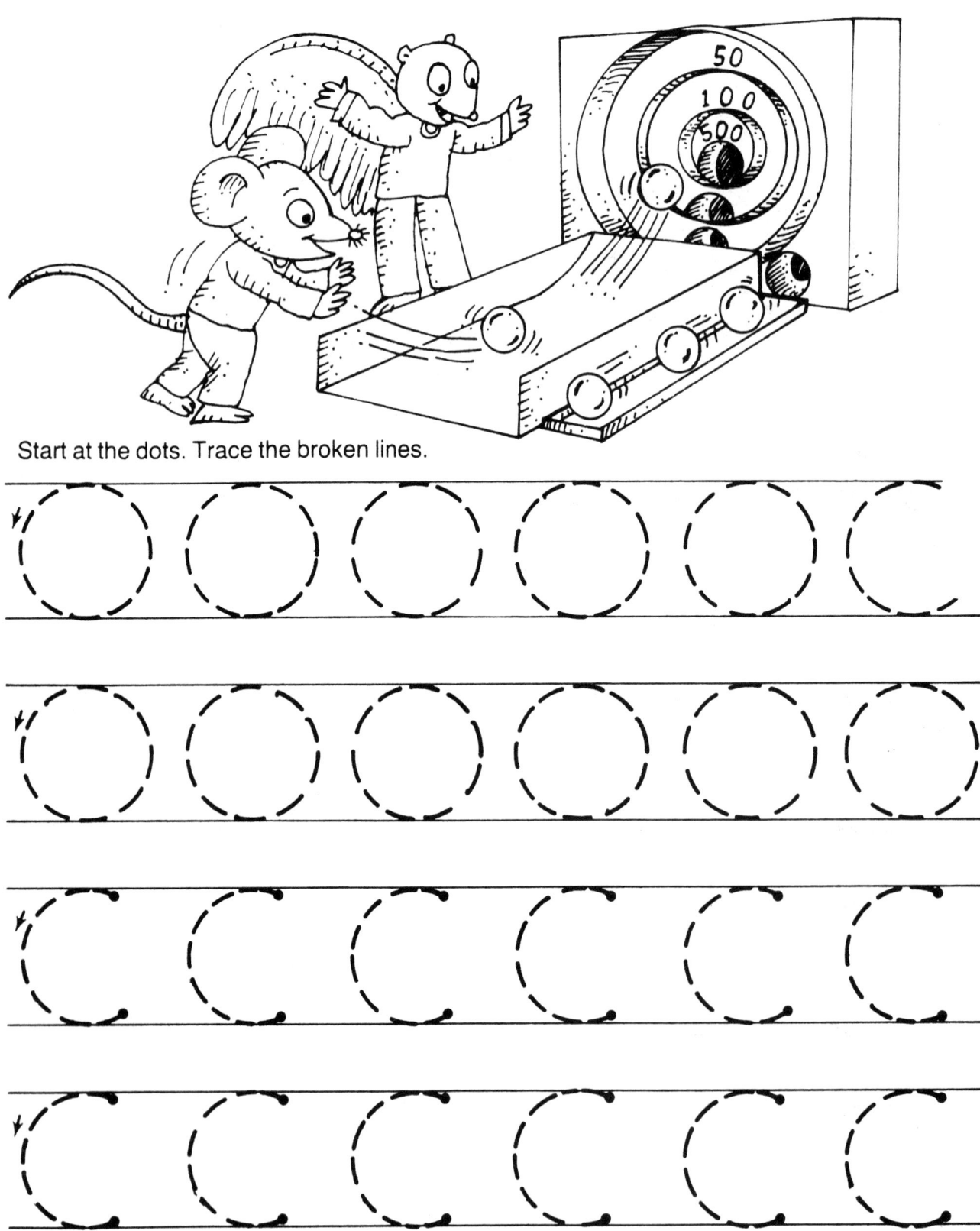

Start at the dots. Trace the broken lines.

Skills: Fine motor skill development; Eye/hand coordination; Forming open and closed curves

HANDWRITING SKILLS

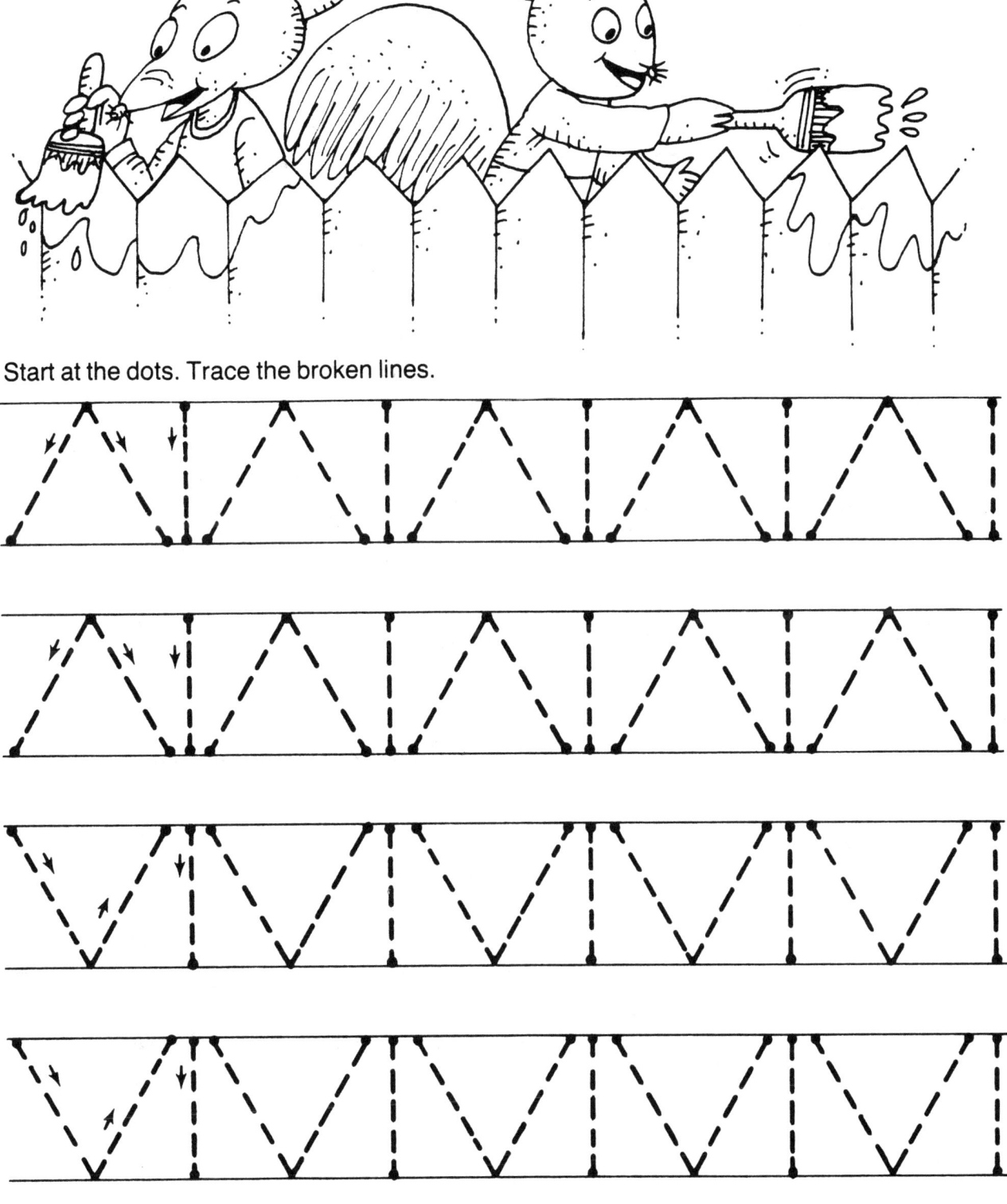

Start at the dots. Trace the broken lines.

Skills: Fine motor skill development; Eye/hand coordination; Forming vertical and diagonal lines

HANDWRITING SKILLS

Start at the dots. Trace the broken lines. Then finish the page.

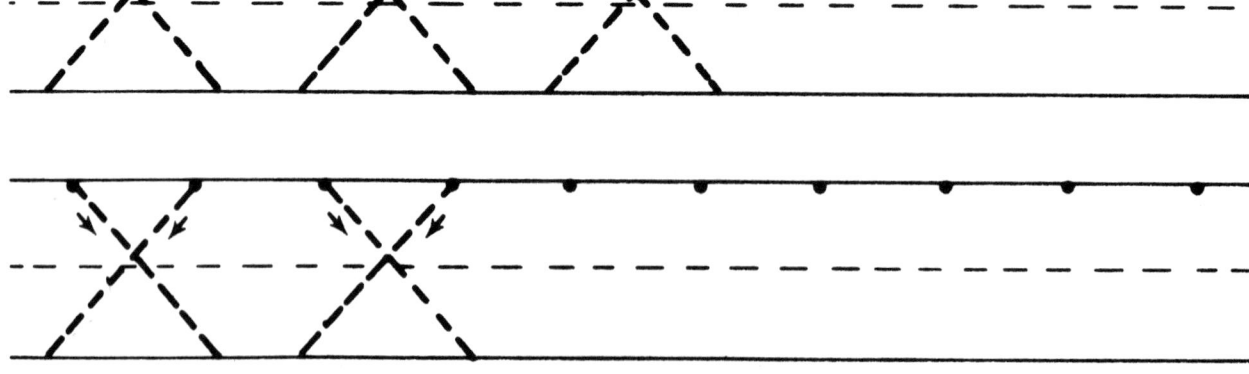

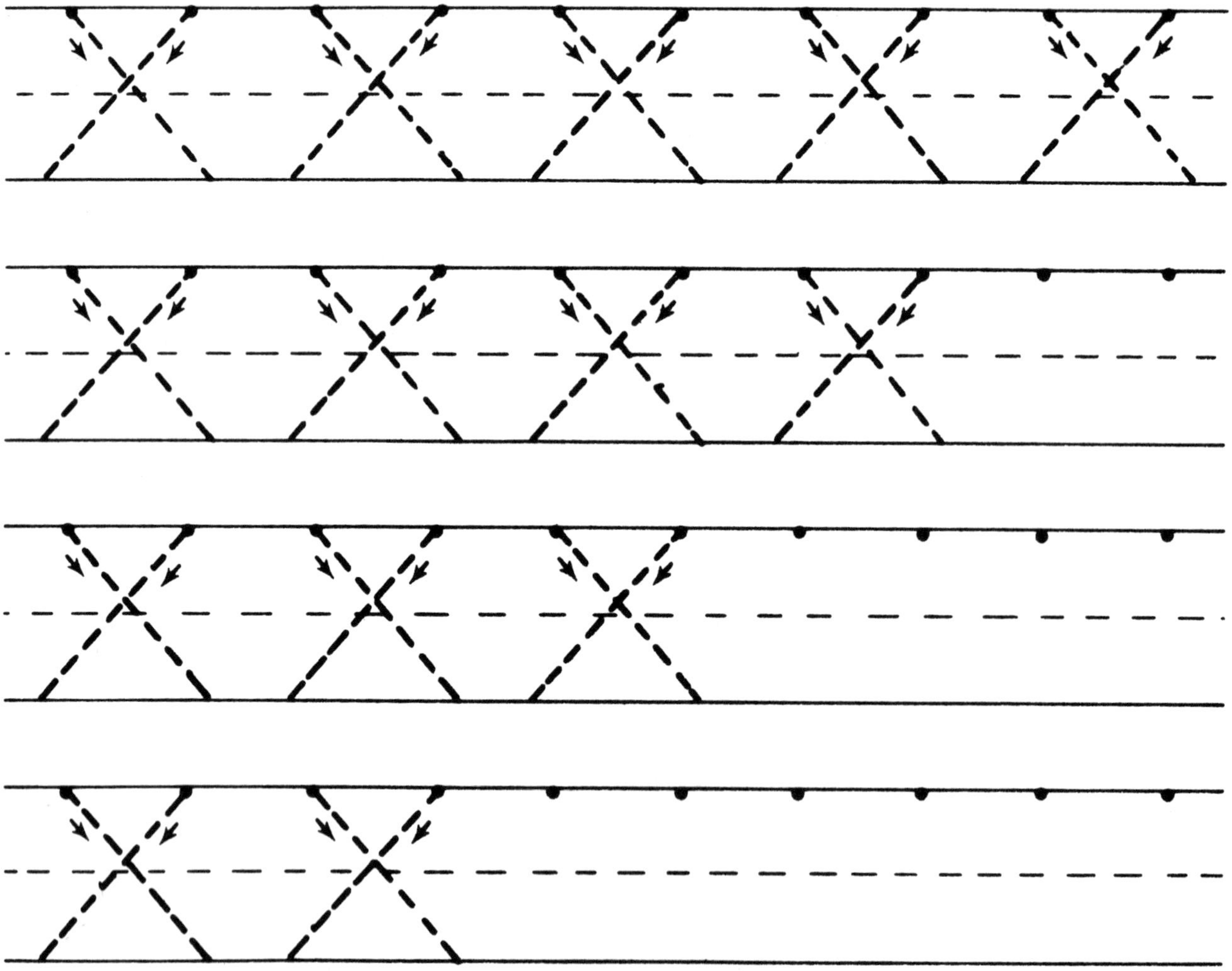

Skills: Fine motor skill development; Eye/hand coordination; Forming diagonal lines in 2 directions

HANDWRITING SKILLS

Start at the dots. Trace the broken lines. Then finish the page.

Skills: Fine motor skill development; Eye/hand coordination; Forming horizontal lines

HANDWRITING SKILLS

Aa

Follow the direction of each arrow. Then practice writing each letter.

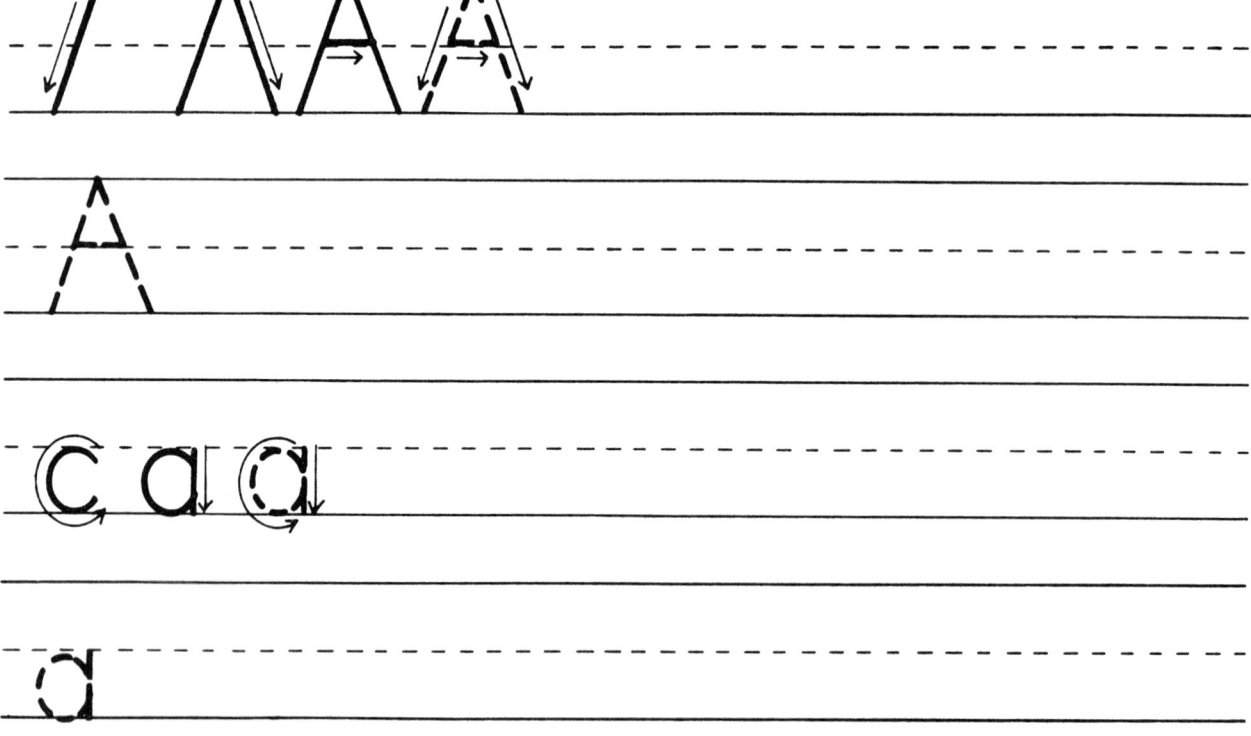

Skills: Forming upper/lower case "a"; Writing left to right

HANDWRITING SKILLS

Bb

Follow the direction of each arrow. Then practice writing each letter.

Skills: Forming upper/lower case "b"; Writing left to right

21

HANDWRITING SKILLS

Cc

Follow the direction of each arrow. Then practice writing each letter.

Skills: Forming upper/lower case "c"; Writing left to right

HANDWRITING SKILLS

Dd

Follow the direction of each arrow. Then practice writing each letter.

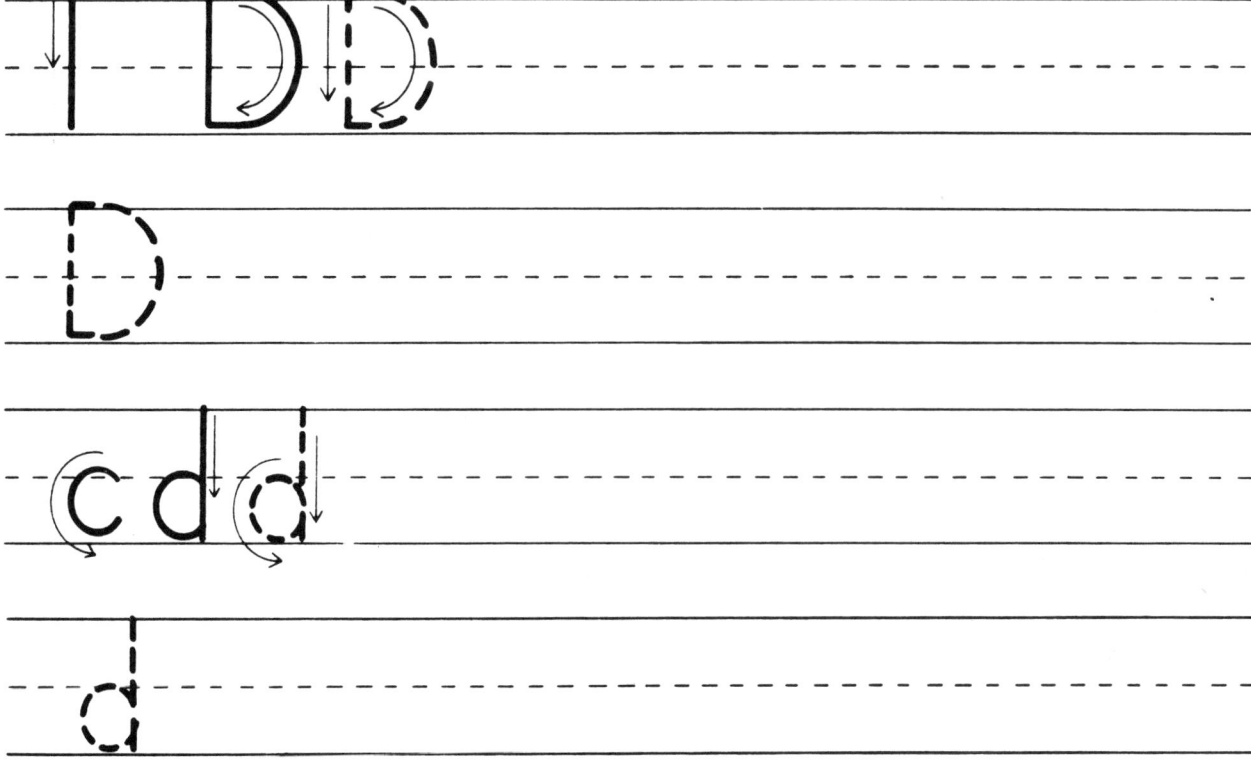

Skills: Forming upper/lower case "d"; Writing left to right

HANDWRITING SKILLS

Ee

Follow the direction of each arrow. Then practice writing each letter.

Skills: Forming upper/lower case "e"; Writing left to right

24

HANDWRITING SKILLS

Ff

Follow the direction of each arrow. Then practice writing each letter.

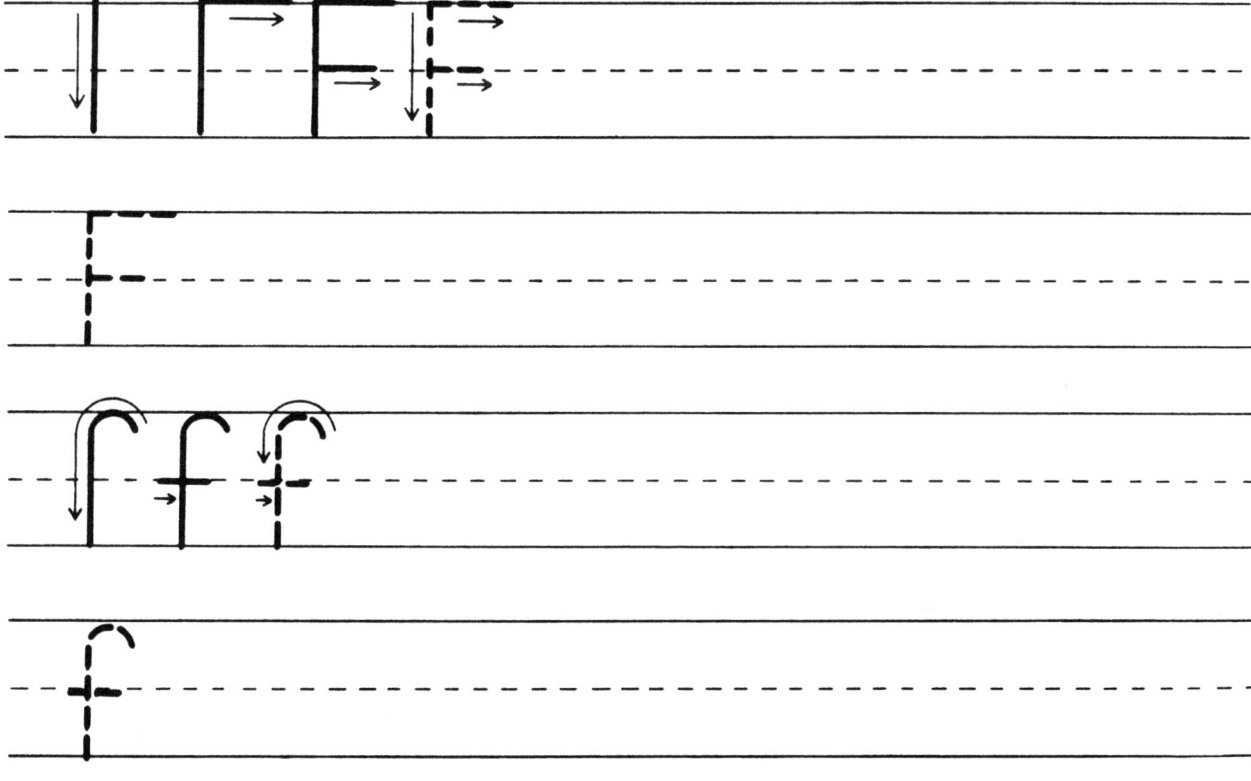

Skills: Forming upper/lower case "f"; Writing left to right

25

HANDWRITING SKILLS

Gg

Follow the direction of each arrow. Then practice writing each letter.

Skills: Forming upper/lower case "g"; Writing left to right

HANDWRITING SKILLS

Follow the direction of each arrow. Then practice writing each letter.

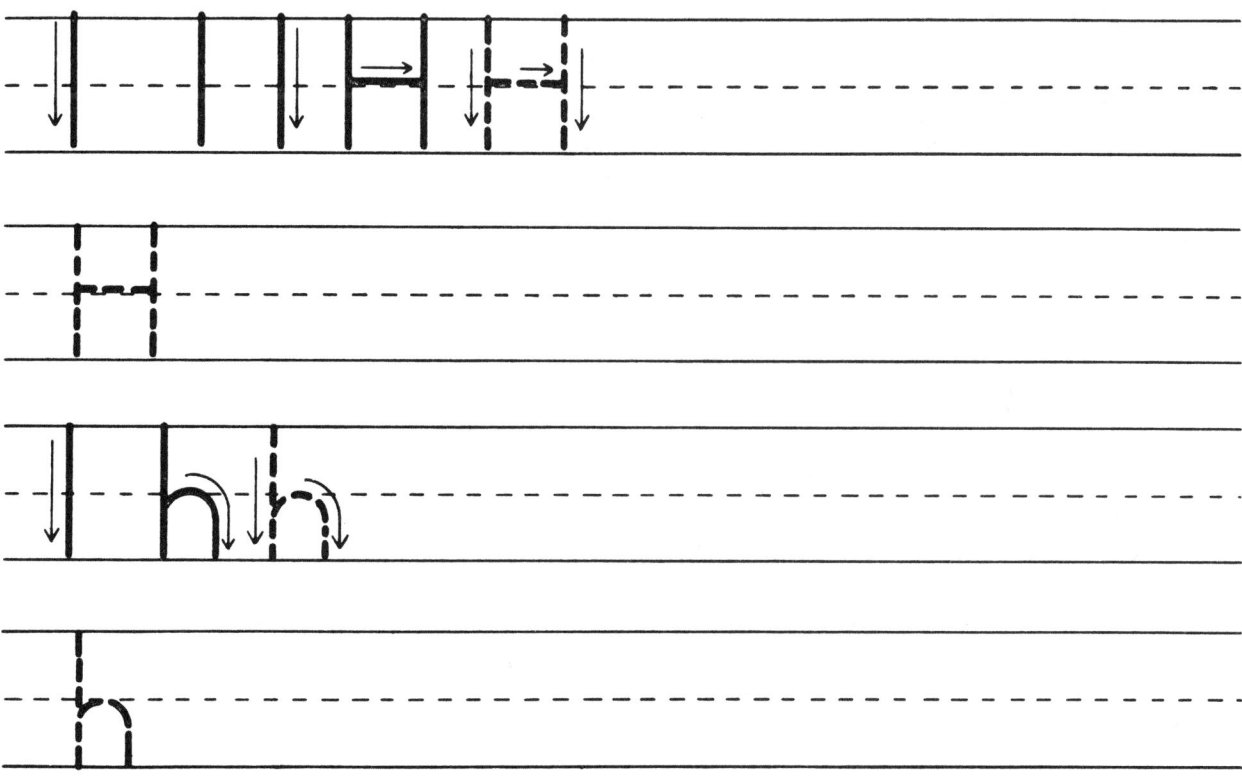

Skills: Forming upper/lower case "h"; Writing left to right

HANDWRITING SKILLS

Follow the direction of each arrow. Then practice writing each letter.

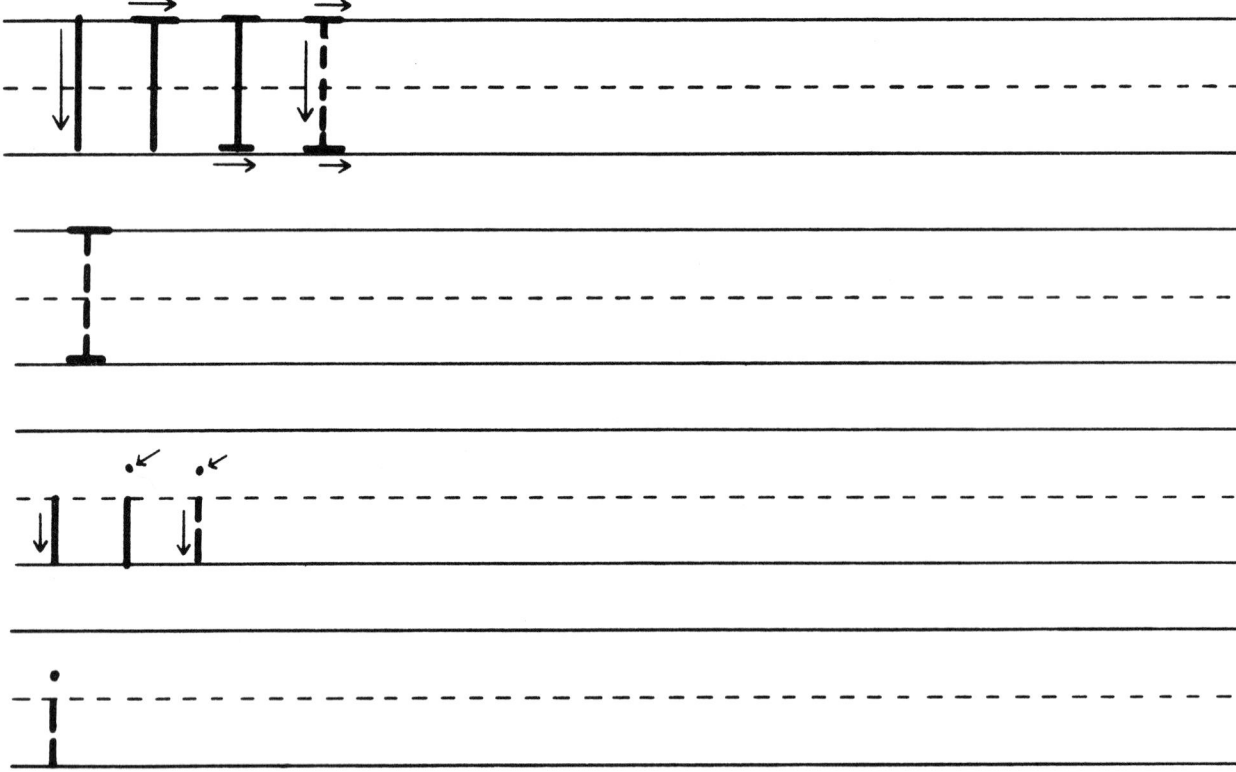

Skills: Forming upper/lower case "i"; Writing left to right

28

HANDWRITING SKILLS

Jj

Follow the direction of each arrow. Then practice writing each letter.

Skills: Forming upper/lower case "j"; Writing left to right

29

HANDWRITING SKILLS

Follow the direction of each arrow. Then practice writing each letter.

Skills: Forming upper/lower case "k"; Writing left to right

HANDWRITING SKILLS

Ll

Follow the direction of each arrow. Then practice writing each letter.

Skills: Forming upper/lower case "l"; Writing left to right

HANDWRITING SKILLS

Mm

Follow the direction of each arrow. Then practice writing each letter.

Skills: Forming upper/lower case "m"; Writing left to right

HANDWRITING SKILLS

Nn

Follow the direction of each arrow. Then practice writing each letter.

Skills: Forming upper/lower case "n"; Writing left to right

33

HANDWRITING SKILLS

Oo

Follow the direction of each arrow. Then practice writing each letter.

Skills: Forming upper/lower case "o"; Writing left to right

HANDWRITING SKILLS

Pp

Follow the direction of each arrow. Then practice writing each letter.

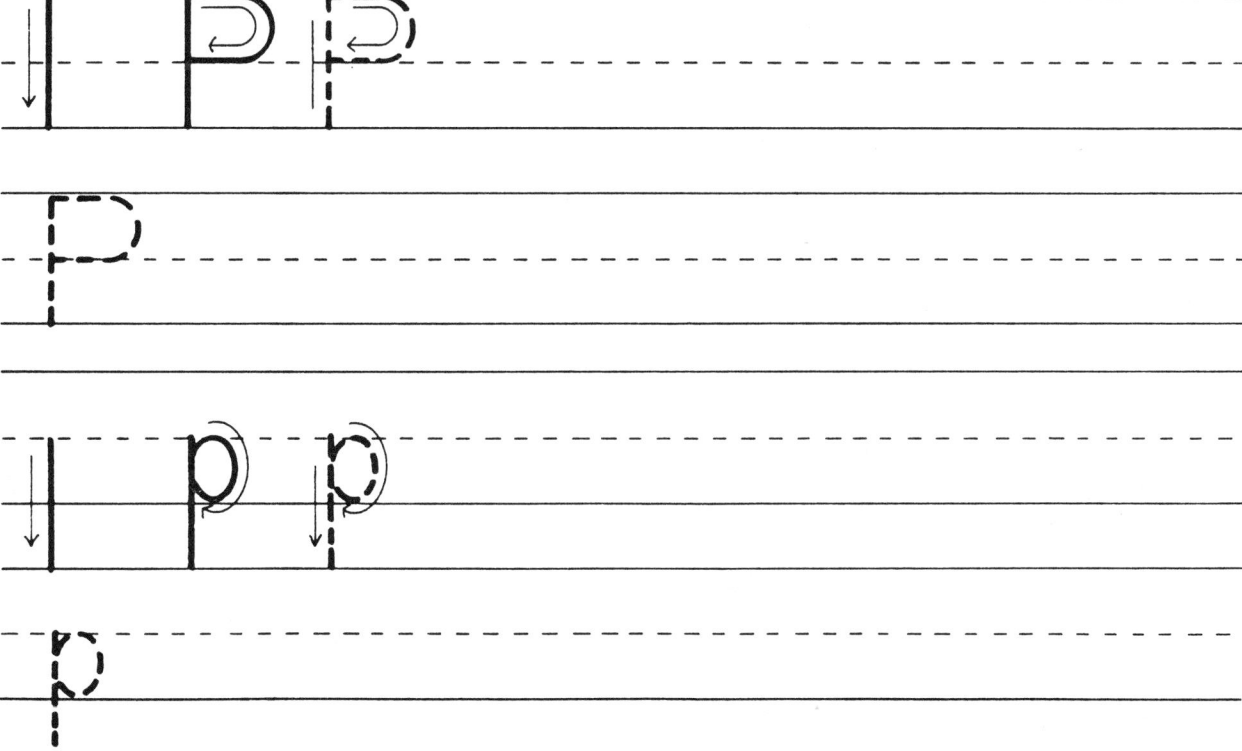

Skills: Forming upper/lower case "p"; Writing left to right

HANDWRITING SKILLS

Follow the direction of each arrow. Then practice writing each letter.

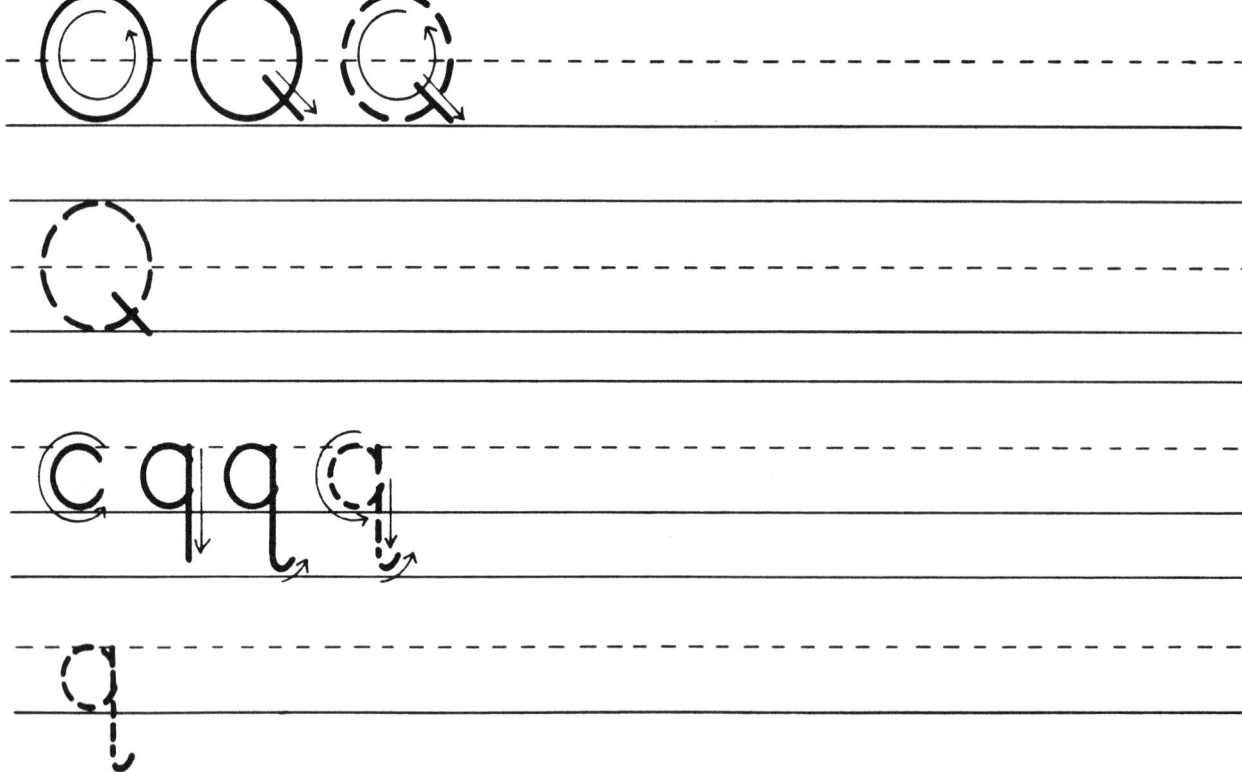

Skills: Forming upper/lower case "q"; Writing left to right

HANDWRITING SKILLS

Rr

Follow the direction of each arrow. Then practice writing each letter.

I P R R

R

l r r

r

Skills: Forming upper/lower case "r"; Writing left to right

HANDWRITING SKILLS

Ss

Follow the direction of each arrow. Then practice writing each letter.

Skills: Forming upper/lower case "s"; Writing left to right

HANDWRITING SKILLS

Tt

Follow the direction of each arrow. Then practice writing each letter.

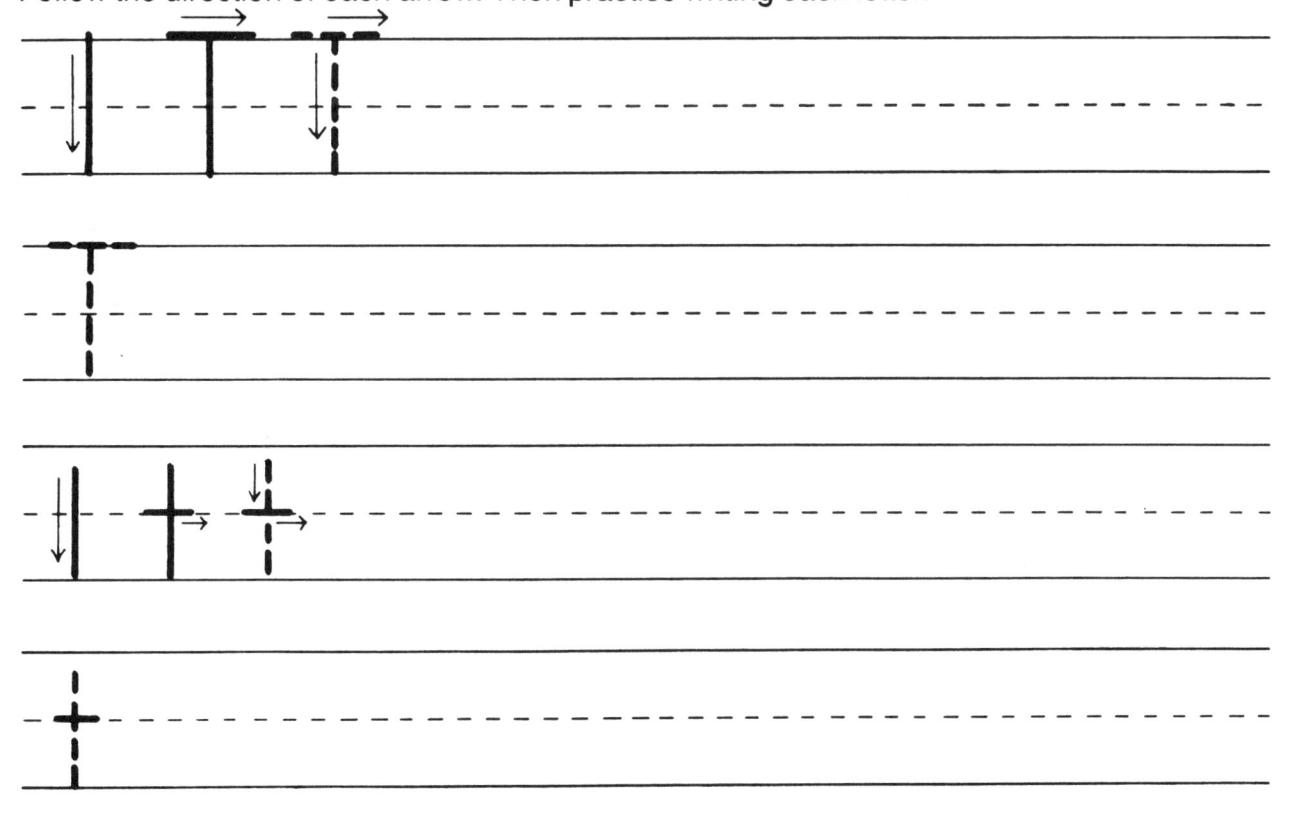

Skills: Forming upper/lower case "t"; Writing left to right

HANDWRITING SKILLS

Uu

Follow the direction of each arrow. Then practice writing each letter.

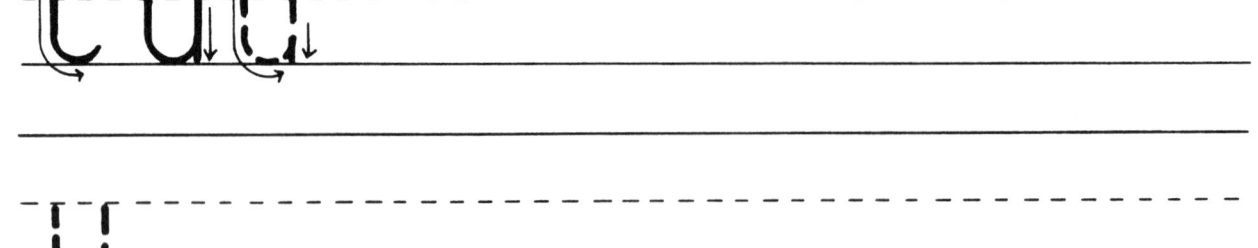

Skills: Forming upper/lower case "u"; Writing left to right

HANDWRITING SKILLS

Vv

Follow the direction of each arrow. Then practice writing each letter.

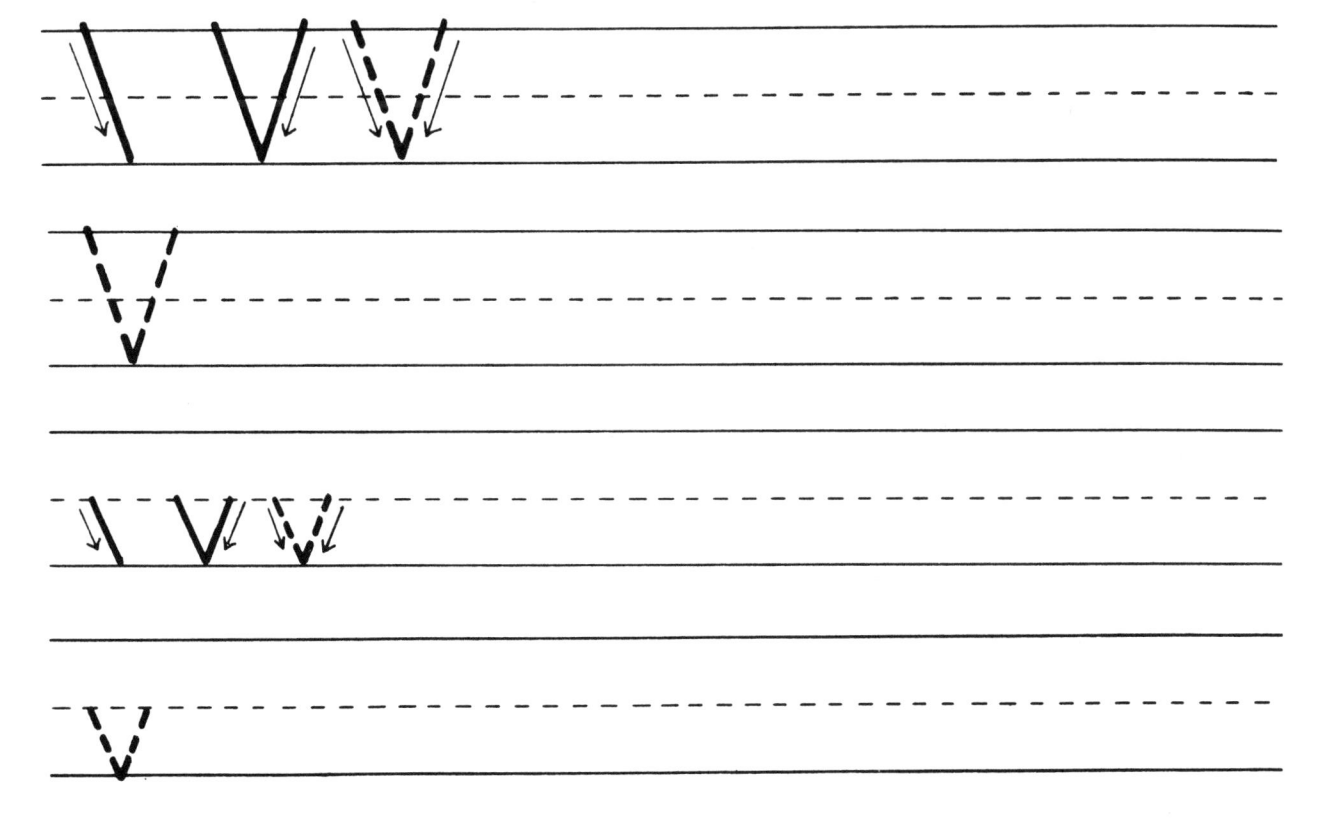

Skills: Forming upper/lower case "v"; Writing left to right

HANDWRITING SKILLS

Ww

Follow the direction of each arrow. Then practice writing each letter.

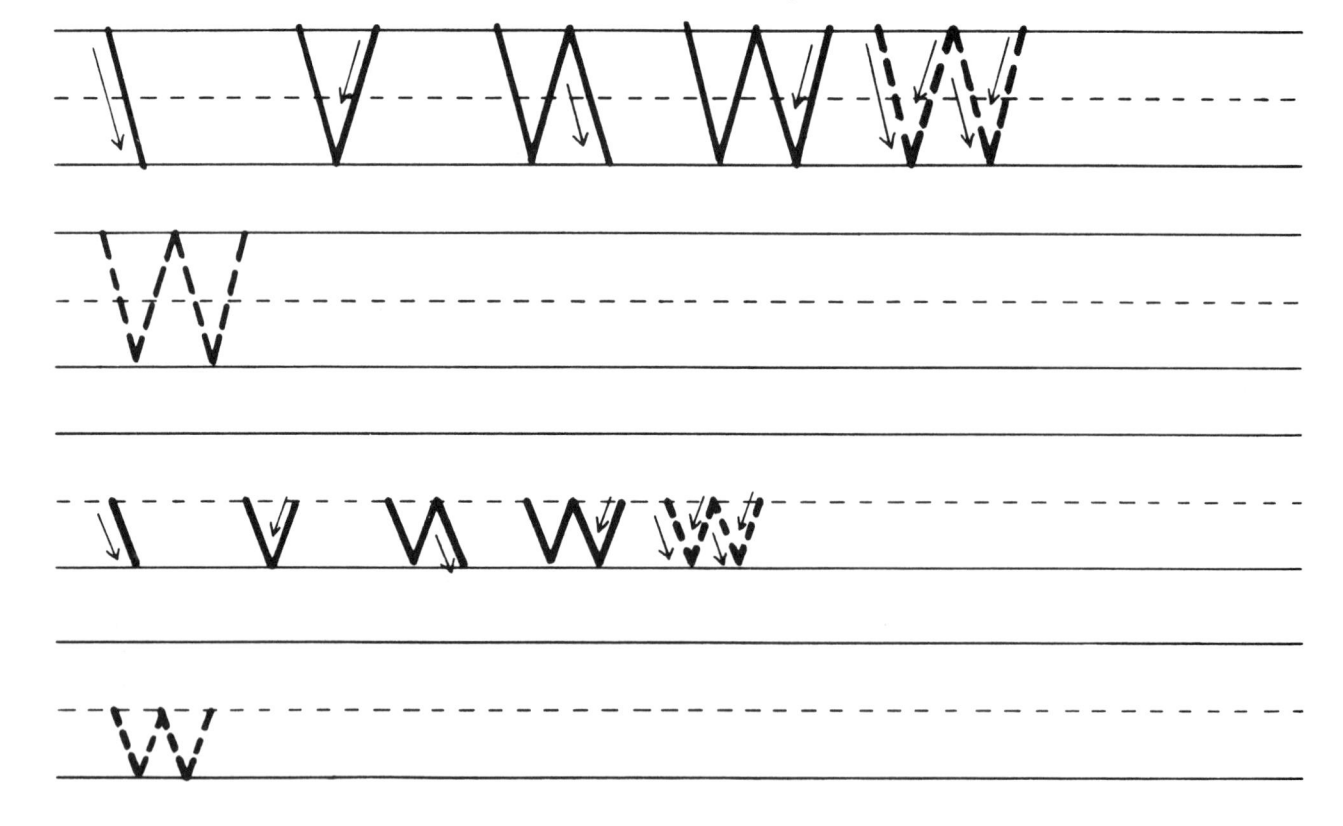

Skills: Forming upper/lower case "w"; Writing left to right

HANDWRITING SKILLS

Xx

Follow the direction of each arrow. Then practice writing each letter.

Skills: Forming upper/lower case "x"; Writing left to right

HANDWRITING SKILLS

Yy

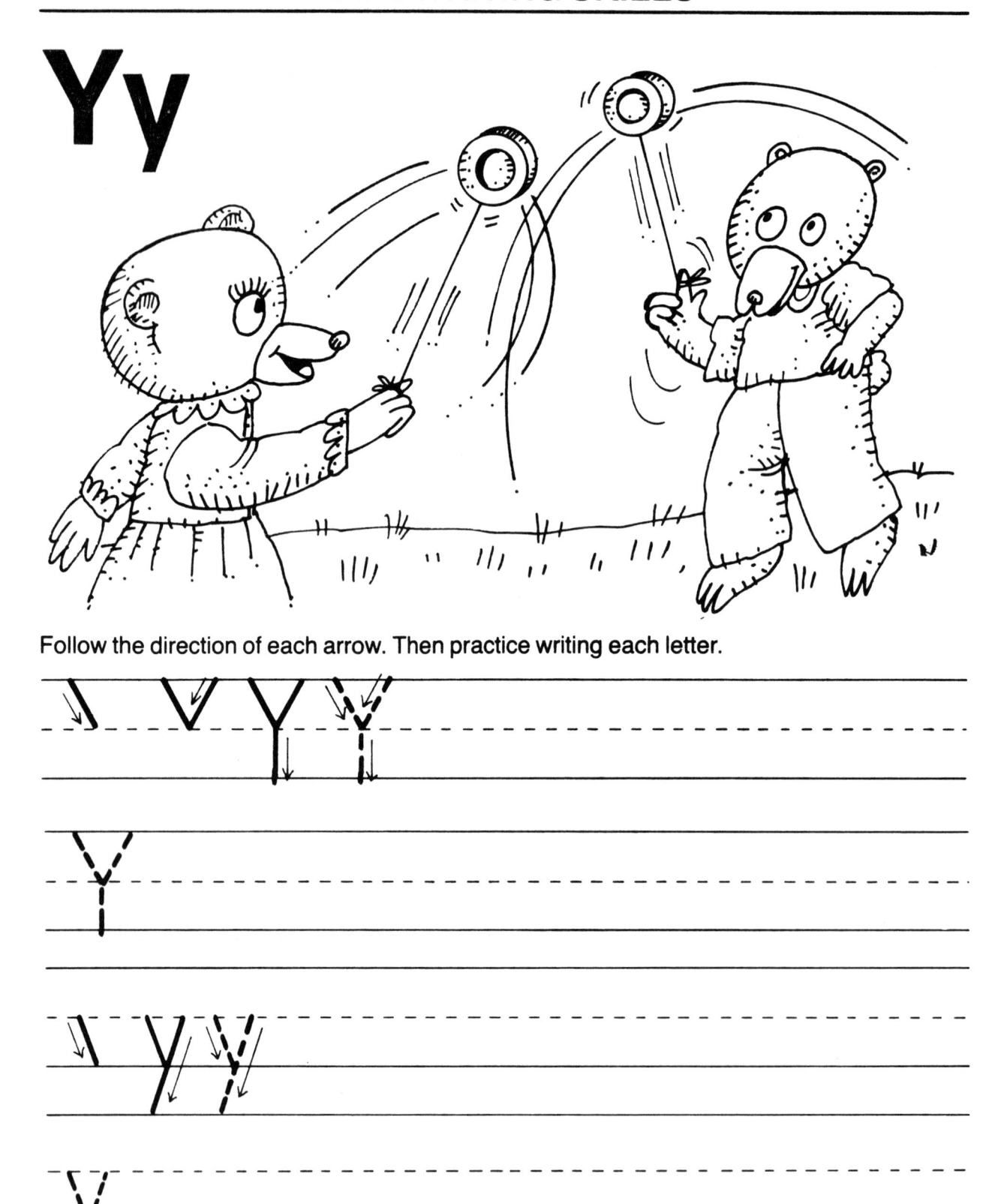

Follow the direction of each arrow. Then practice writing each letter.

Skills: Forming upper/lower case "y"; Writing left to right

HANDWRITING SKILLS

Zz

Follow the direction of each arrow. Then practice writing each letter.

Skills: Forming upper/lower case "z"; Writing left to right

45

HANDWRITING SKILLS

Trace each letter.

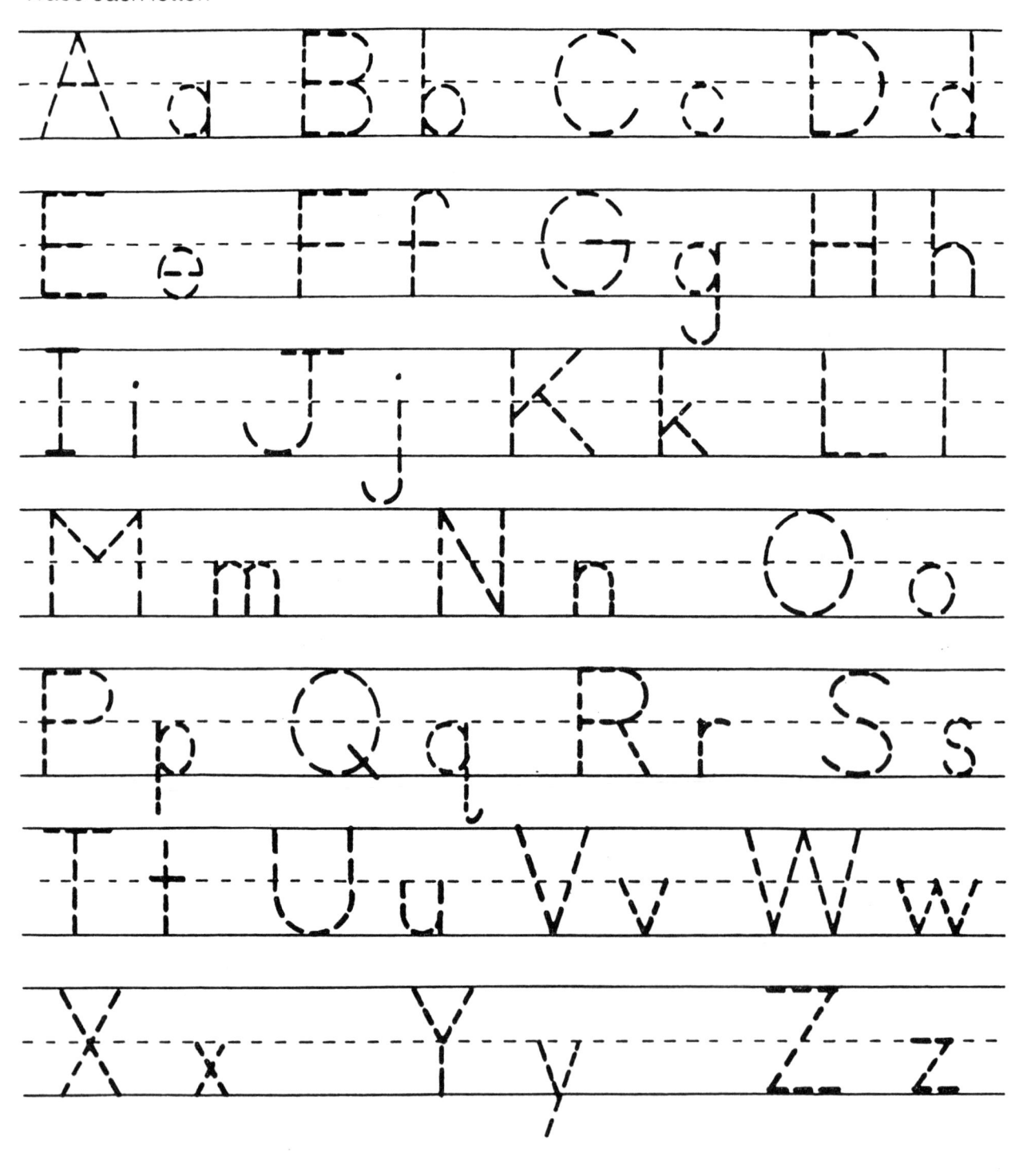

Aa Bb Cc Dd
Ee Ff Gg Hh
Ii Jj Kk Ll
Mm Nn Oo
Pp Qq Rr Ss
Tt Uu Vv Ww
Xx Yy Zz

Skills: Forming upper/lower case letters; Writing the alphabet

HANDWRITING SKILLS

Connect the dots from A to Z to find out what the children are riding. Then color the picture.

Skills: Letter order; Recognition of upper case letters

47

HANDWRITING SKILLS

Connect the dots from a to z to find out who is hiding in this cave. Then color the picture.

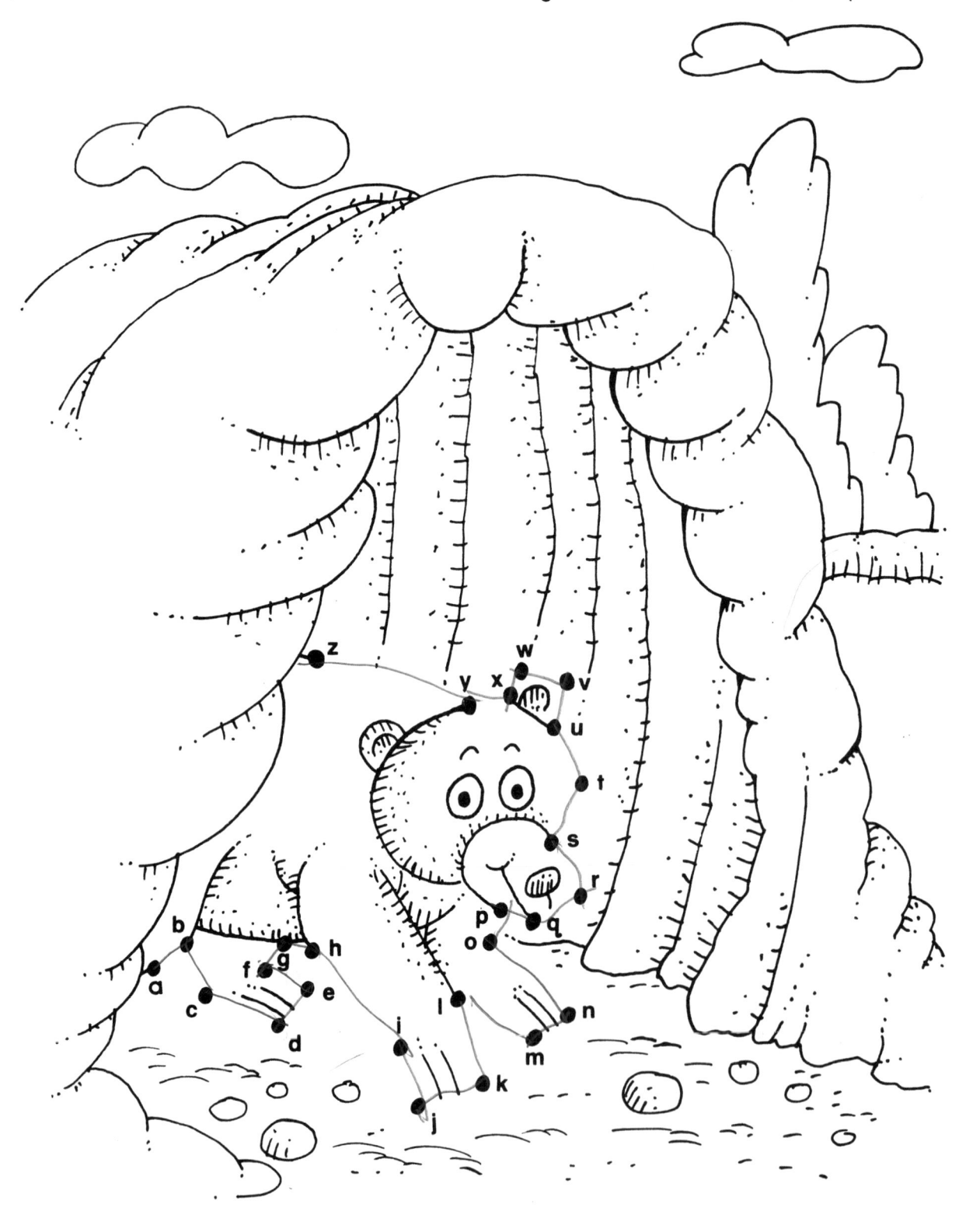

Skills: Letter order; Recognition of lower case letters

COLORS, SHAPES, AND NUMBERS

Trace and print the word.

red red red

Color these things that are red.

Skills: Distinguishing color; Classification; Word recognition

49

COLORS, SHAPES, AND NUMBERS

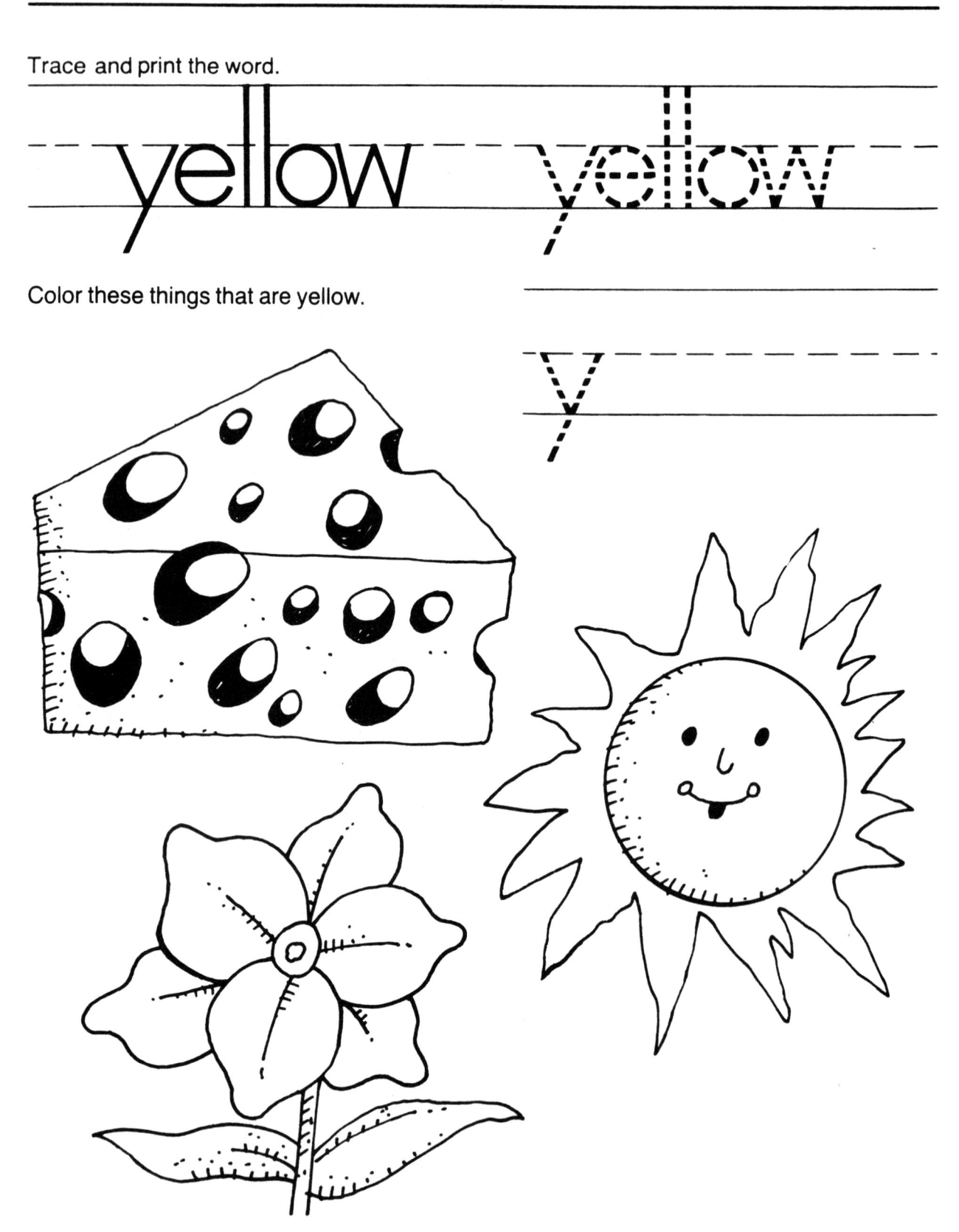

Trace and print the word.

yellow   yellow

Color these things that are yellow.

y

Skills: Distinguishing color; Classification; Word recognition

COLORS, SHAPES, AND NUMBERS

Trace and print the word.

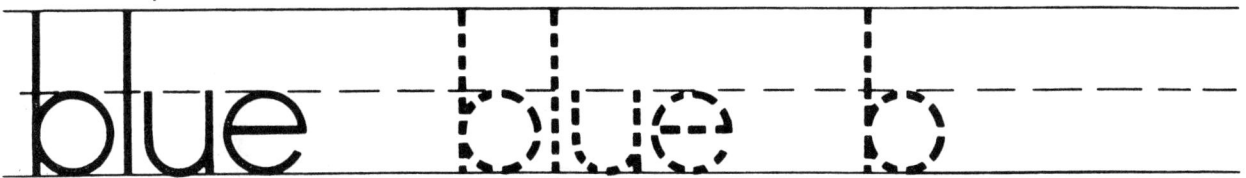

blue   blue   b

Color these things that are blue.

Skills: Distinguishing color; Classification; Word recognition

COLORS, SHAPES, AND NUMBERS

Trace and print the word.

orange   orange

Color these things that are orange.

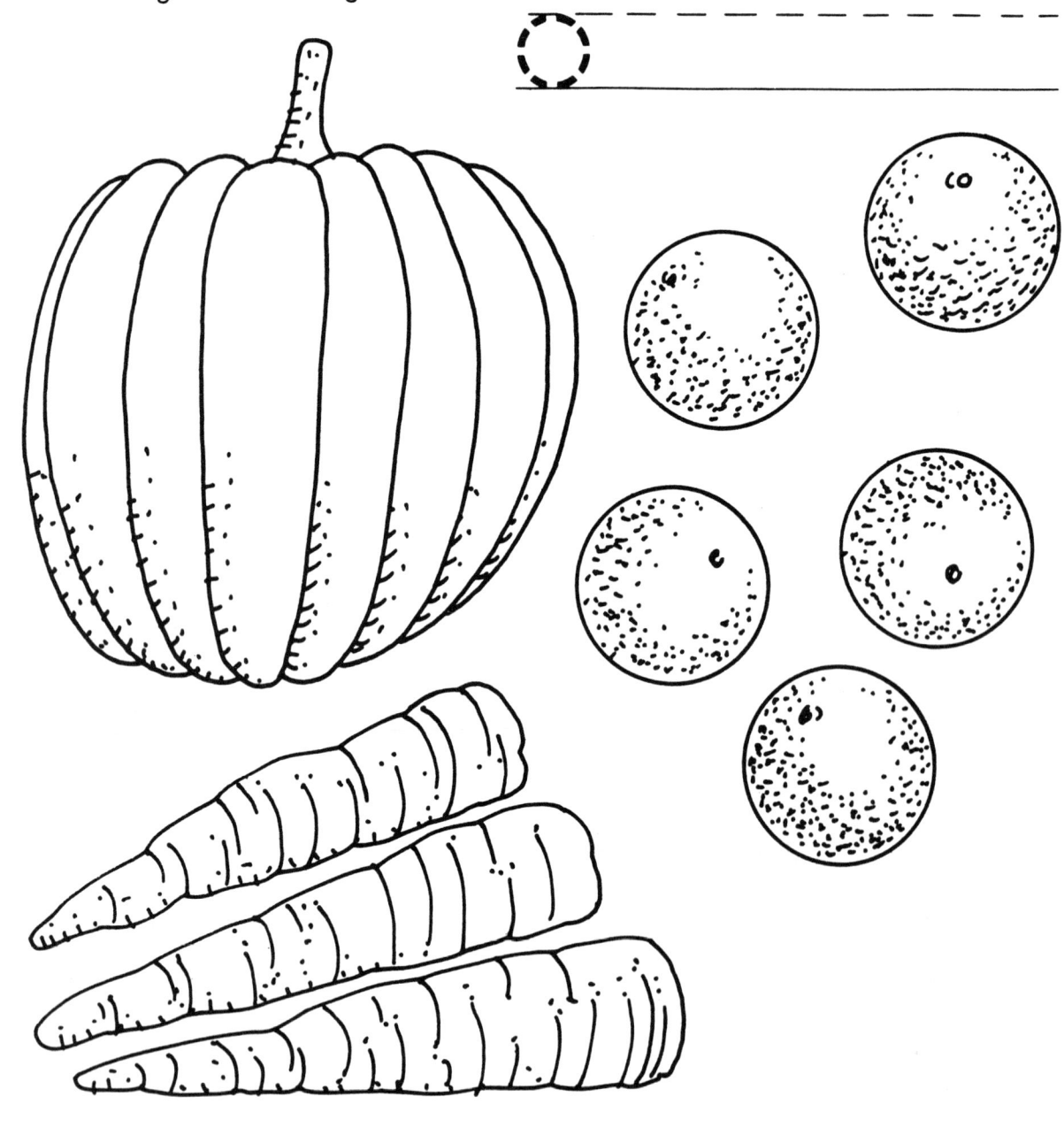

o

Skills: Distinguishing color; Classification; Word recognition

COLORS, SHAPES, AND NUMBERS

Trace and print the word.

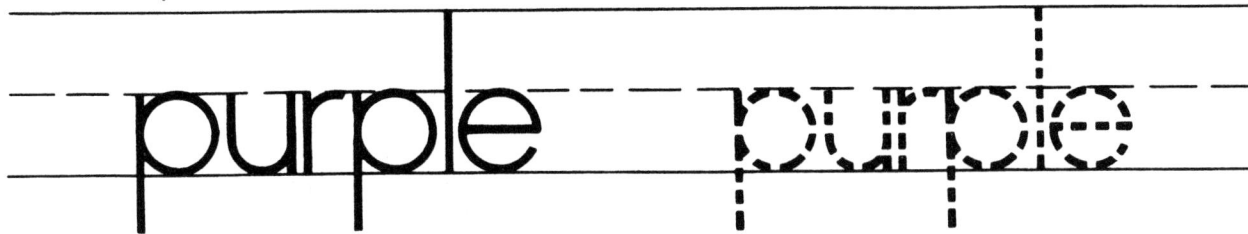

purple   purple

p

Color these things that are purple.

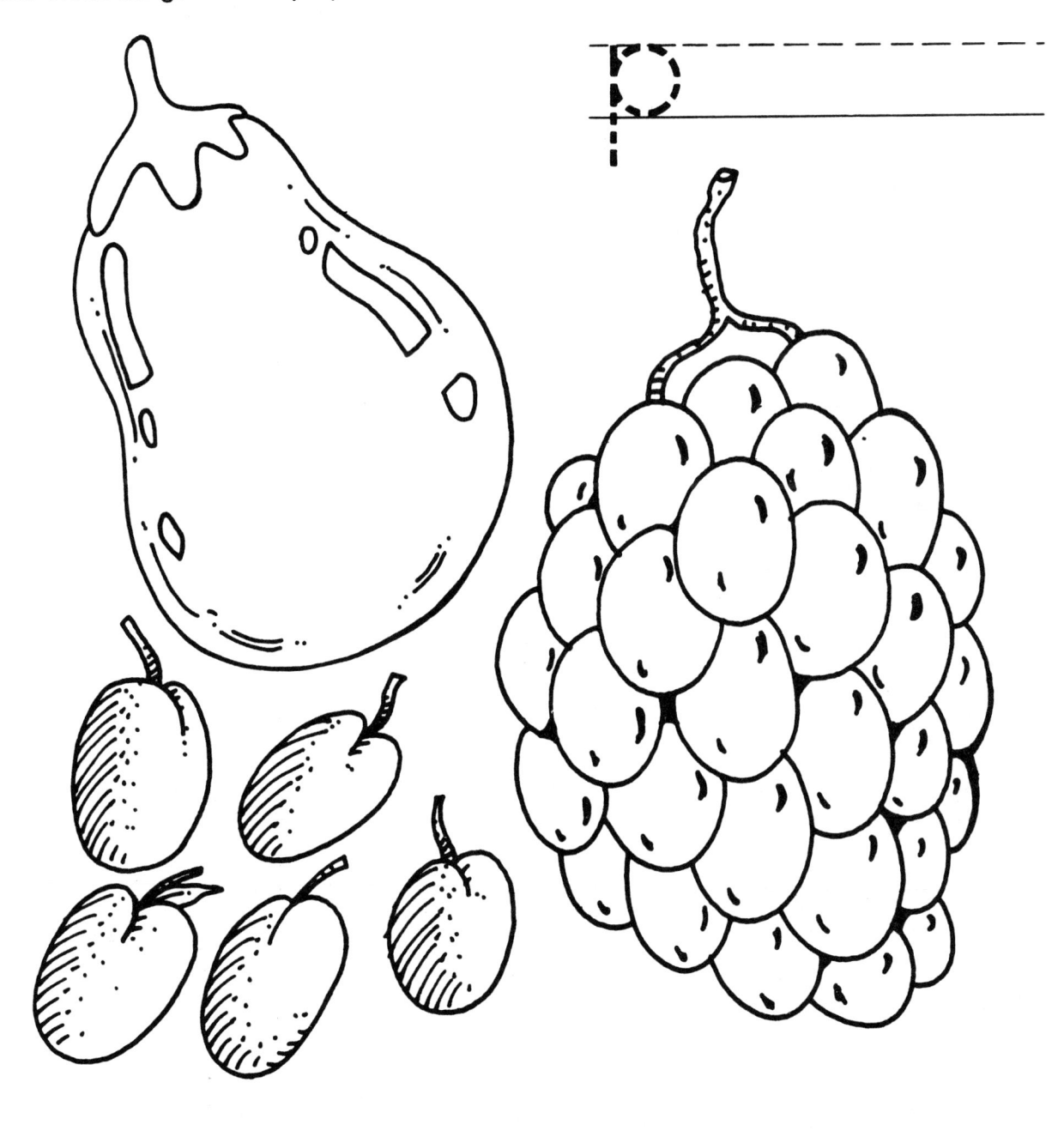

Skills: Distinguishing color; Classification; Word recognition

COLORS, SHAPES, AND NUMBERS

Trace and print the word.

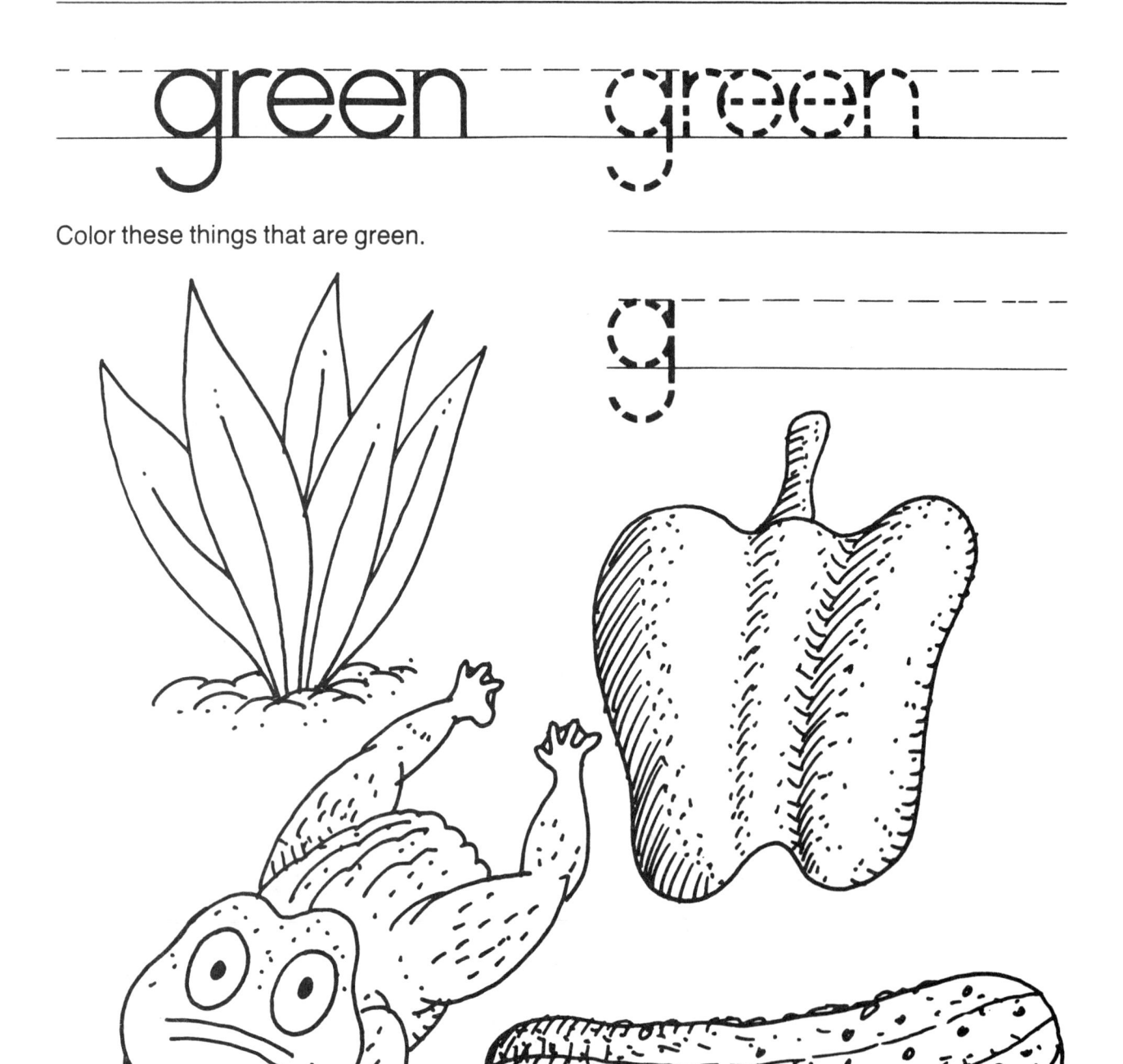

green   green

Color these things that are green.

g

Skills: Distinguishing color; Classification; Word recognition

COLORS, SHAPES, AND NUMBERS

Trace and print the word.

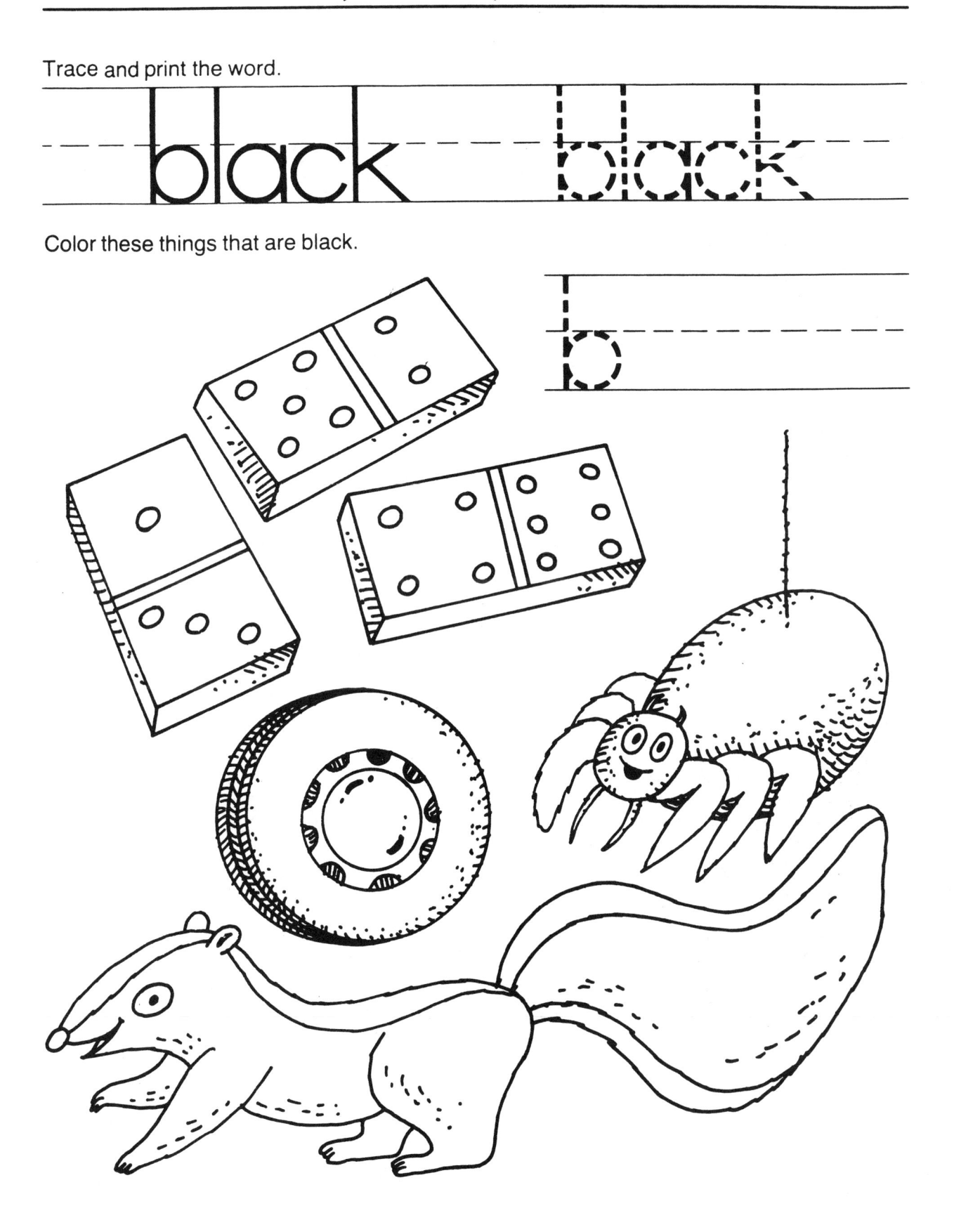

black   black

Color these things that are black.

b

Skills: Distinguishing color; Classification; Word recognition

COLORS, SHAPES, AND NUMBERS

Trace and print the word.

brown   brown

Color these things that are brown.

b

Skills: Distinguishing color; Classification; Word recognition

COLORS, SHAPES, AND NUMBERS

Look at the boats in the lake.
Color each boat to match the color word.
Then color the lake blue.

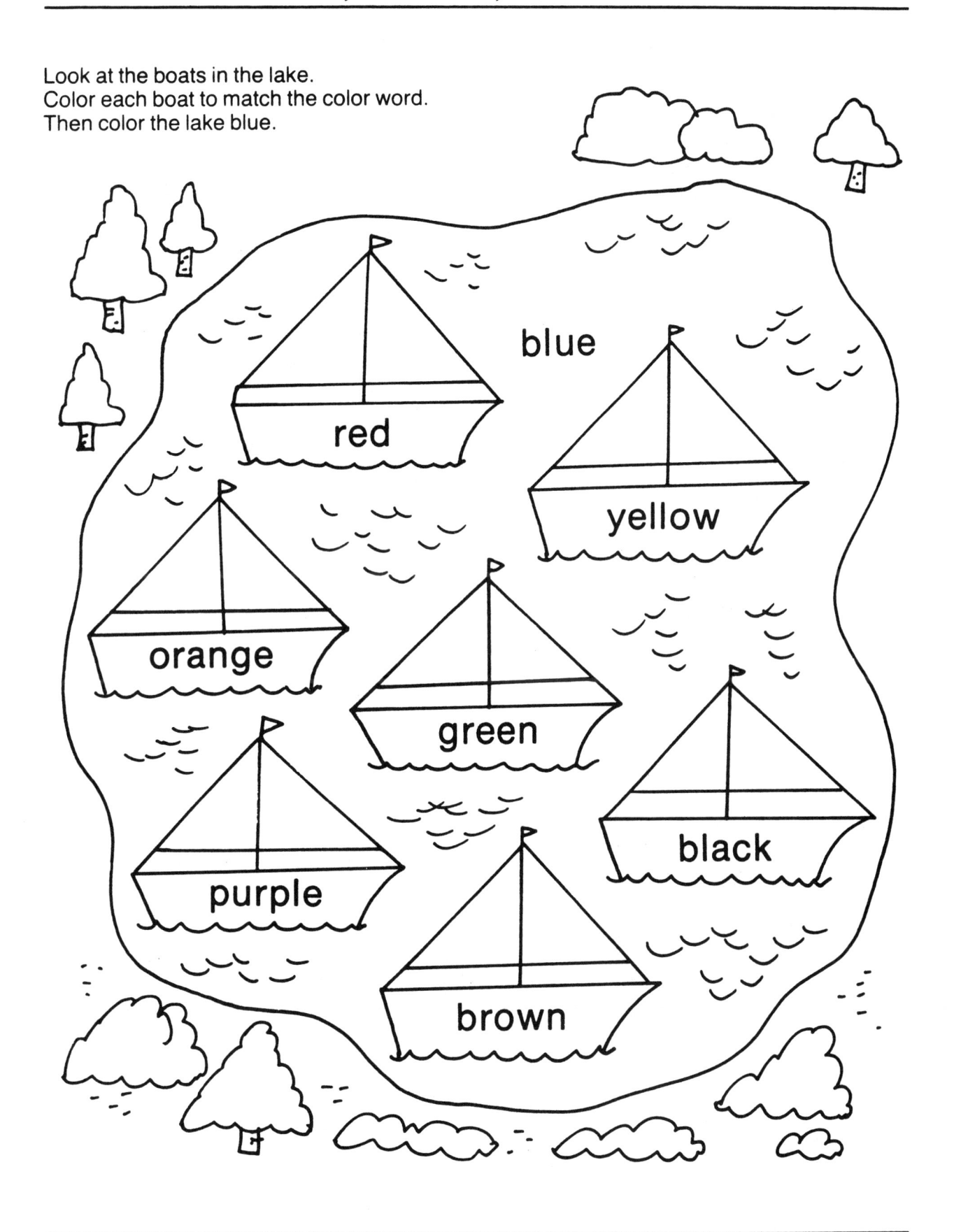

blue

red

yellow

orange

green

purple

black

brown

Skills: Distinguishing color; Word recognition; Fine motor skill development

COLORS, SHAPES, AND NUMBERS

What is hiding in this picture?
Follow these directions to find out.
Color the A spaces red.
Color the B spaces blue.
Color the C spaces yellow.
Color the D spaces green.
Color the E spaces orange.

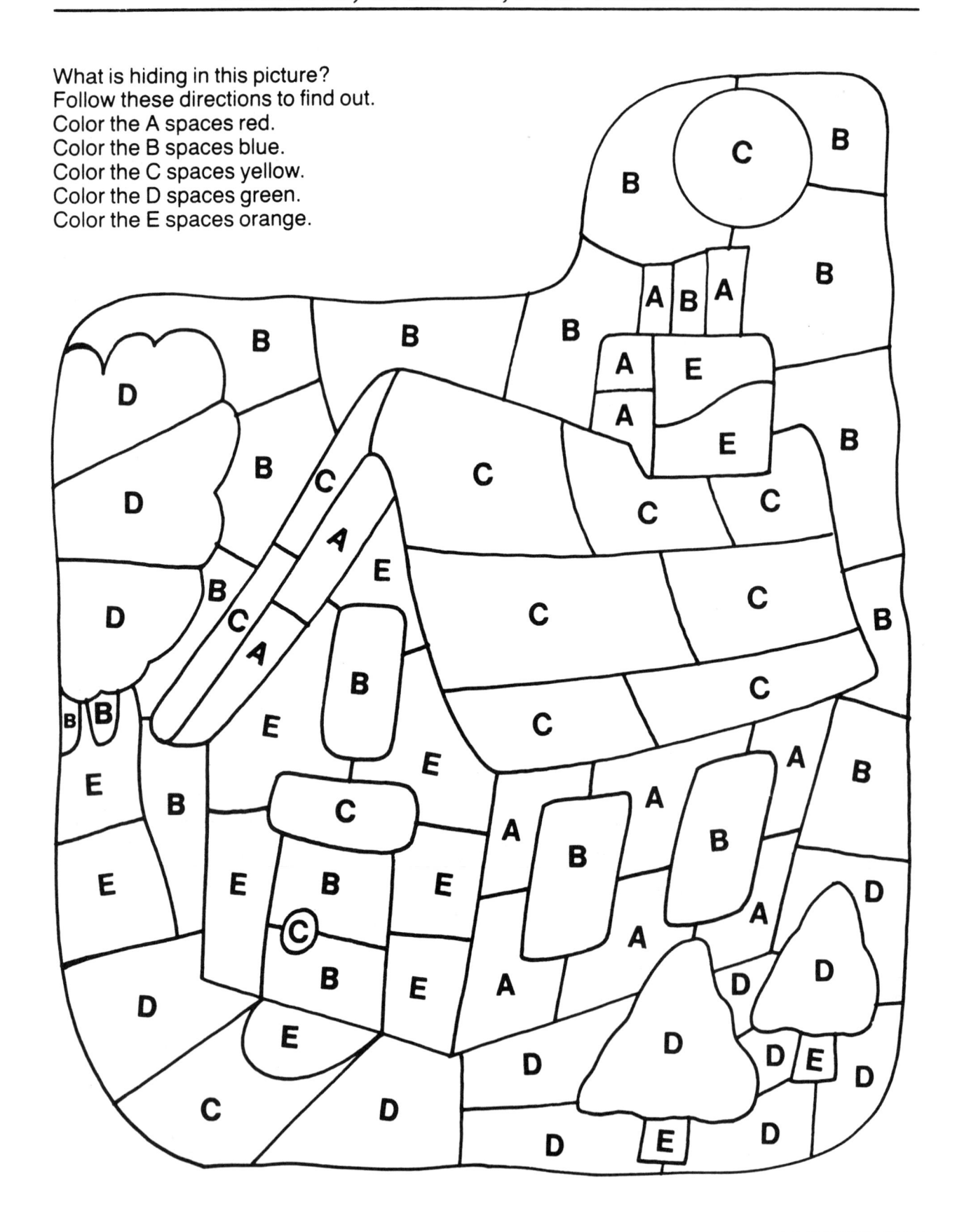

Skills: Distinguishing color; Matching letters to color codes

COLORS, SHAPES, AND NUMBERS

Look at the picture below.
Color the dog brown.
Color the flowers red.
Color the grass green.
Color the sun yellow.
Color the kite blue.
Color the boy's shirt orange.

Skills: Following directions; Matching colors to objects

COLORS, SHAPES, AND NUMBERS

Color each picture at the top to match the color word.
Then look at the color in each box.
Draw something that is that color.

red   **blue**   **yellow**   **green**

red	blue

yellow	green

Skills: Following directions; Matching colors to color words; Responding creatively

COLORS, SHAPES, AND NUMBERS

Trace the circles at the top of the page.
Draw your own circles on the bottom.
Then color the shapes.

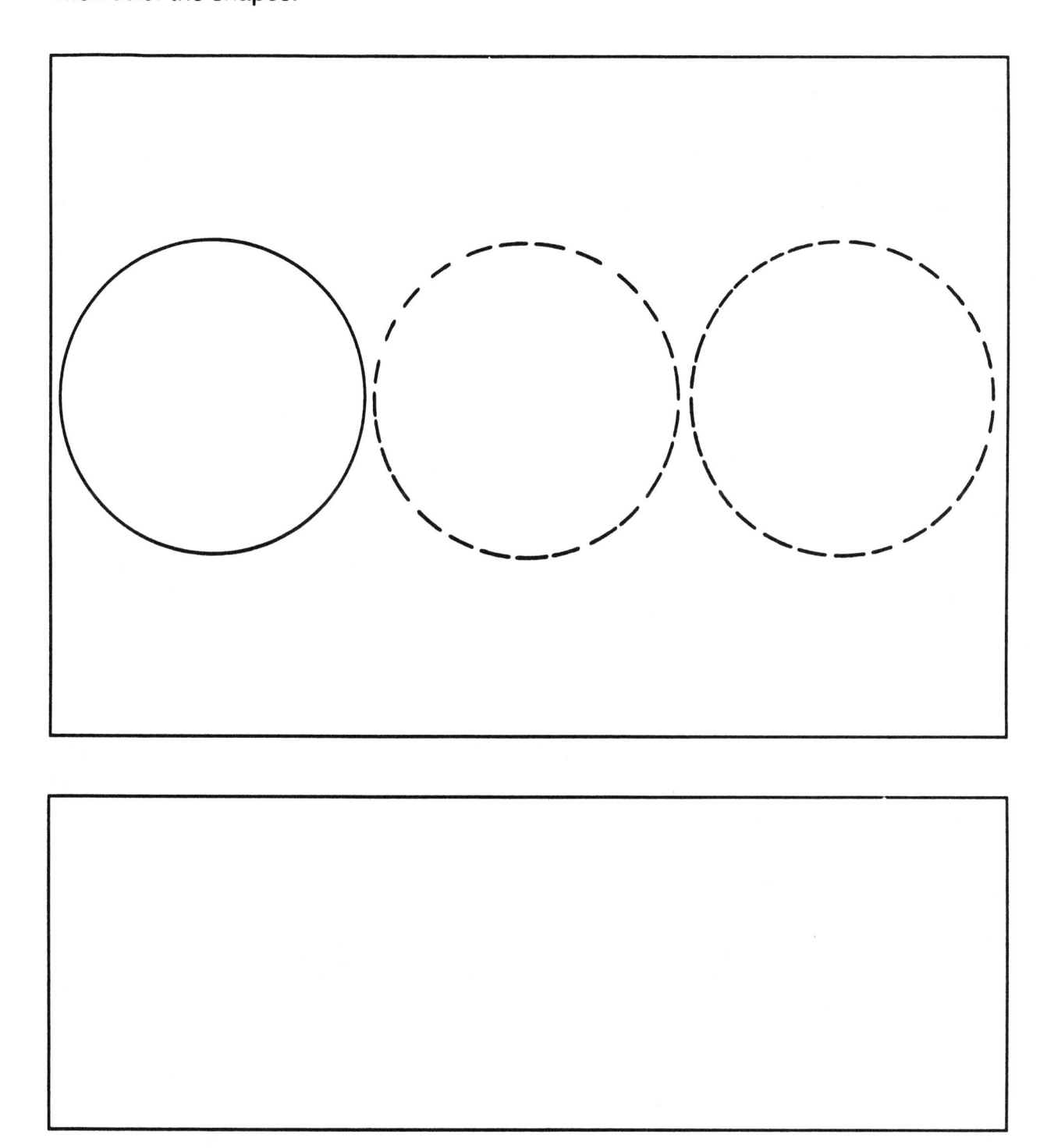

Skills: Recognizing shapes; Forming geometric shapes

COLORS, SHAPES, AND NUMBERS

Look at the circles at the top of the page.
Write the word. Then color the circles.

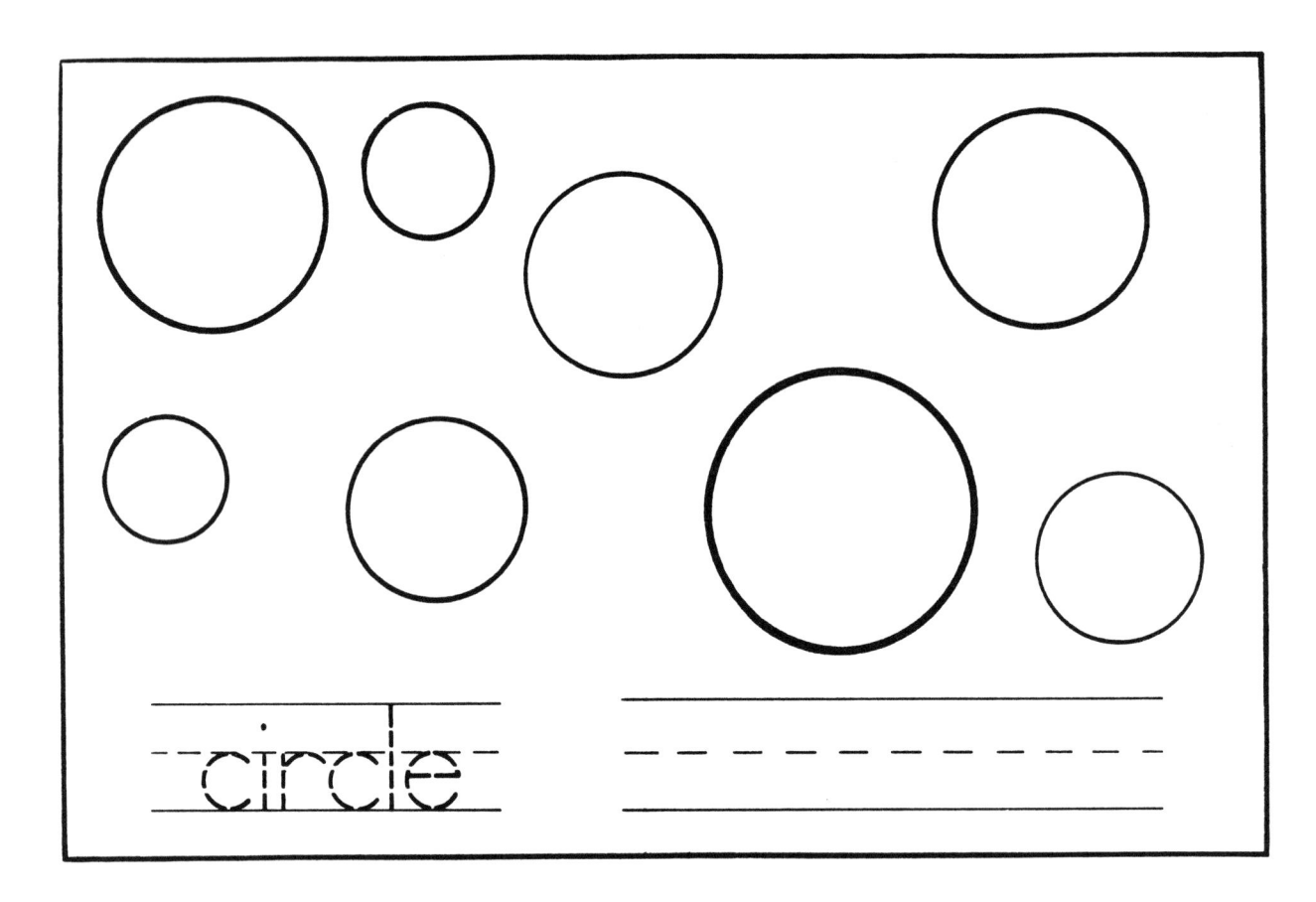

circle

Draw something that is shaped like a circle.

Skills: Fine motor skill development; Sight vocabulary recognition; Association between sight vocabulary and shapes

COLORS, SHAPES, AND NUMBERS

Trace the squares at the top of the page.
Draw your own squares on the bottom.
Then color the shapes.

Skills: Recognizing shapes; Forming geometric shapes

63

COLORS, SHAPES, AND NUMBERS

Look at the squares at the top of the page.
Write the word. Then color the squares.

square

Draw something that is shaped like a square.

Skills: Fine motor skill development; Sight vocabulary recognition; Association between sight vocabulary and shapes

COLORS, SHAPES, AND NUMBERS

Trace the triangles at the top of the page.
Draw your own triangles on the bottom.
Then color the shapes.

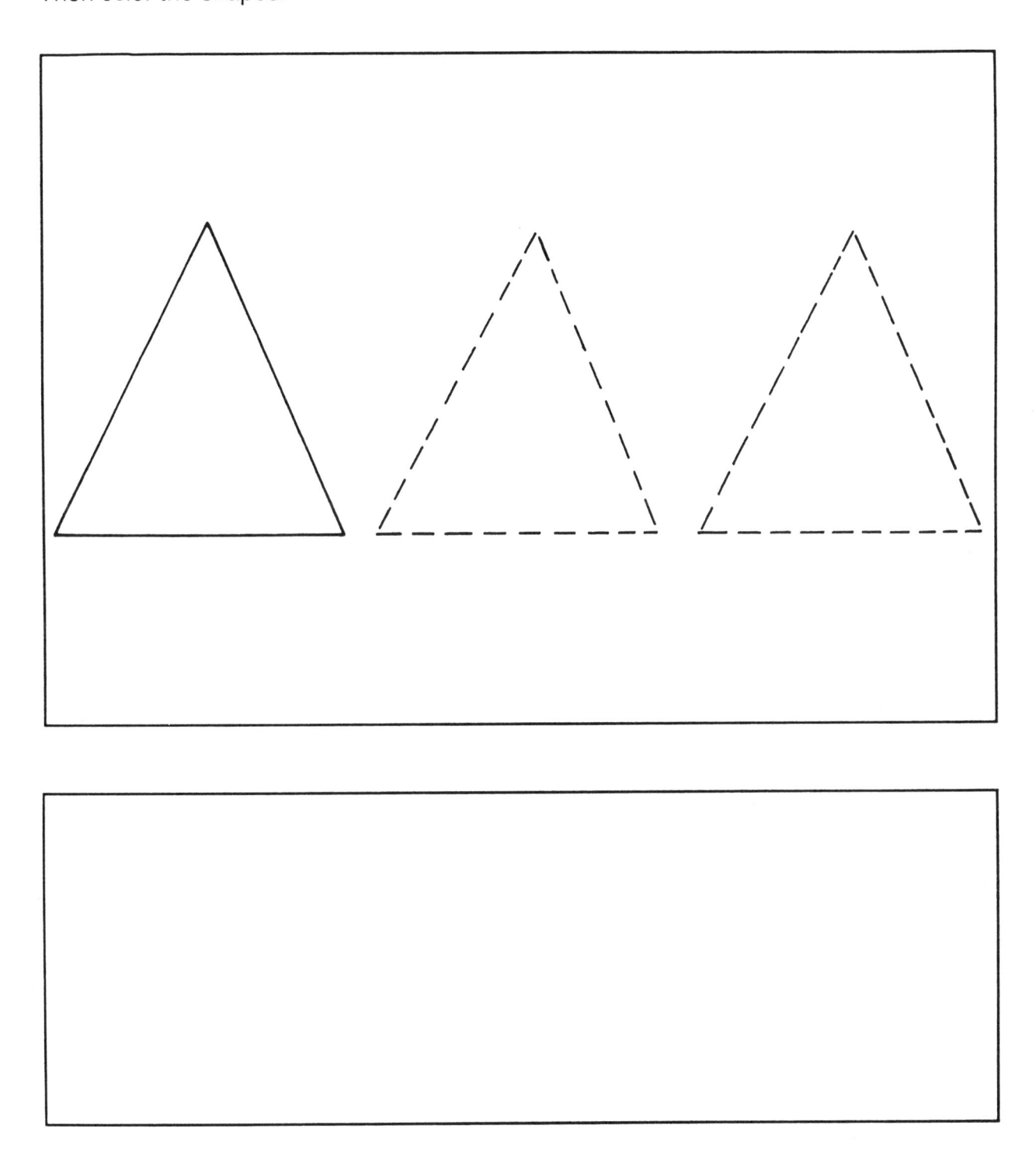

Skills: Recognizing shapes; Forming geometric shapes

COLORS, SHAPES, AND NUMBERS

Look at the triangles at the top of the page.
Write the word. Then color the triangles.

triangle

Draw something that is shaped like a triangle.

Skills: Fine motor skill development; Sight vocabulary recognition; Association between sight vocabulary and shapes

COLORS, SHAPES, AND NUMBERS

Trace the rectangles at the top of the page.
Draw your own rectangles on the bottom.
Then color the shapes.

Skills: Recognizing shapes; Forming geometric shapes

COLORS, SHAPES, AND NUMBERS

Look at the rectangles at the top of the page.
Write the word. Then color the rectangles.

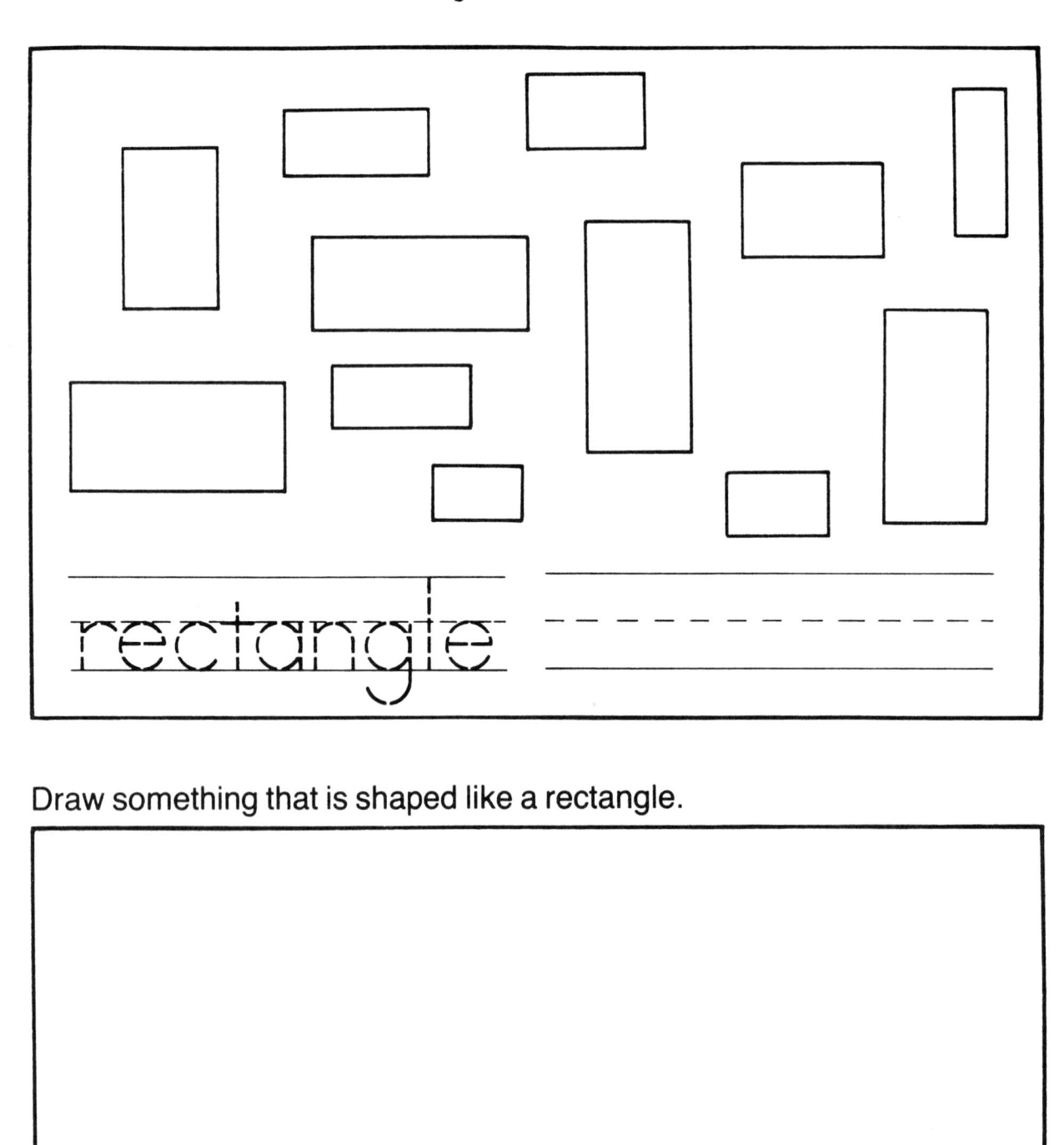

rectangle

Draw something that is shaped like a rectangle.

Skills: Fine motor skill development; Sight vocabulary recognition; Association between sight vocabulary and shapes

COLORS, SHAPES, AND NUMBERS

Look at the circles at the top of the page.
Circle the objects that are shaped like circles.

Skills: Recognizing shapes in objects

COLORS, SHAPES, AND NUMBERS

Look at the squares at the top of the page.
Circle the objects that are shaped like squares.

Skills: Recognizing shapes in objects

COLORS, SHAPES, AND NUMBERS

Look at the triangles at the top of the page.
Circle the objects that are shaped like triangles.

Skills: Recognizing shapes in objects

71

COLORS, SHAPES, AND NUMBERS

Look at the rectangles at the top of the page.
Circle the objects that are shaped like rectangles.

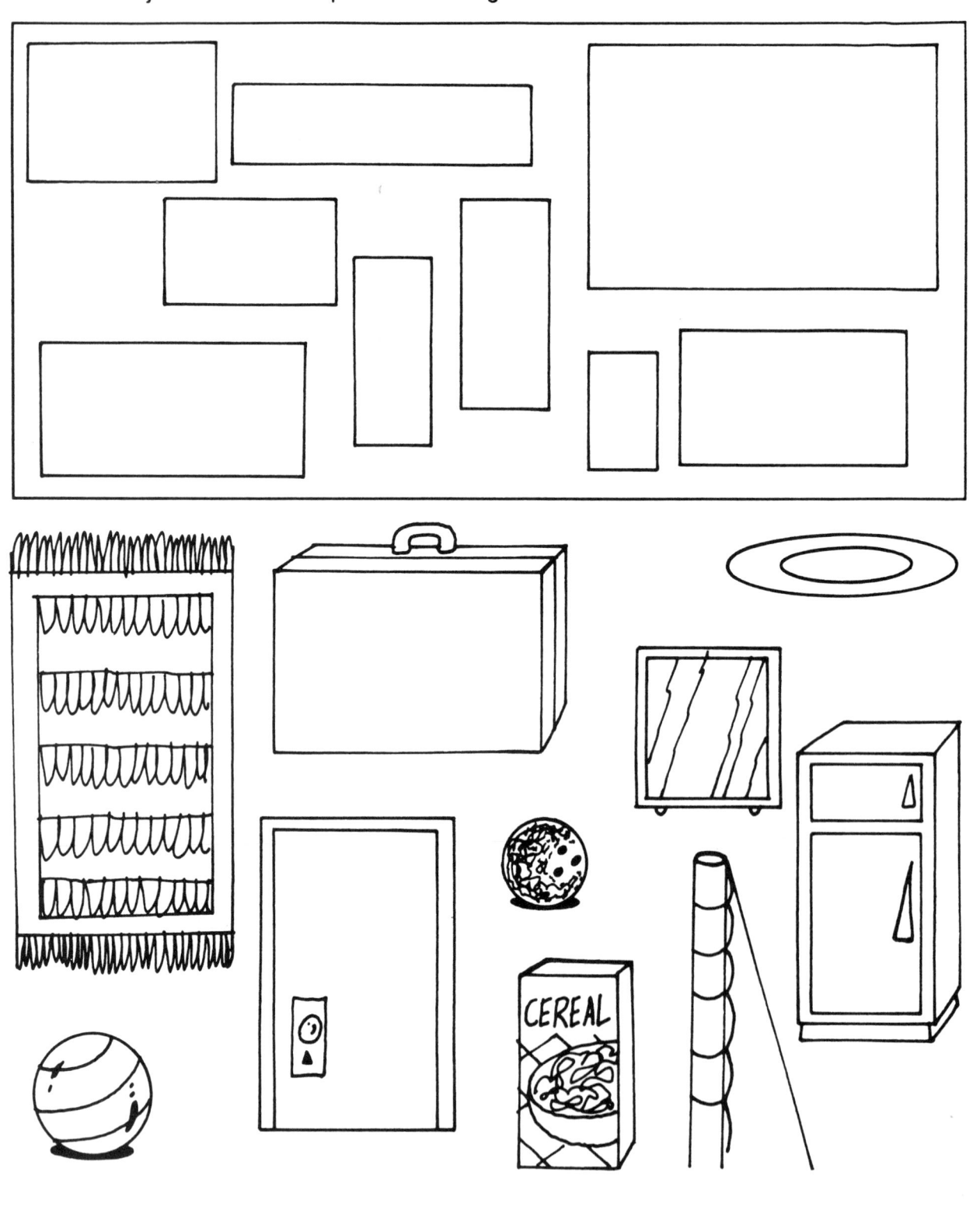

Skills: Recognizing shapes in objects

COLORS, SHAPES, AND NUMBERS

Color the shape that matches the word.

Triangle	○ □ △ ▭
Square	△ □ ▭ ○
Circle	▭ △ ○ □
Rectangle	□ ▭ ○ △

Skills: Following directions; Association between sight vocabulary and shapes; Sight vocabulary recognition

COLORS, SHAPES, AND NUMBERS

Look at the shapes.
Color the circles red.
Color the triangles yellow.
Color the squares blue.
Color the rectangles green.

Skills: Following directions; Association between sight vocabulary and shapes

COLORS, SHAPES, AND NUMBERS

Color the squares red.
Color the circles blue.
Color the triangles yellow.
Color the rectangles green.

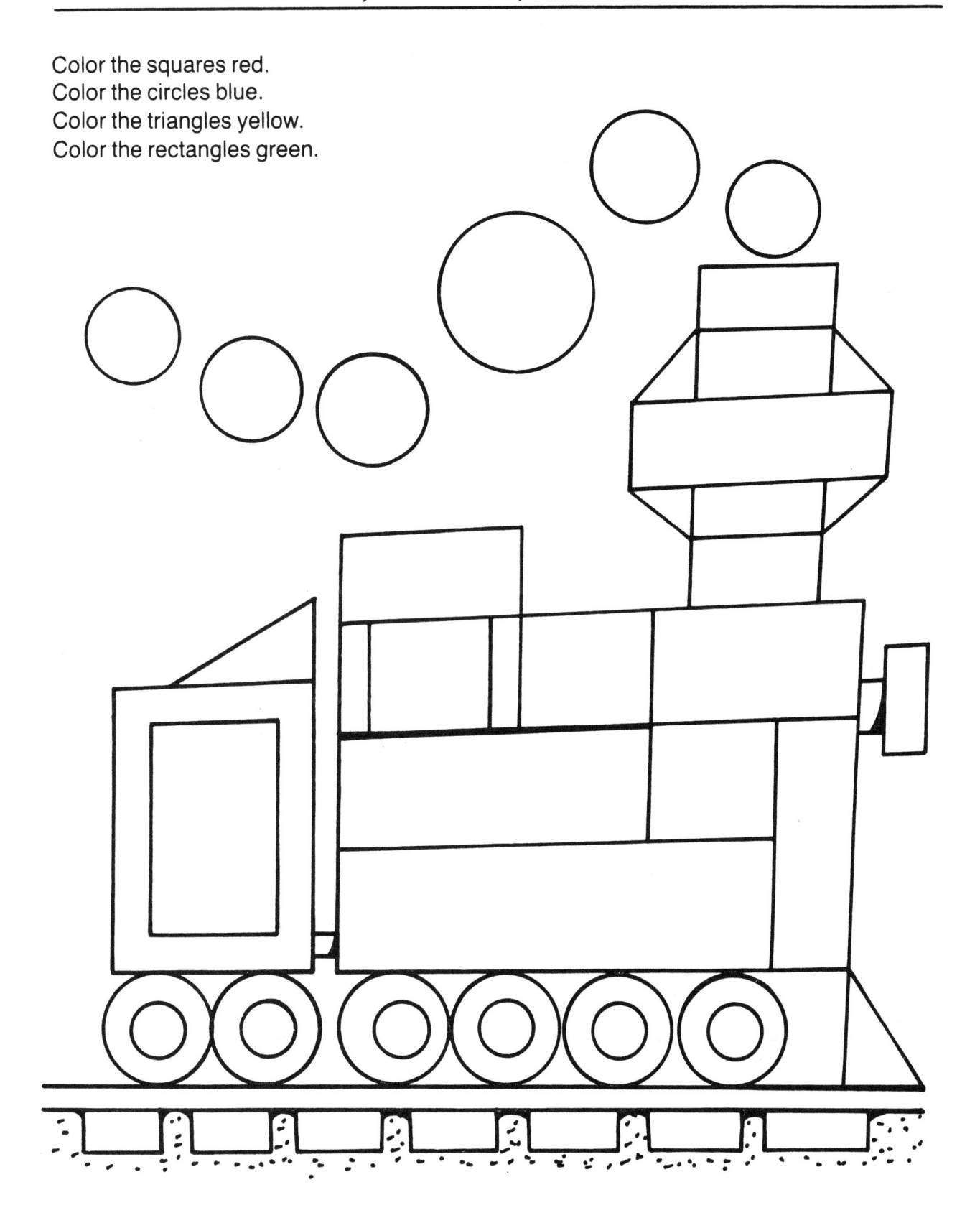

Skills: Following directions; Association between sight vocabulary and shapes

COLORS, SHAPES, AND NUMBERS

Look at each shape.
Find and circle the shapes that have two sides that match.
Then color all of the shapes.

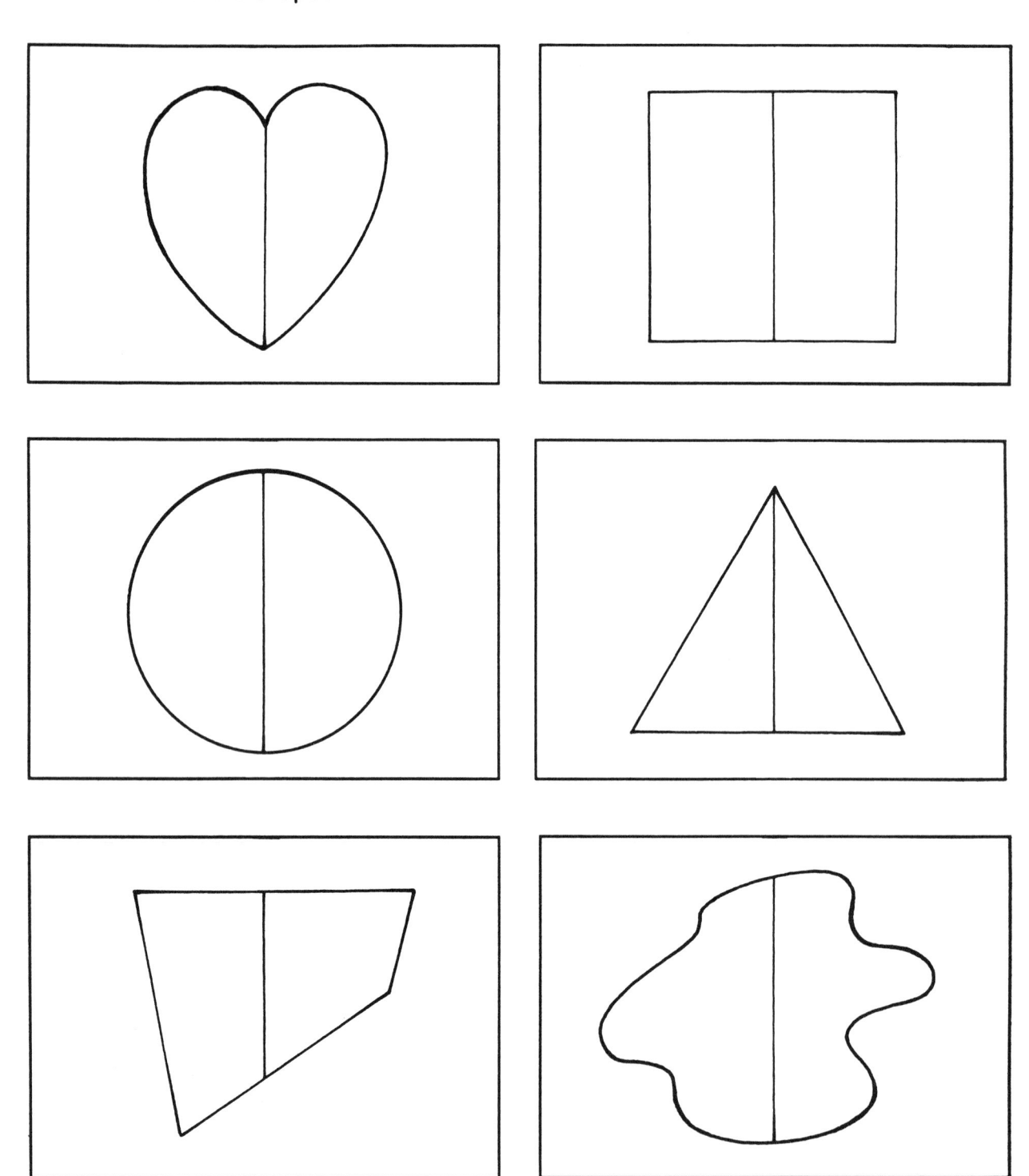

Skills: Recognizing symmetrical shapes

76

COLORS, SHAPES, AND NUMBERS

Look at each picture.
Find and circle the pictures that have two sides that match.
Then color all of the pictures.

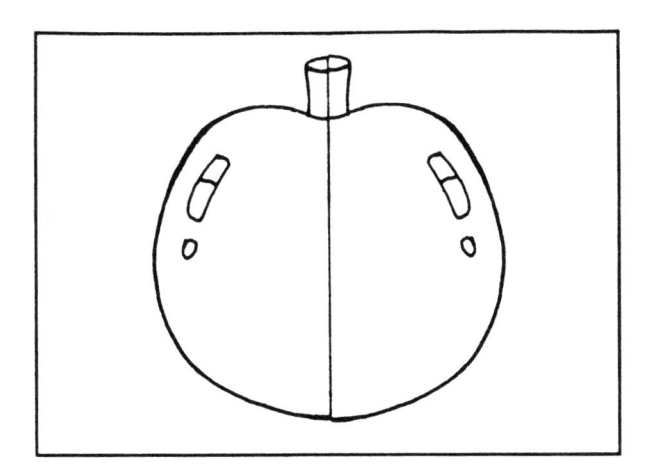

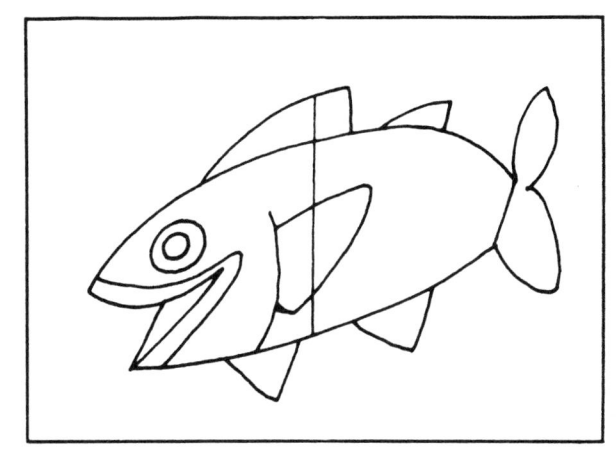

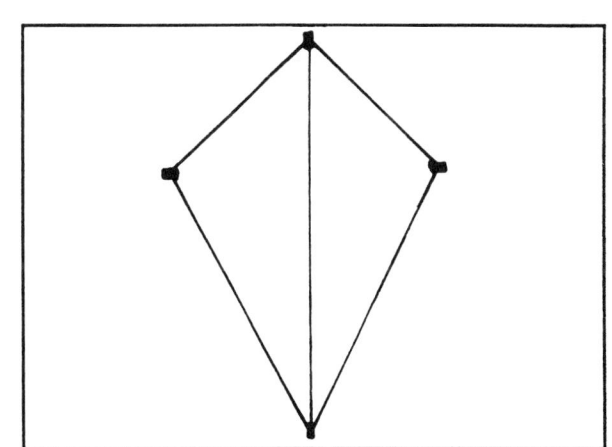

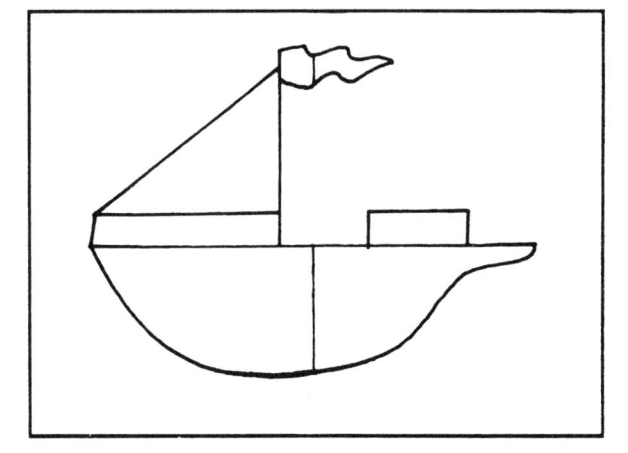

Skills: Recognizing symmetry in objects

77

COLORS, SHAPES, AND NUMBERS

How many objects are in each set?
Draw a line to match the sets with the same number of objects.

Skills: Identifying sets; Matching

COLORS, SHAPES, AND NUMBERS

Circle the correct numeral.

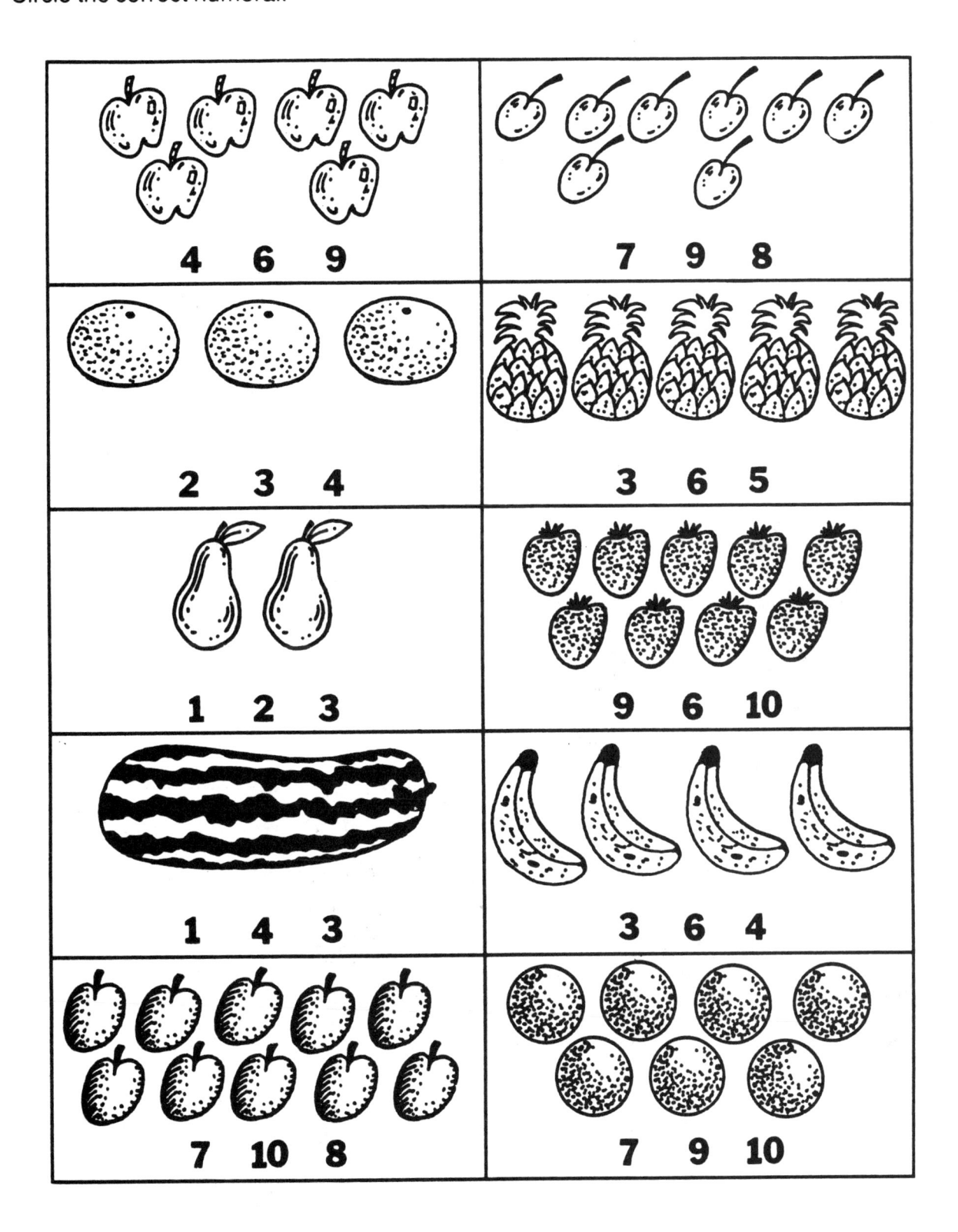

4 6 9	7 9 8
2 3 4	3 6 5
1 2 3	9 6 10
1 4 3	3 6 4
7 10 8	7 9 10

Skills: Recognizing sets of objects and the corresponding numeral; Following directions

COLORS, SHAPES, AND NUMBERS

Print the correct numeral.

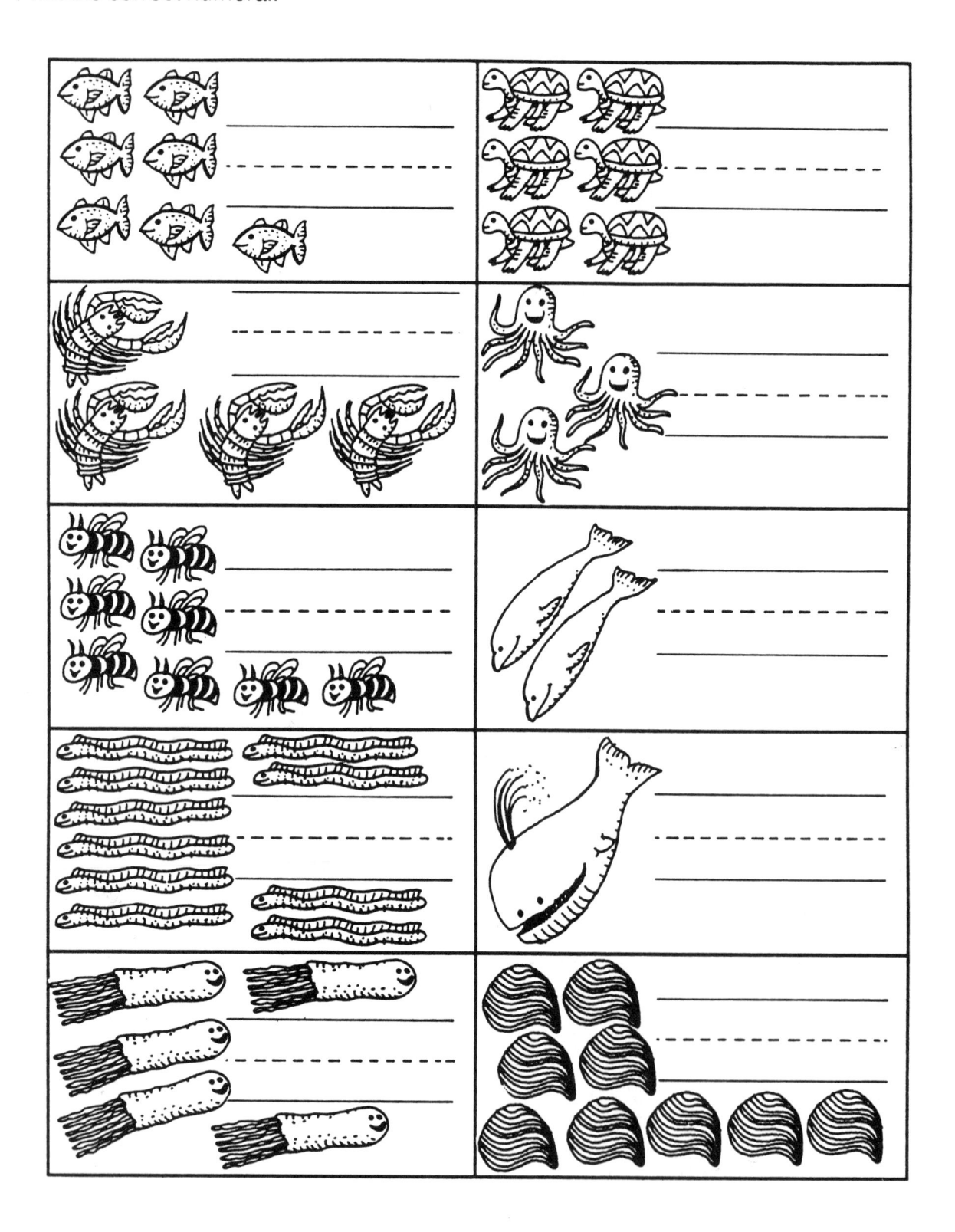

Skills: Recognizing sets of objects; Forming numerals

COLORS, SHAPES, AND NUMBERS

Trace and print the numerals and the number words.

1 one	2 two
1 one	2 two

Skills: Recognizing sets of one and two; Association between sight vocabulary, numerals and sets

81

COLORS, SHAPES, AND NUMBERS

Trace and print the numerals and the number words.

3 three

4 four

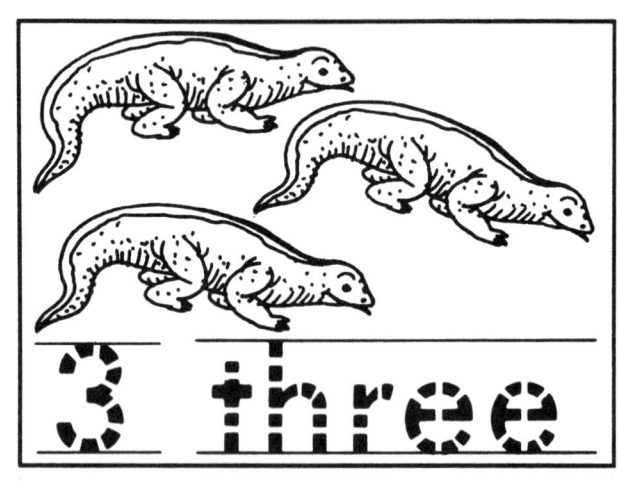

3 three

4 four

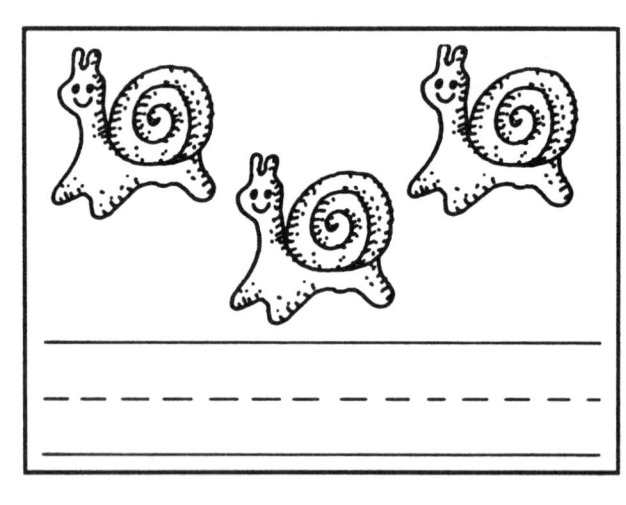

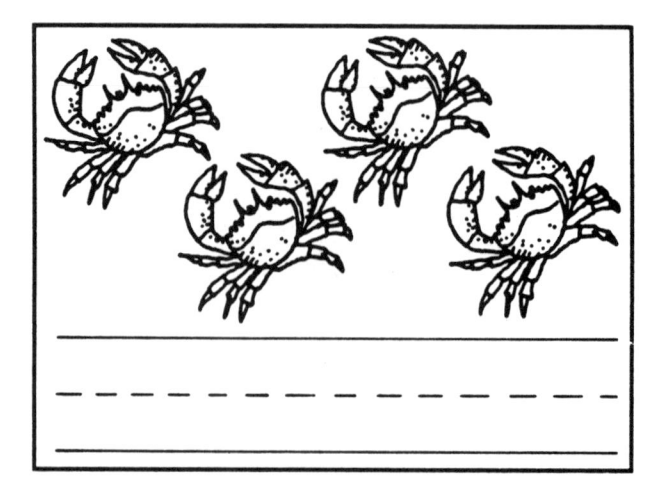

Skills: Recognizing sets of three and four; Association between sight vocabulary, numerals and sets

COLORS, SHAPES, AND NUMBERS

Trace and print the numerals and the number words.

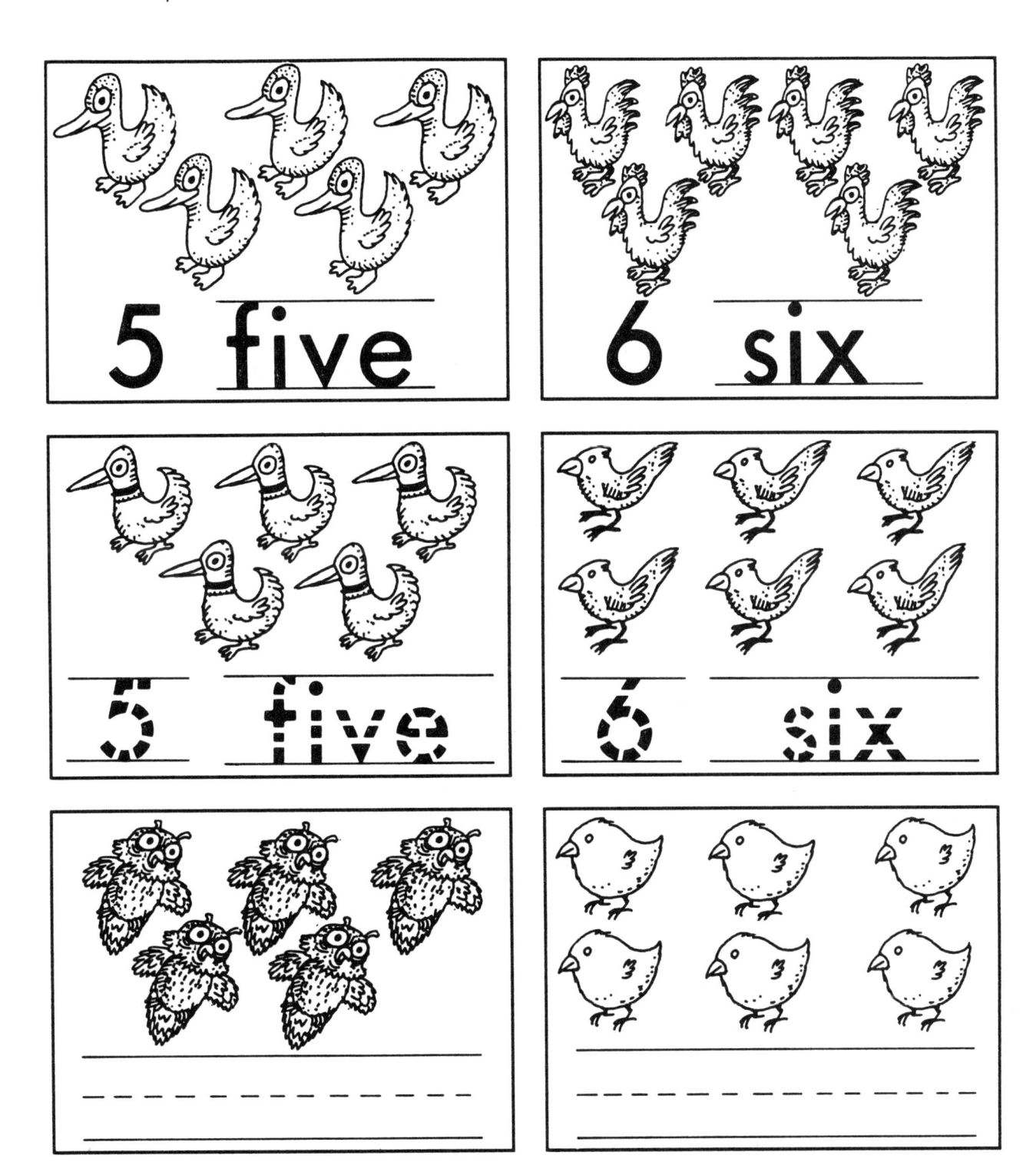

5 five	6 six
5 five	6 six

Skills: Recognizing sets of five and six; Association between sight vocabulary, numerals and sets

COLORS, SHAPES, AND NUMBERS

Trace and print the numerals and the number words.

| 7 seven | 8 eight |
| 7 seven | 8 eight |

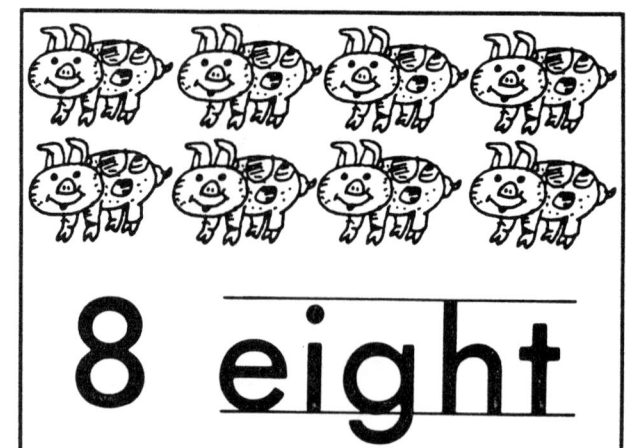

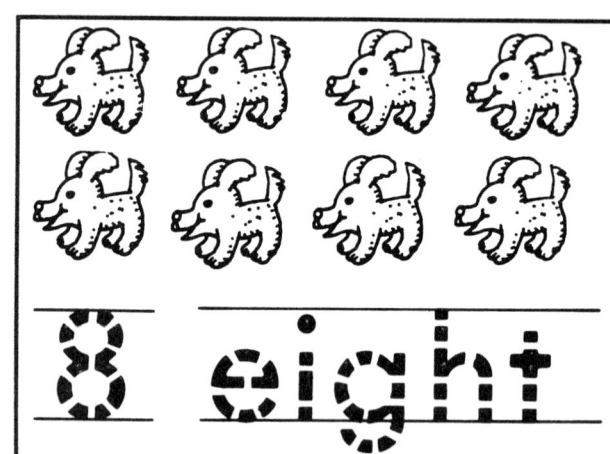

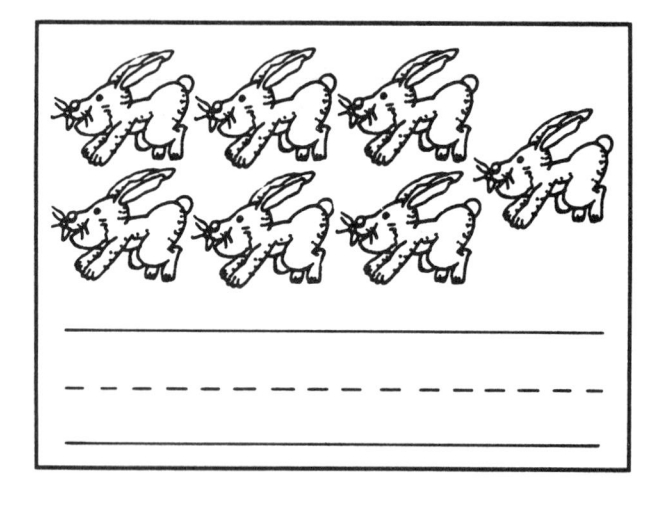

Skills: Recognizing sets of seven and eight; Association between sight vocabulary, numerals and sets

COLORS, SHAPES, AND NUMBERS

Trace and print the numerals and the number words.

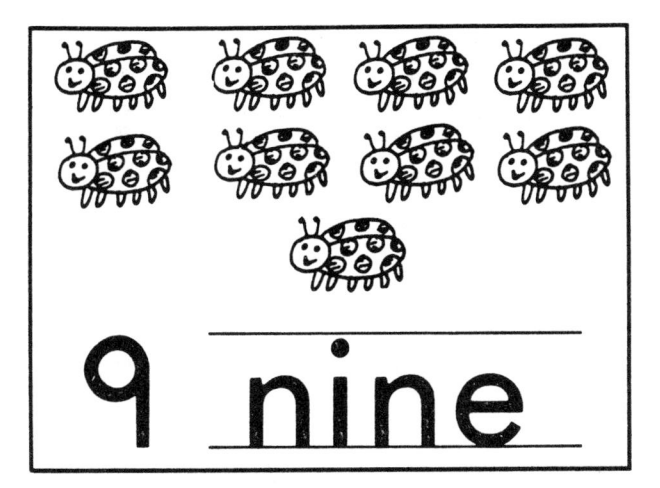

9 nine

10 ten

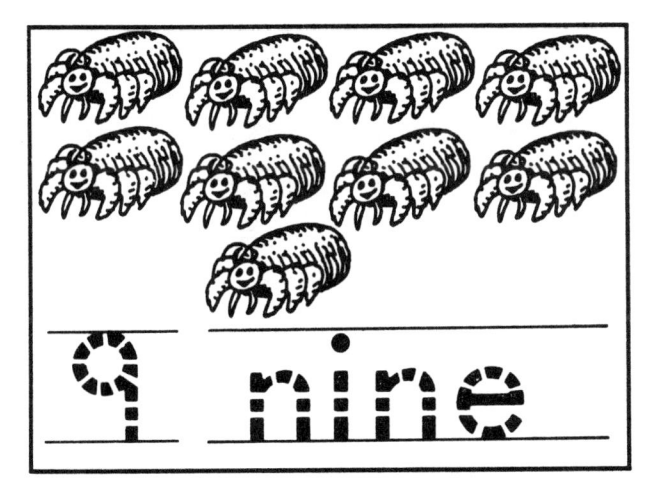

9 nine

10 ten

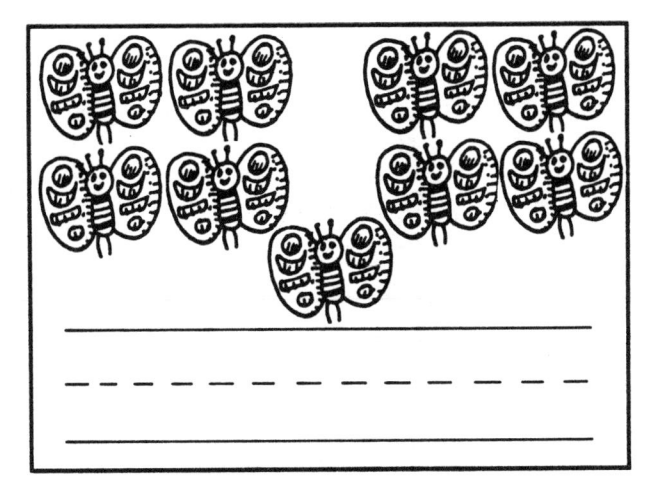

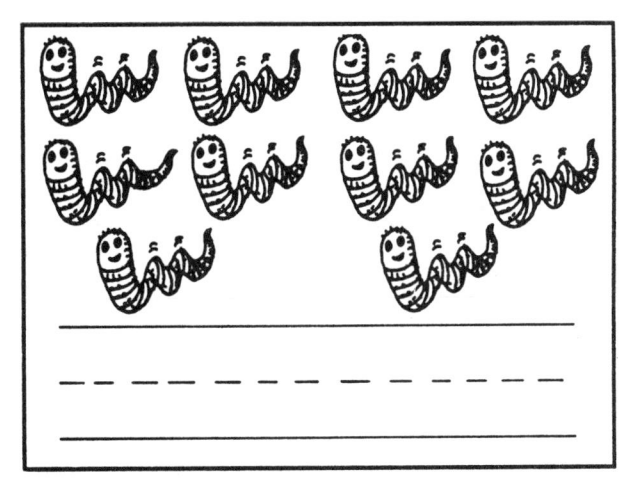

Skills: Recognizing sets of nine and ten; Association between sight vocabulary, numerals and sets

85

COLORS, SHAPES, AND NUMBERS

Trace the numerals and the number words.
Match the numerals and the words.

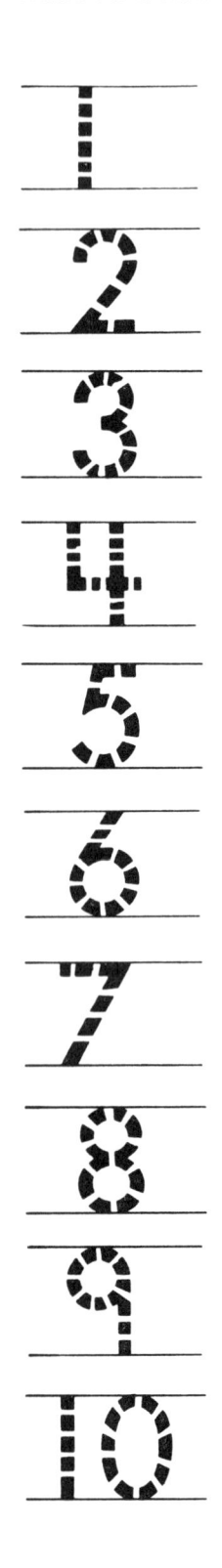

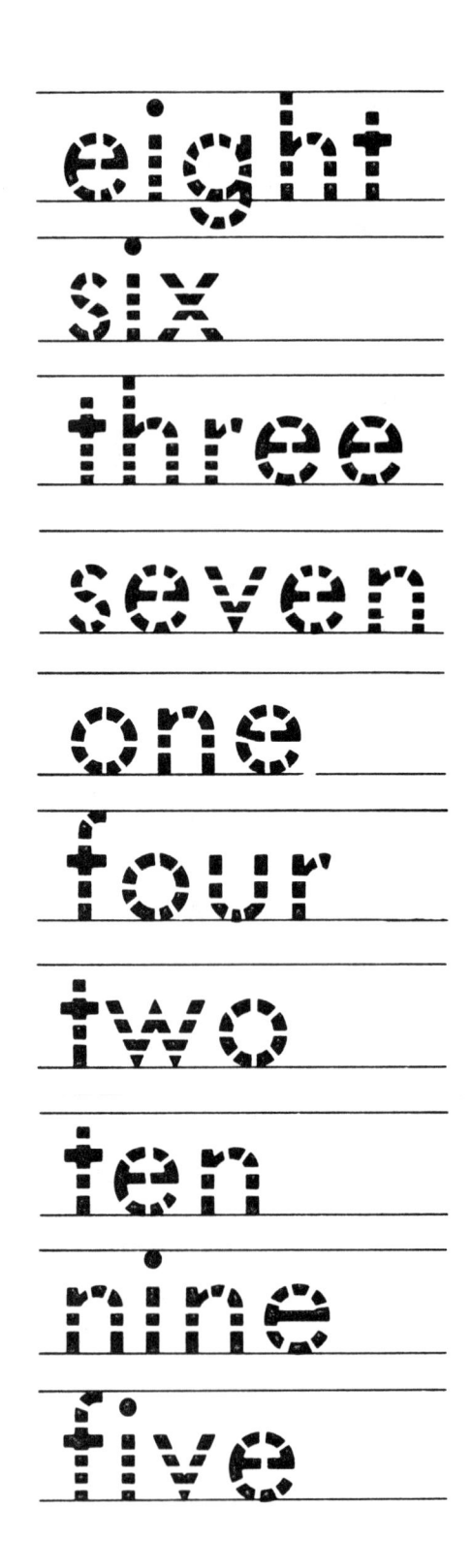

1	eight
2	six
3	three
4	seven
5	one
6	four
7	two
8	ten
9	nine
10	five

Skills: Following directions; Recognizing numerals and the corresponding number word

COLORS, SHAPES, AND NUMBERS

Circle the correct number.

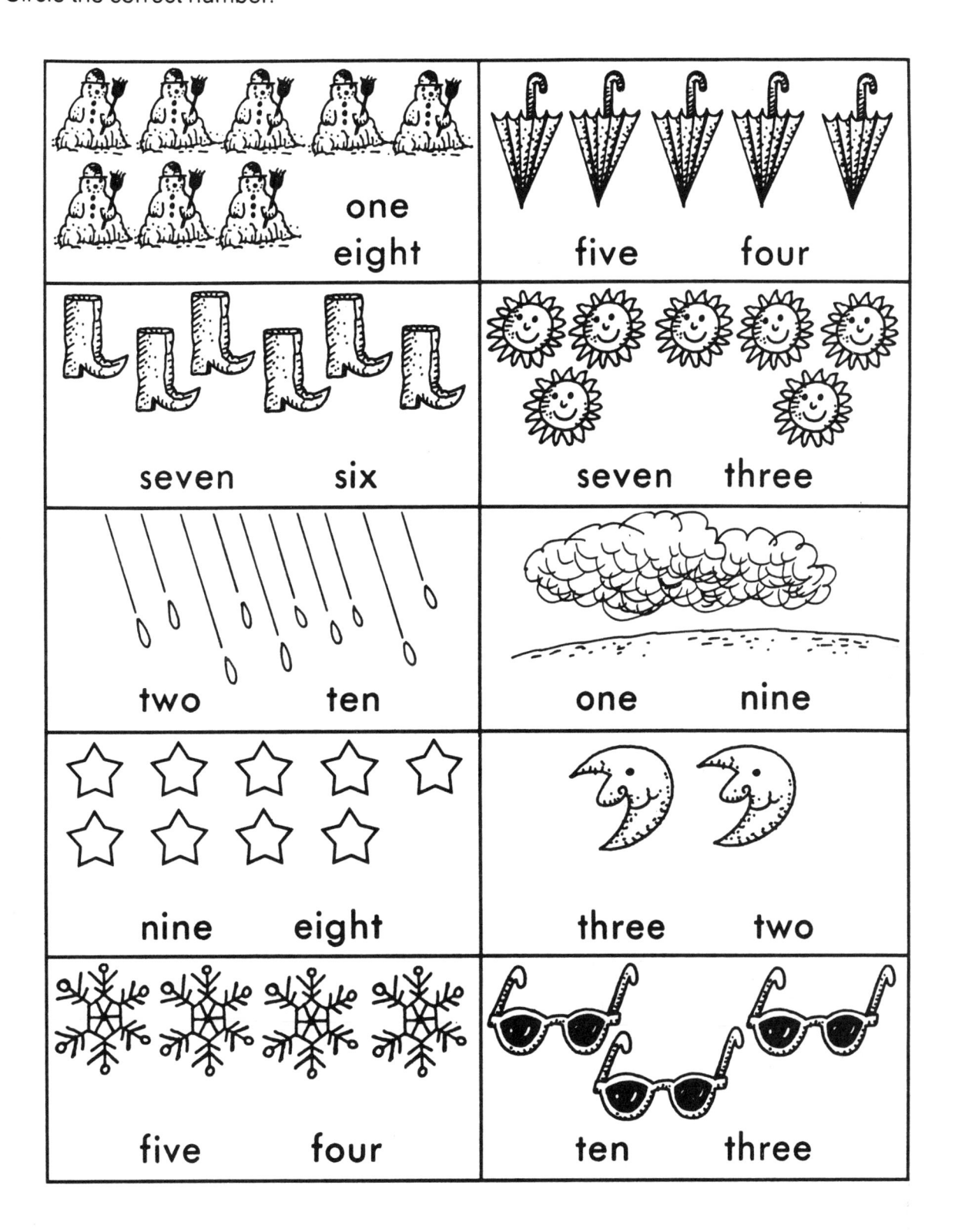

one / eight	five / four
seven / six	seven / three
two / ten	one / nine
nine / eight	three / two
five / four	ten / three

Skills: Recognizing sets of objects and the corresponding number word

COLORS, SHAPES, AND NUMBERS

Look at the large picture below.
Then look at the pictures in each small box.
Write the numeral that tells how many of each object you see.

Skills: Recognizing sets of objects; Classifying and recording information; Writing numerals

COLORS, SHAPES, AND NUMBERS

Count how many of each and write that numeral in each box. Then color the pictures.

Skills: Recognizing sets of objects; Classifying and recording information; Writing numerals

COLORS, SHAPES, AND NUMBERS

Count how many of each and write that numeral in each box. Then color the pictures.

Skills: Recognizing sets of objects; Classifying and recording information; Writing numerals

COLORS, SHAPES, AND NUMBERS

Trace the numerals and the number words.
Then draw that many objects.

1 one	2 two
3 three	4 four

Skills: Recognizing numerals; Writing number words; Forming corresponding sets of objects

COLORS, SHAPES, AND NUMBERS

Trace the numerals and the number words.
Then draw that many objects.

5 five	6 six
7 seven	8 eight

Skills: Recognizing numerals; Writing number words; Forming corresponding sets of objects

COLORS, SHAPES, AND NUMBERS

Trace the numerals and the number words.
Then draw that many objects.

9 nine

10 ten

Skills: Recognizing numerals; Writing number words; Forming corresponding sets of objects

COUNTING AND MATH SKILLS

Trace the numbers from 1 to 100.

1	2	3	4	5	6	7	8	9	10
11	12	13	14	15	16	17	18	19	20
21	22	23	24	25	26	27	28	29	30
31	32	33	34	35	36	37	38	39	40
41	42	43	44	45	46	47	48	49	50
51	52	53	54	55	56	57	58	59	60
61	62	63	64	65	66	67	68	69	70
71	72	73	74	75	76	77	78	79	80
81	82	83	84	85	86	87	88	89	90
91	92	93	94	95	96	97	98	99	100

Skills: Counting to 100; Forming numerals

COUNTING AND MATH SKILLS

Look at the balloons.
What number comes next?

5, 6, 7, ___

2, ___, 4, ___

1, ___, 3, ___

8, ___, 9, ___

Skills: Ordering numbers to 10; Writing numerals

COUNTING AND MATH SKILLS

Look at the jars.
What number comes next?

6, ___   4, ___

9, ___   7, ___

2, ___   5, ___

3, ___   8, ___

Skills: Ordering numbers to ten; Writing numerals

COUNTING AND MATH SKILLS

Look at the umbrellas.
Write the missing numbers.

4 5 __   7 __ 9

__ 3 4   6 7 __

8 9 __   1 2 __

Skills: Ordering numbers to ten; Writing numerals

COUNTING AND MATH SKILLS

Look at each group of cupcakes.
What number comes between?

4   5   6   8   ___   10

1   ___   3   6   ___   8

2   ___   4   5   ___   7

Skills: Ordering numbers to 10; Writing numerals

COUNTING AND MATH SKILLS

Look at the party bags.
Write the missing numbers.

8 9 10   2 3 ___

___ 5 6   4 5 ___

1 ___ 3   7 ___ 9

Skills: Ordering numbers to 10; Writing numerals

COUNTING AND MATH SKILLS

Look at the sets in each box.
Circle the number that tells how many.
Then color the pictures.

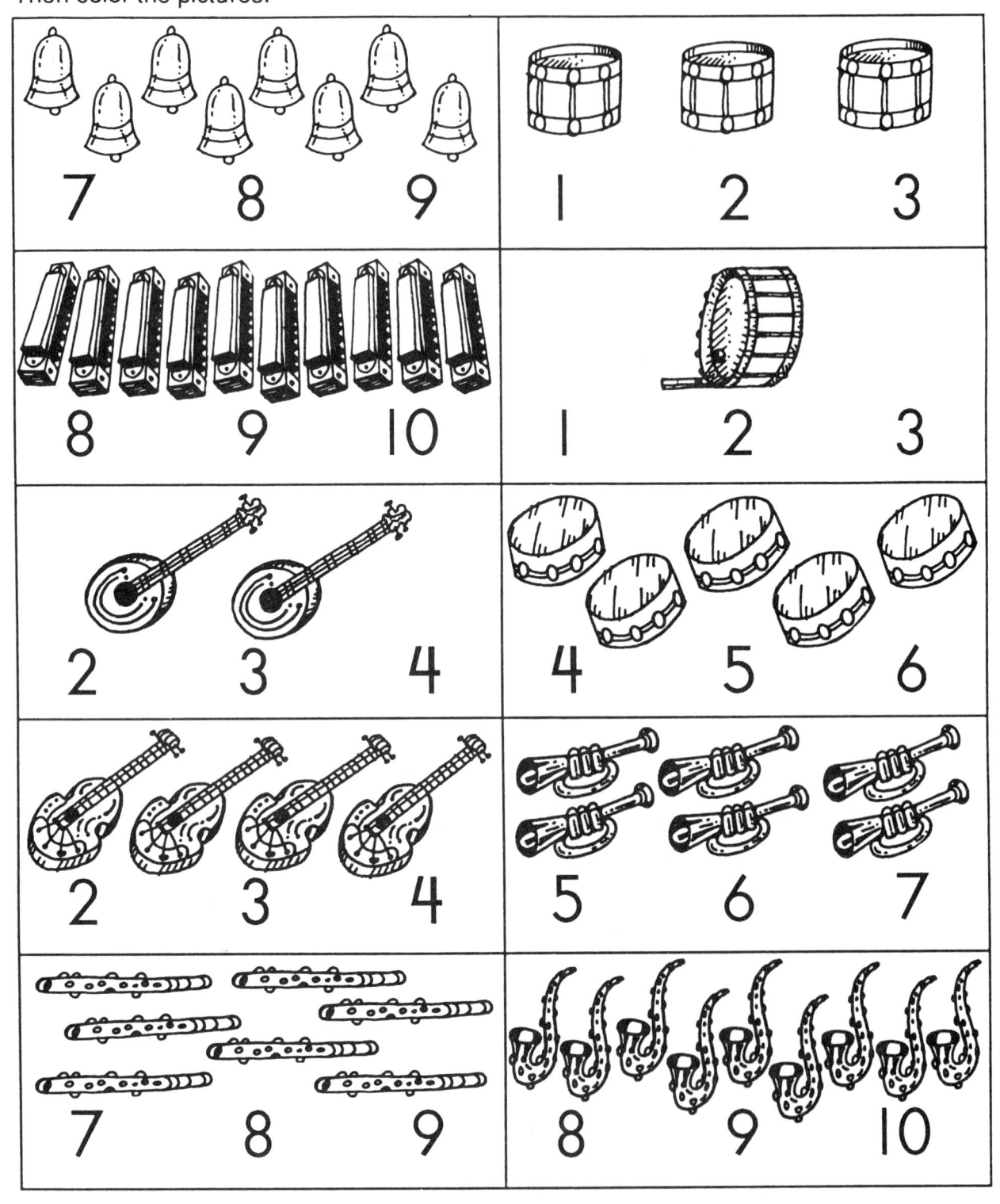

7 8 9	1 2 3
8 9 10	1 2 3
2 3 4	4 5 6
2 3 4	5 6 7
7 8 9	8 9 10

Skills: Recognizing sets of objects and the corresponding numeral

COUNTING AND MATH SKILLS

How many objects are in each set?
Draw a line to match the sets with the same number of objects.

Skills: Identifying and matching sets

101

COUNTING AND MATH SKILLS

Look at the numeral on each necklace.
Draw that many beads on each necklace.

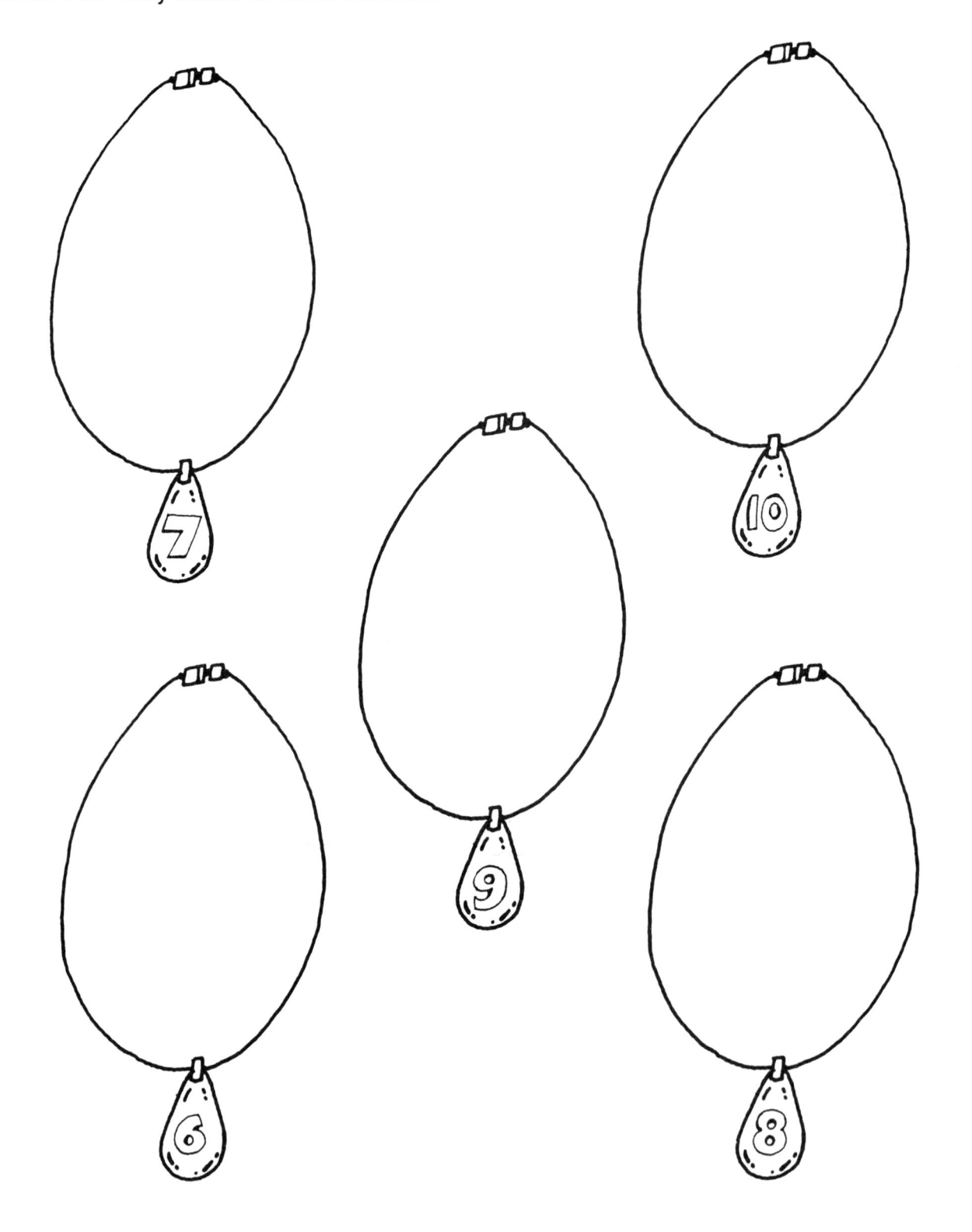

Skills: Recognizing numerals; Creating sets to show an amount

COUNTING AND MATH SKILLS

Look at the numeral at the beginning of each row.
Circle that **number** of fruits.

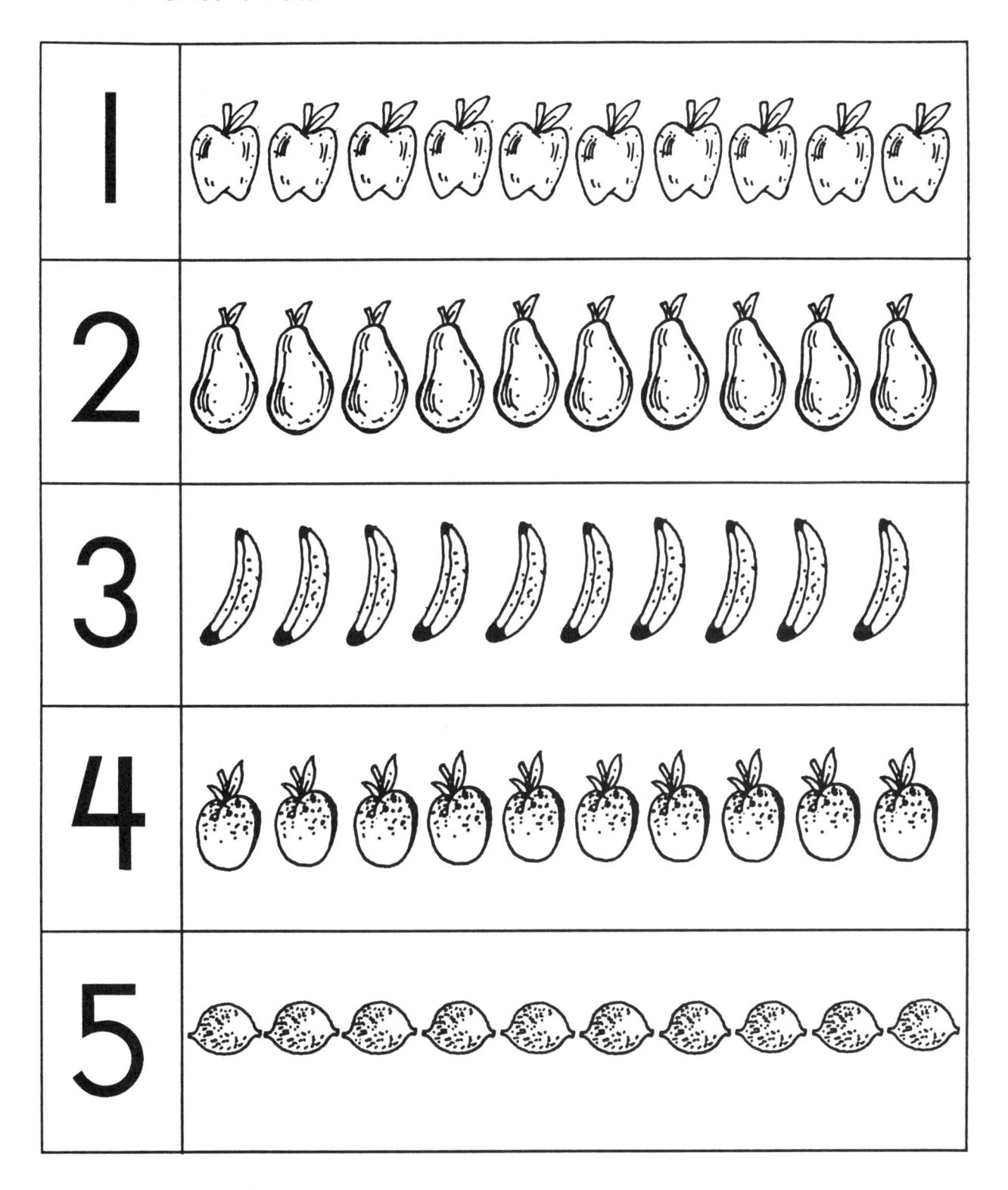

1	🍎🍎🍎🍎🍎🍎🍎🍎🍎🍎
2	🍐🍐🍐🍐🍐🍐🍐🍐🍐🍐
3	🍌🍌🍌🍌🍌🍌🍌🍌🍌🍌
4	🍓🍓🍓🍓🍓🍓🍓🍓🍓🍓
5	🍋🍋🍋🍋🍋🍋🍋🍋🍋🍋

Skills: Creating sets of objects; Recognizing numerals

COUNTING AND MATH SKILLS

Look at the numeral at the beginning of each row.
Circle that number of objects.

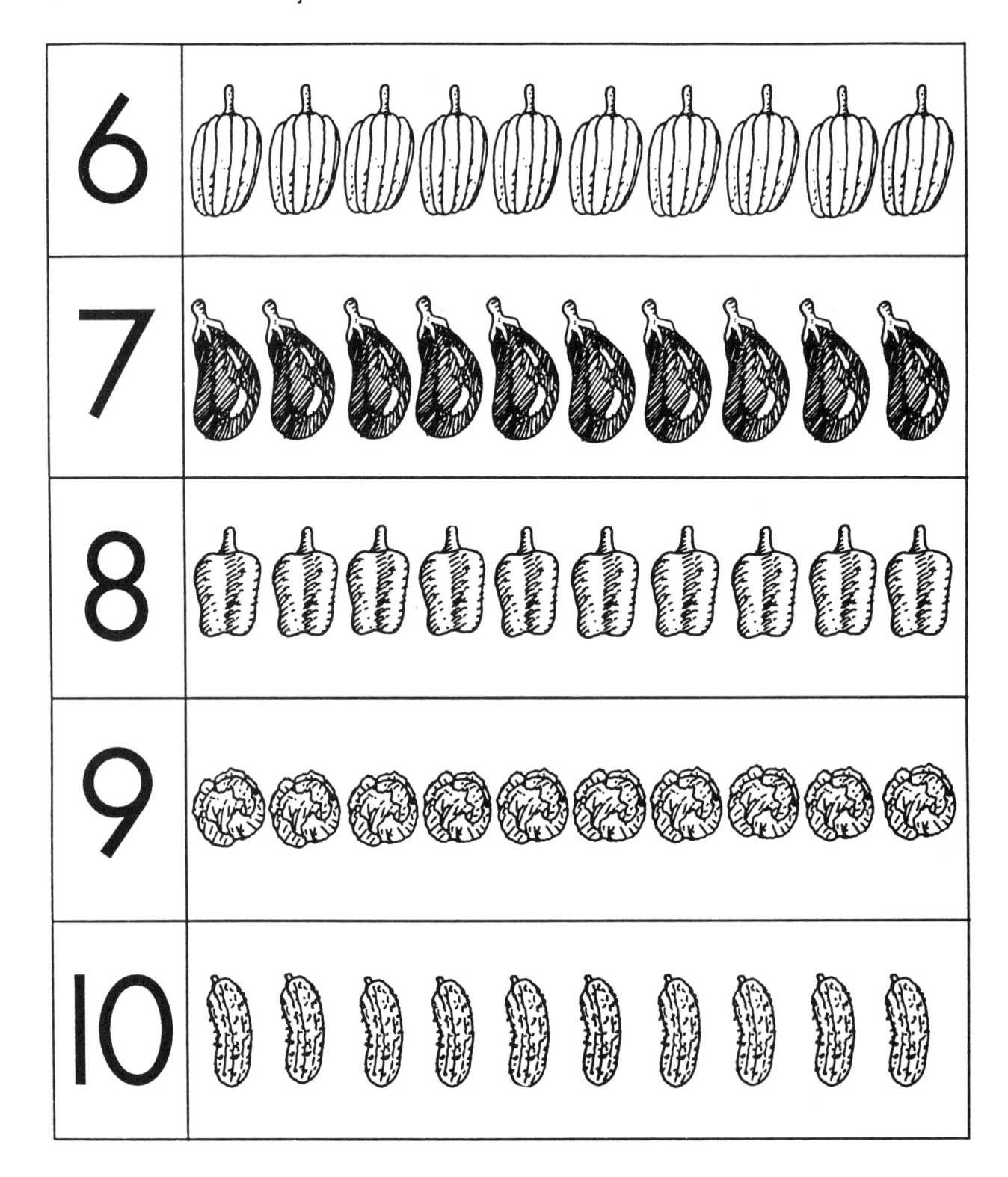

6	🎃🎃🎃🎃🎃🎃🎃🎃🎃🎃
7	🍆🍆🍆🍆🍆🍆🍆🍆🍆🍆
8	🫑🫑🫑🫑🫑🫑🫑🫑🫑
9	🥦🥦🥦🥦🥦🥦🥦🥦🥦🥦
10	🥒🥒🥒🥒🥒🥒🥒🥒🥒🥒

Skills: Creating sets of objects; Recognizing numerals

COUNTING AND MATH SKILLS

Look at the objects in each row.
Count the objects in each row.
Write the number in each box.
Then color the page.

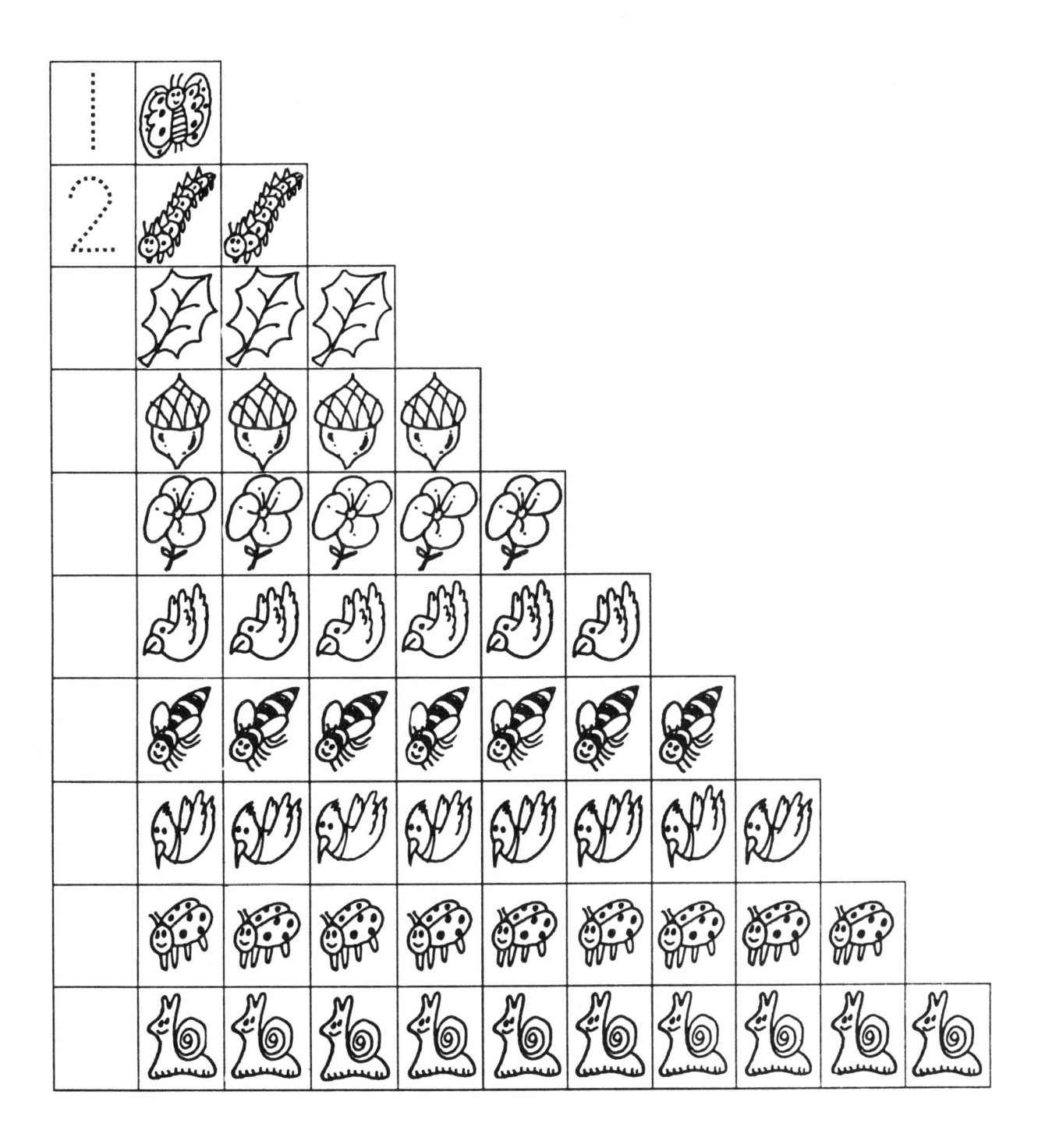

Skills: Recognizing sets of objects; Forming numerals

COUNTING AND MATH SKILLS

Follow the dots from one to ten to find out what is in the air.

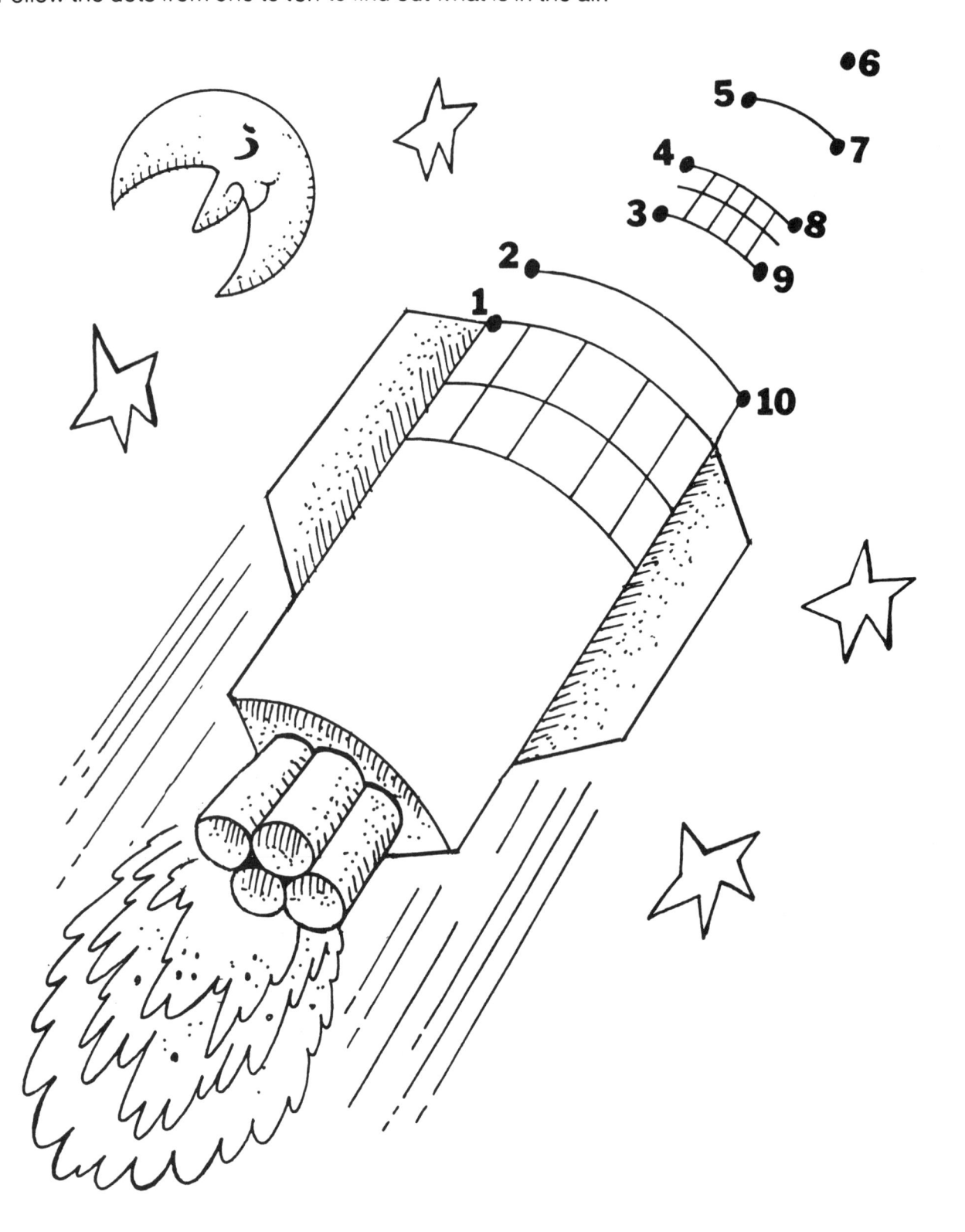

Skills: Order of numerals from one to ten; Following directions

COUNTING AND MATH SKILLS

Follow the dots from 1 to 25 to find out what is on the beach.

Skills: Ordering numerals from 1 to 25

COUNTING AND MATH SKILLS

Color all the numbers that are greater than 20.

18, 49, 33, 27, 36, 46, 11, 12, 19, 43, 47, 16, 38, 45, 31, 13, 9, 32, 42, 24, 17, 37, 48, 23

Skills: Comparing numbers

COUNTING AND MATH SKILLS

Color all the numbers that are less than 50.

Skills: Comparing numbers

COUNTING AND MATH SKILLS

Follow the dots from 1 to 50 to find out who is jumping through the hoop.

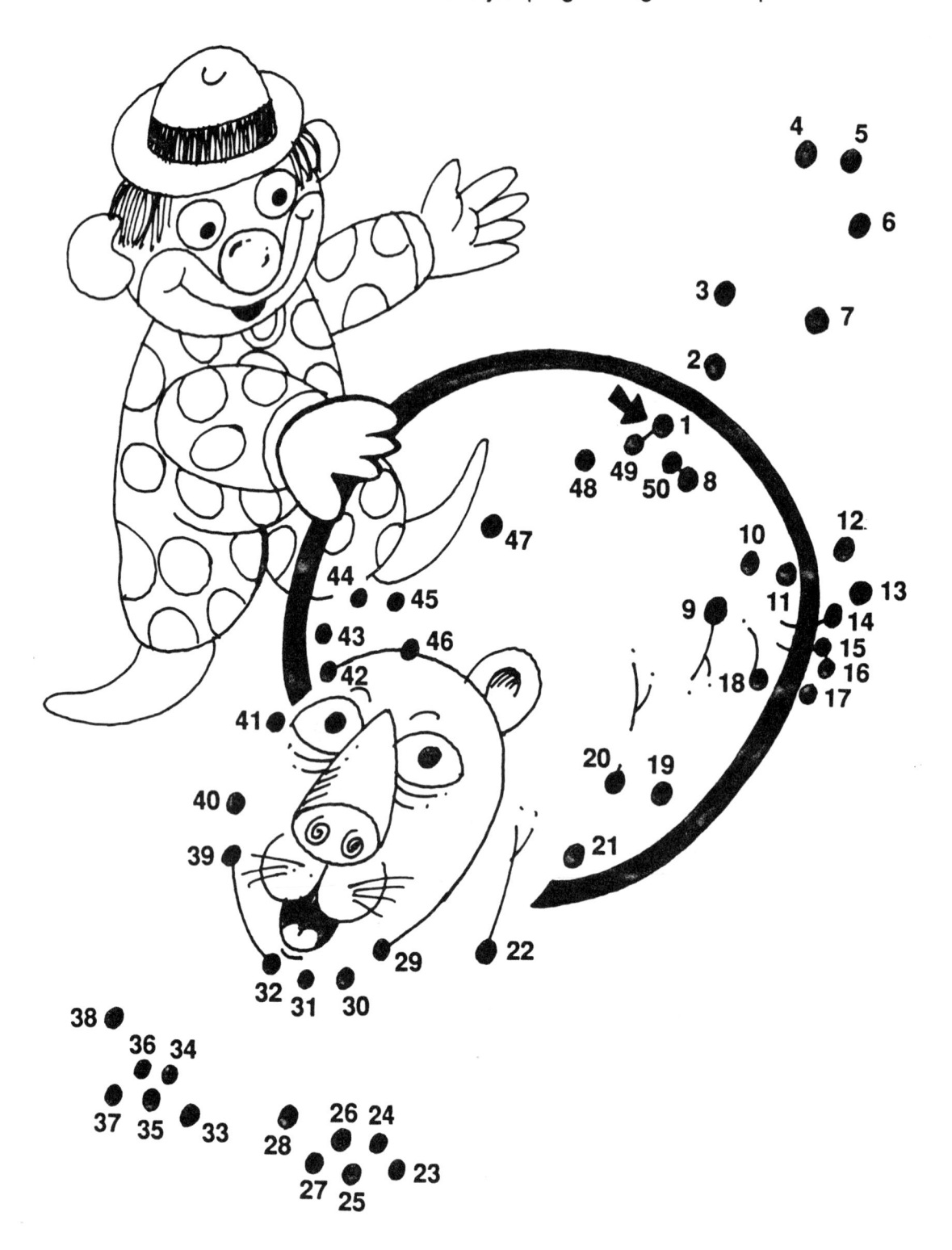

Skills: Ordering numerals from 1 to 50

COUNTING AND MATH SKILLS

Look at the seesaws.
Circle the number that is larger.

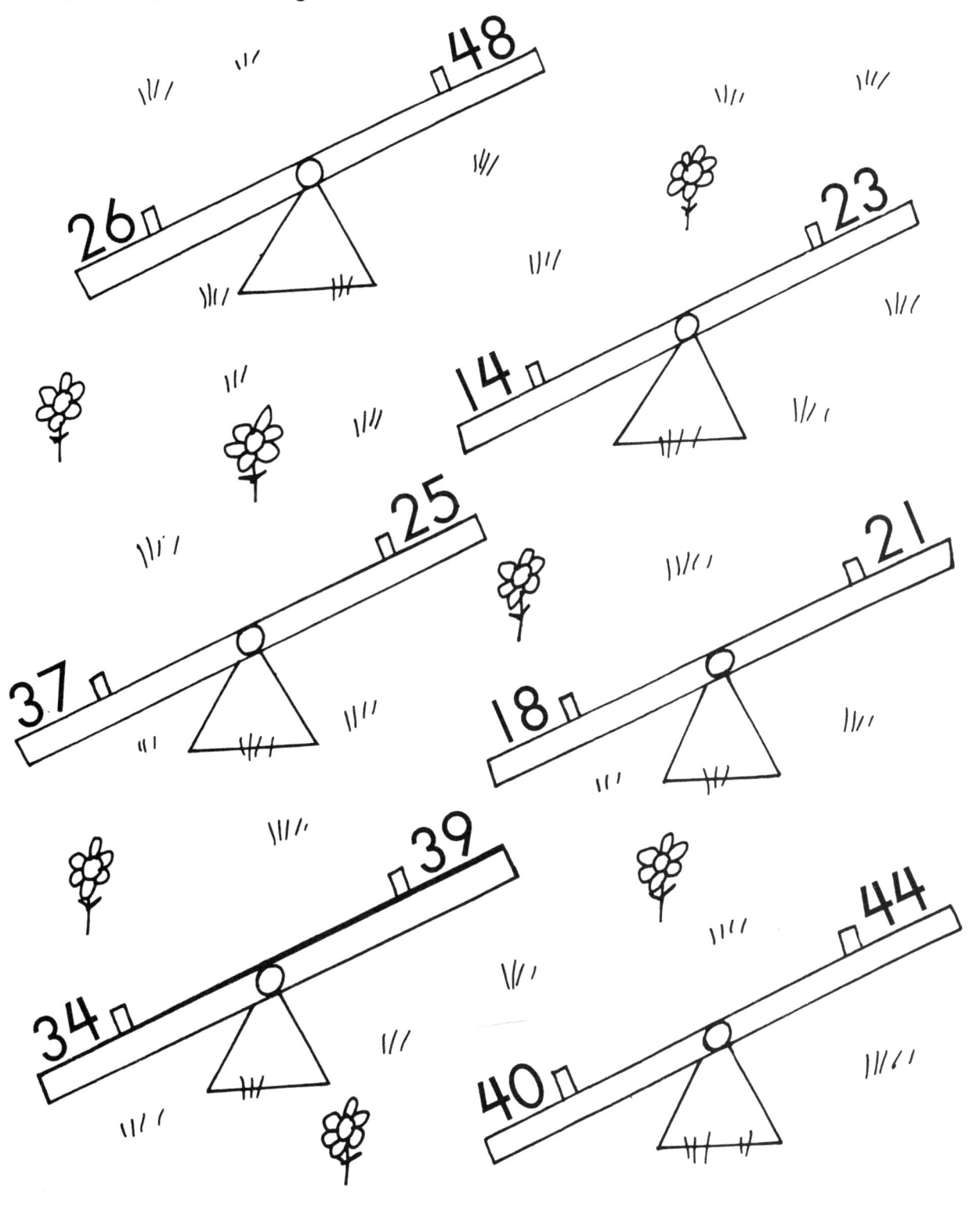

Skills: Comparing numbers

111

COUNTING AND MATH SKILLS

Look at the bicycles.
Circle the number that is smaller.

- 15, 42
- 25, 18
- 33, 41
- 27, 35
- 46, 22
- 20, 39

Skills: Comparing numbers

COUNTING AND MATH SKILLS

Can you count to 100?
Write the missing numbers.

1	2			5		7	8		10
11		13	14		16			19	20
	22	23	24			27			
31			34	35			38		40
		43			46	47		49	
51	52						58		60
			64	65	66				
	72				76		78		
81				85	86		88	89	
								99	

Skills: Counting to 100; Forming numerals

COUNTING AND MATH SKILLS

Follow the dots from 1 to 100 to find out who lives near the castle.

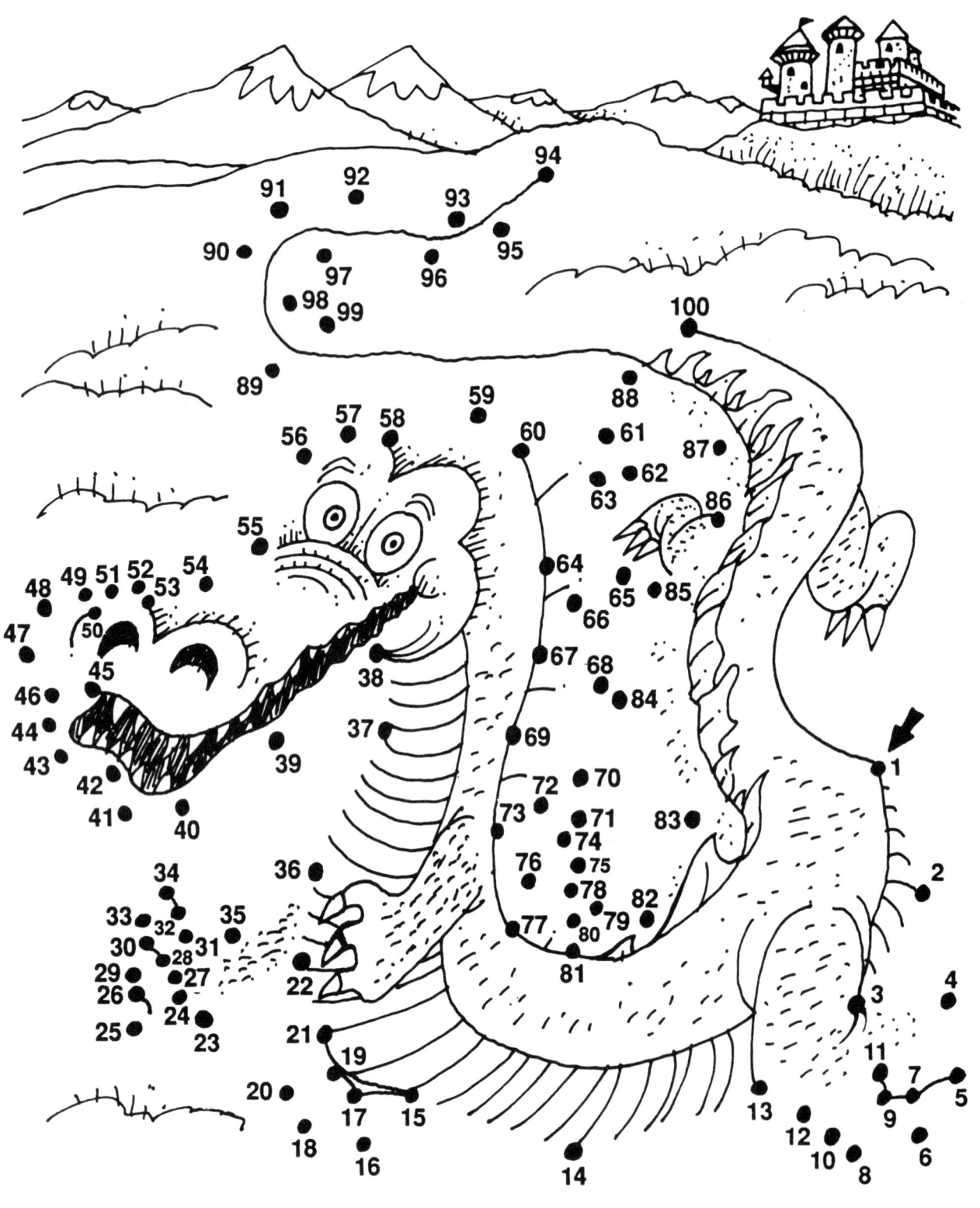

Skills: Ordering numerals from 1 to 100

COUNTING AND MATH SKILLS

Look at the even numbers.
Look at the odd numbers.
Fill in the missing numbers.

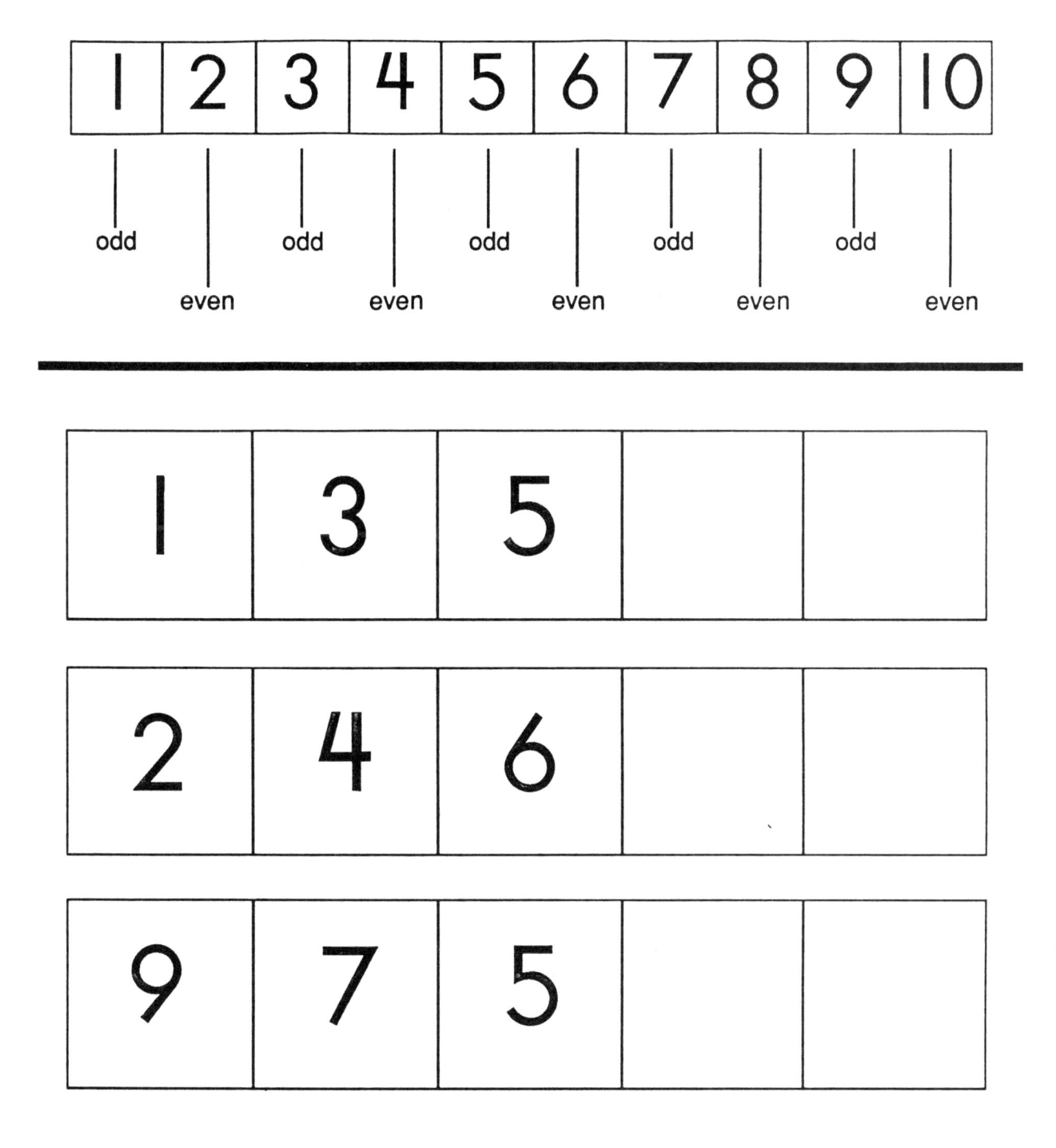

| 1 | 2 | 3 | 4 | 5 | 6 | 7 | 8 | 9 | 10 |

odd — even — odd — even — odd — even — odd — even — odd — even

| 1 | 3 | 5 | | |

| 2 | 4 | 6 | | |

| 9 | 7 | 5 | | |

Skills: Recognizing and using odd and even numbers

COUNTING AND MATH SKILLS

Follow the dots.
Start with 2 and count by 2s.

Skills: Counting by 2s to 50

COUNTING AND MATH SKILLS

Color the odd numbers to see which animal is swimming in the pond.

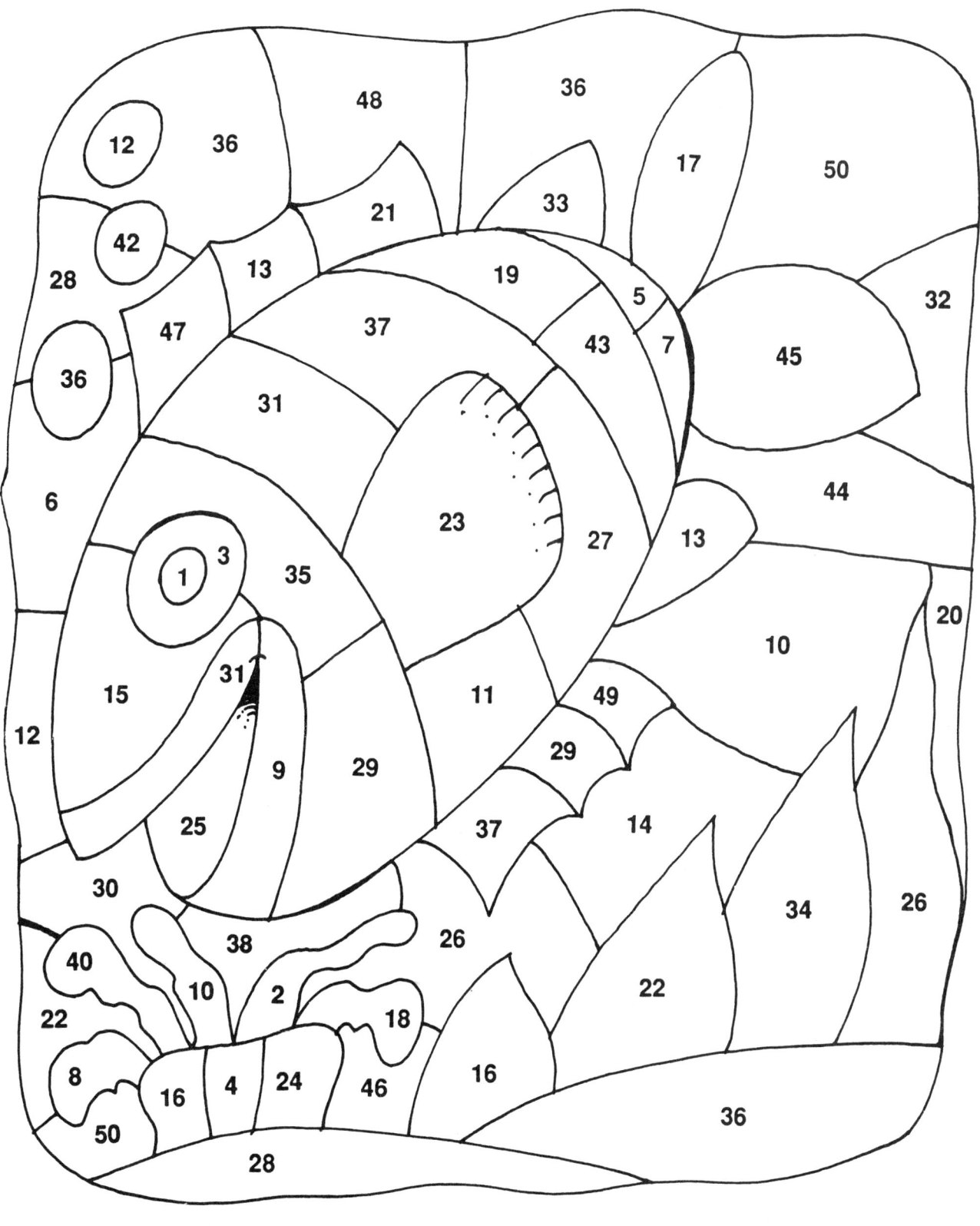

Skills: Identifying odd numbers

117

COUNTING AND MATH SKILLS

Color the even numbers to see which animal is hiding in the jungle.

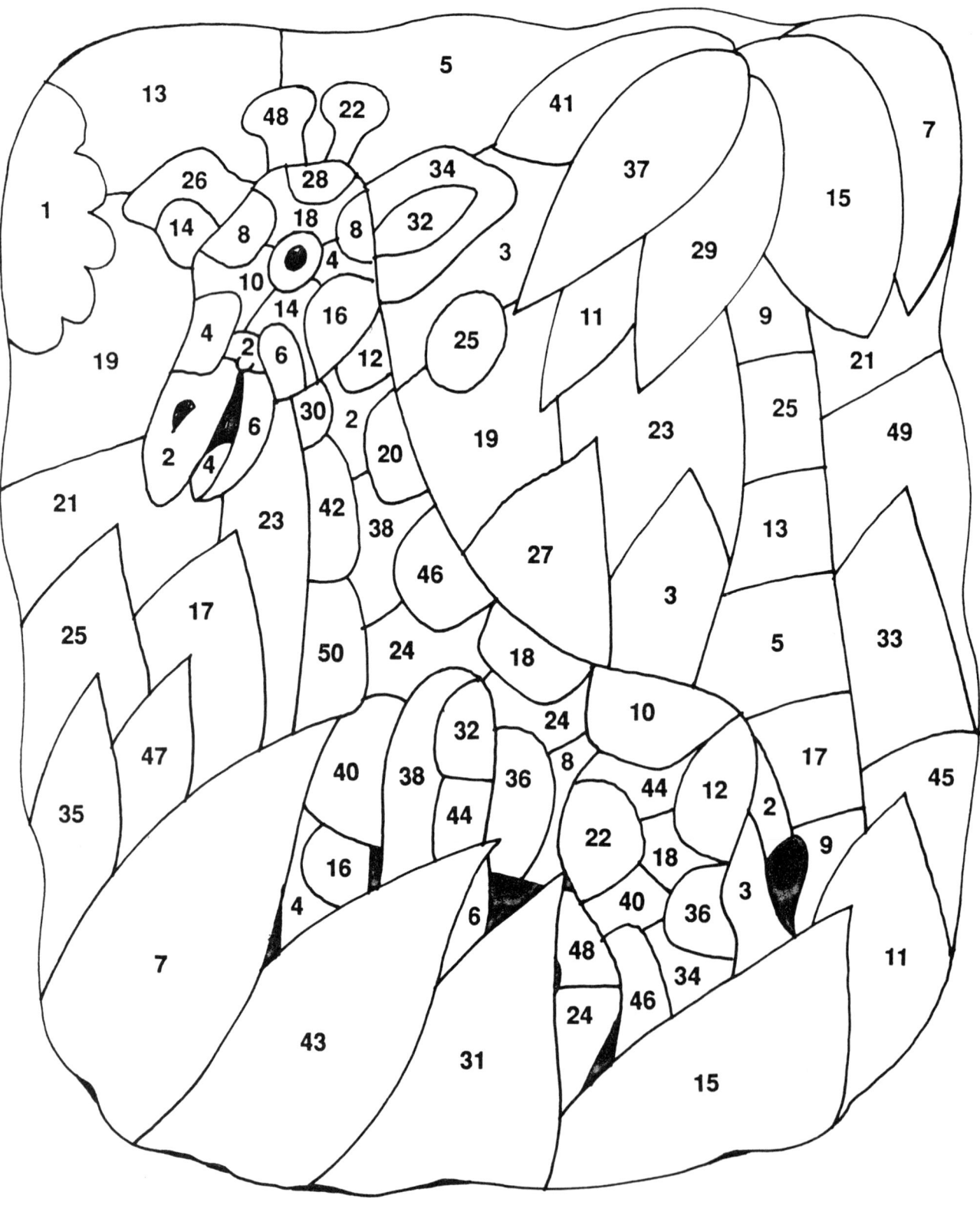

Skills: Identifying even numbers

COUNTING AND MATH SKILLS

Look at the acrobats.
Start with 2 and count by 2 s.

Skills: Counting by 2 s to 12

119

COUNTING AND MATH SKILLS

Follow the dots.
Start with 5 and count by 5 s.

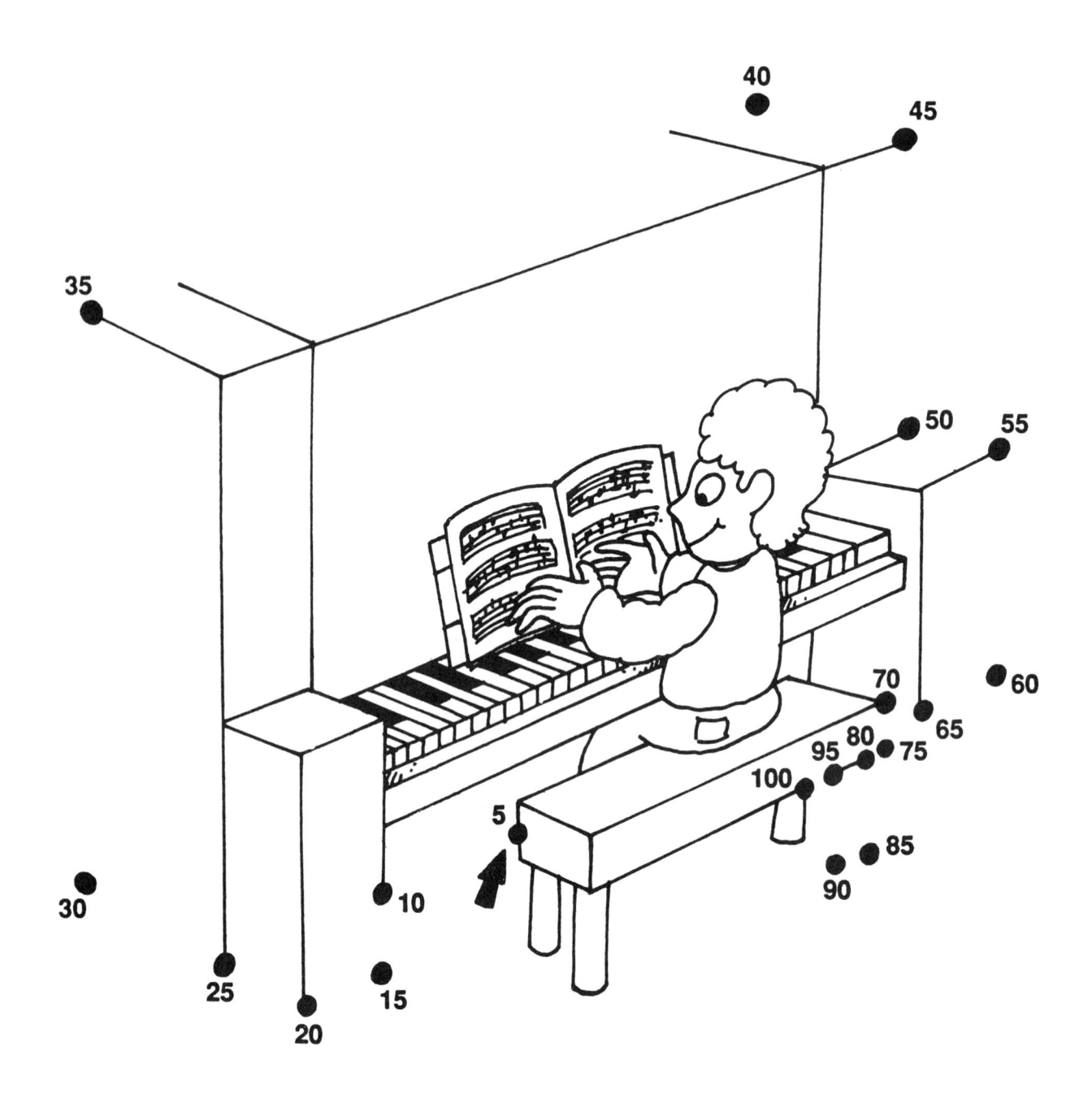

Skills: Counting by 5 s to 100

COUNTING AND MATH SKILLS

Look at the jugglers.
Start with 5 and count by 5 s.

Skills: Counting by 5 s to 25

COUNTING AND MATH SKILLS

Look at these marbles.
Make them into groups of 10.

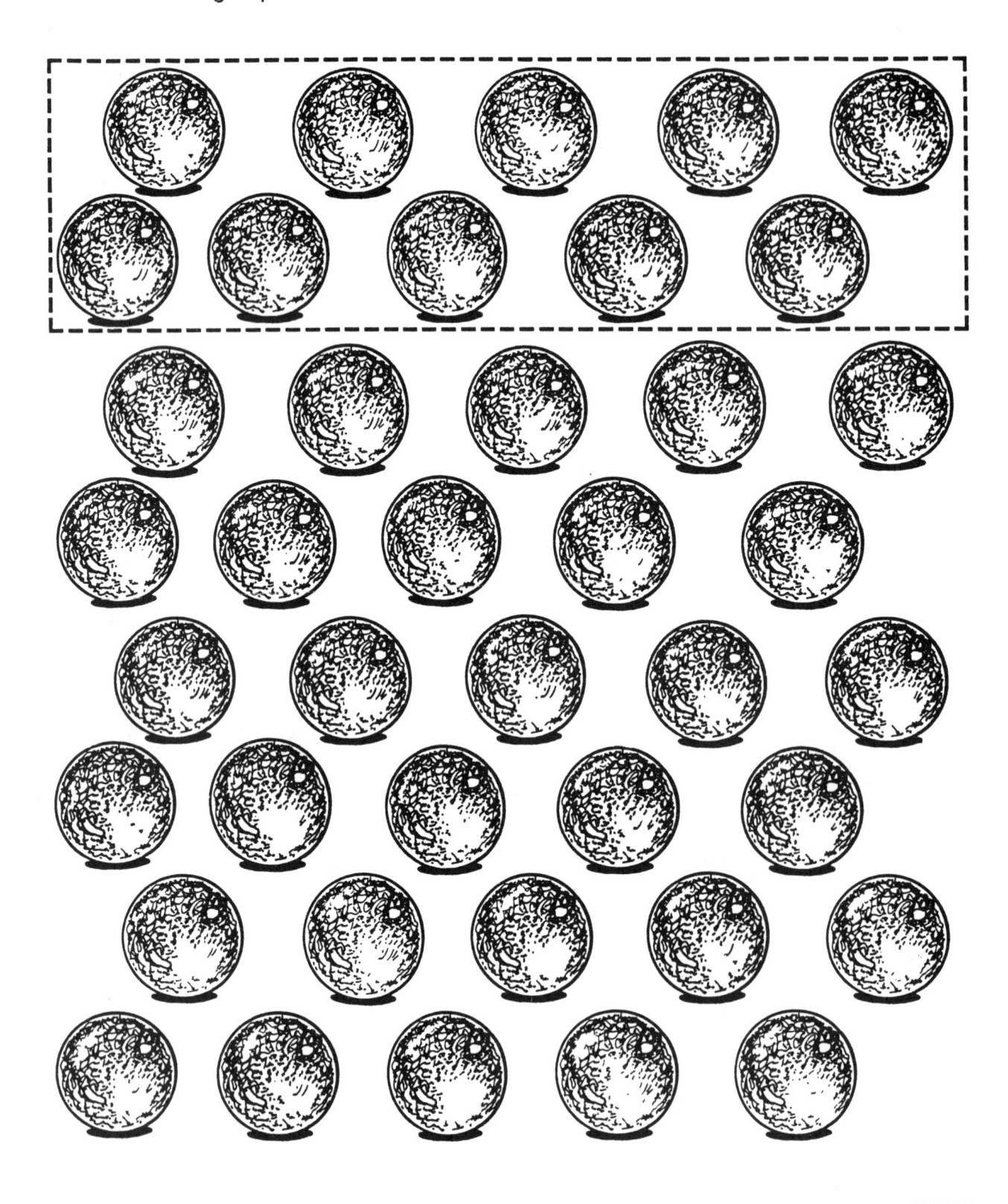

Skills: Forming groups of 10; Counting objects to form groups

COUNTING AND MATH SKILLS

Look at these crayons.
Make them into groups of 10.
How many groups are there? _____

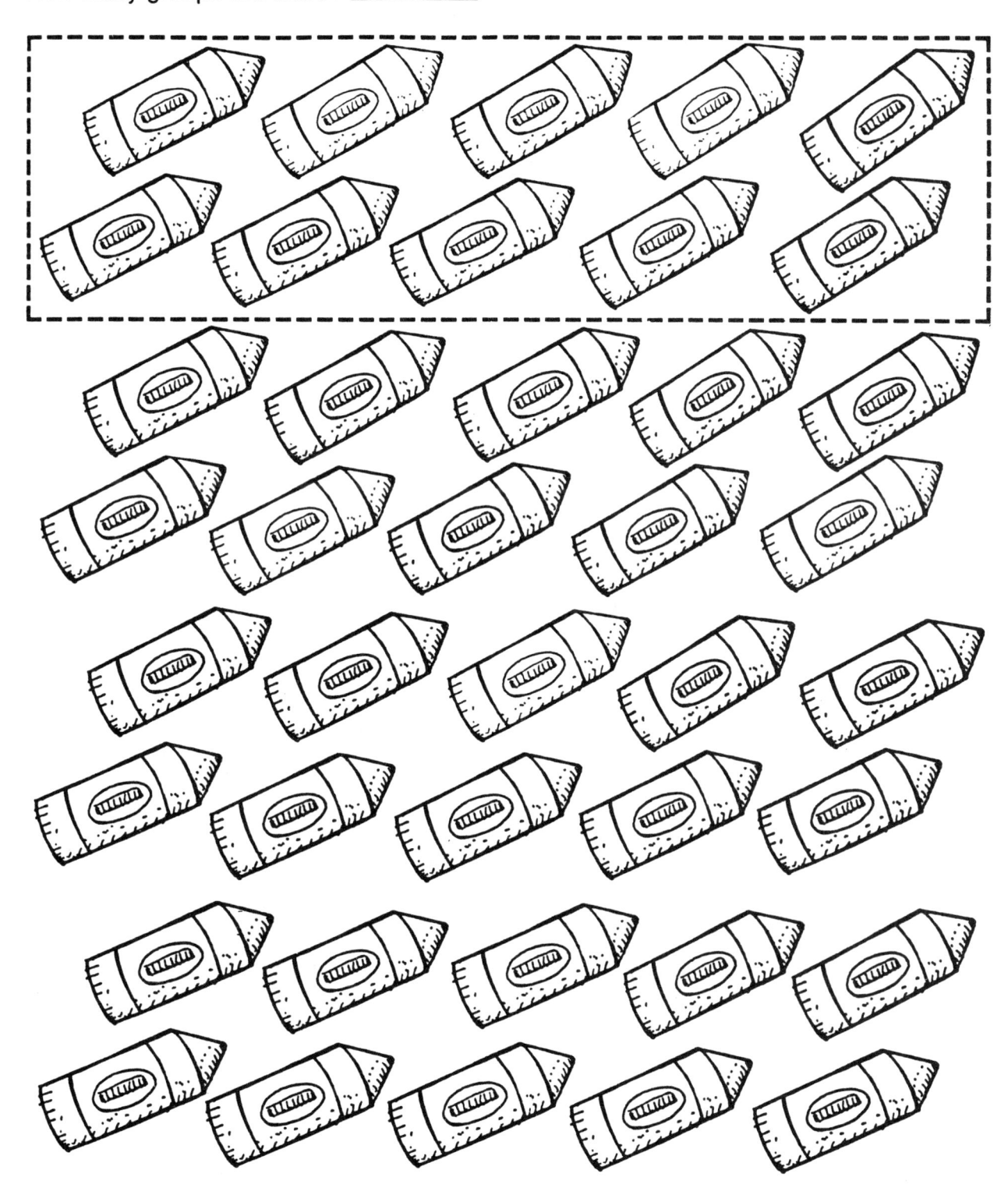

Skills: Forming groups of 10; Counting objects to form groups

COUNTING AND MATH SKILLS

Look at these fish. Make them into groups of ten.
How many groups of ten are there?

Skills: Forming groups of ten; Counting objects to form groups

COUNTING AND MATH SKILLS

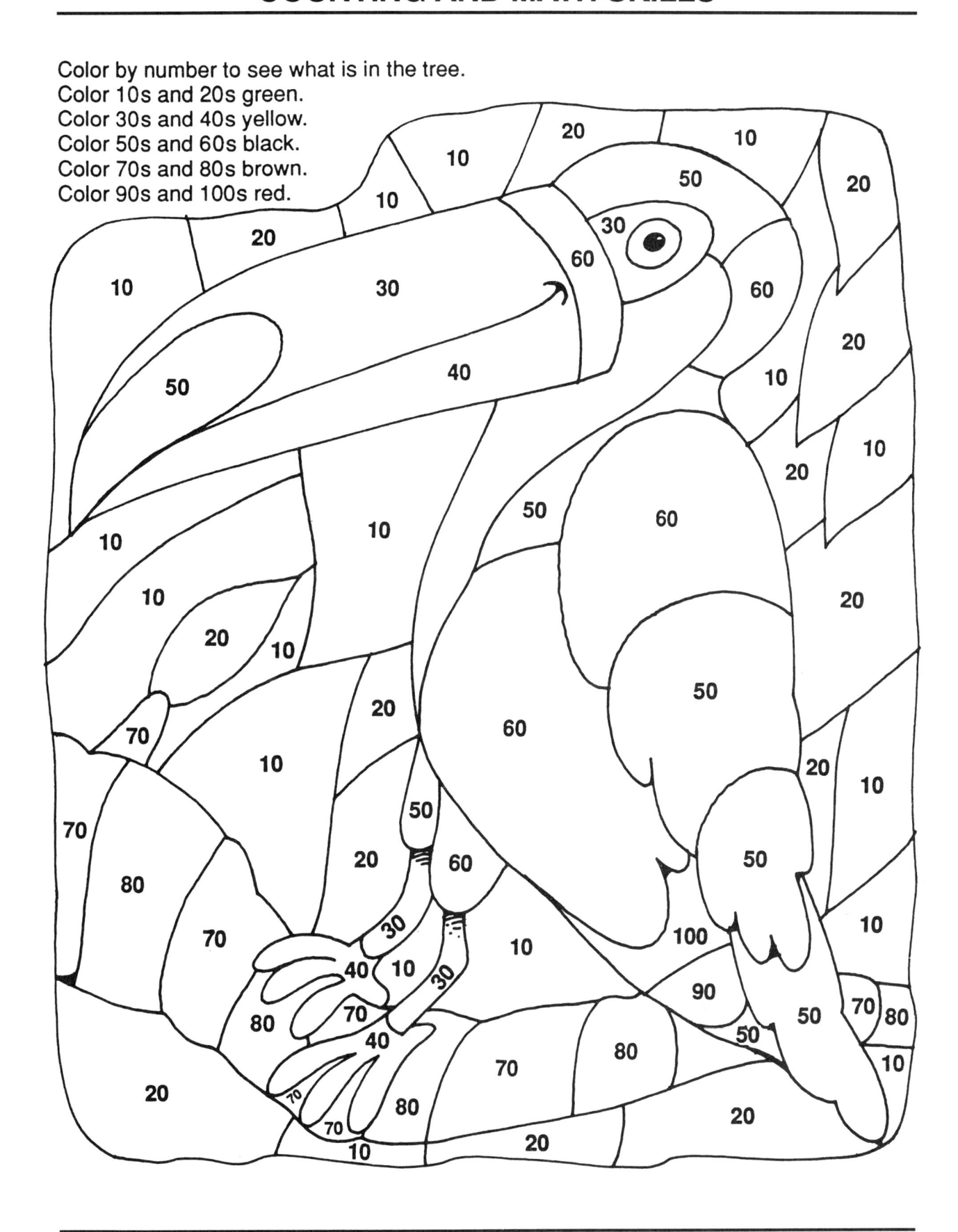

Color by number to see what is in the tree.
Color 10s and 20s green.
Color 30s and 40s yellow.
Color 50s and 60s black.
Color 70s and 80s brown.
Color 90s and 100s red.

Skills: Recognizing decade numbers

COUNTING AND MATH SKILLS

Look closely at this picture.
Find and circle these numbers hidden in the picture:
10, 20, 30, 40, 50, 60, 70, 80, 90, 100.
Then color the picture.

Skills: Recognizing decade numbers

COUNTING AND MATH SKILLS

Look at the numbers in each box.
Draw a line to match the numbers that are the same.

24	36
51	47
36	24
47	51

4	9
13	8
8	13
9	4

67	90
82	75
90	82
75	67

14	63
68	19
63	14
19	68

Skills: Recognizing and matching numerals

COUNTING AND MATH SKILLS

Look at each picture.
How many are in the first group?
How many are in the second group?
How many in all?

__3__ and __2__ is __5__

___ and ___ is ___

___ and ___ is ___

Skills: Recognizing sets of objects and writing corresponding numerals; Adding groups of objects; Understanding addition sentences

COUNTING AND MATH SKILLS

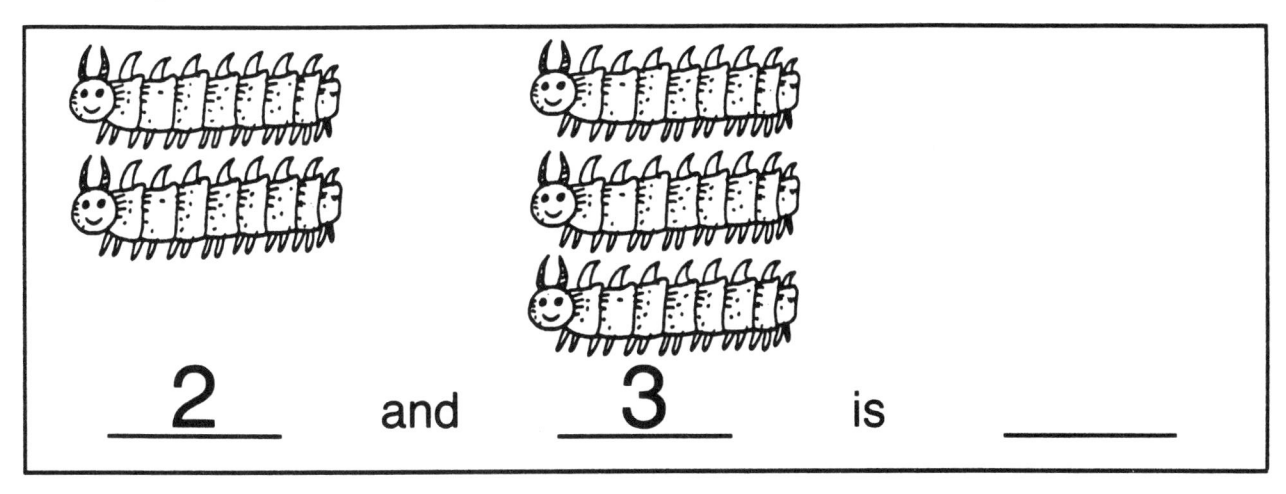

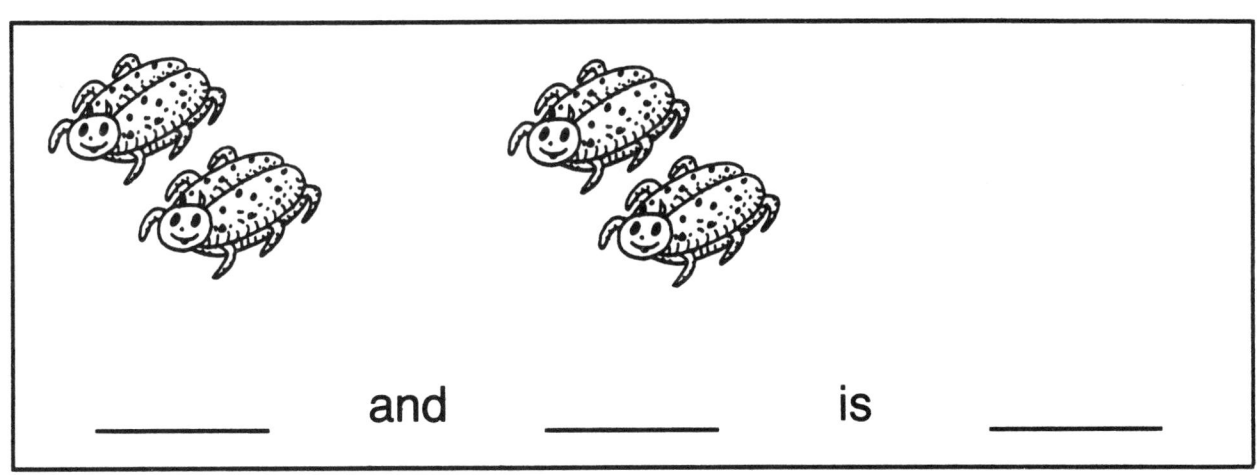

Look at each picture.
How many are in the first group?
How many are in the second group?
How many in all?

___2___ and ___3___ is _____

_____ and _____ is _____

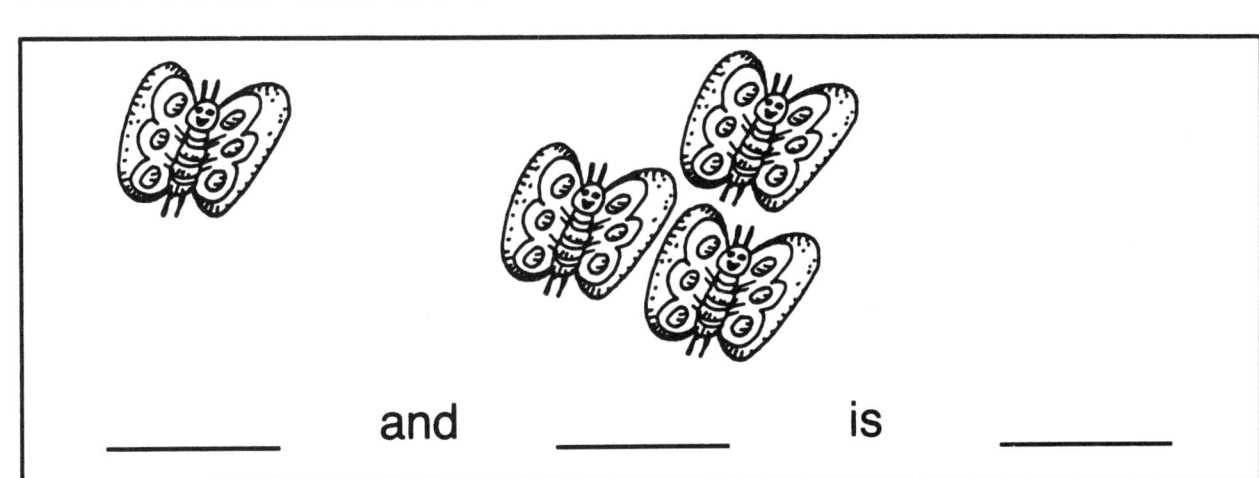

_____ and _____ is _____

Skills: Recognizing sets of objects and writing corresponding numerals; Adding groups of objects; Understanding addition sentences

COUNTING AND MATH SKILLS

Look at each picture.
How many are in the first group?
How many are in the second group?
How many in all?

$\underline{1}$ and $\underline{1}$ is $\underline{2}$
$\underline{1}$ + $\underline{1}$ = $\underline{2}$

___ and ___ is ___
___ + ___ = ___

___ and ___ is ___
___ + ___ = ___

Skills: Recognizing sets of objects and writing corresponding numerals; Adding groups of objects; Understanding addition sentences

COUNTING AND MATH SKILLS

Look at each picture.
How many are in the first group?
How many are in the second group?
How many in all?

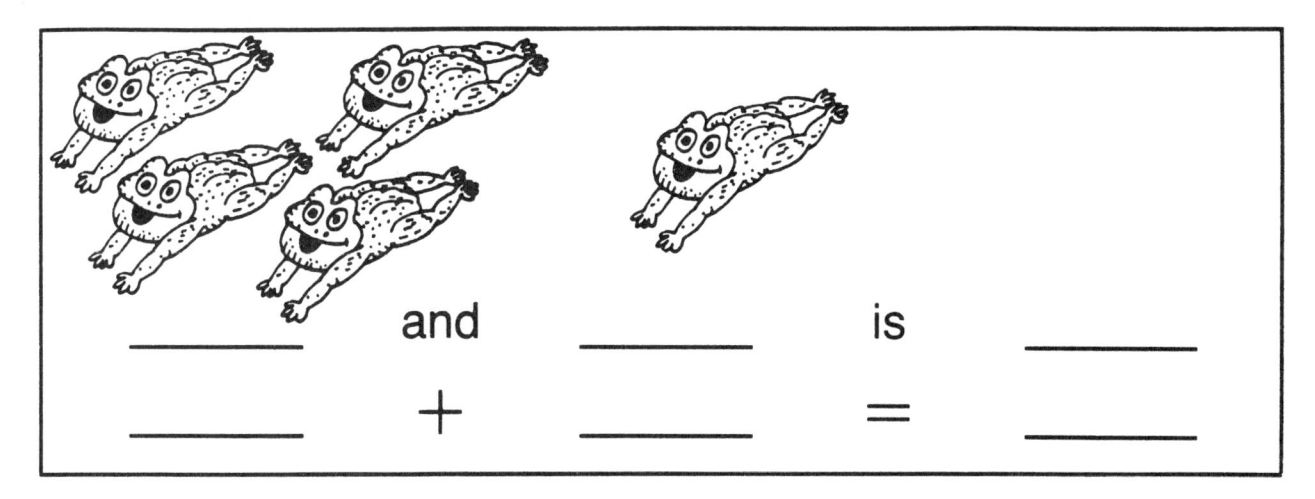

____ and ____ is ____
____ + ____ = ____

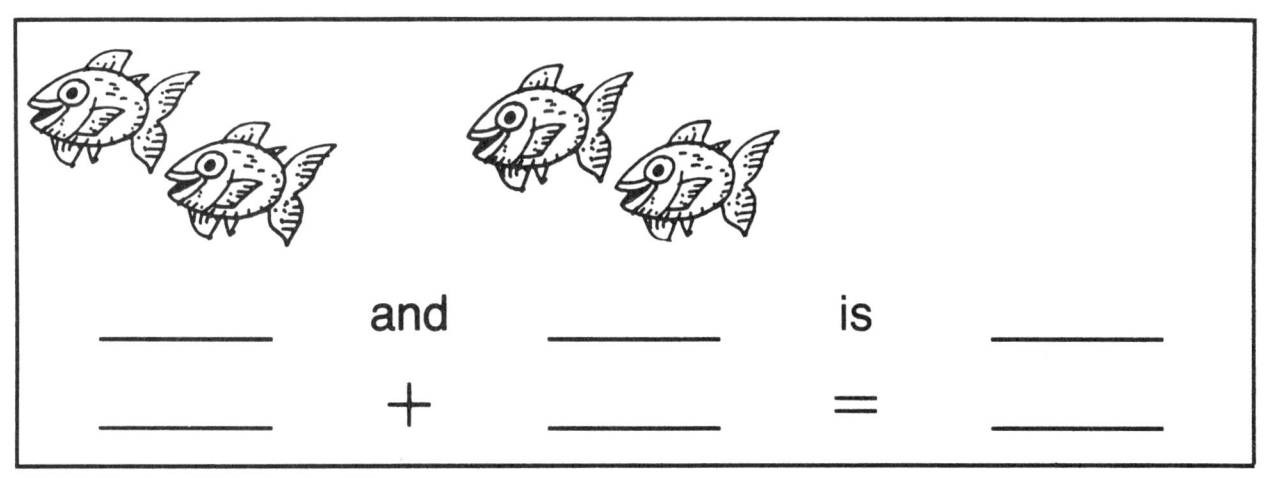

____ and ____ is ____
____ + ____ = ____

____ and ____ is ____
____ + ____ = ____

Skills: Recognizing sets of objects and writing corresponding numerals; Adding groups of objects; Understanding addition sentences

COUNTING AND MATH SKILLS

Look at each picture.
How many are in the first group?
How many are in the second group?
How many in all?

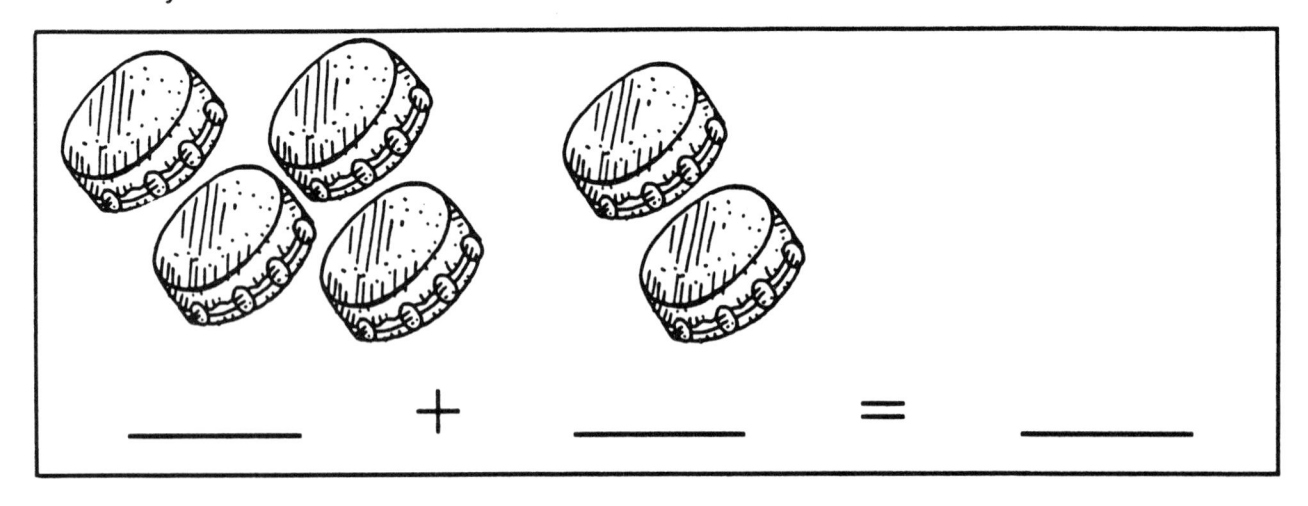

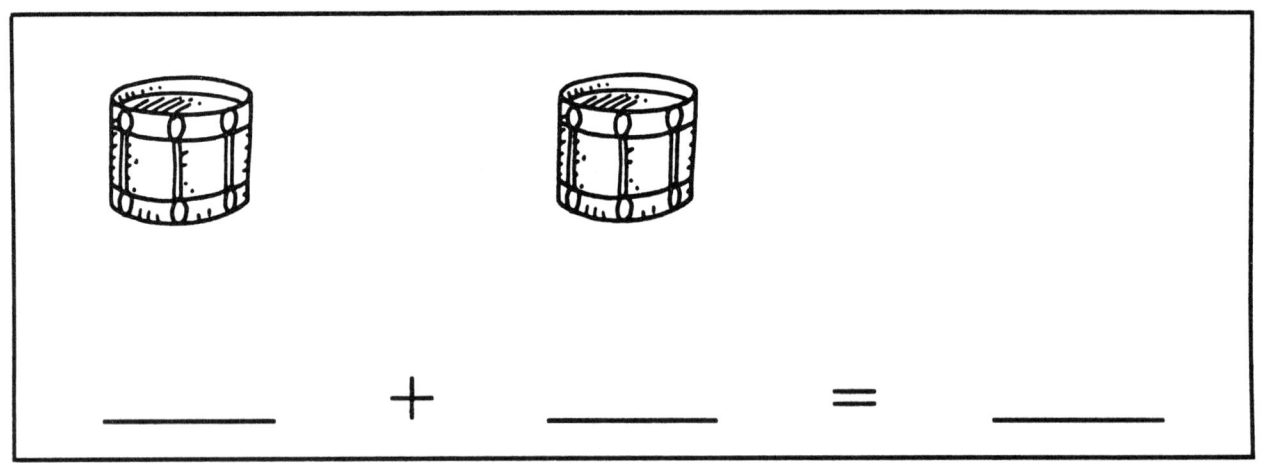

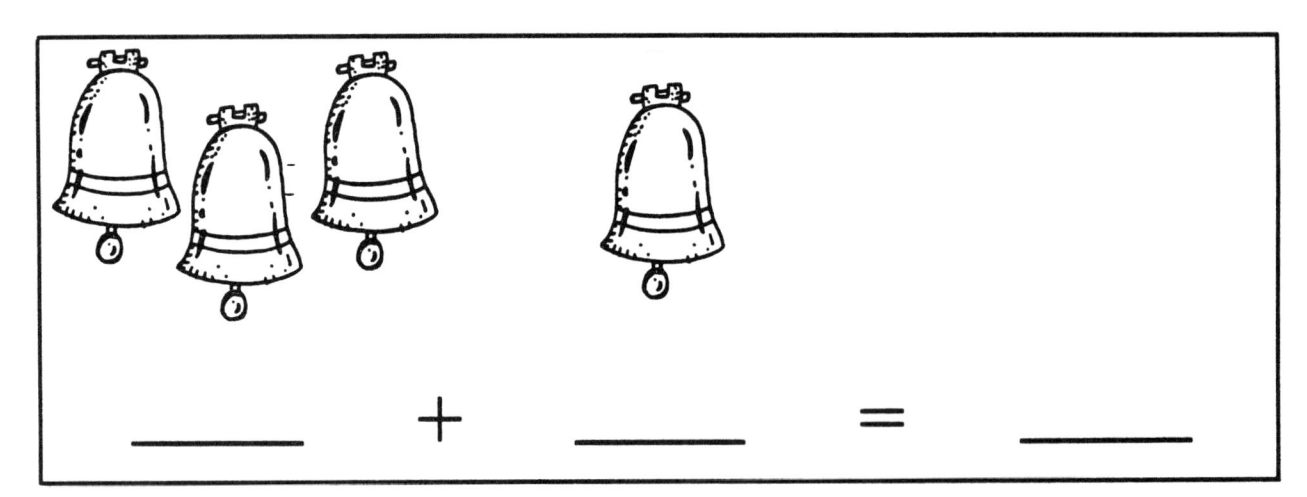

___ + ___ = ___

___ + ___ = ___

___ + ___ = ___

Skills: Recognizing sets of objects and writing corresponding numerals; Adding groups of objects; Practicing addition problems

COUNTING AND MATH SKILLS

Look at each picture.
How many are in the first group?
How many are in the second group?
How many in all?

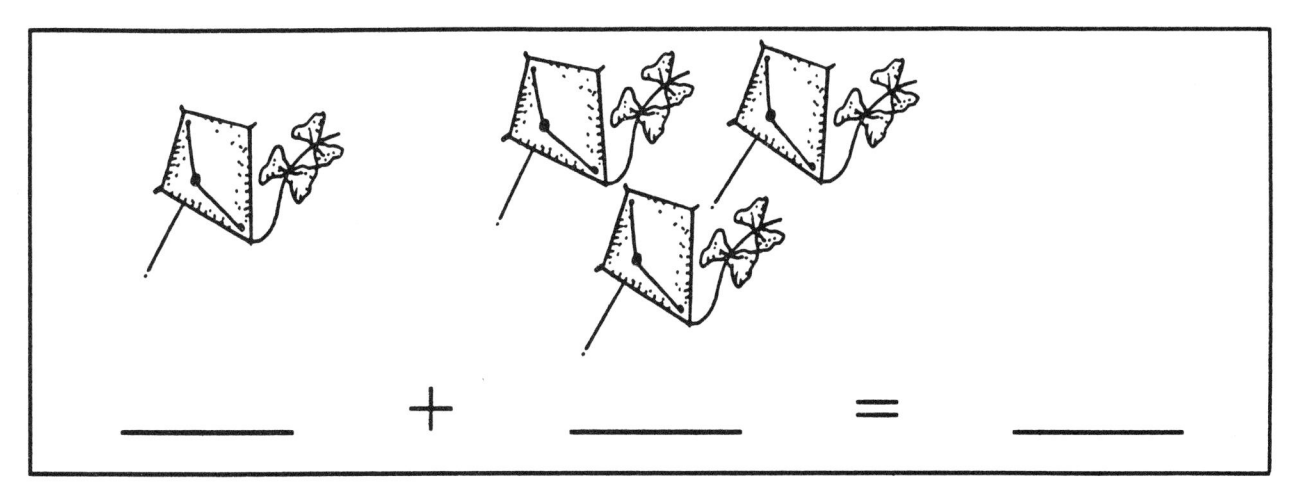

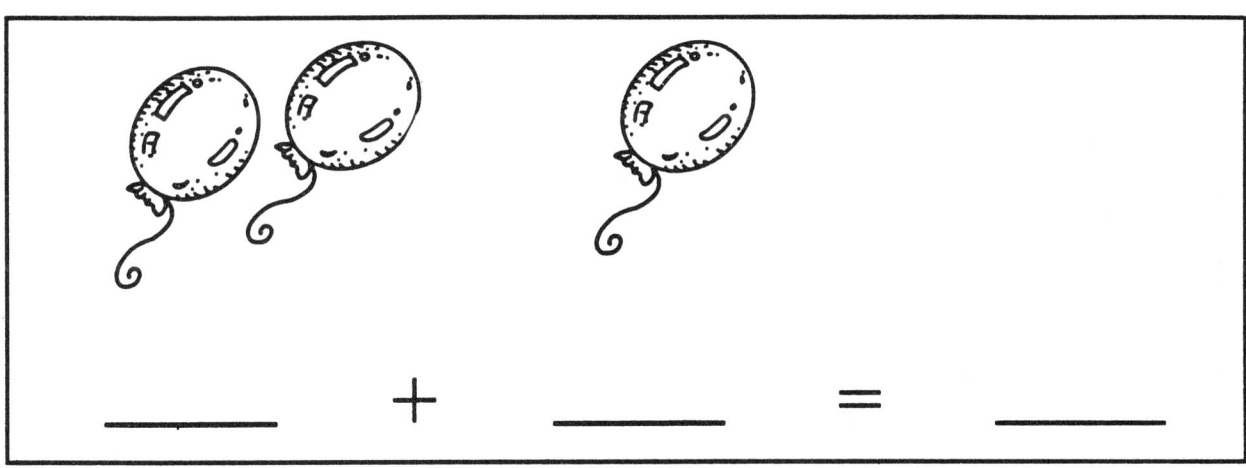

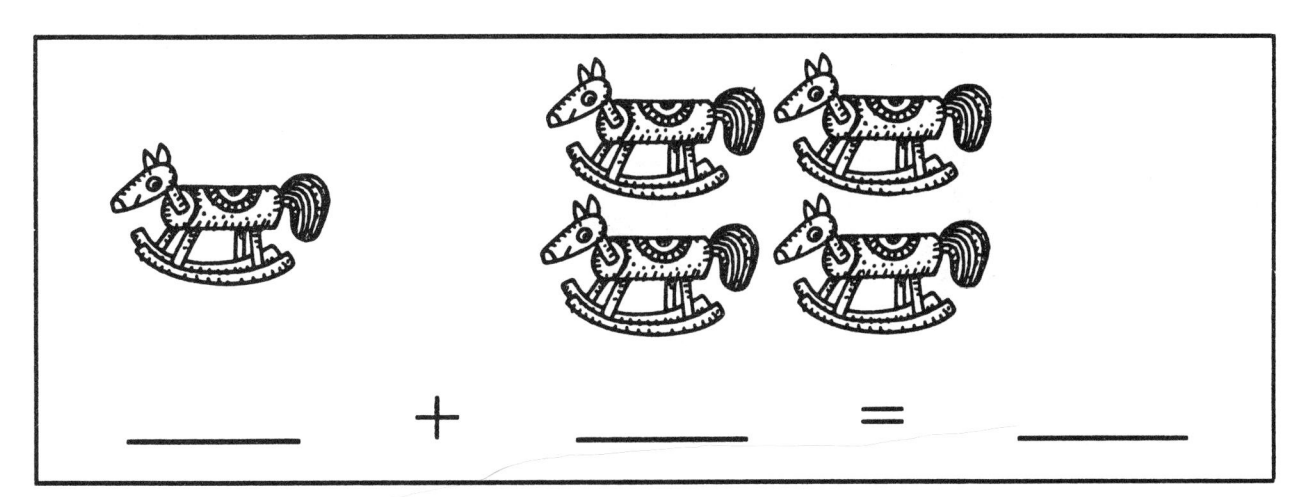

___ + ___ = ___

___ + ___ = ___

___ + ___ = ___

Skills: Adding groups of objects; Practicing addition problems

COUNTING AND MATH SKILLS

Look at each picture.
How many are in the first group?
How many are in the second group?
How many in all?

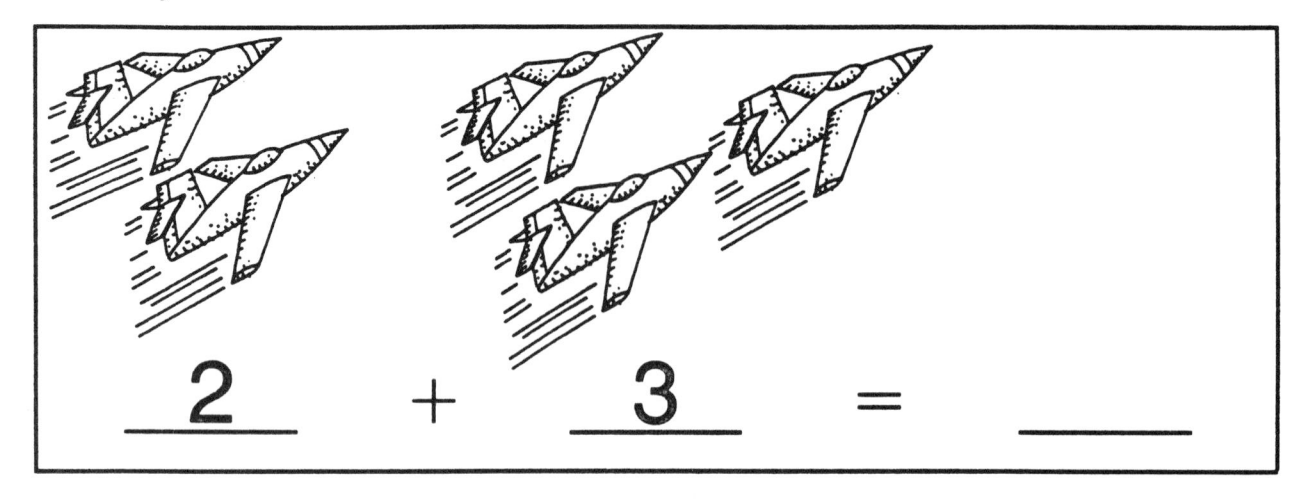

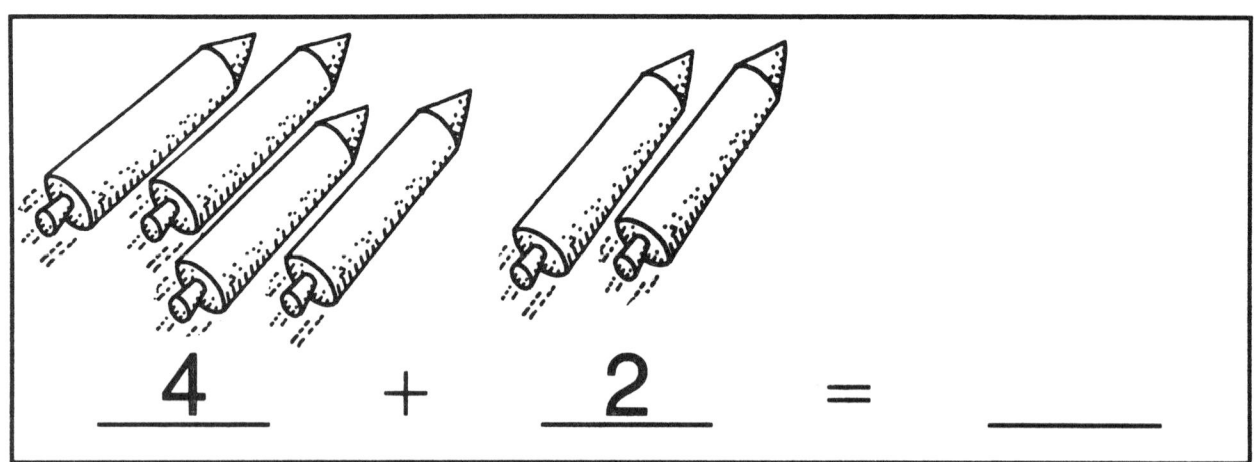

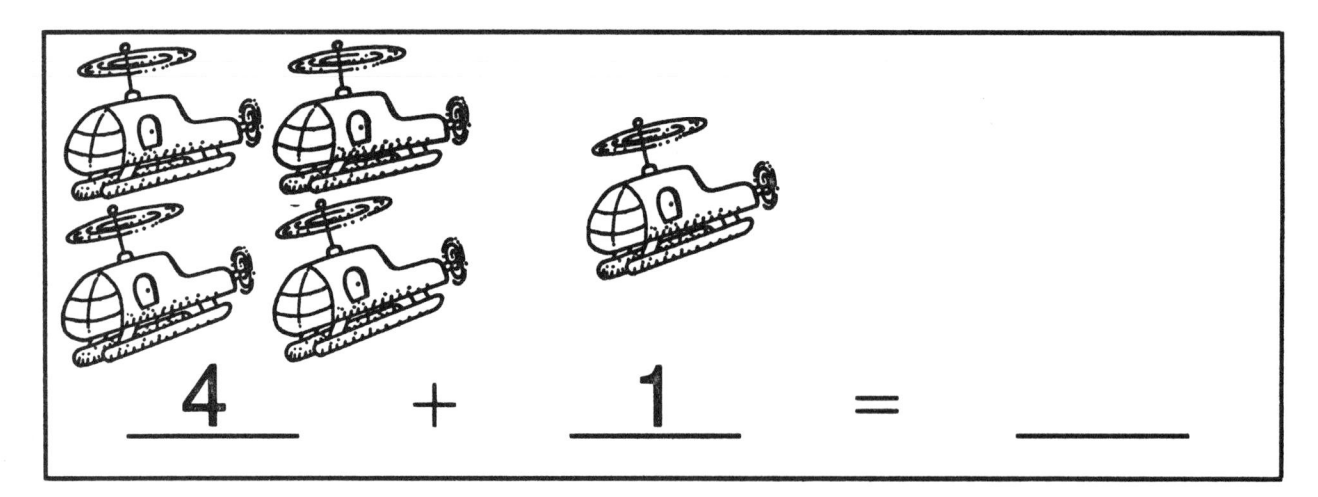

__2__ + __3__ = _____

__4__ + __2__ = _____

__4__ + __1__ = _____

Skills: Adding groups of objects; Practicing addition problems

COUNTING AND MATH SKILLS

How many in all?
Add them to find out.

$\begin{array}{r} 2 \\ +3 \\ \hline \end{array}$

$\begin{array}{r} 2 \\ +2 \\ \hline \end{array}$

$\begin{array}{r} 3 \\ +1 \\ \hline \end{array}$

$\begin{array}{r} 4 \\ +1 \\ \hline \end{array}$

Skills: Solving vertical problems; Writing numeral problems

COUNTING AND MATH SKILLS

How many in all?
Add them to find out.

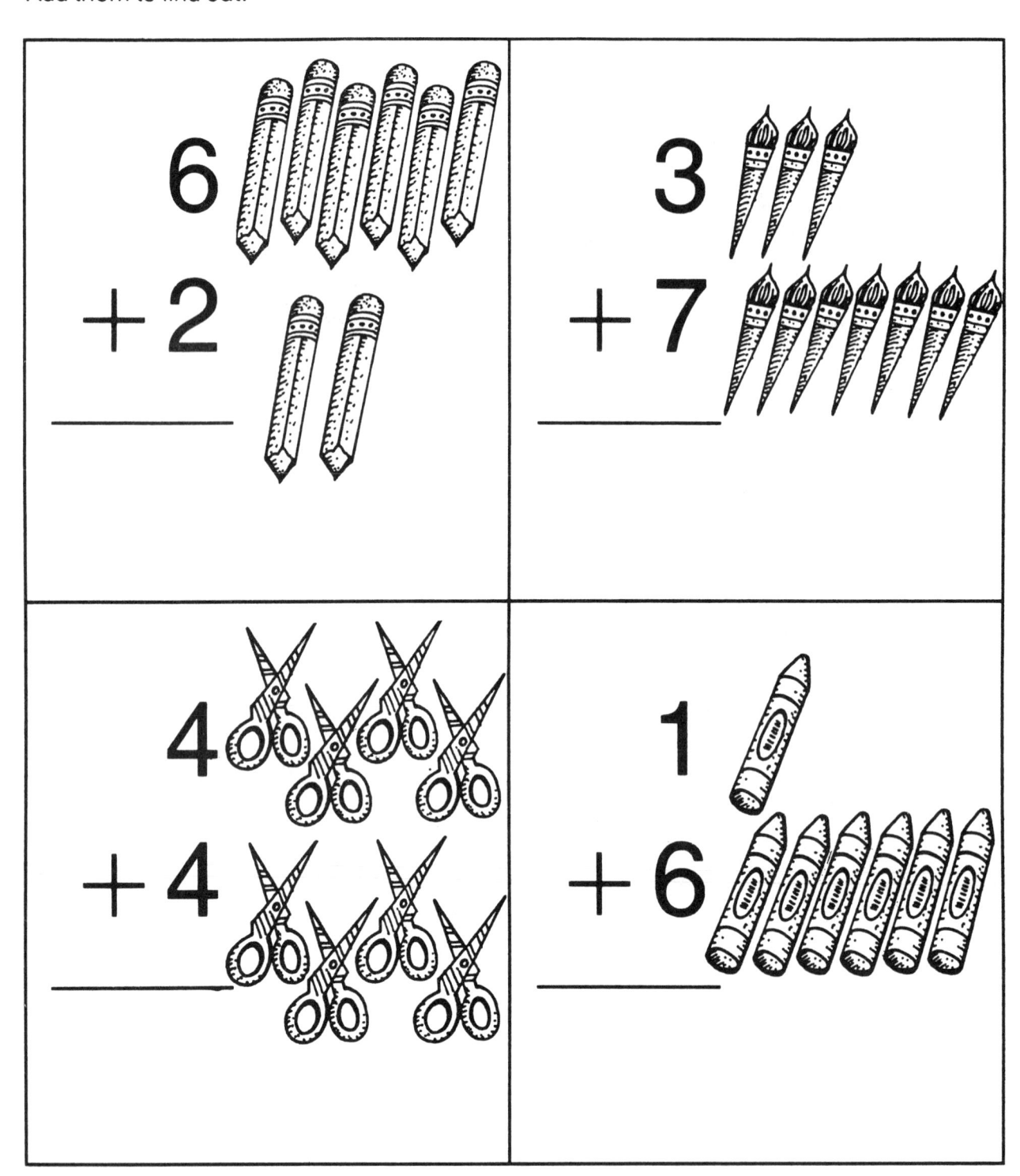

```
  6
+ 2
____
```

```
  3
+ 7
____
```

```
  4
+ 4
____
```

```
  1
+ 6
____
```

Skills: Solving vertical addition problems to ten; Writing numeral problems

COUNTING AND MATH SKILLS

Add the numbers in each flower.
If the answer is six, color it yellow.
If the answer is seven, color it red.
If the answer is eight, color it orange.

$$3 + 3$$

$$4 + 3$$

$$2 + 4$$

$$5 + 3$$

$$2 + 6$$

Skills: Solving vertical addition problems; Writing numerals

COUNTING AND MATH SKILLS

Add the numbers in each dolphin.
If the answer is 7, color it green.
If the answer is 8, color it brown.
If the answer is 9, color it yellow.

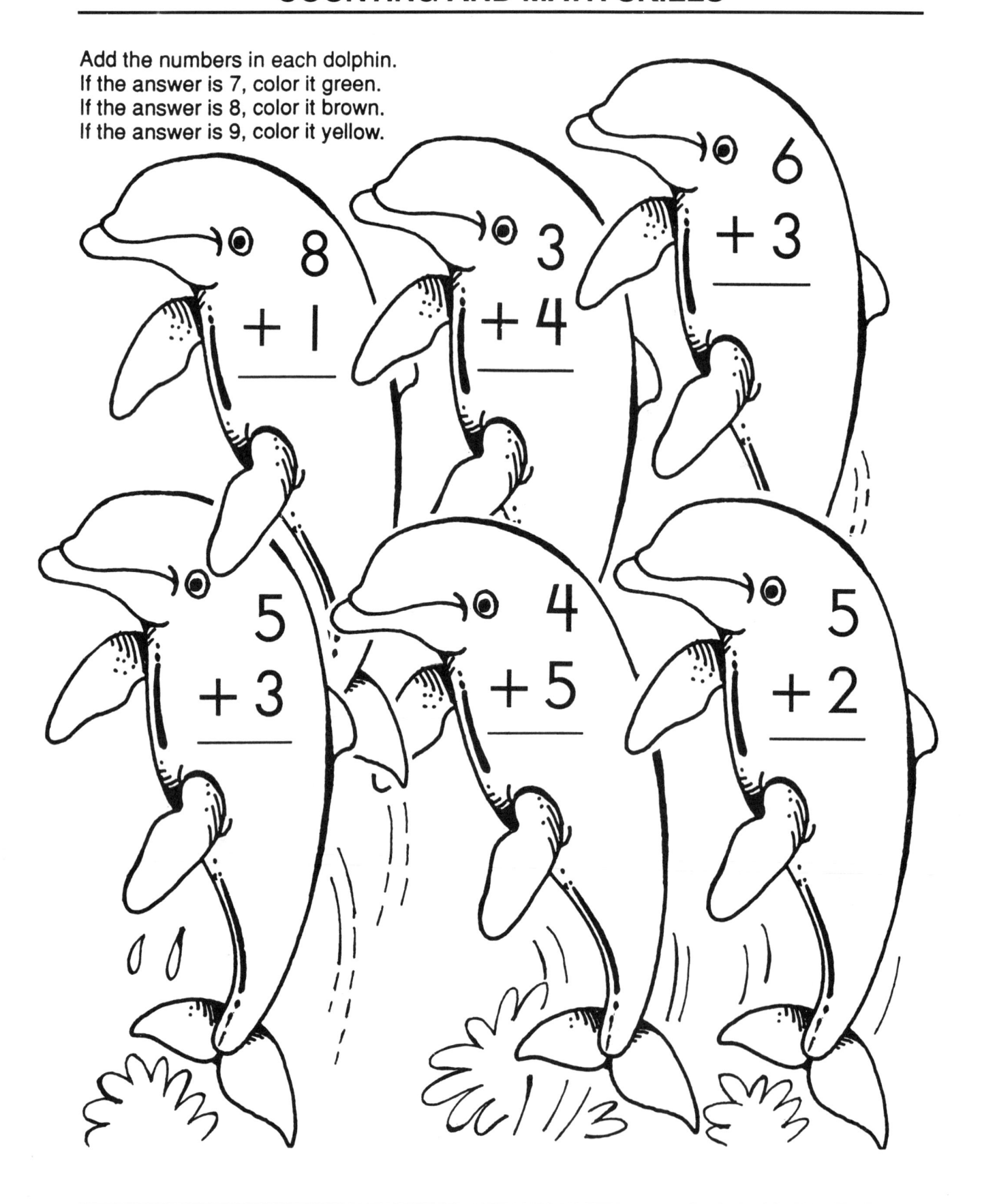

8 + 1

3 + 4

6 + 3

5 + 3

4 + 5

5 + 2

Skills: Solving vertical addition problems; Writing numerals

COUNTING AND MATH SKILLS

How many in all?
Add to find out.

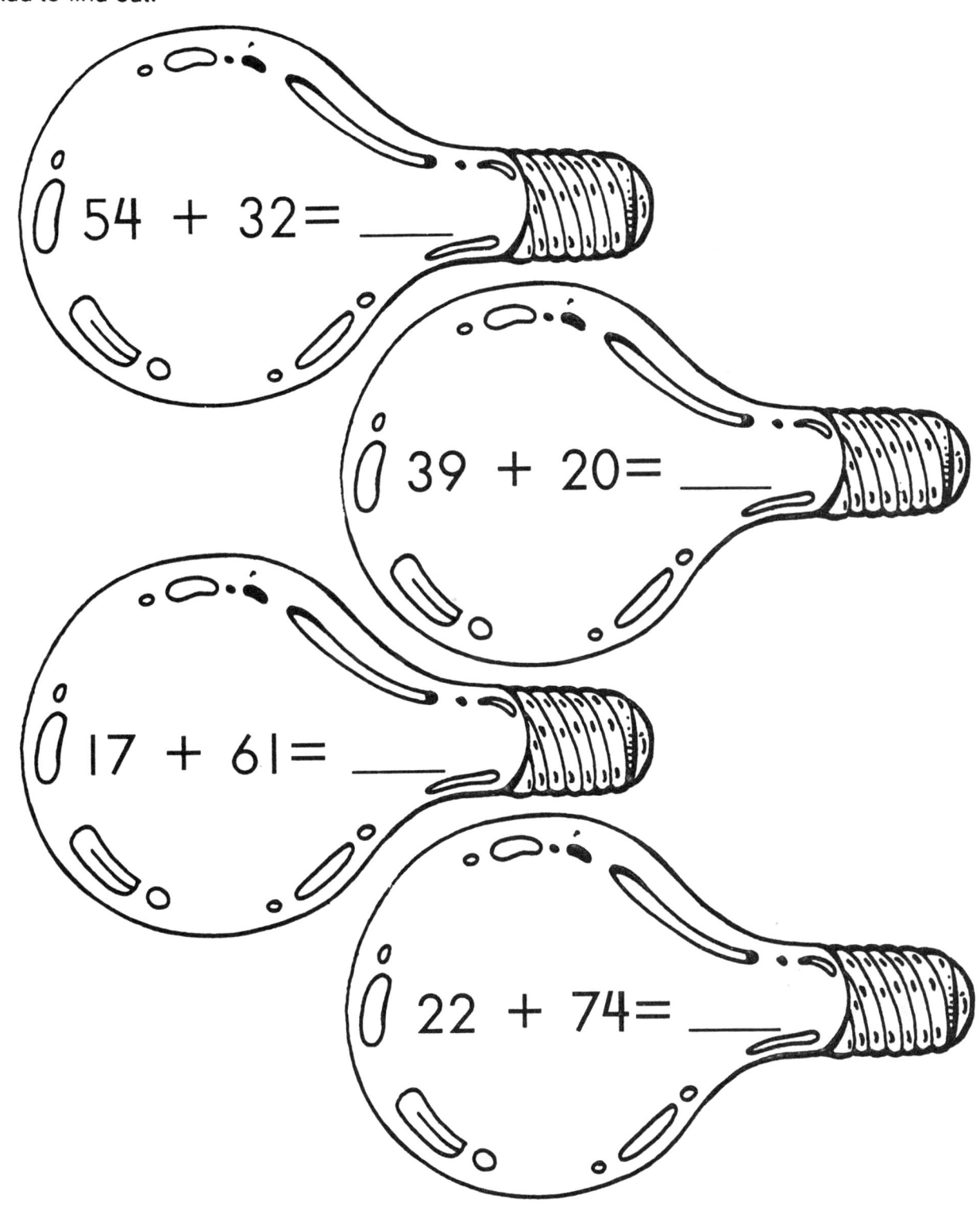

54 + 32 = _____

39 + 20 = _____

17 + 61 = _____

22 + 74 = _____

Skills: Solving 2-digit addition problems; Writing numerals

COUNTING AND MATH SKILLS

How many in all?
Add to find out.

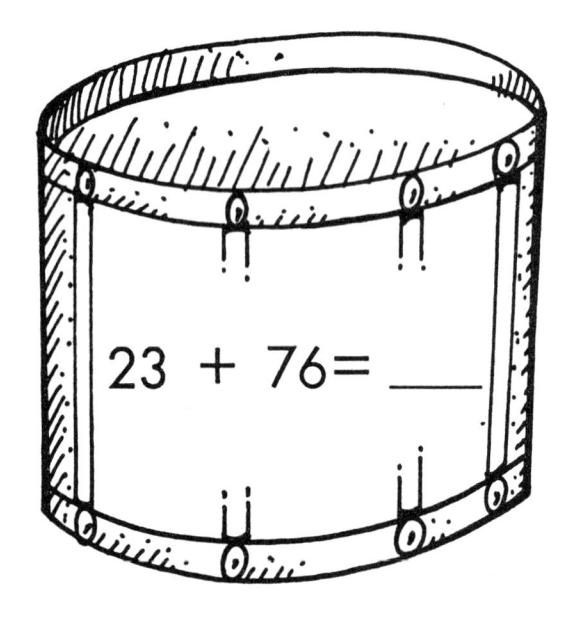

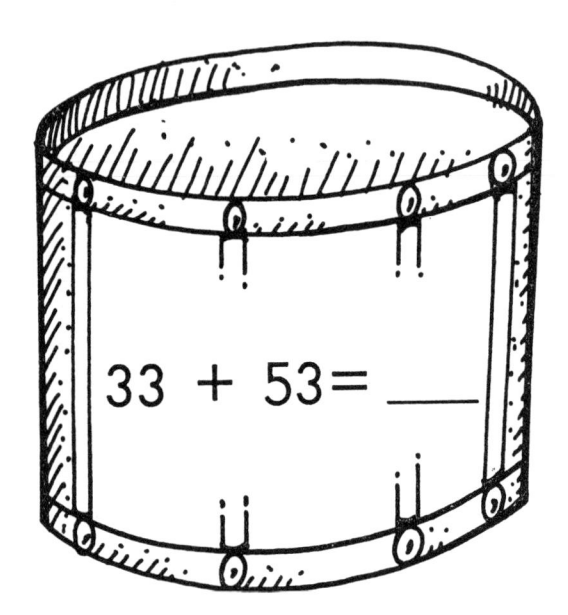

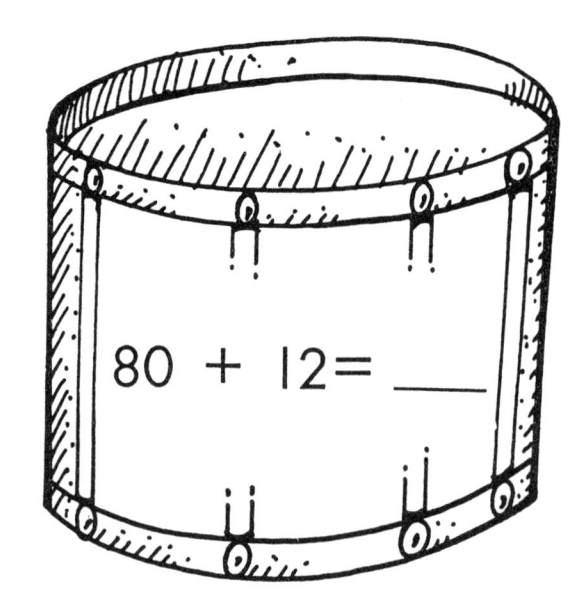

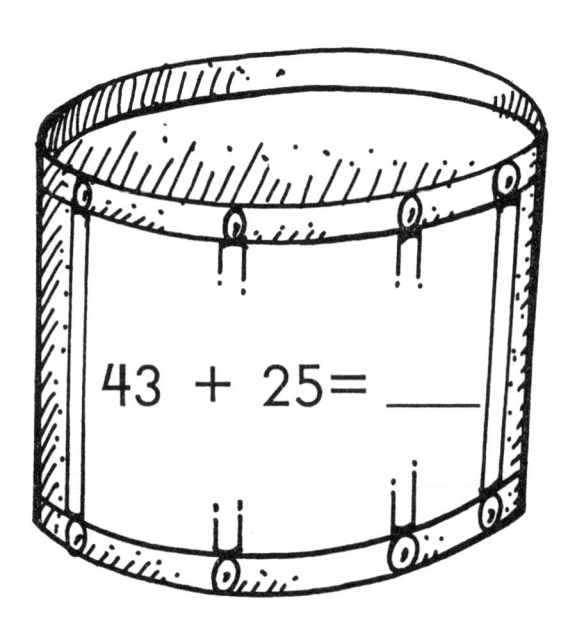

80 + 12 = ____

23 + 76 = ____

43 + 25 = ____

33 + 53 = ____

Skills: Solving 2-digit addition problems; Writing numerals

COUNTING AND MATH SKILLS

Add the numbers in each section.
If the answer is 18, color it orange.
If the answer is 27, color it black.
If the answer is 15, color it brown.

15 + 12

20 + 7

14 + 4

10 + 8

10 + 5

9 + 6

16 + 2

11 + 4

21 + 6

12 + 3

12 + 6

13 + 14

Skills: Solving 2-digit addition problems; Writing numerals

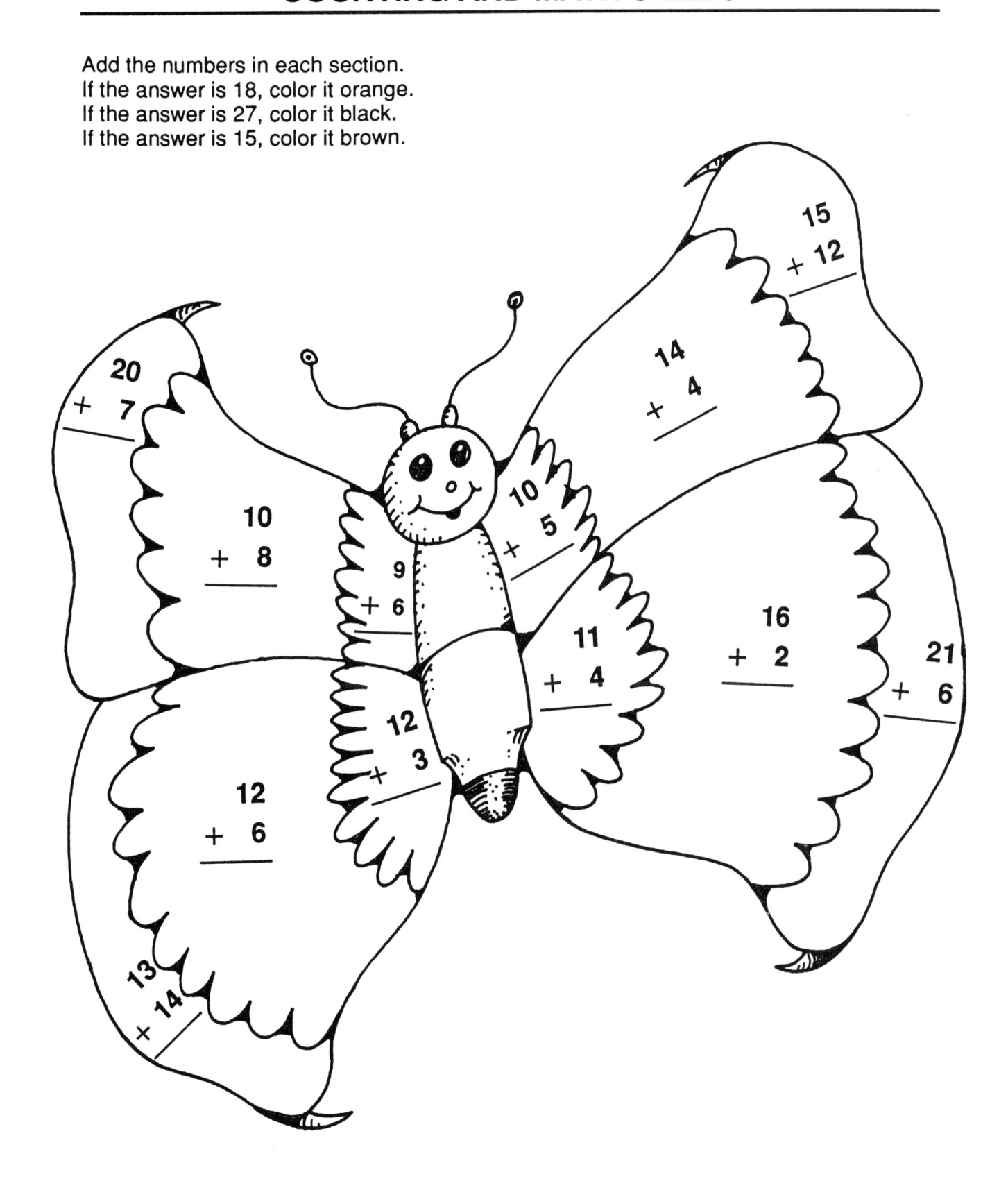

COUNTING AND MATH SKILLS

Add the numbers in each sea horse.
If the answer is 24, color it red.
If the answer is 36, color it blue.
If the answer is 45, color it yellow.

12
+ 12

23
+ 22

25
+ 11

32
+ 13

14
+ 22

10
+ 14

Skills: Solving 2-digit addition problems; Writing numerals

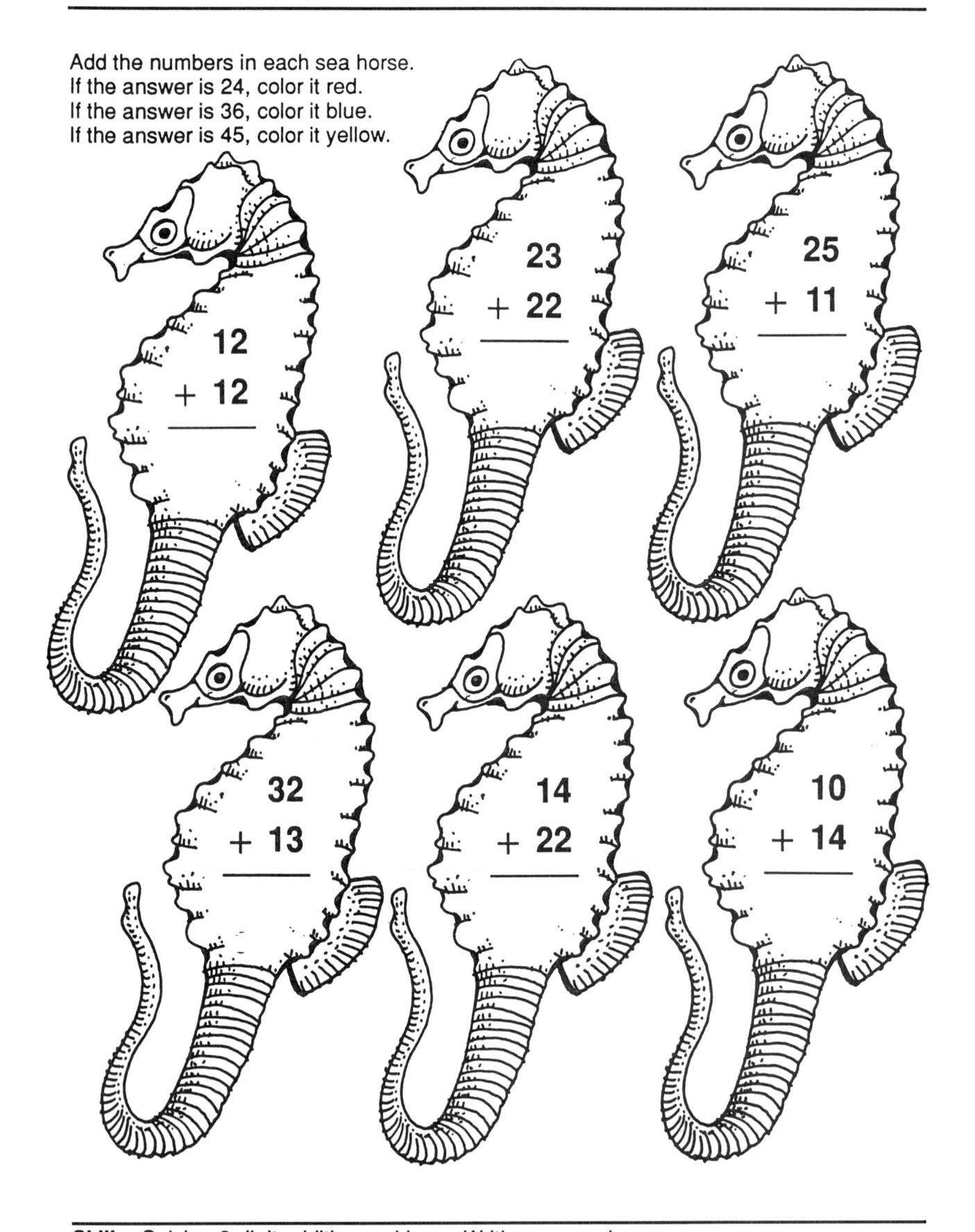

COUNTING AND MATH SKILLS

Look at each picture.
How many are left?

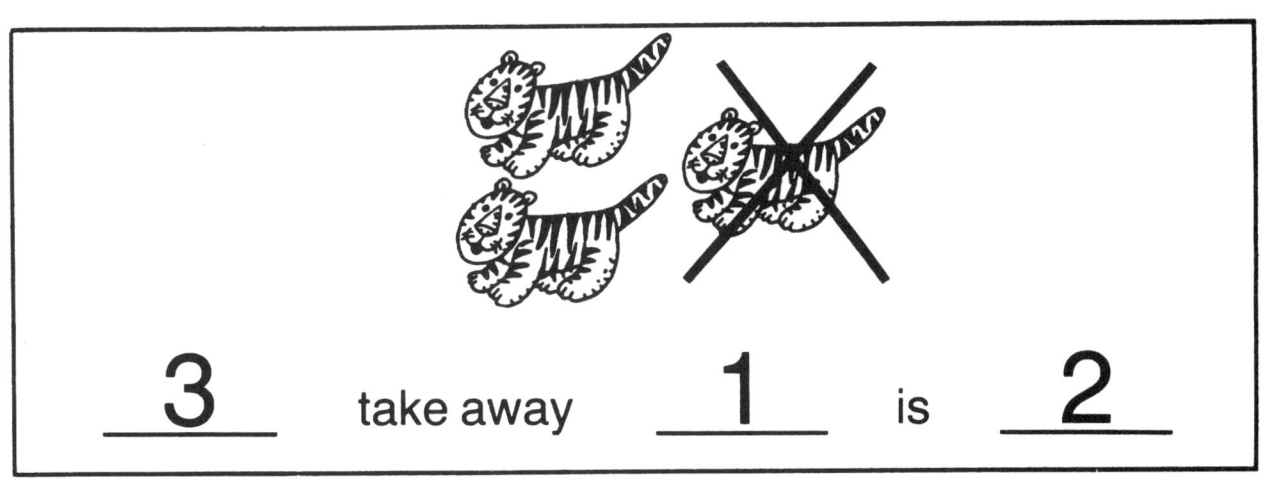

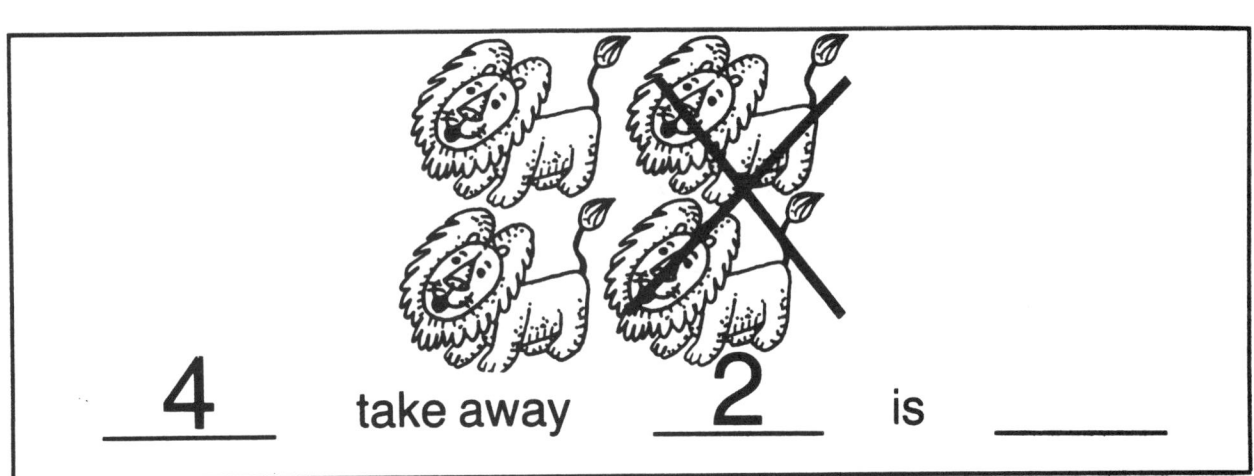

__3__ take away __1__ is __2__

__4__ take away __2__ is ____

__5__ take away __4__ is ____

Skills: Recognizing sets of objects and writing corresponding numerals; Subtracting groups of objects; Practicing subtraction problems

143

COUNTING AND MATH SKILLS

Look at each picture.
How many are left?

___4___ take away ___3___ is _____

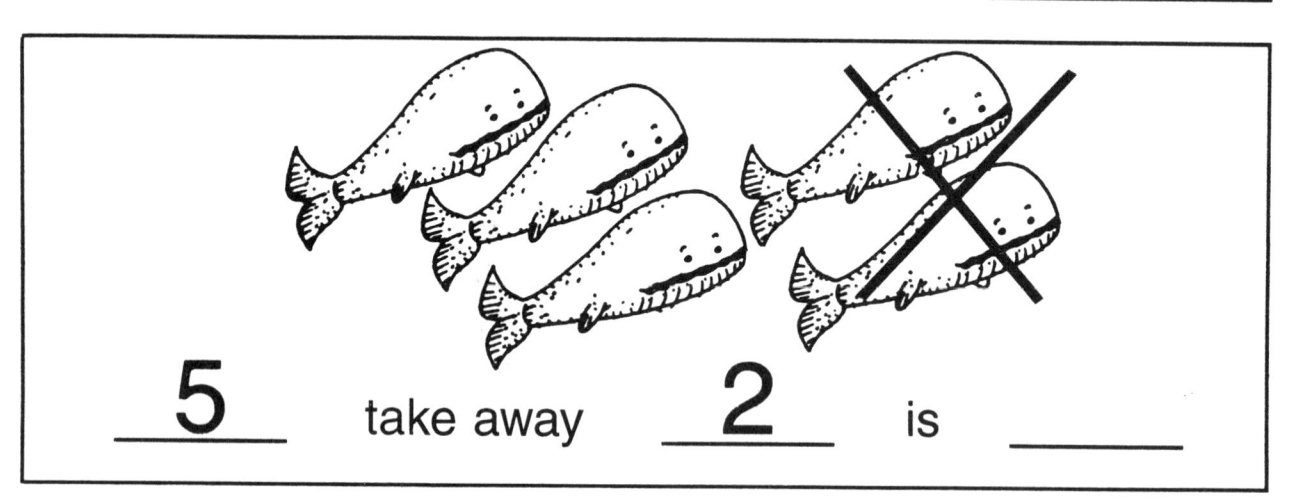

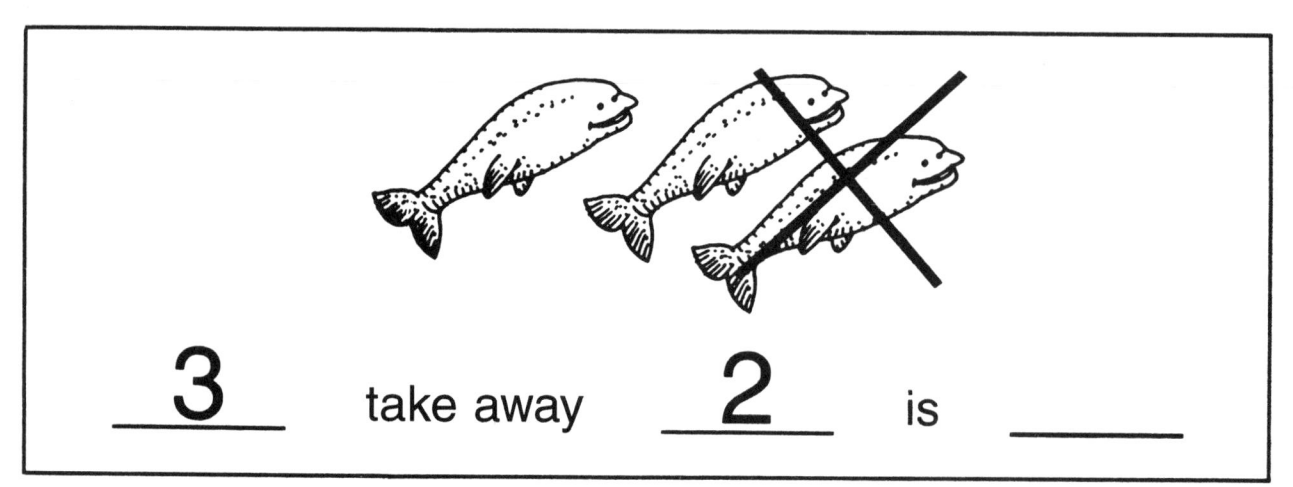

___5___ take away ___2___ is _____

___3___ take away ___2___ is _____

Skills: Recognizing sets of objects and writing corresponding numerals; Subtracting groups of objects; Practicing subtraction problems

COUNTING AND MATH SKILLS

Look at each picture.
How many are left?

  2   take away ____ is ____
  2   —   ____ =   ____

  4   take away ____ is ____
  4   —   ____ =   ____

  5   take away ____ is ____
  5   —   ____ =   ____

Skills: Recognizing sets of objects and writing corresponding numerals; Subtracting groups of objects; Understanding subtraction sentences

COUNTING AND MATH SKILLS

Look at each picture.
How many are left?

__5__ take away _____ is _____

__5__   −   _____   =   _____

__3__ take away _____ is _____

__3__   −   _____   =   _____

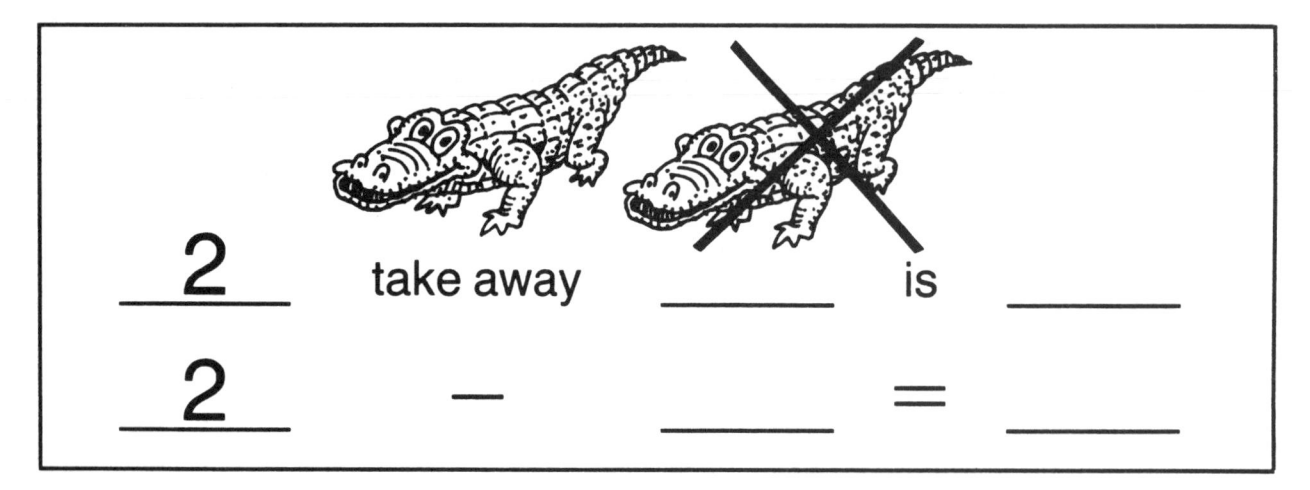

__2__ take away _____ is _____

__2__   −   _____   =   _____

Skills: Recognizing sets of objects and writing corresponding numerals; Subtracting groups of objects; Understanding subtraction sentences

COUNTING AND MATH SKILLS

Look at each picture.
How many are left?

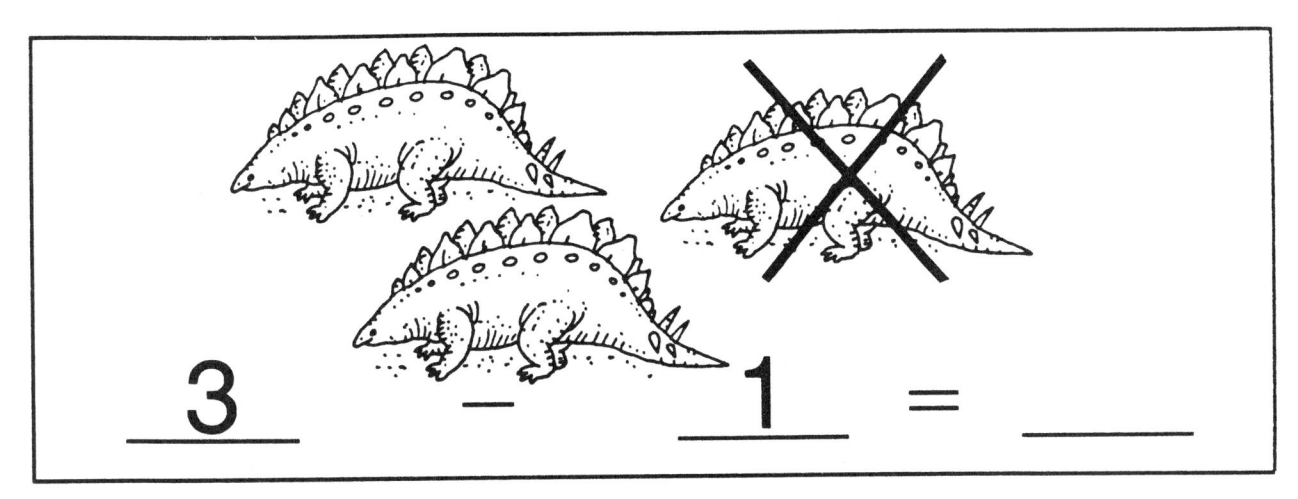

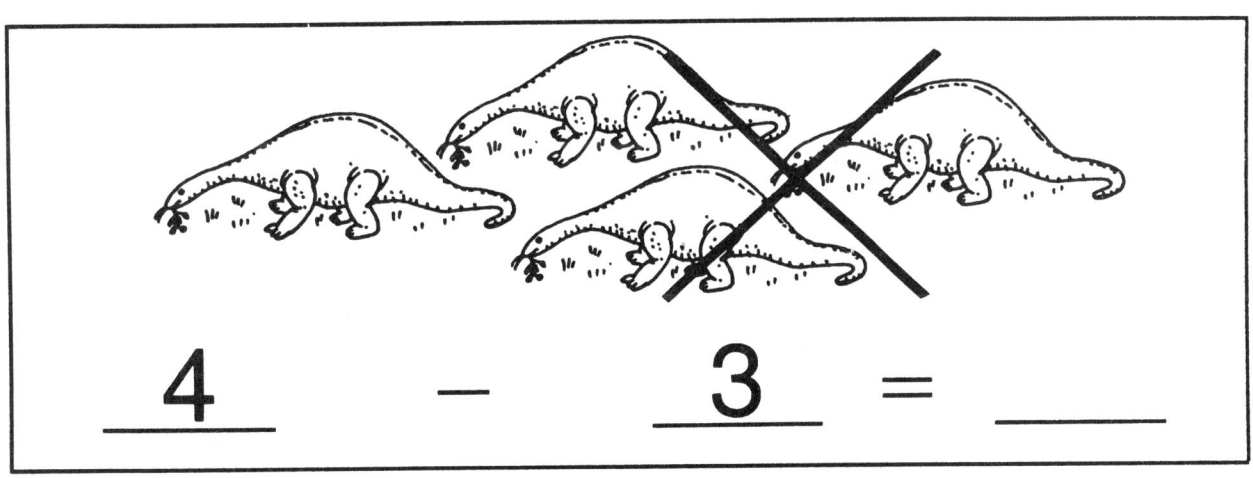

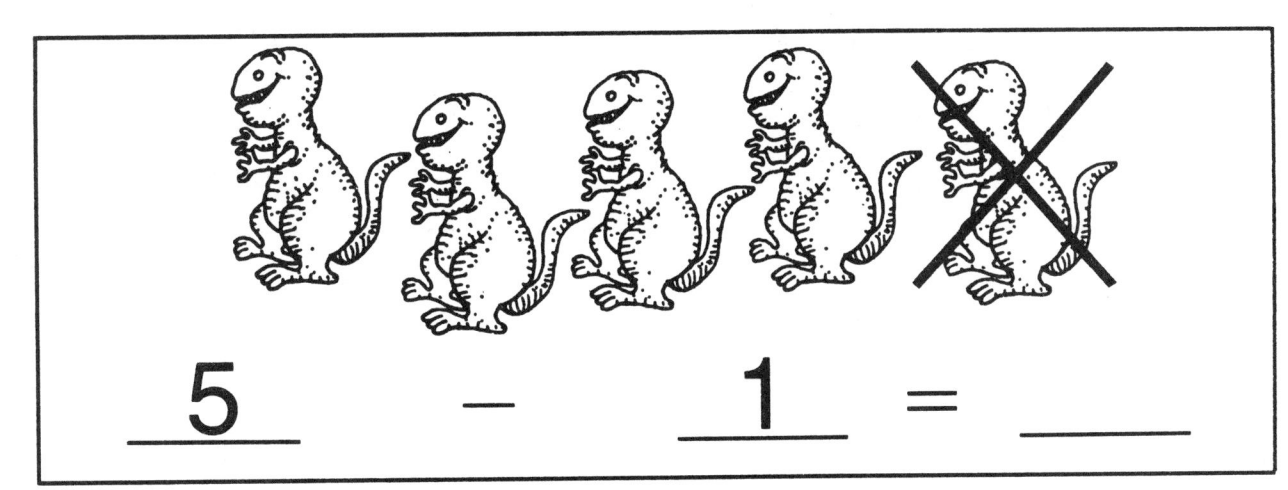

 3   −   1   = ___

 4   −   3   = ___

 5   −   1   = ___

Skills: Recognizing sets of objects and writing corresponding numerals; Subtracting groups of objects; Practicing subtraction problems

COUNTING AND MATH SKILLS

How many are left?
Subtract to find out.

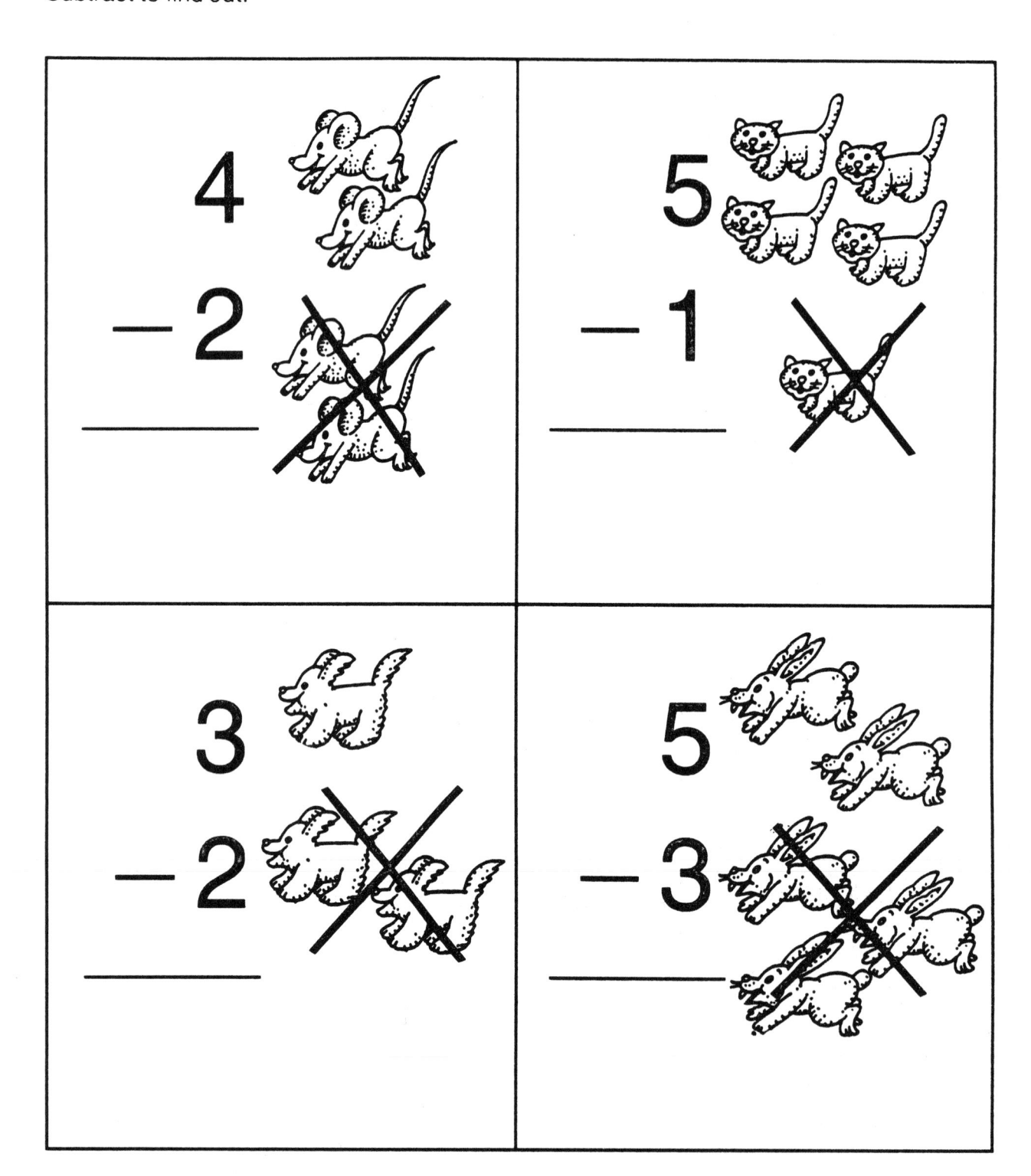

4	5
-2	-1

3	5
-2	-3

Skills: Solving vertical subtraction problems; Writing numerals

COUNTING AND MATH SKILLS

How many are left?
Subtract to find out.

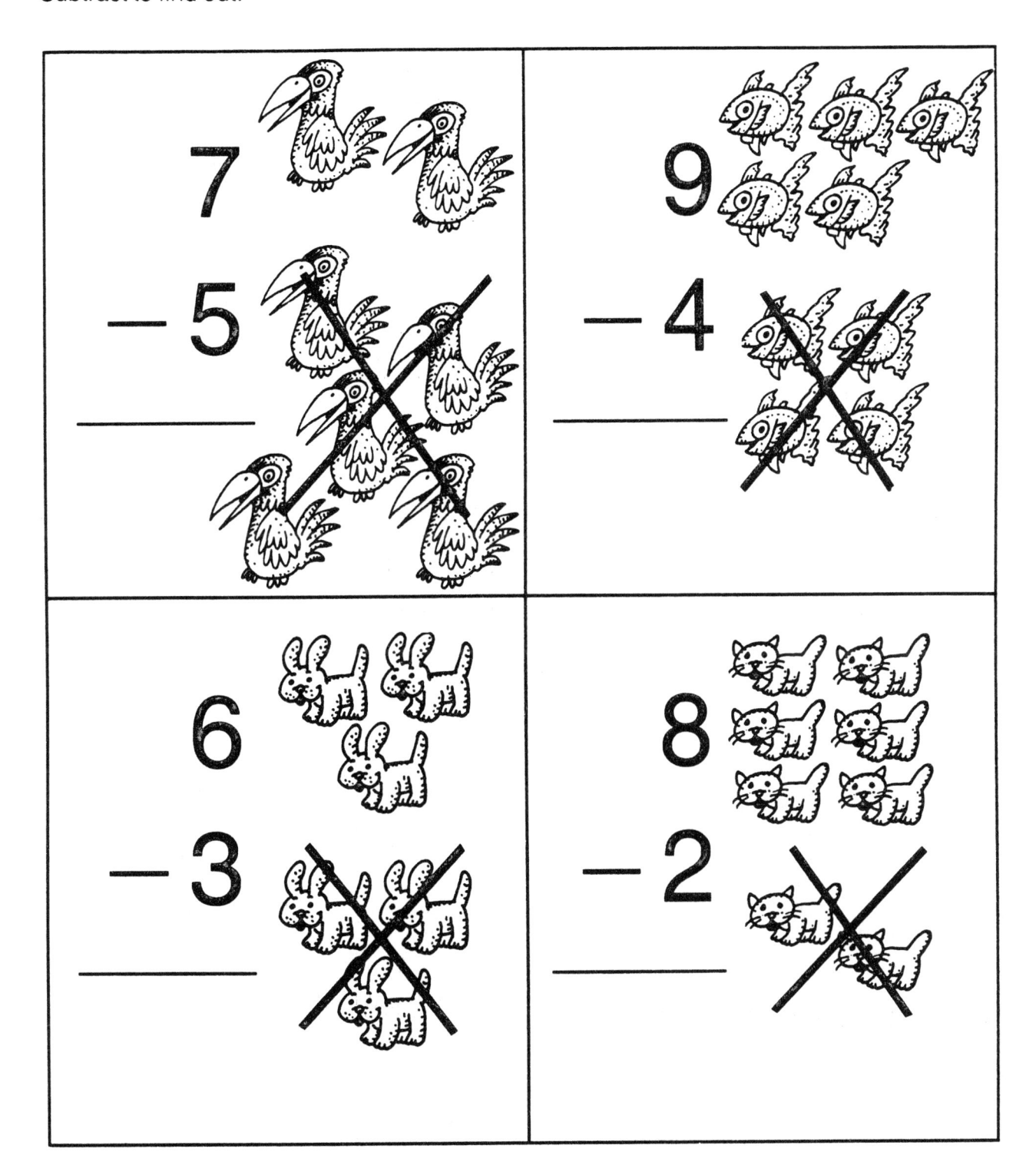

| 7 − 5 = ___ | 9 − 4 = ___ |
| 6 − 3 = ___ | 8 − 2 = ___ |

Skills: Solving vertical subtraction problems to ten; Writing numerals

COUNTING AND MATH SKILLS

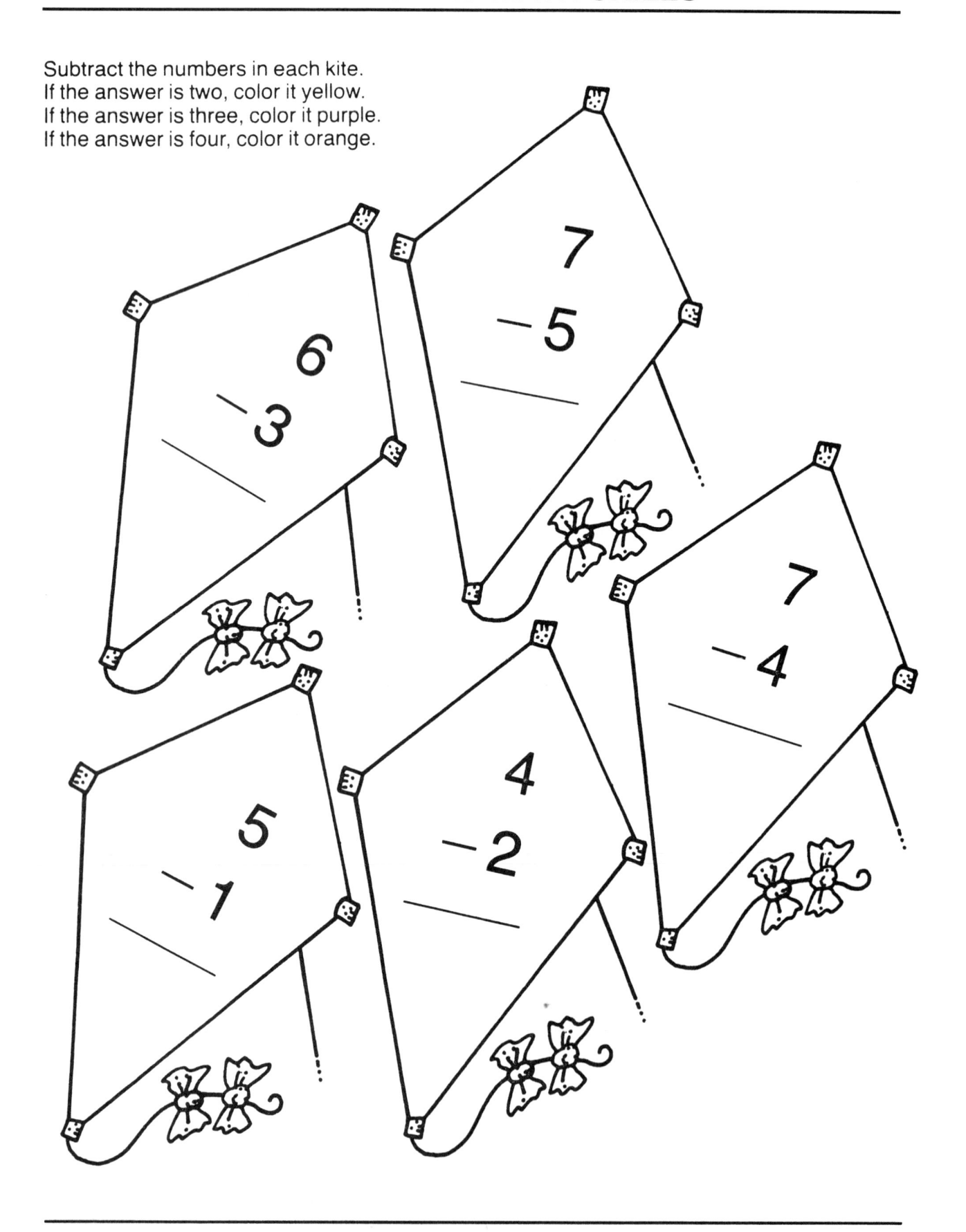

Subtract the numbers in each kite.
If the answer is two, color it yellow.
If the answer is three, color it purple.
If the answer is four, color it orange.

$6 - 3$

$7 - 5$

$7 - 4$

$5 - 1$

$4 - 2$

Skills: Solving vertical subtraction problems; Writing numerals

COUNTING AND MATH SKILLS

Subtract the numbers in each piggy bank.
If the answer is 2, color it green.
If the answer is 3, color it blue.
If the answer is 4, color it yellow.

$$6 - 3$$

$$7 - 4$$

$$6 - 2$$

$$8 - 4$$

$$9 - 7$$

Skills: Solving vertical subtraction problems; Writing numerals

COUNTING AND MATH SKILLS

How many are left?
Subtract to find out.

$$85 - 43$$

$$46 - 25$$

$$78 - 57$$

$$96 - 32$$

Skills: Solving 2-digit subtraction problems; Writing numerals

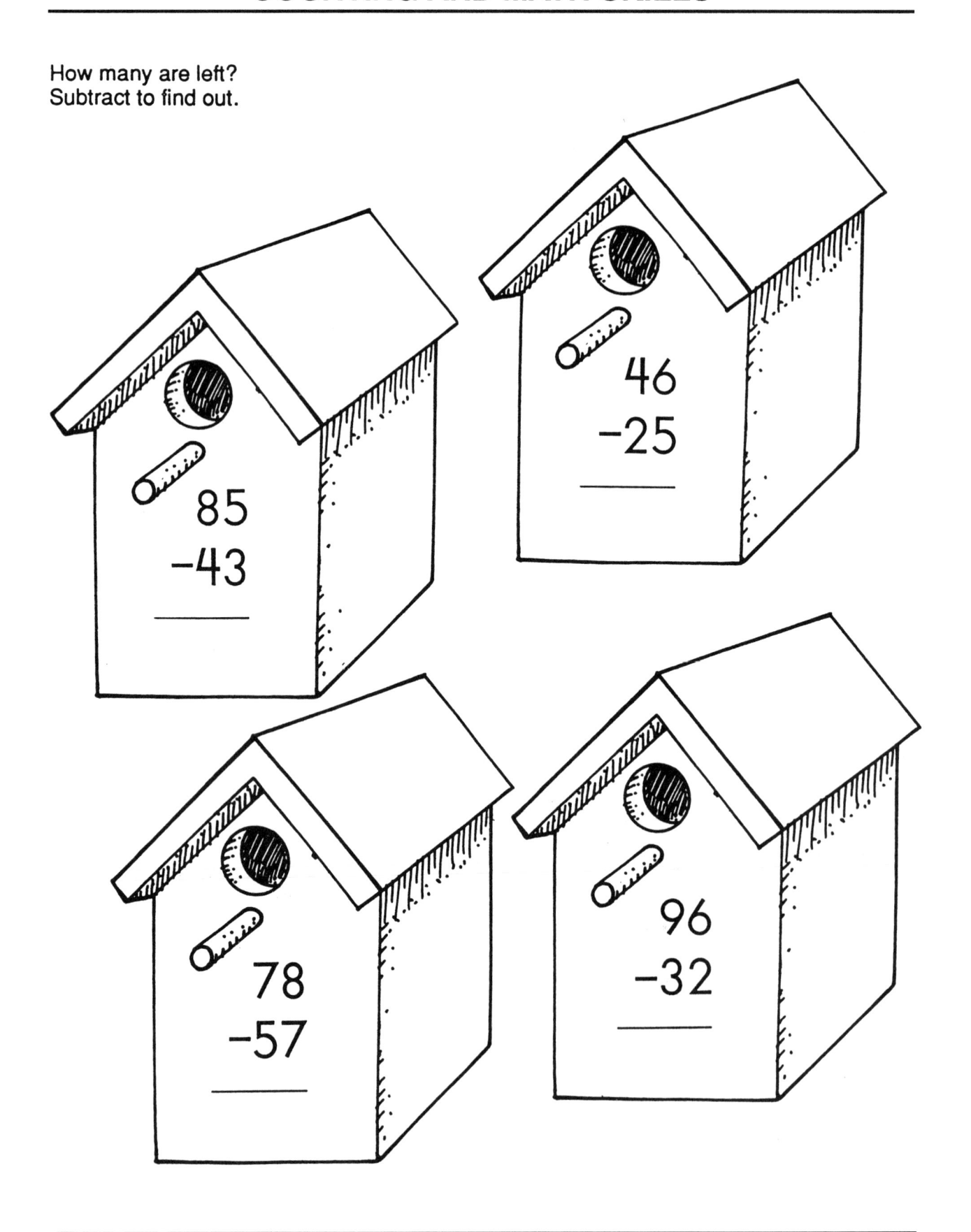

COUNTING AND MATH SKILLS

Subtract the numbers in each teapot.
If the answer is 12, color it red.
If the answer is 24, color it blue.
If the answer is 33, color it yellow.

37
−13
___

48
−36
___

49
−16
___

45
−12
___

46
−22
___

26
−14
___

Skills: Solving 2-digit subtraction problems; Writing numerals

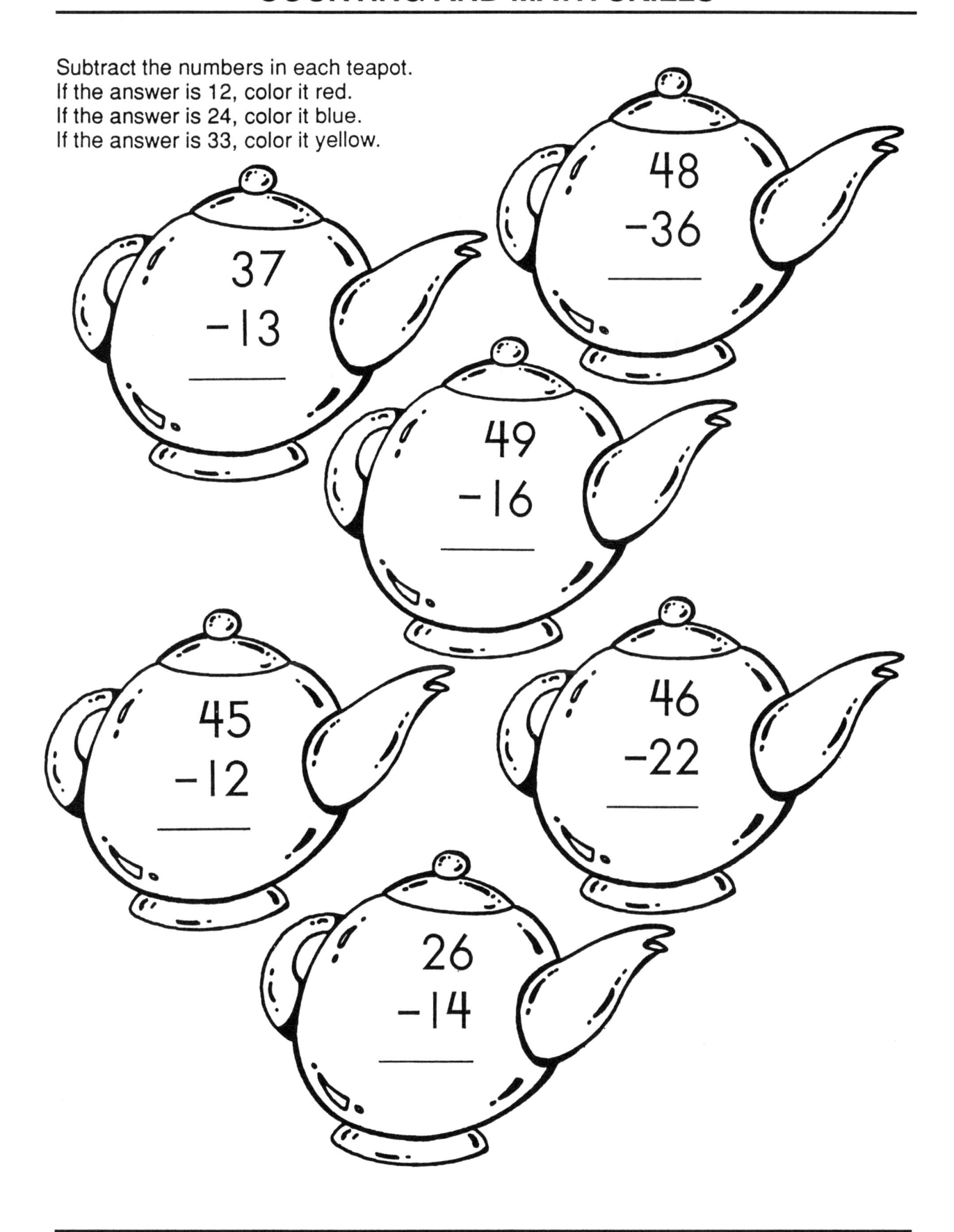

COUNTING AND MATH SKILLS

Subtract the numbers in each fish.
If the answer is 34, color it purple.
If the answer is 21, color it pink.
If the answer is 43, color it green.

67
−33

56
−22

48
− 5

51
−30

56
−13

48
−14

32
−11

69
−26

47
−26

Skills: Solving 2-digit subtraction problems; Writing numerals

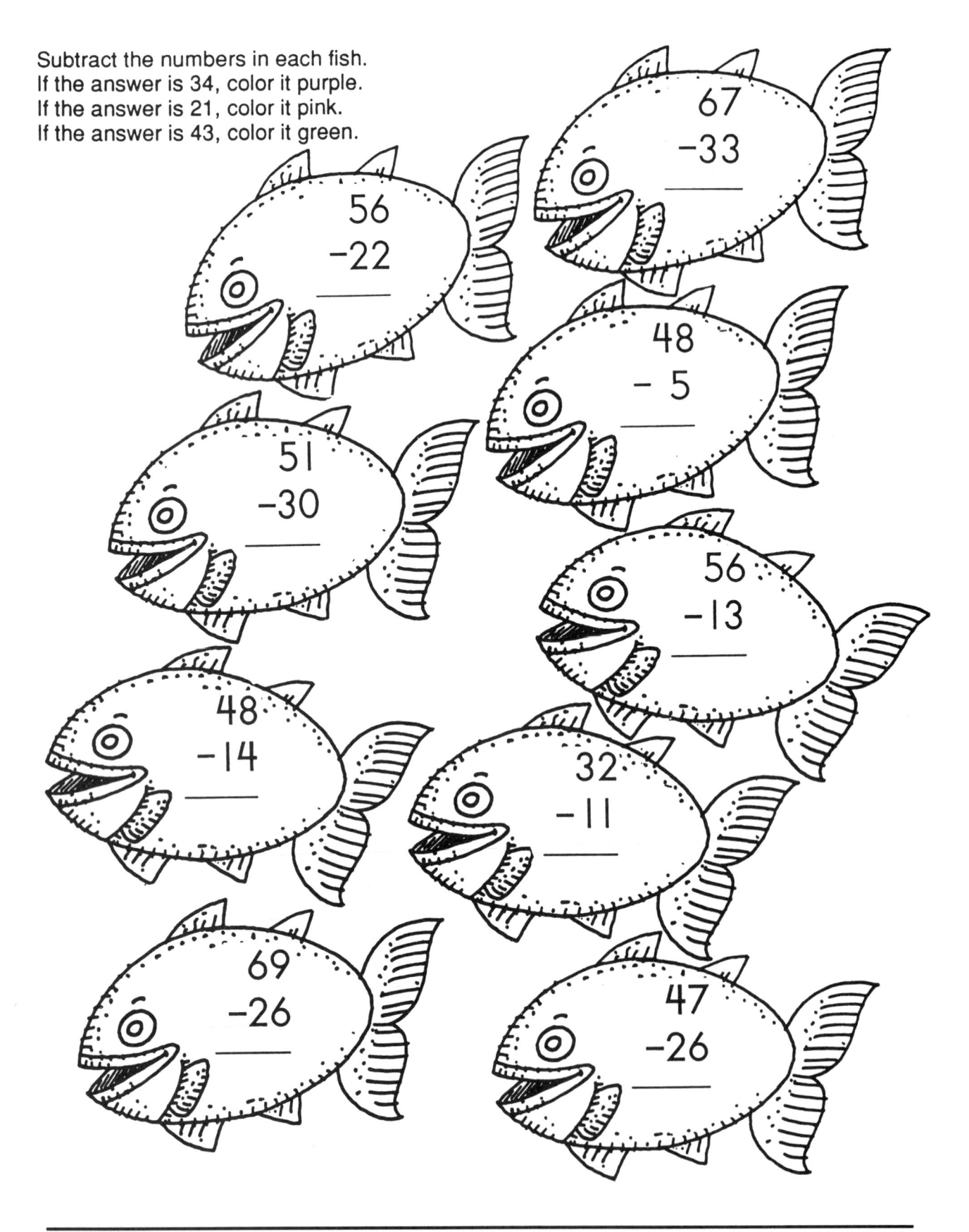

COUNTING AND MATH SKILLS

Subtract the numbers in each kite.
If the answer is 25, color it red.
If the answer is 42, color it blue.
If the answer is 36, color it yellow.

39
−14
____

48
−12
____

63
−21
____

58
−16
____

46
−21
____

57
−21
____

86
−50
____

75
−33
____

75
−50
____

Skills: Solving 2-digit subtraction problems; Writing numerals

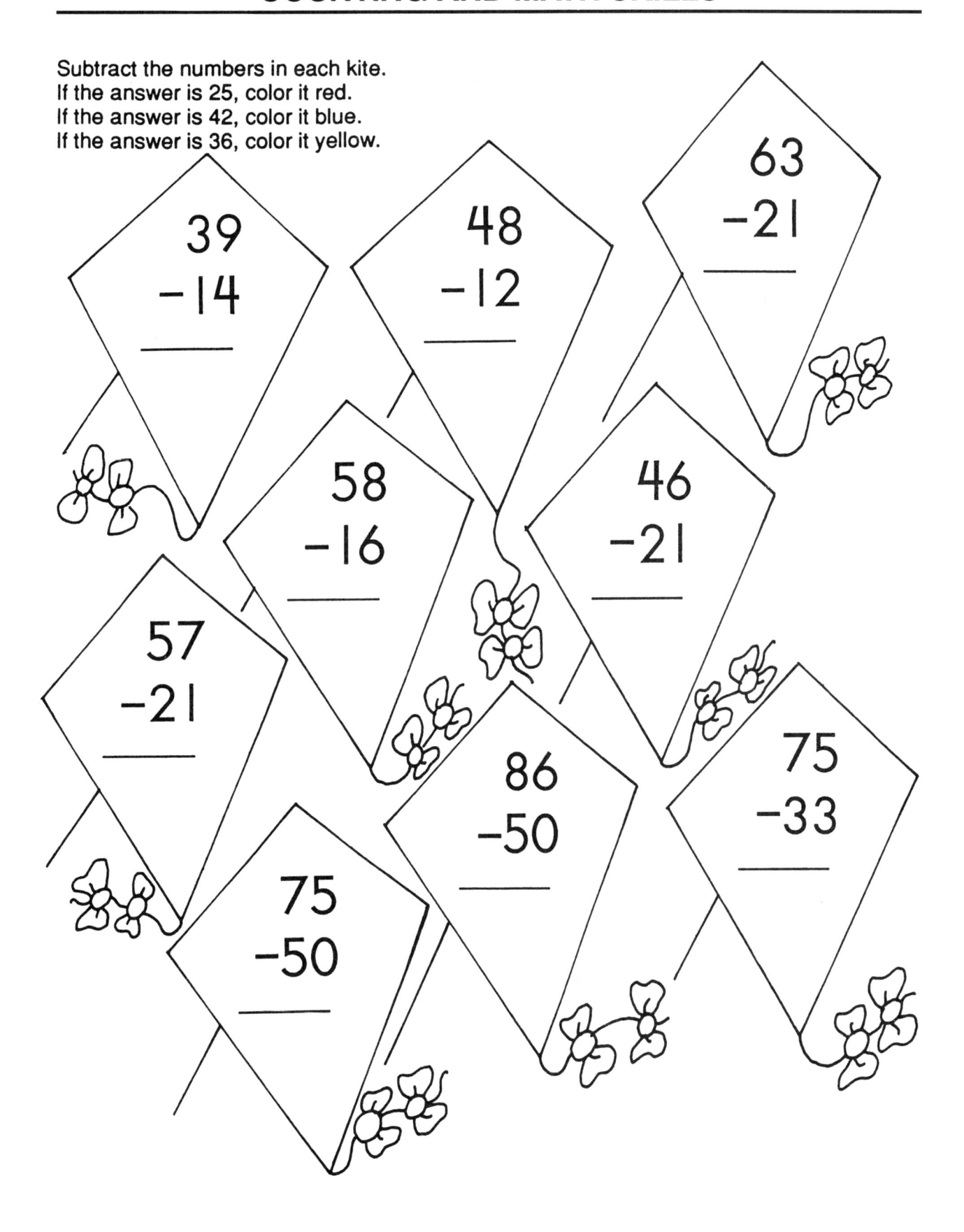

MEASURING

Look at the pictures in each box.
Circle the ones that are the same length.
Then color the pictures.

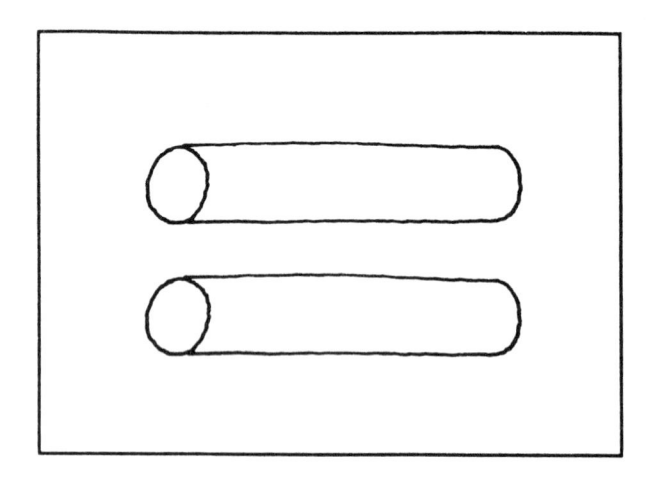

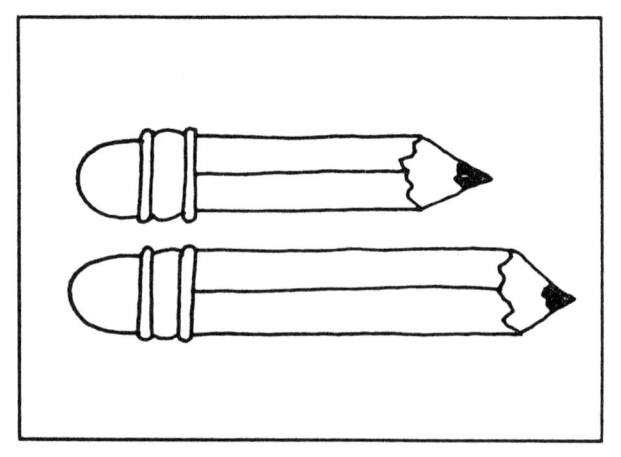

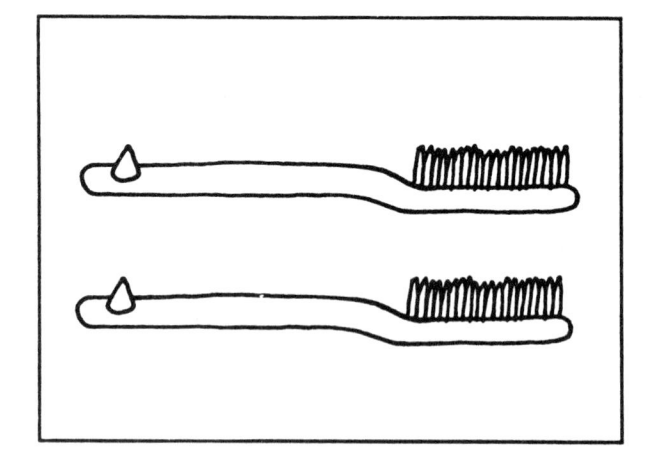

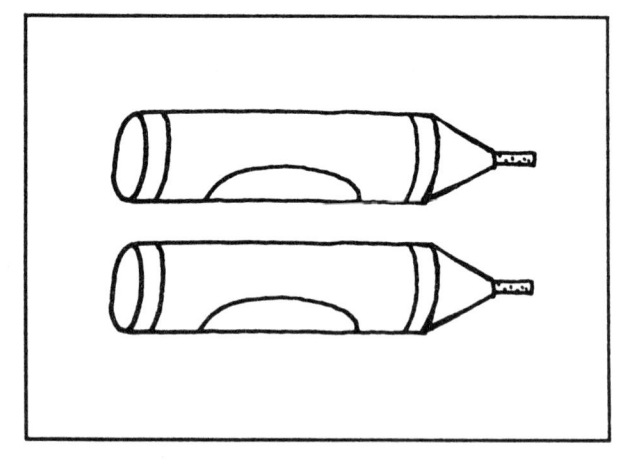

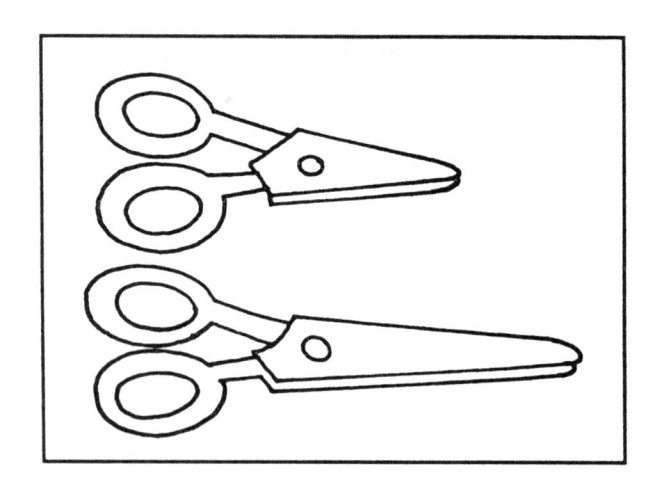

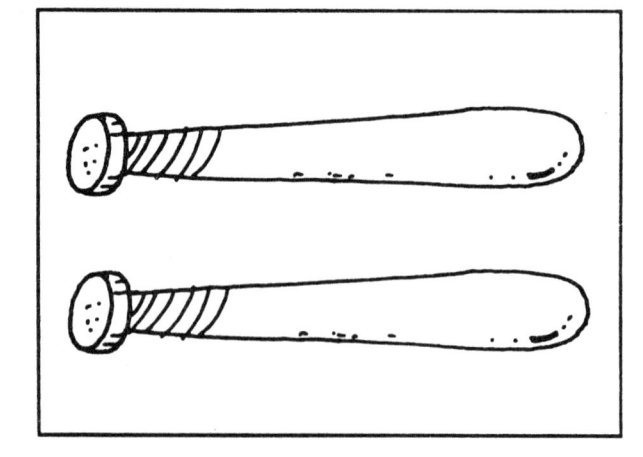

Skills: Recognizing objects that are the same length

MEASURING

Look at the pictures in each box.
Which one is shorter?
Circle the one that is shorter.
Then color the pictures.

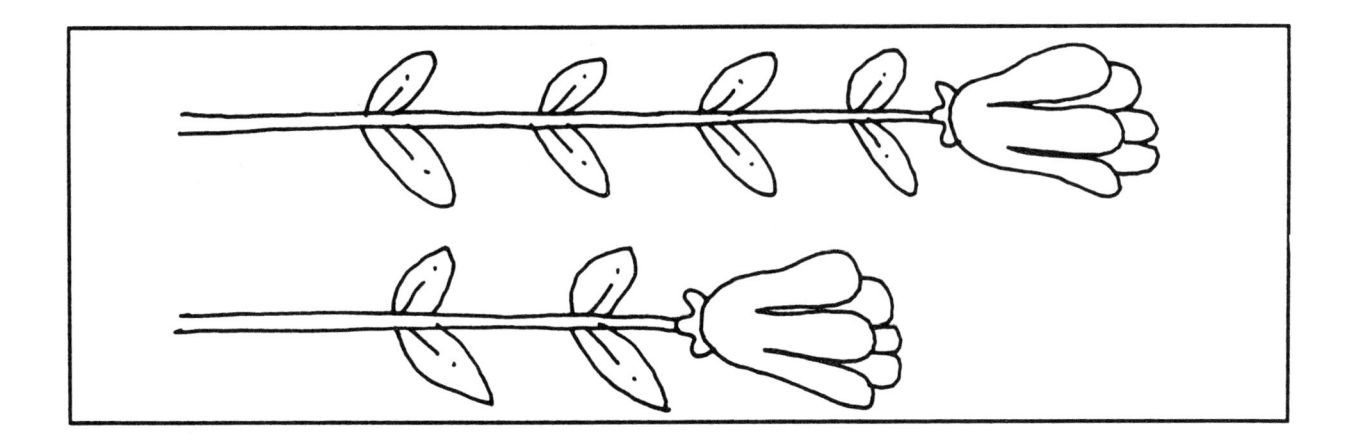

Skills: Comparing length

157

MEASURING

Look at the pictures in each box.
Which one is longer?
Circle the one that is longer.
Then color the pictures.

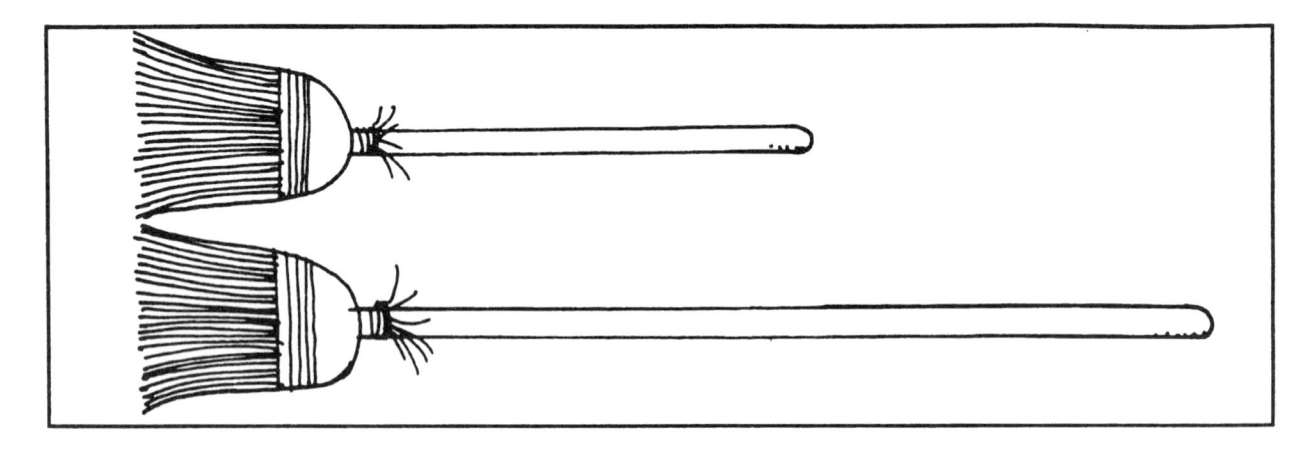

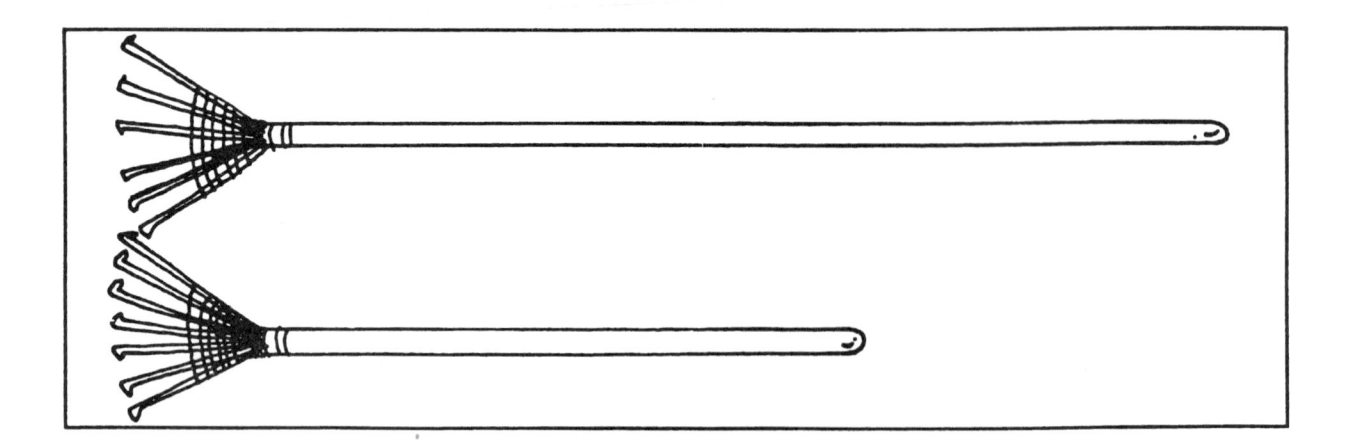

Skills: Comparing length

158

MEASURING

Which one is longer?
Look at the pictures in each box and circle the one that is longer.
Then color the picture.

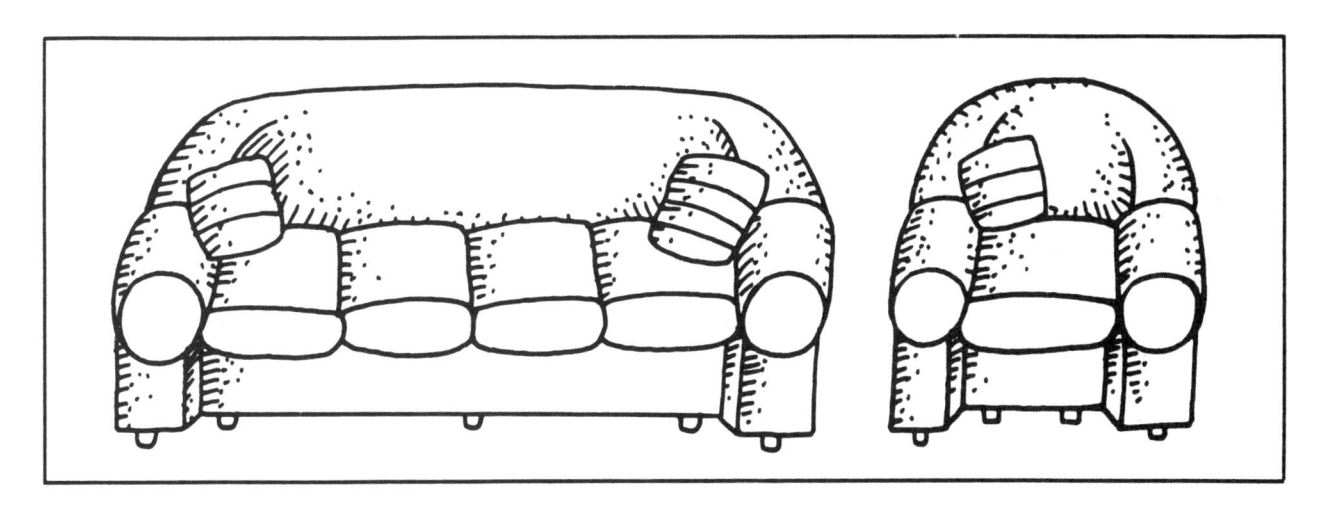

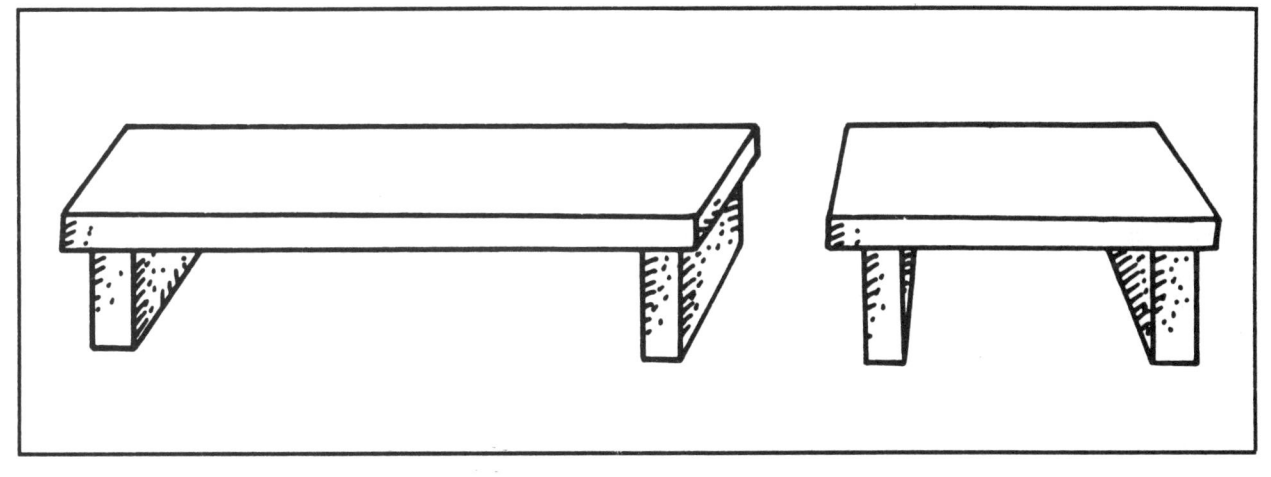

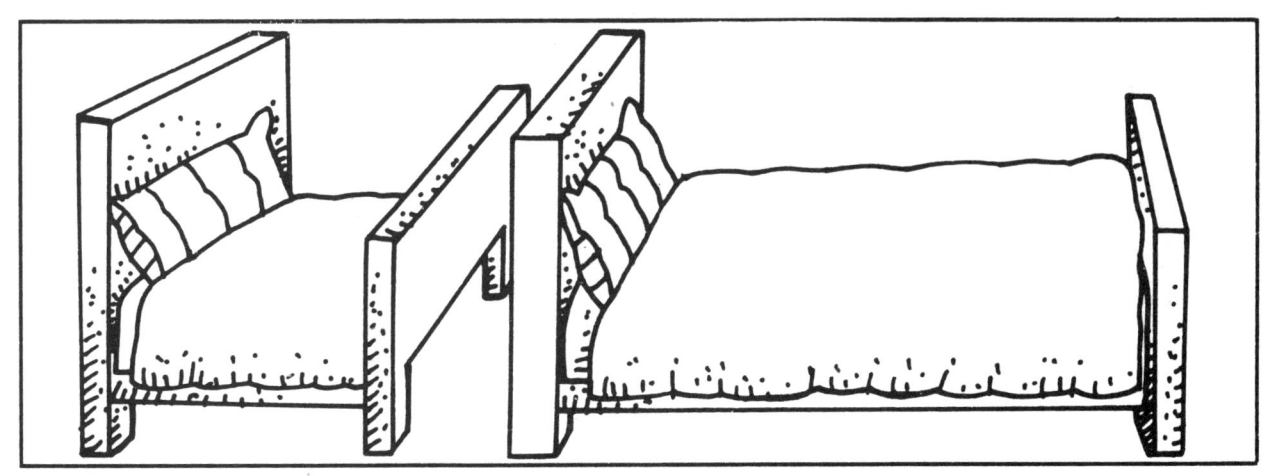

Skills: Making comparisons; Visual discrimination; Vocabulary

MEASURING

Which one is shorter?
Look at the pictures in each box and circle the one that is shorter.
Then color the picture.

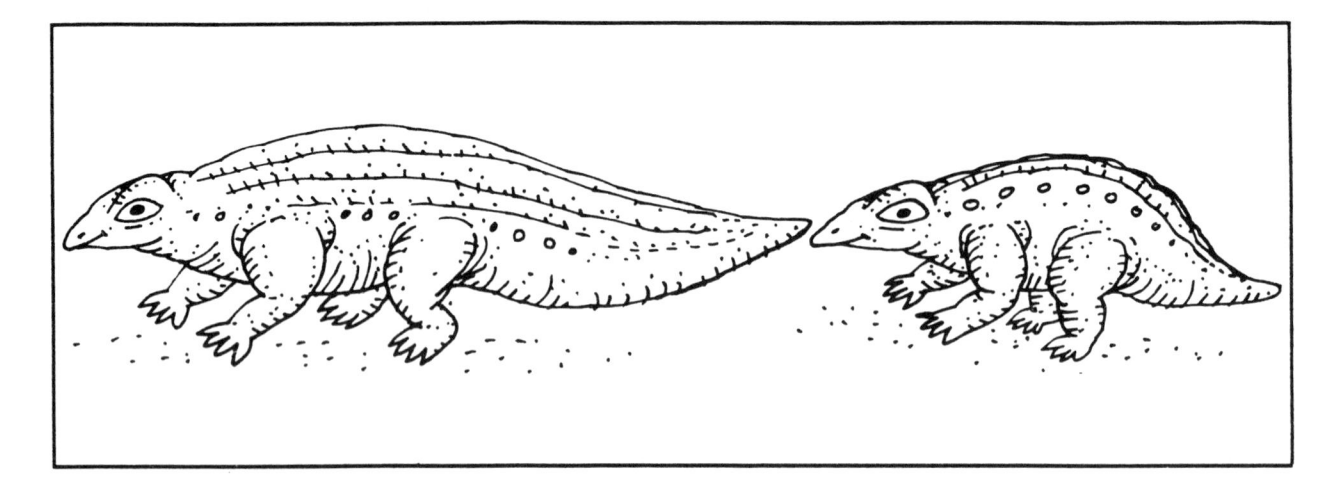

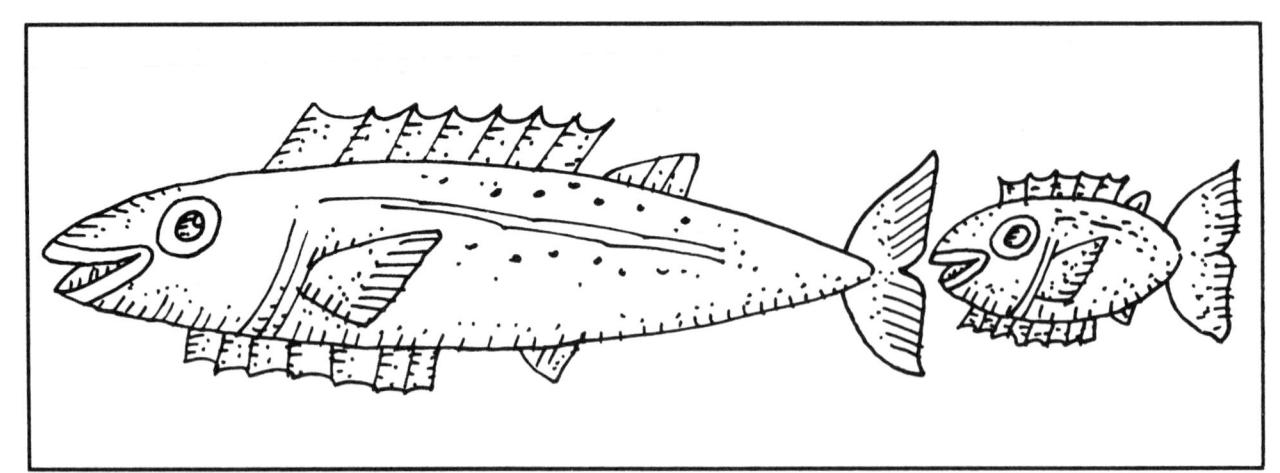

Skills: Making comparisons; Visual discrimination; Vocabulary

MEASURING

Look at the picture in each box.
Count how many paper clips long it is.
Then write that number on the line.

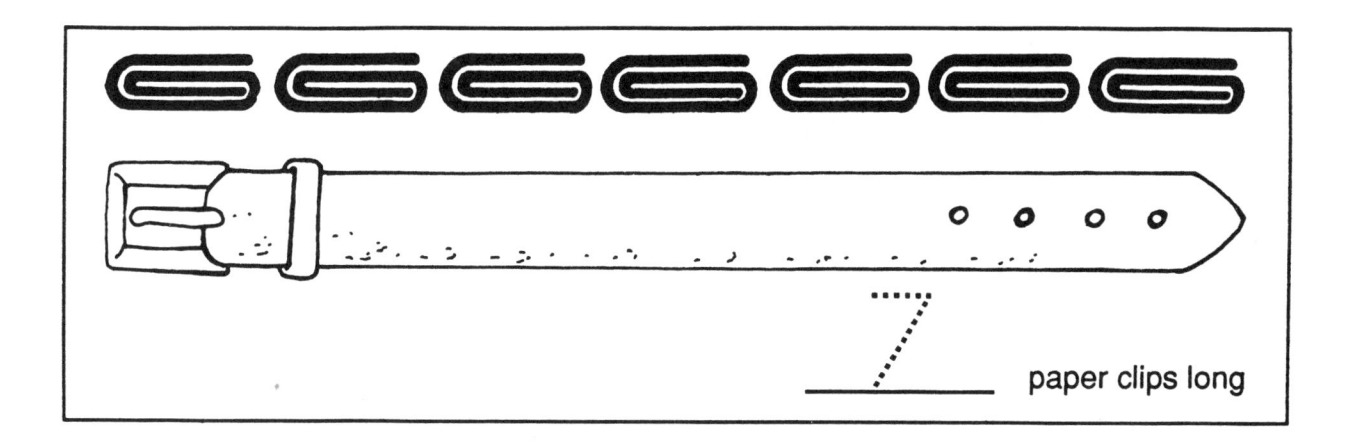

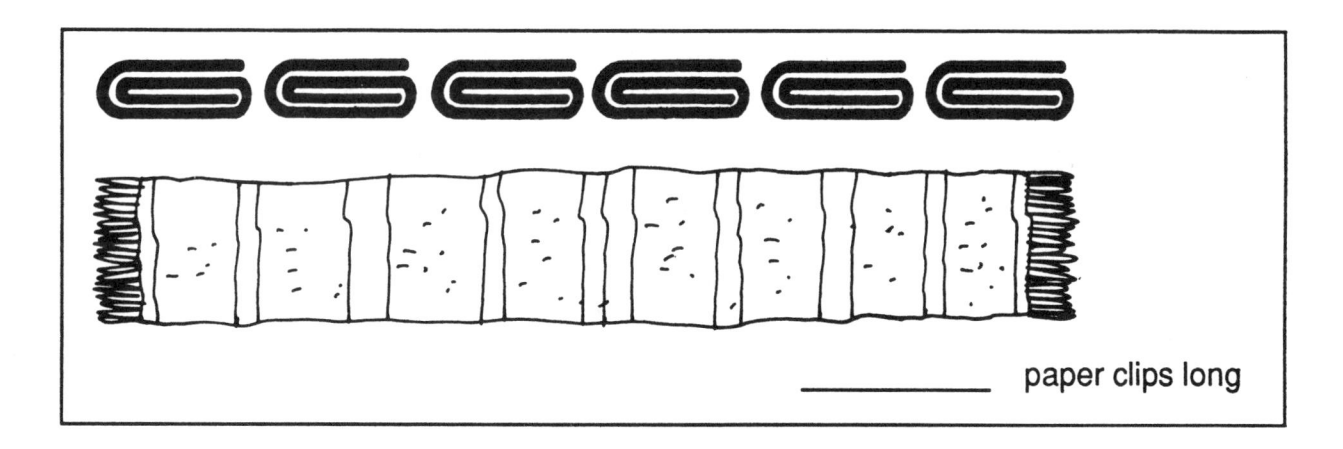

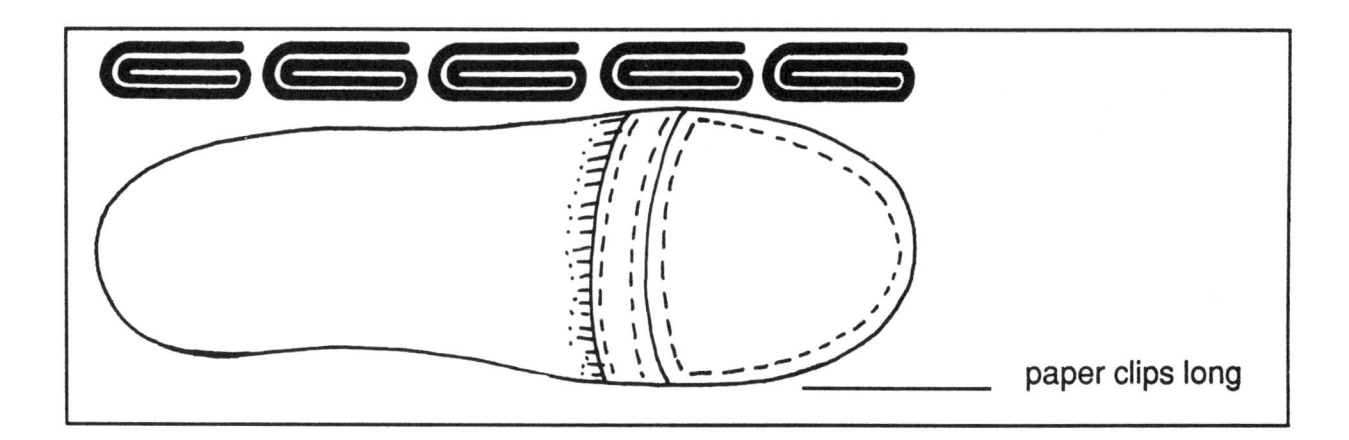

_7_ paper clips long

_____ paper clips long

_____ paper clips long

Skills: Measuring lengths; Using nonstandard units

MEASURING

Look at the picture in each box.
Count how many paper clips long it is.
Then write that number on the line.

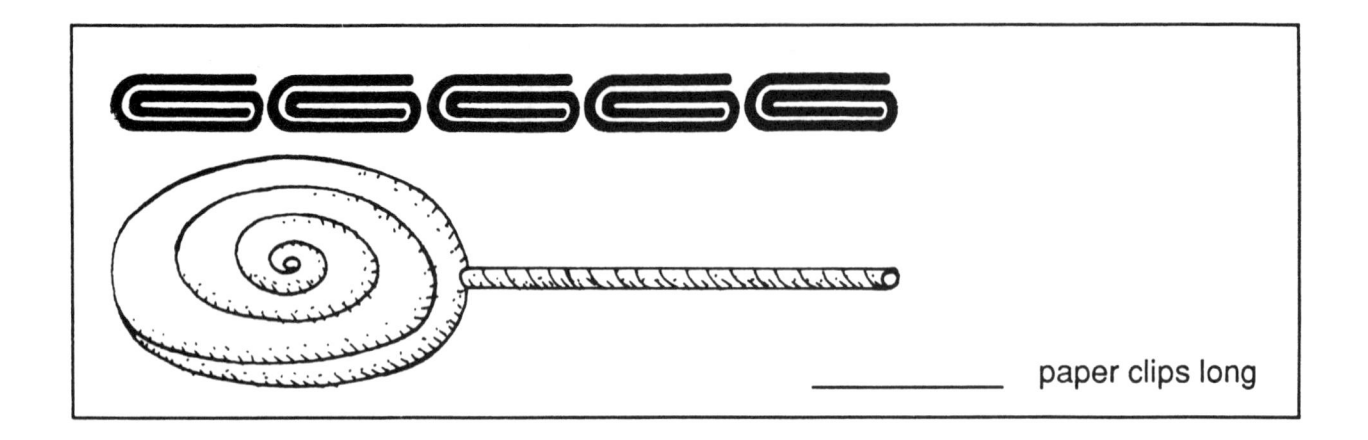

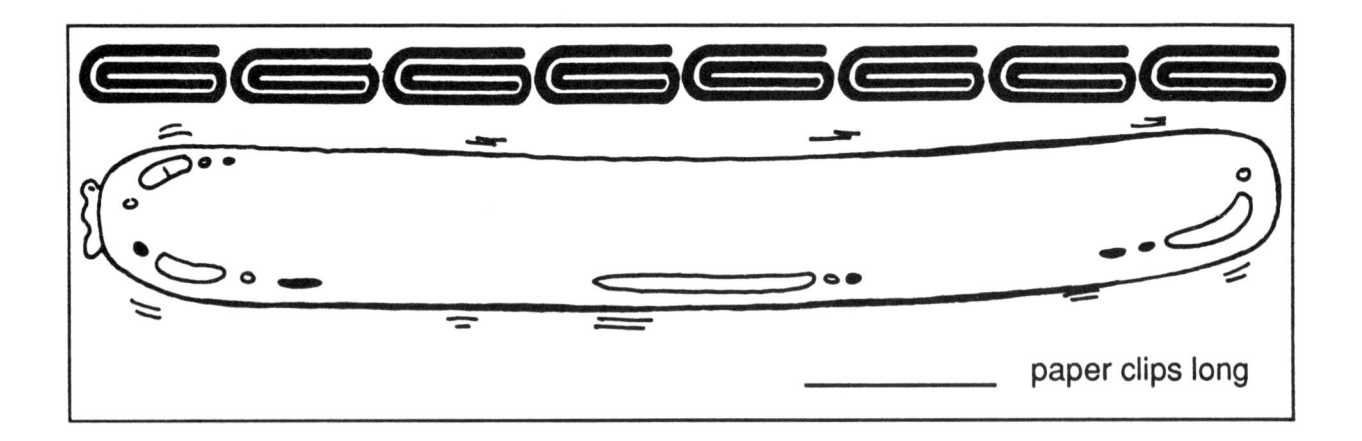

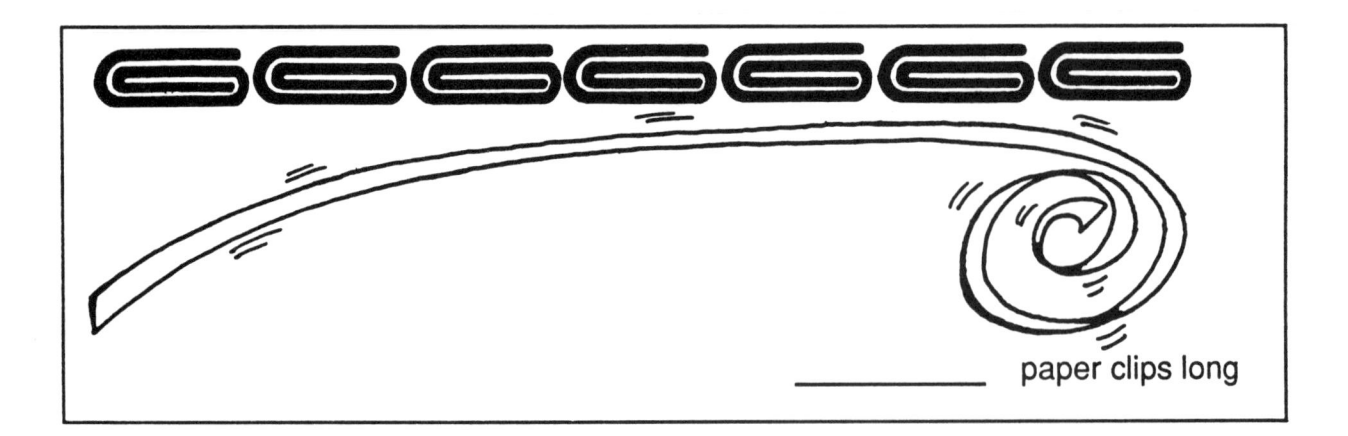

_____ paper clips long

_____ paper clips long

_____ paper clips long

Skills: Measuring lengths; Using nonstandard units

MEASURING

Look at the picture in each box.
Count how many paper clips long it is.
Then write that number on the line.

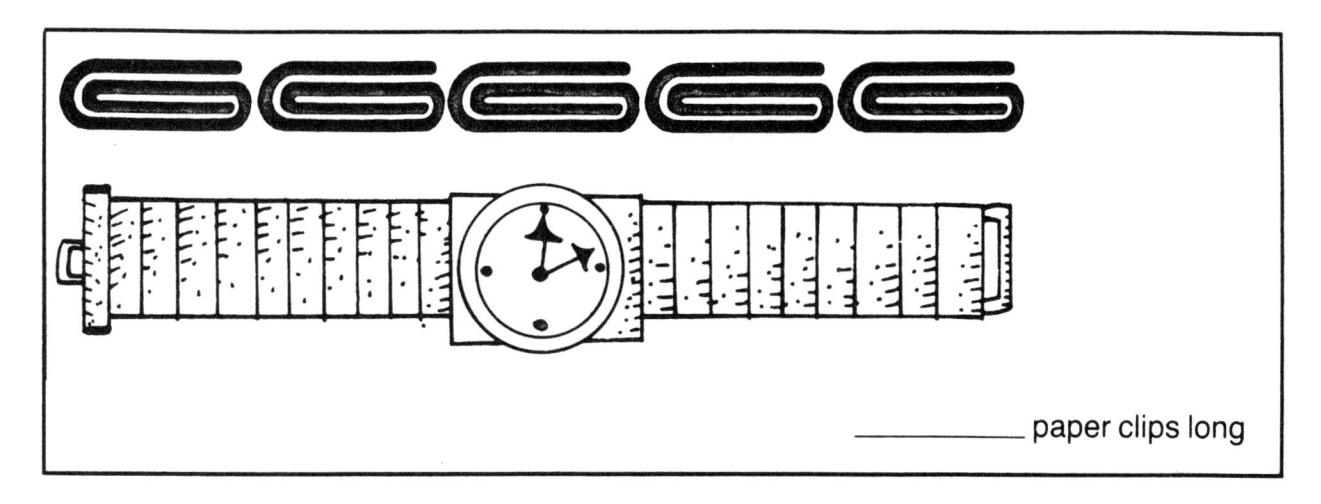

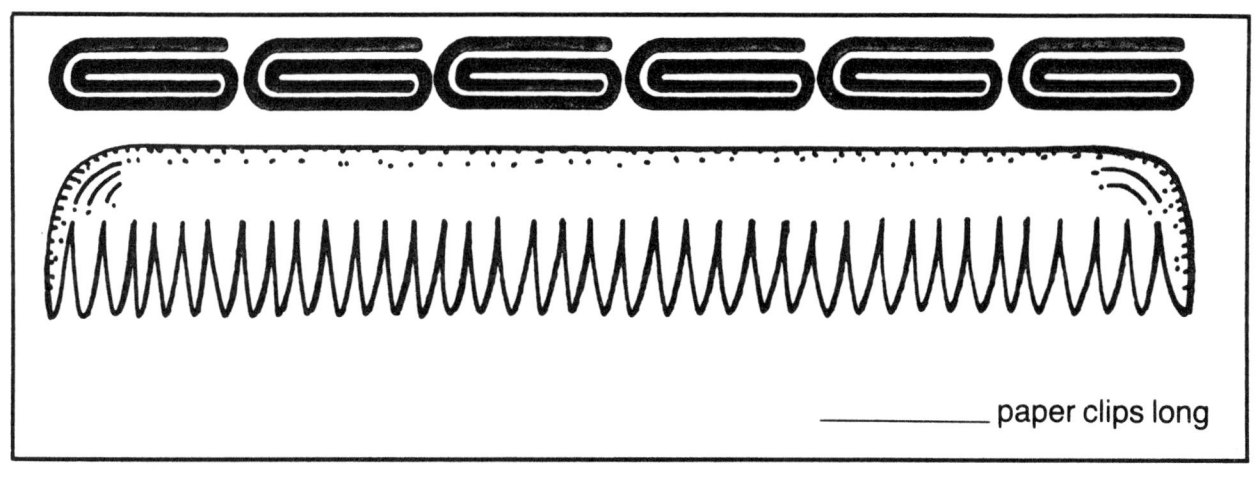

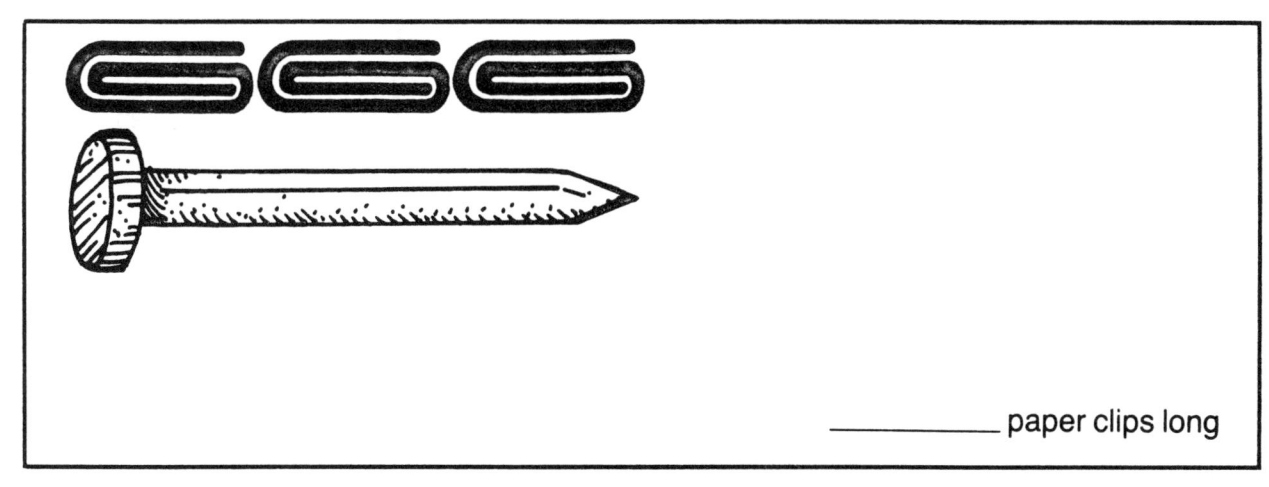

_____ paper clips long

_____ paper clips long

_____ paper clips long

Skills: Measuring lengths; Following directions; Using number concepts

MEASURING

Look at the pictures in each box.
Circle the picture of the person that is taller.
Then color the pictures.

Skills: Comparing height

164

MEASURING

Look at the pictures in each box.
Circle the picture of the person that is shorter.
Then color the pictures.

Skills: Comparing height

MEASURING

Look at the pictures in each box.
Which one holds more?
Circle the one that holds more.
Then color the pictures.

Skills: Comparing capacity

166

MEASURING

Look at the pictures in each box.
Which one holds less?
Circle the one that holds less.
Then color the pictures.

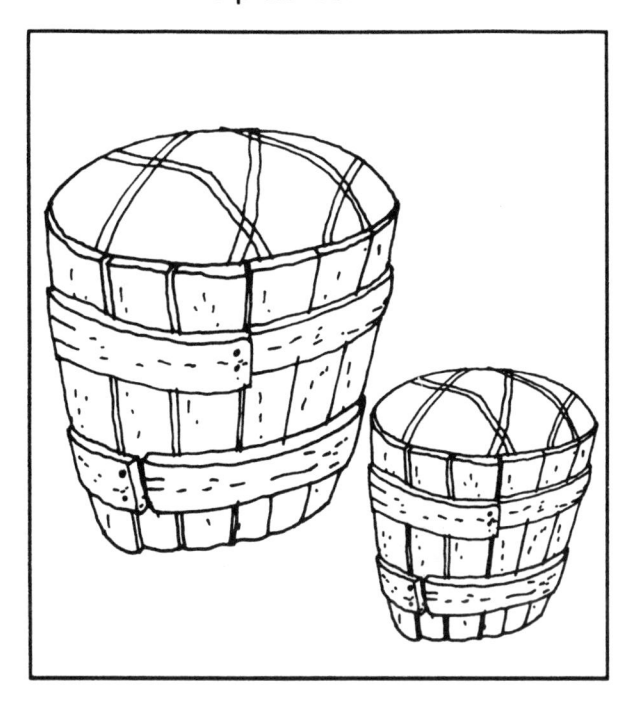

Skills: Comparing capacity

MEASURING

Look at the pictures in each box.
Which one is heavier?
Circle the one that is heavier.
Then color the pictures.

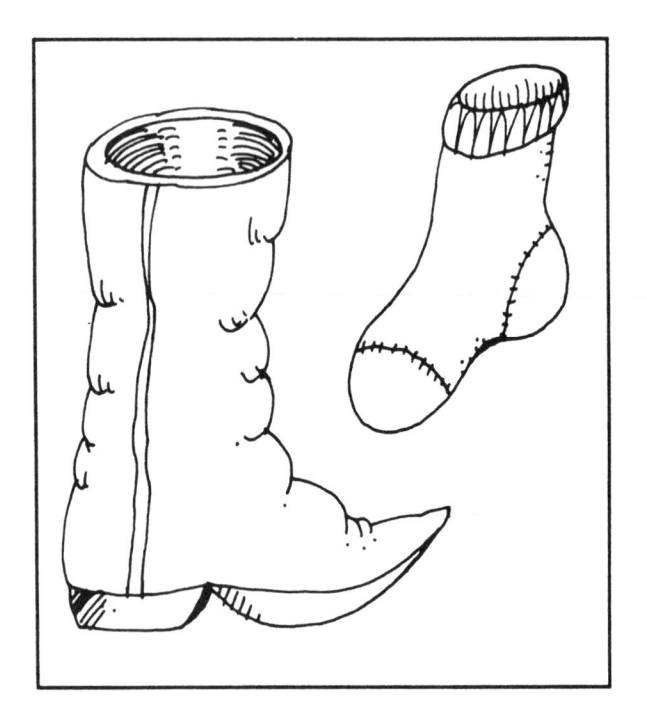

Skills: Comparing weight

MEASURING

Look at the pictures in each box.
Which one is lighter?
Circle the one that is lighter.
Then color the pictures.

Skills: Comparing weight

169

MEASURING

Look at the pictures in each row.
Which one is small?
Circle the one that is small.
Then color the pictures.

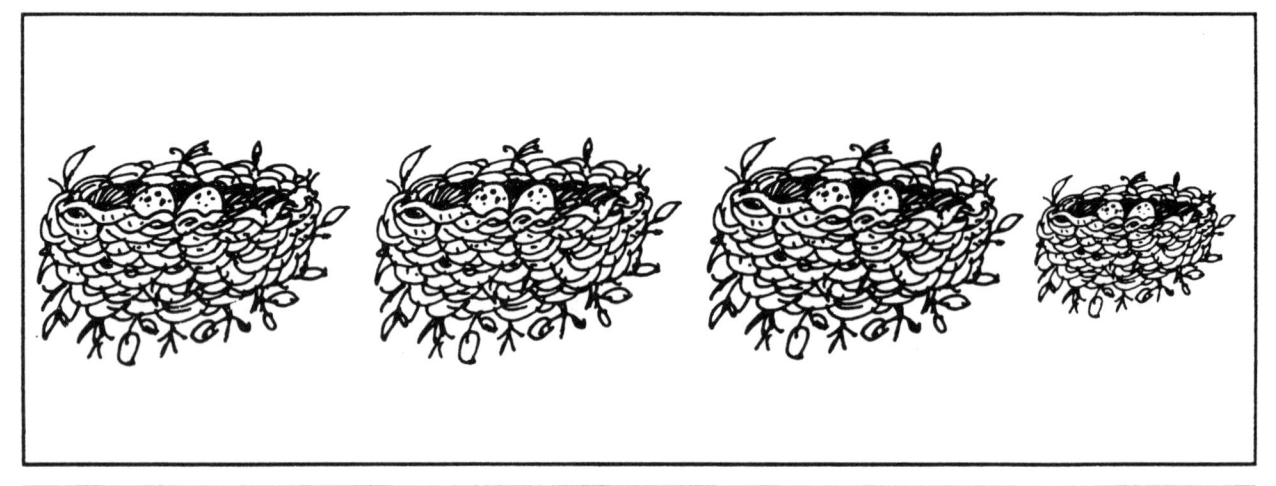

Skills: Comparing size

170

MEASURING

Look at the pictures in each row.
Which one is large?
Circle the one that is large.
Then color the pictures.

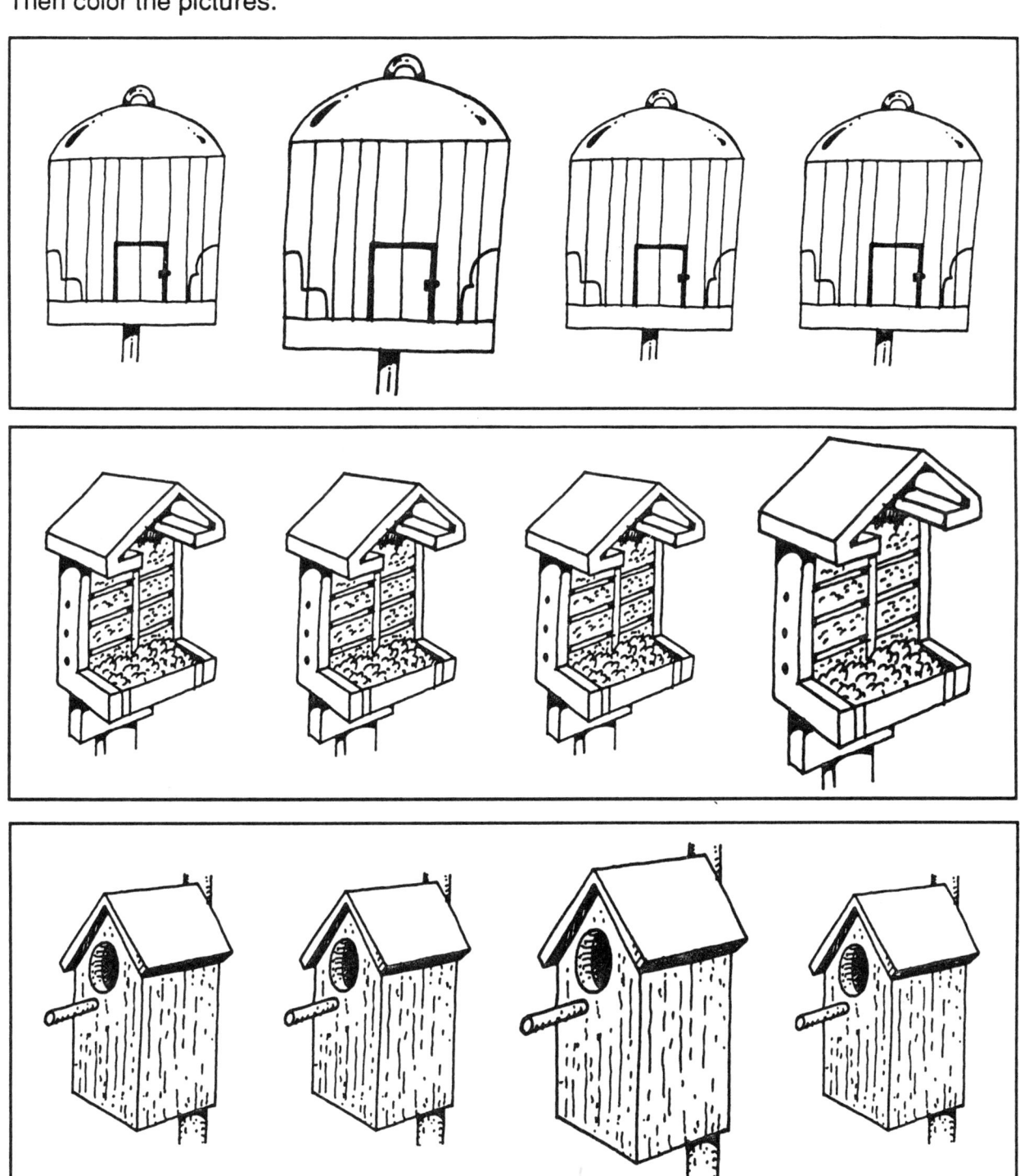

Skills: Comparing size

MEASURING

Look at the pictures in each box.
Color the small pictures purple.
Color the large pictures orange.

Skills: Comparing size

MEASURING

Look at the pictures in each box.
Color the small pictures red.
Color the large pictures blue.

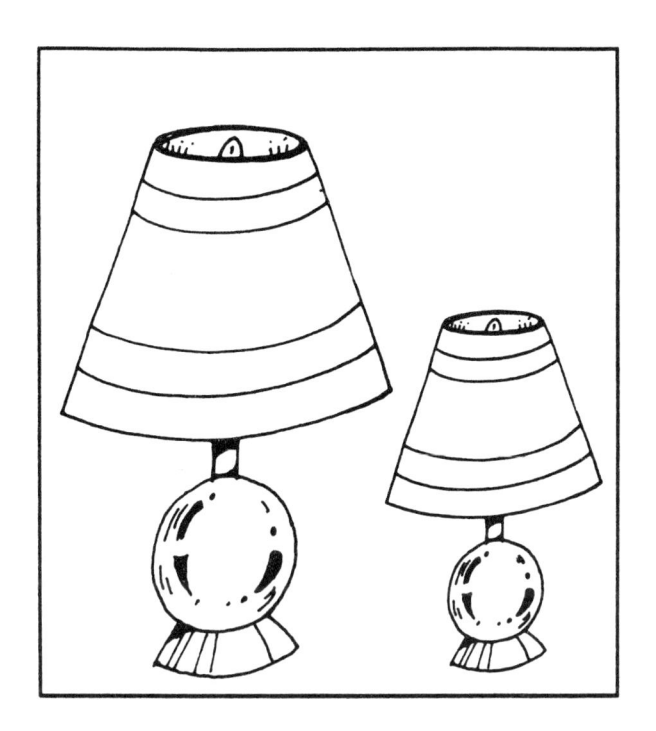

Skills: Comparing size

MEASURING

Look at the pictures in each box.
Color the small pictures orange.
Color the large pictures yellow.

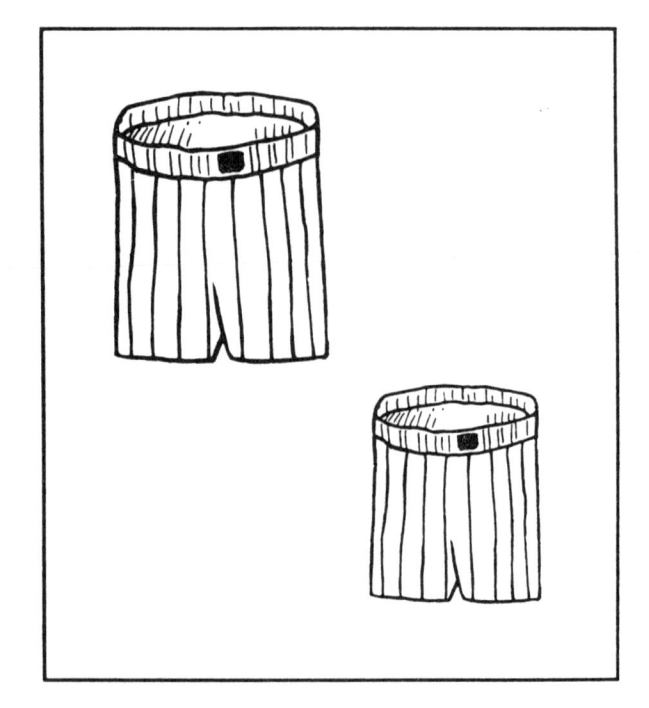

Skills: Comparing size

TIME AND MONEY

Look at the pictures in each row.
Which activity takes longer to do?
Color that picture.

Skills: Determining time duration

175

TIME AND MONEY

Look at the clock.
Trace the numbers.
Then color the picture.

Skills: Identifying and tracing the numbers on the clock

TIME AND MONEY

Look at the clock in each box.
Write the time in the space below each clock.

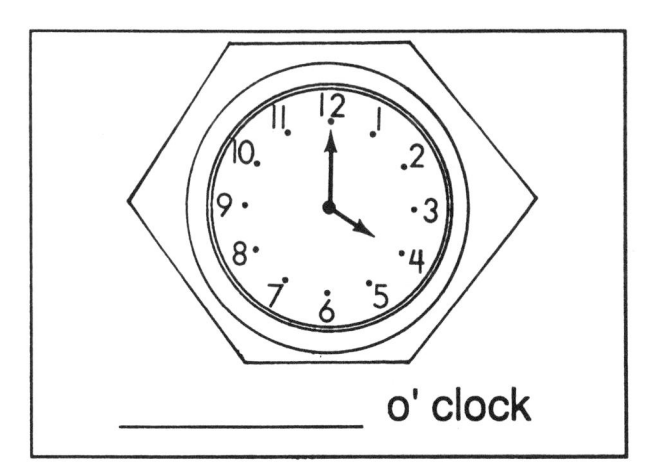

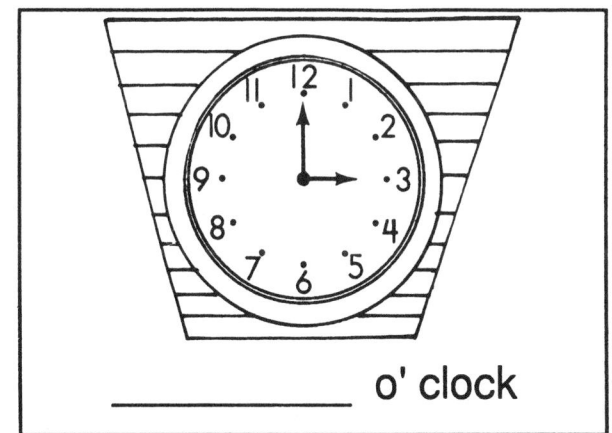

_2_ o' clock

____ o' clock

____ o' clock

____ o' clock

____ o' clock

____ o' clock

Skills: Identifying time to the hour

TIME AND MONEY

Look at the clock in each box.
Write the time in the space below each clock.

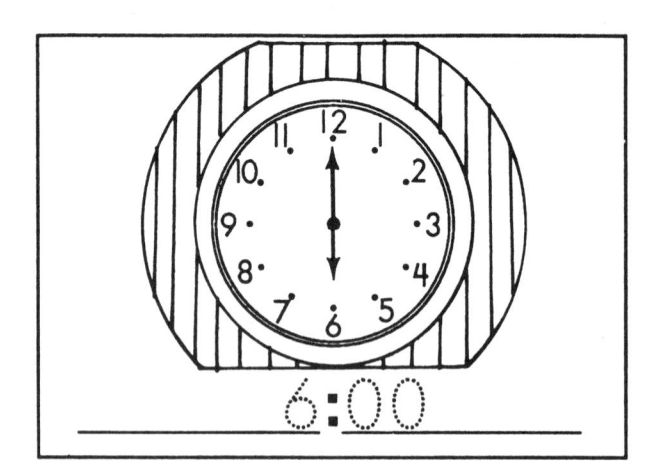

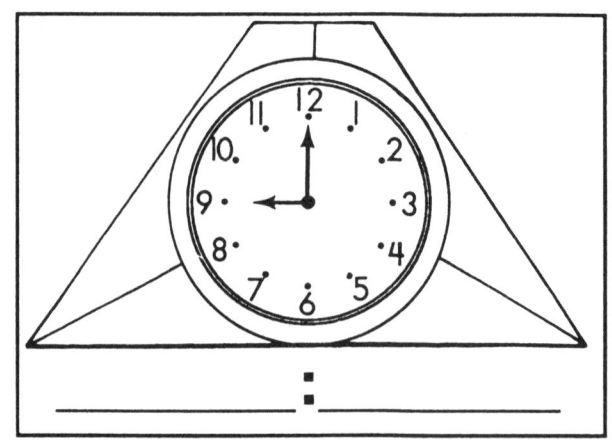

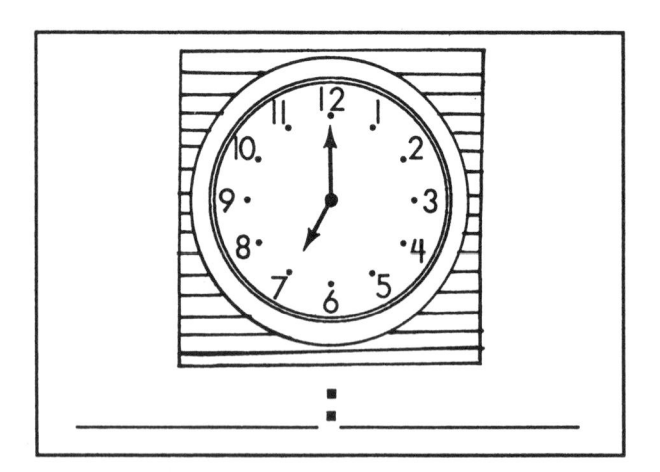

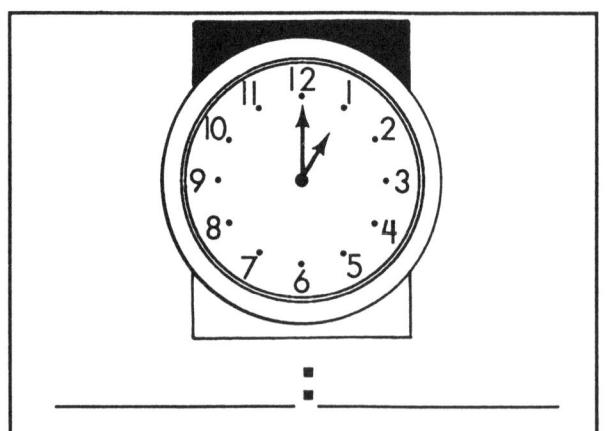

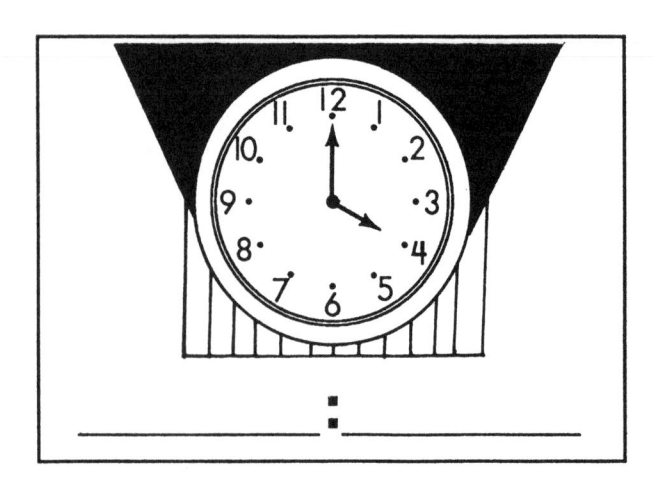

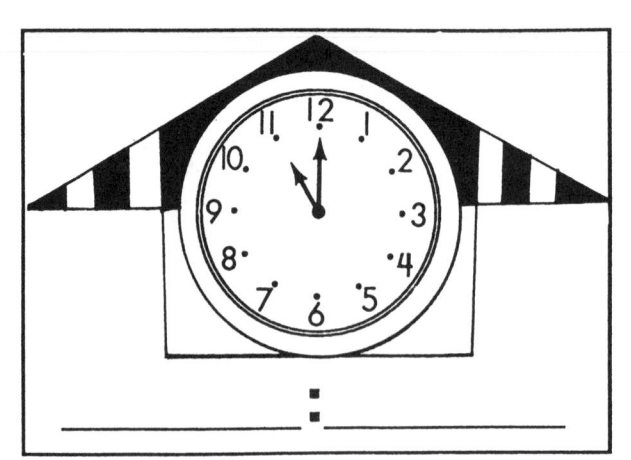

6:00

Skills: Identifying time to the hour

TIME AND MONEY

60 minutes is one hour.

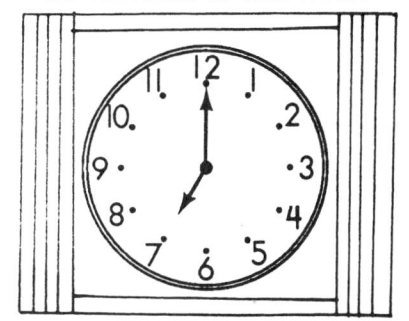

30 minutes is one half hour.

7:00   **7:30**

Look at the clock in each box.
Write the time in the space below each clock.

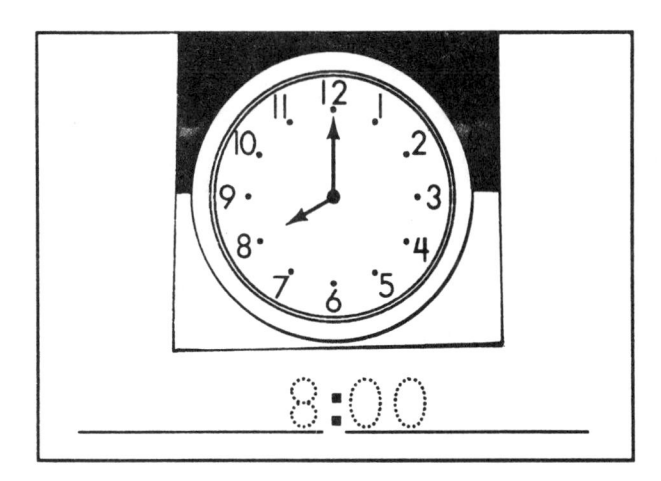

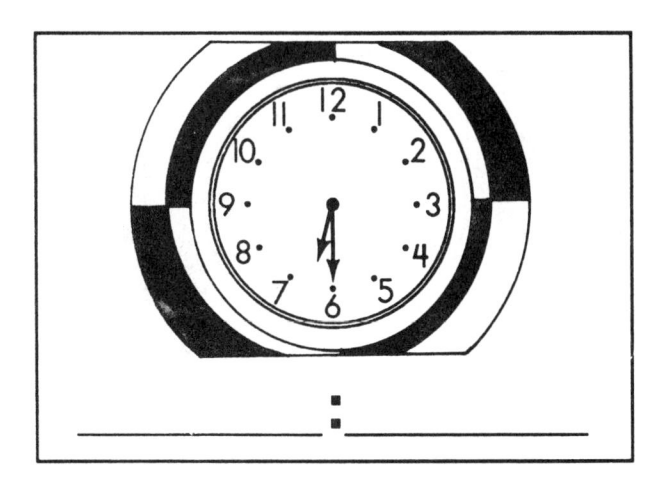

8:00

___:___

___:___   ___:___

Skills: Identifying time to the hour and half hour

TIME AND MONEY

Look at the clock in each box.
Write the time in the space below each clock.

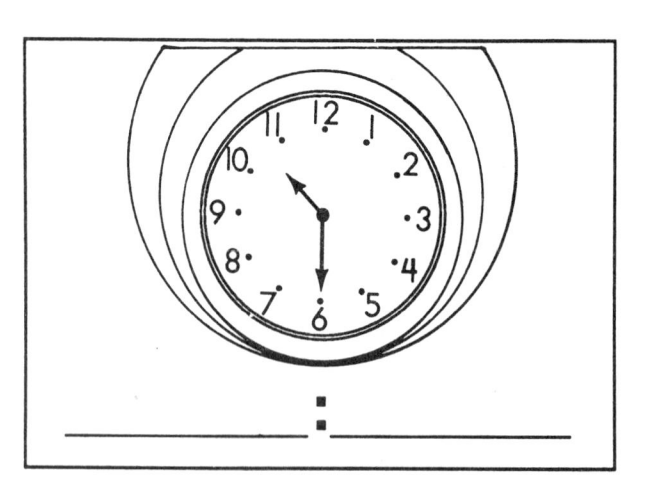

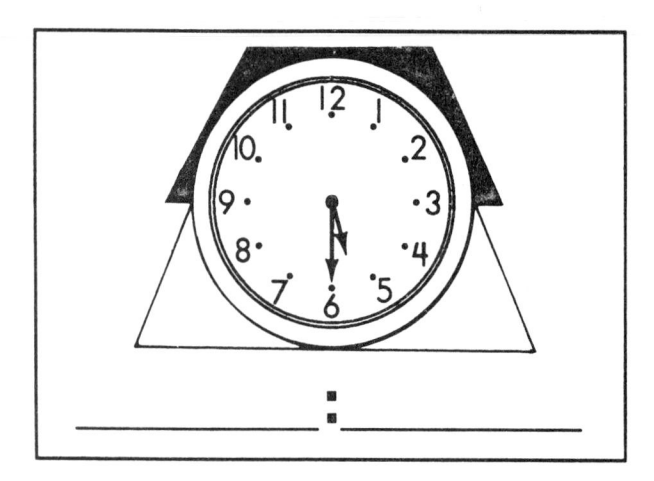

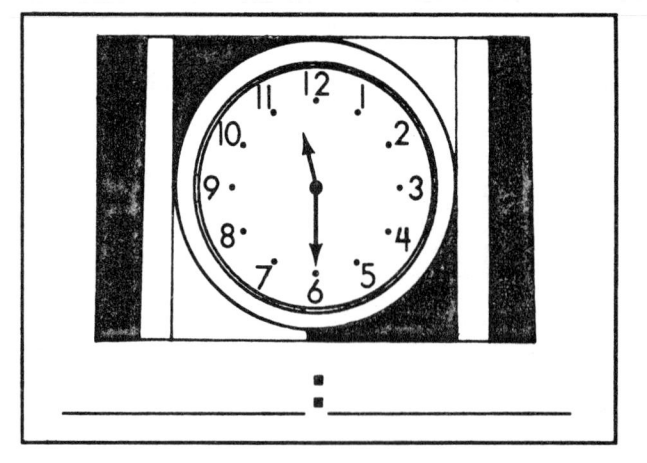

3:30

Skills: Identifying time to the hour and half hour

TIME AND MONEY

Look at the clocks on each side of the page.
Match the clocks that show the same time.
Then color the pictures.

11:00

7:00

1:00

3:00

Skills: Using number skills to determine the same time

TIME AND MONEY

Look at the clocks on each side of the page.
Match the clocks that show the same time.
Then color the pictures.

Skills: Using number skills to determine the same time

TIME AND MONEY

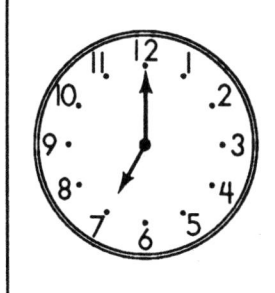

Look at the first clock in each row.
Find and circle a clock that shows the same time.
Then color the pictures.

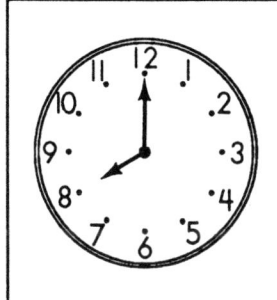

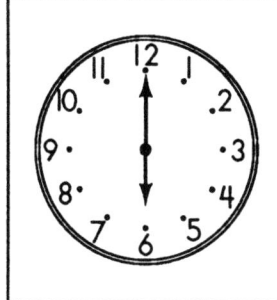

Skills: Using number skills to determine the same time

TIME AND MONEY

Look at the first clock in each row.
Find and circle a clock that shows the same time.
Then color the pictures.

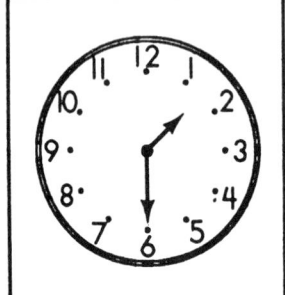

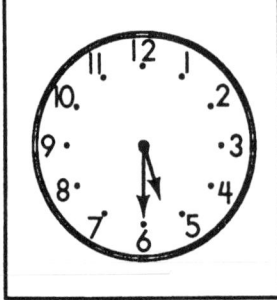

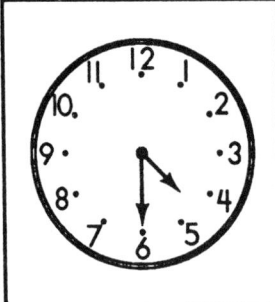

Skills: Using number skills to determine the same time

TIME AND MONEY

Look at the minute hand on each clock.
Draw the hour hand to show the correct time.
Then color the pictures.

9:00

2:00

4:00

10:00

5:00

1:00

Skills: Showing time to the hour on the clock

TIME AND MONEY

Look at the minute hand on each clock.
Draw the hour hand to show the correct time.
Then color the pictures.

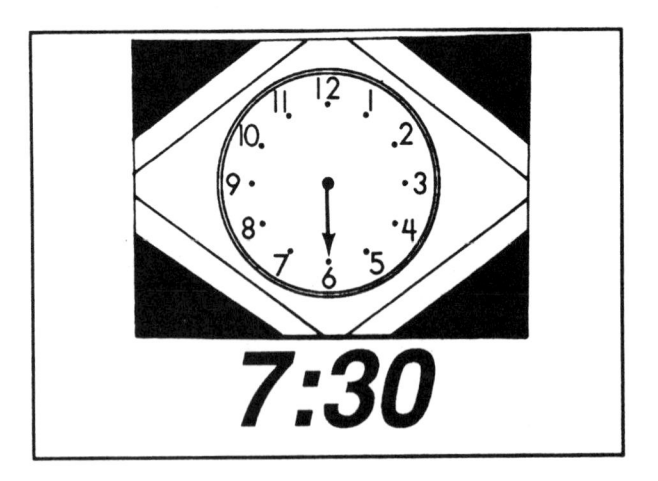

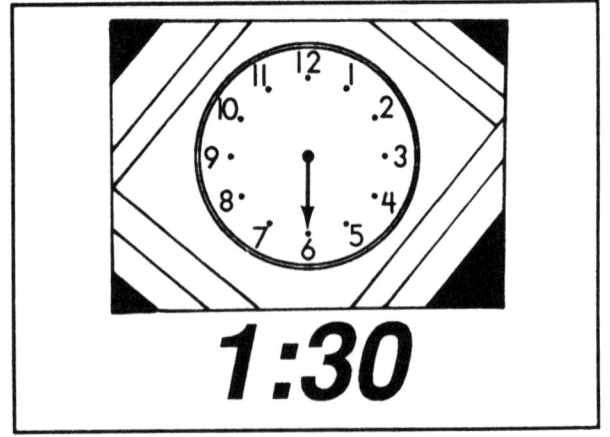

3:30

5:30

7:30

12:30

9:30

1:30

Skills: Showing time to the half hour on the clock

TIME AND MONEY

Look at the coins.
Draw a circle around each penny.
Draw a square around each nickel.
Draw a line under each dime.

Skills: Identifying pennies, nickels and dimes

TIME AND MONEY

Look at the coins in each box.
Circle how many cents.

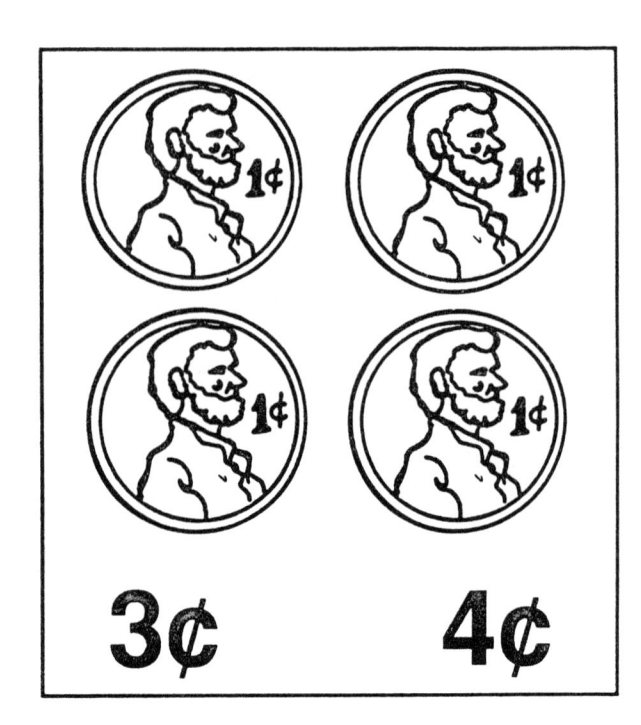

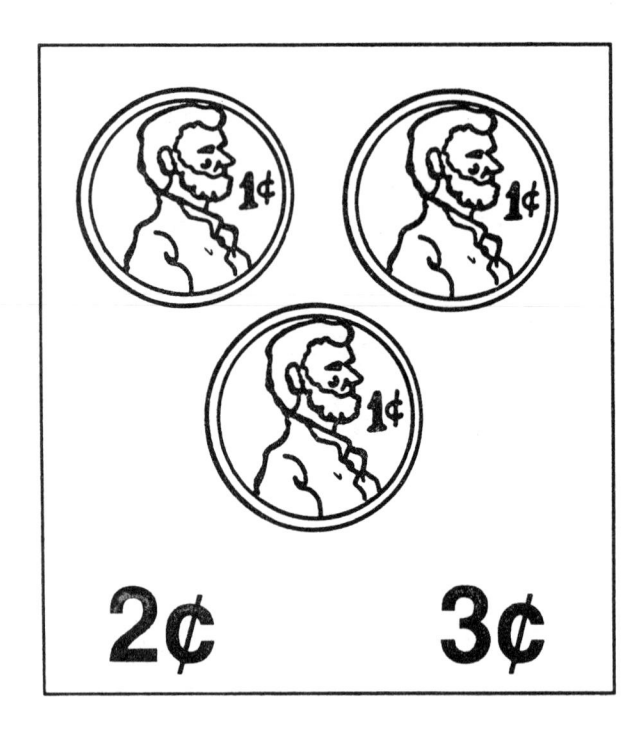

(2 pennies) **1¢** **2¢**	(4 pennies) **3¢** **4¢**
(3 pennies) **2¢** **3¢**	(1 penny) **1¢** **2¢**

Skills: Identifying amounts of money

TIME AND MONEY

Look at the coins in each box.
Circle how many cents.

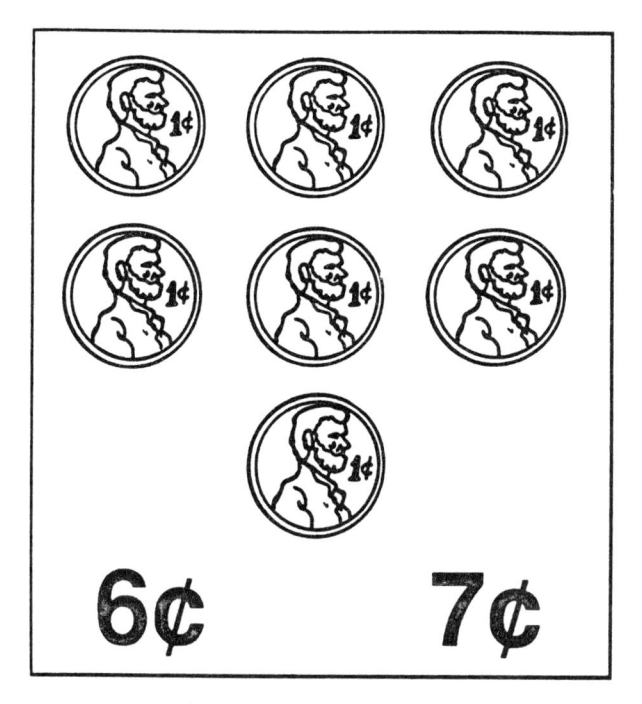

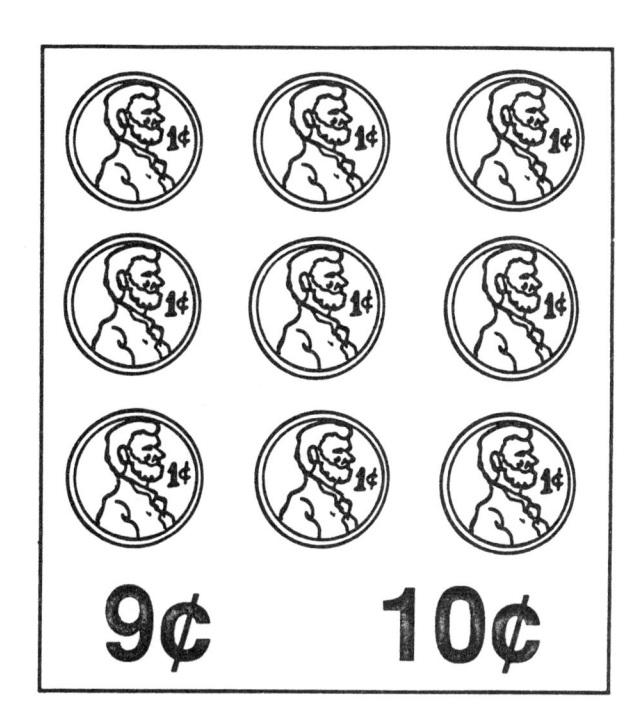

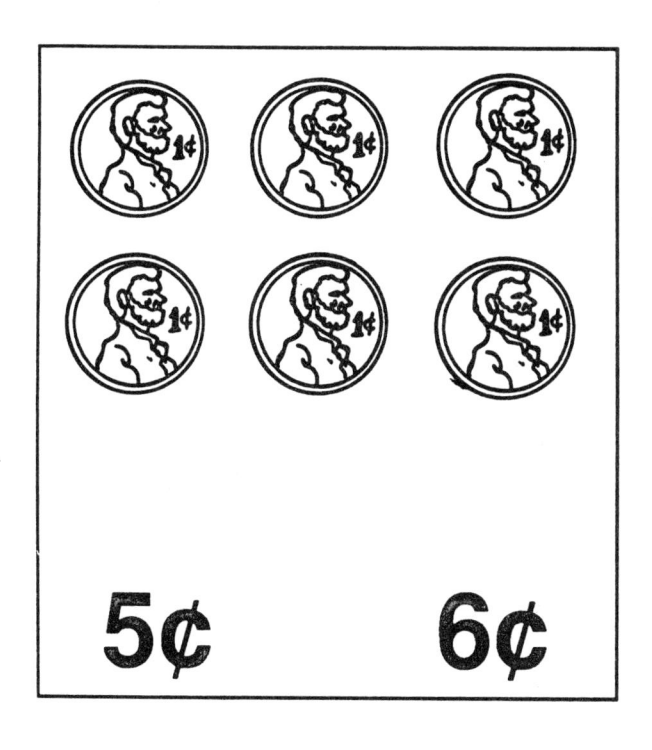

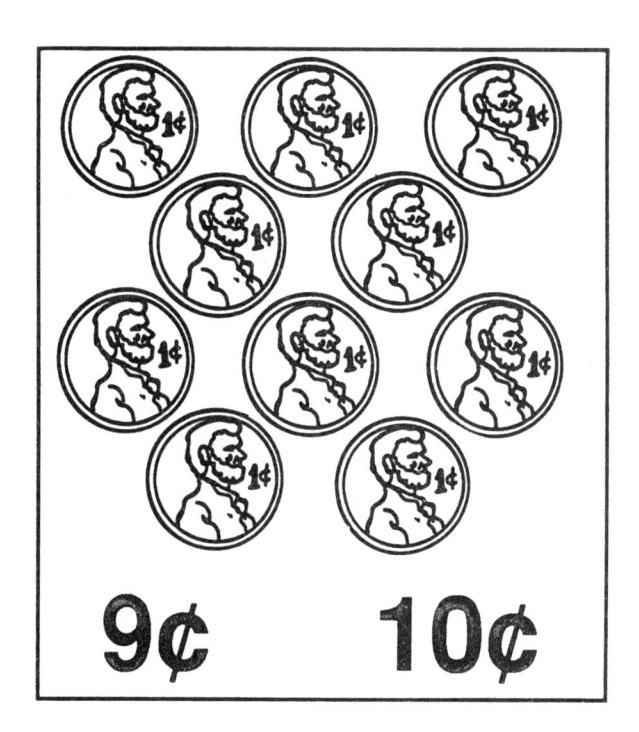

6¢ 7¢

9¢ 10¢

5¢ 6¢

9¢ 10¢

Skills: Identifying amounts of money

TIME AND MONEY

5 pennies are the same as 1 nickel.
Look at the amounts of money on this page.
Circle the amounts that show 5¢

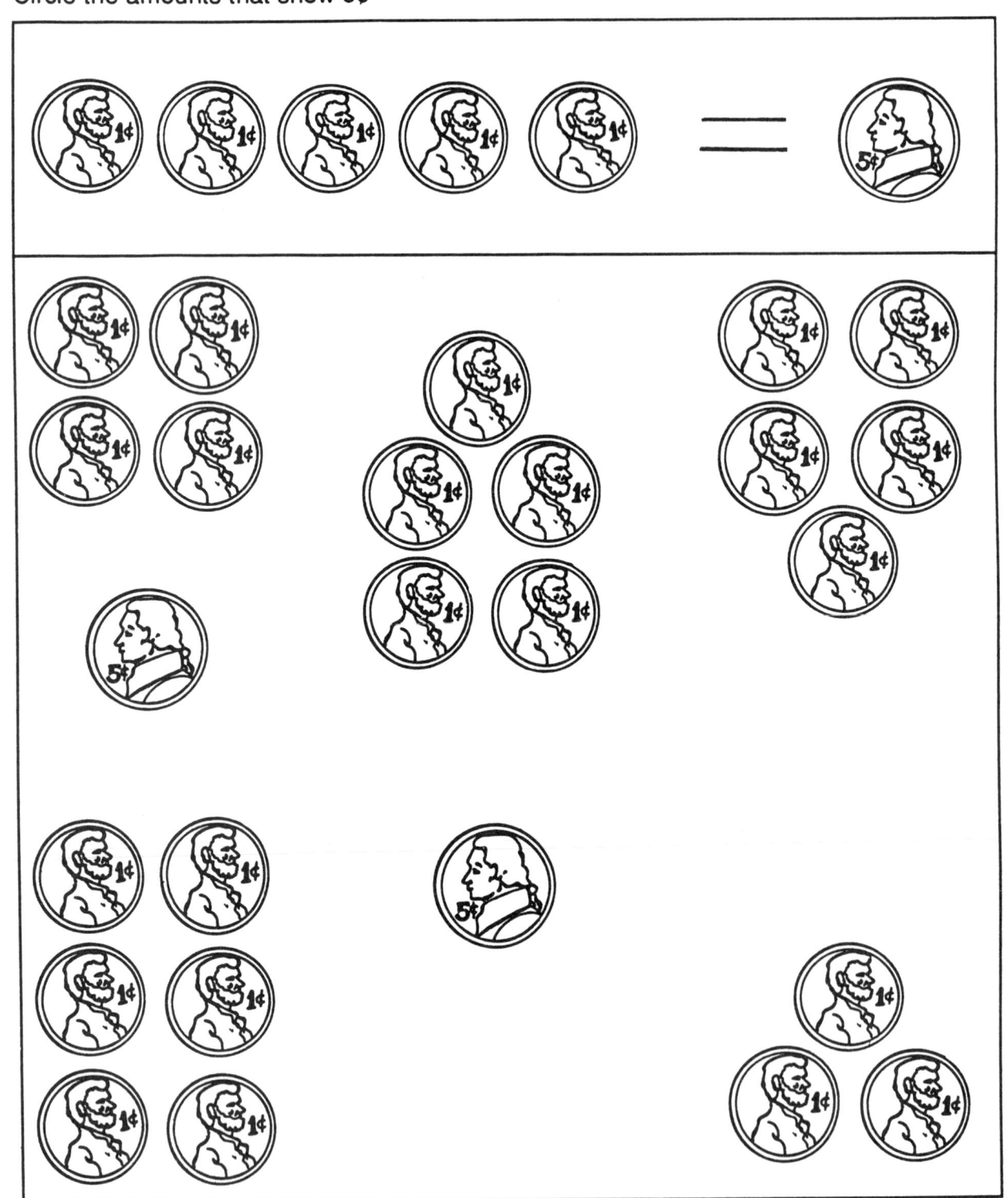

Skills: Identifying amounts of money

TIME AND MONEY

Look at the money on each side of the page.
Match the groups of coins that show the amount of money.
Then color the pictures.

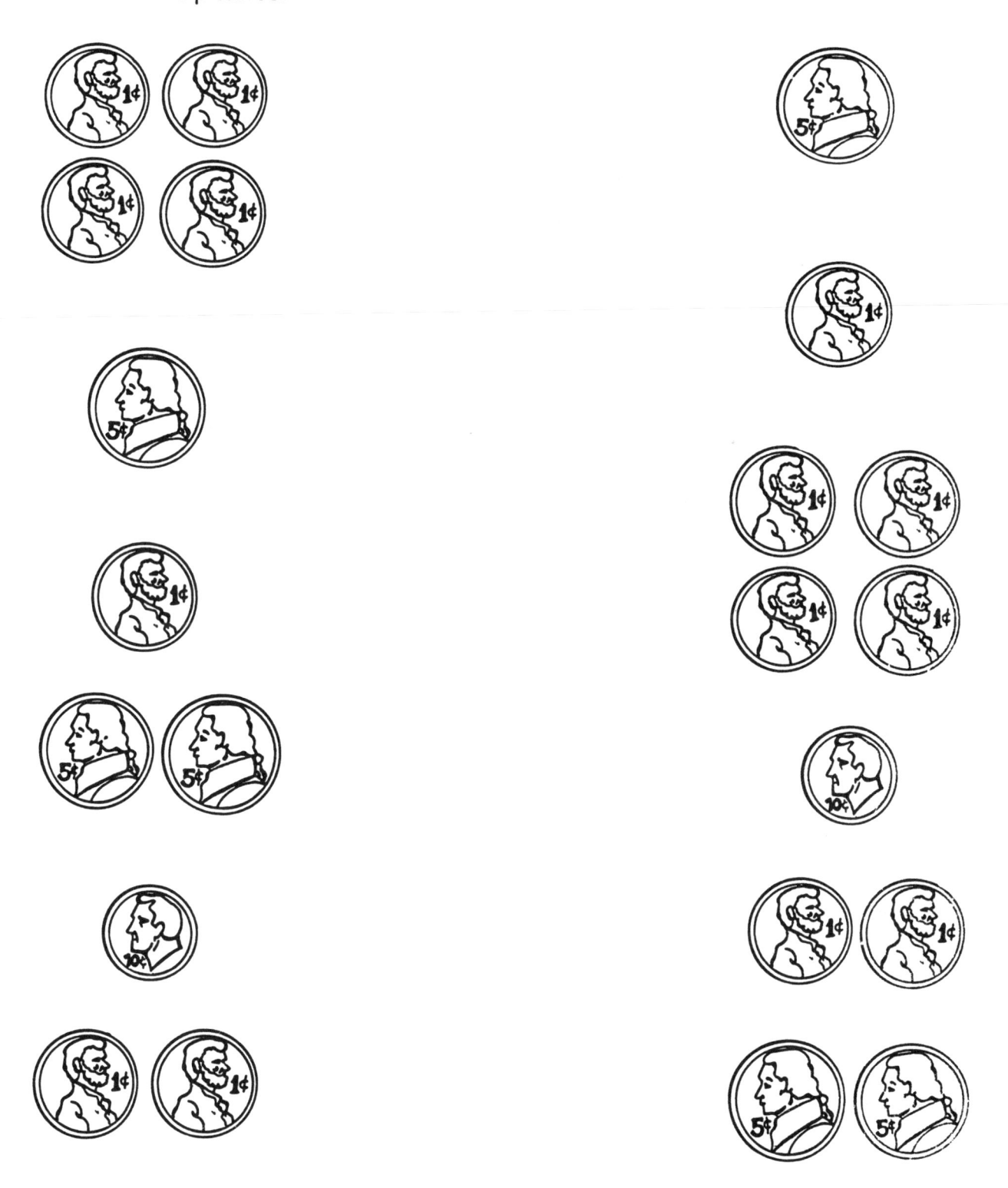

Skills: Identifying amounts of money; Matching same amounts of money

TIME AND MONEY

10 pennies are the same as 1 dime.
2 nickels are the same as 1 dime.

Look at the amounts of money on this page.
Circle the amounts that show 10¢.

Skills: Identifying amounts of money

TIME AND MONEY

Look at the coins in each purse.
Write the amount of money that is in each purse.

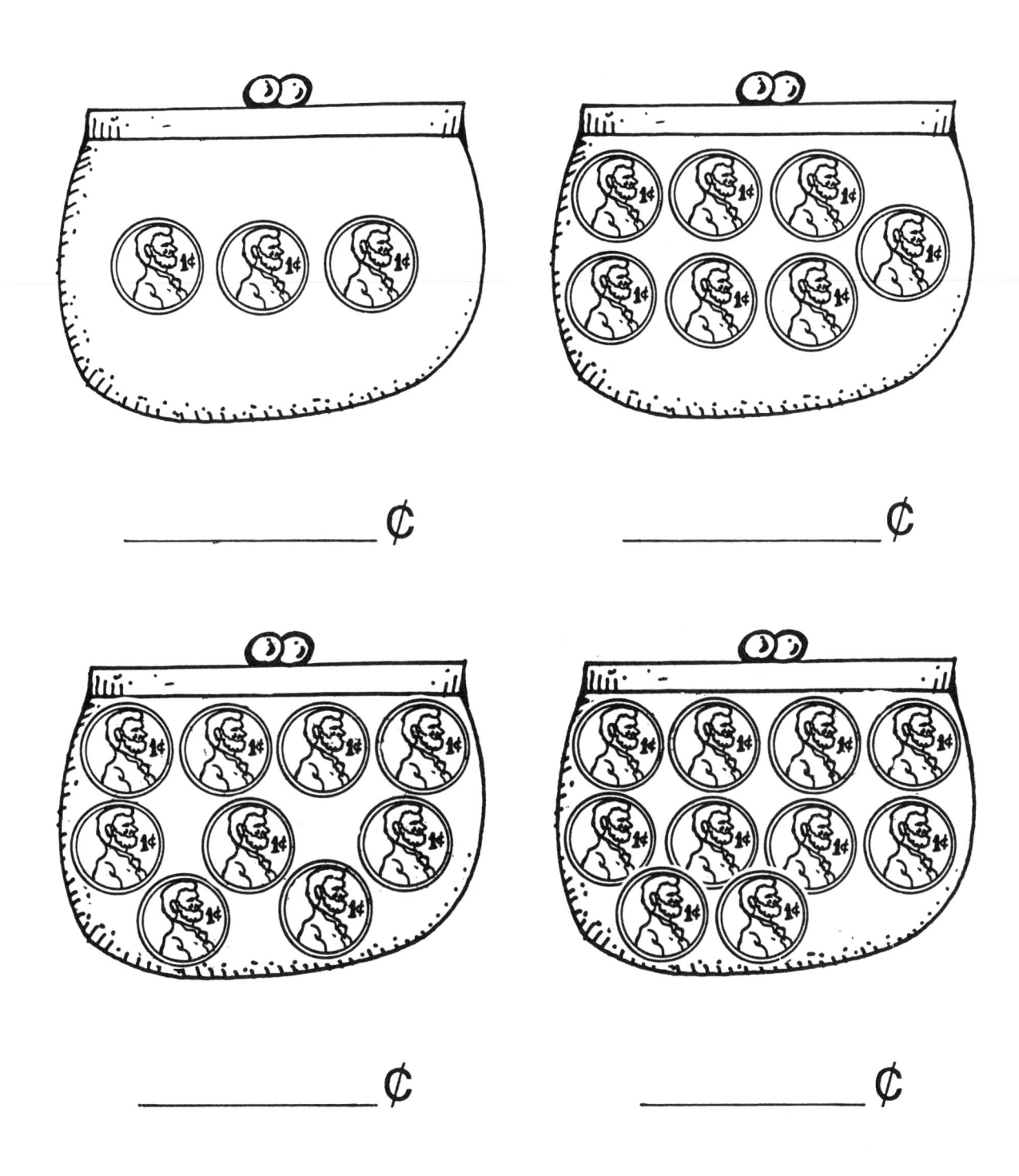

_____ ¢   _____ ¢

_____ ¢   _____ ¢

Skills: Identifying amounts of money

193

TIME AND MONEY

Look at the coins in each piggy bank.
Write the amount of money that is in each piggy bank.

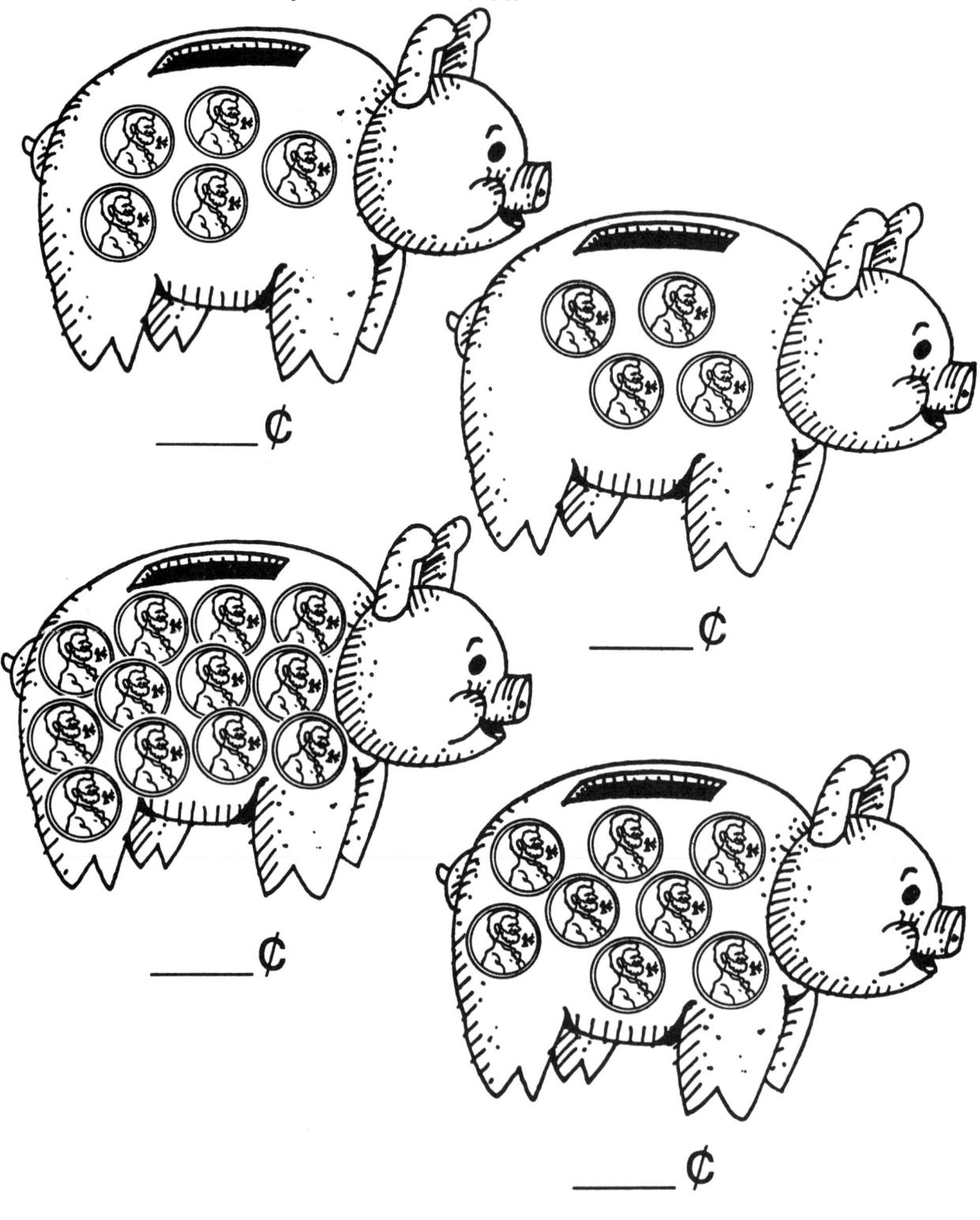

_____ ¢

_____ ¢

_____ ¢

_____ ¢

Skills: Identifying amounts of money

TIME AND MONEY

Look at the objects in each box.
Circle the amount of money that each object costs.

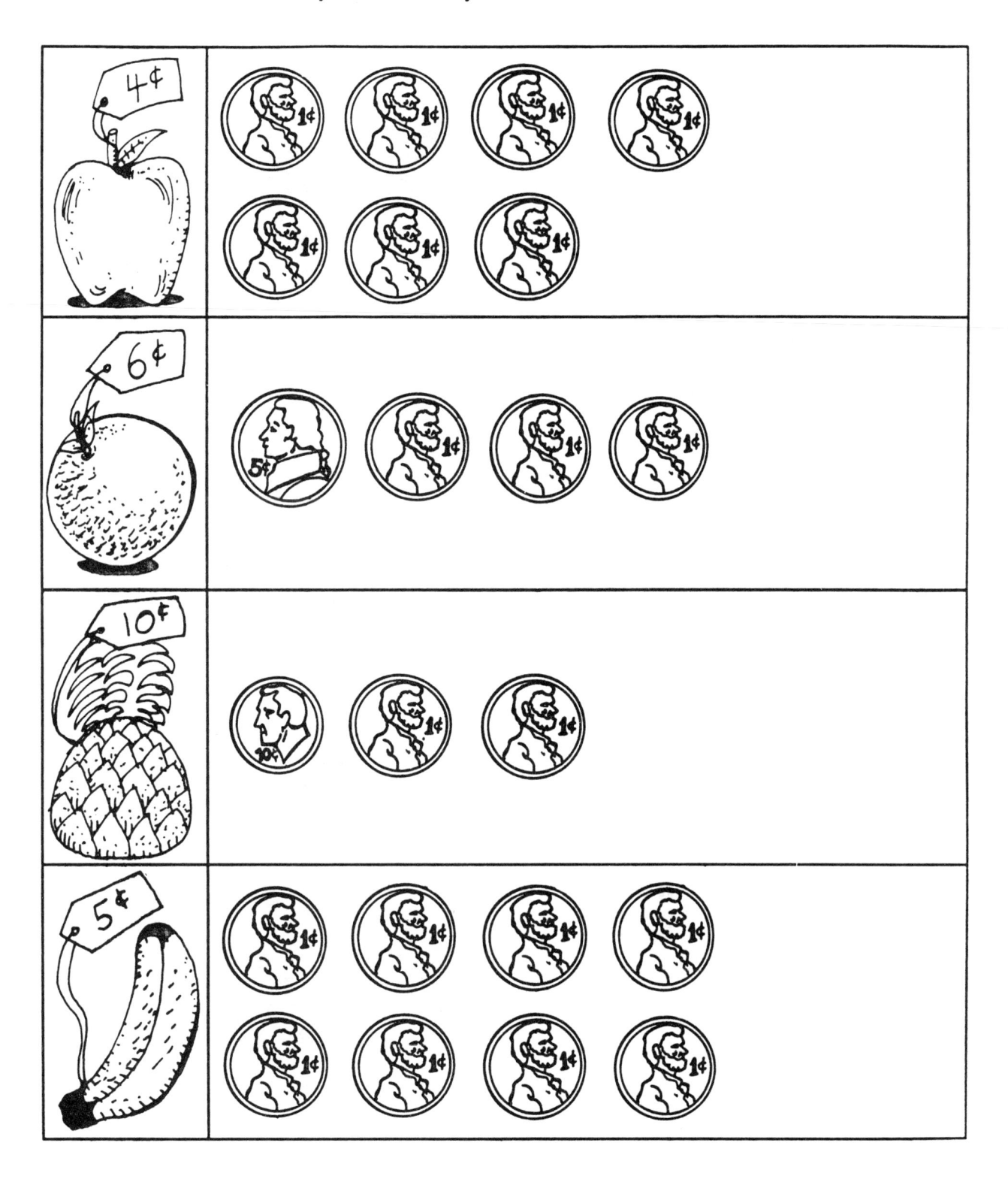

Skills: Understanding the use of money

READING READINESS

Look at each picture.
Draw a line to match the pictures that look the same.
Then color the pictures.

Skills: Association; Visual discrimination

196

READING READINESS

Look at the pictures on this page.
Draw lines to match the pictures that look the same.
Then color the pictures.

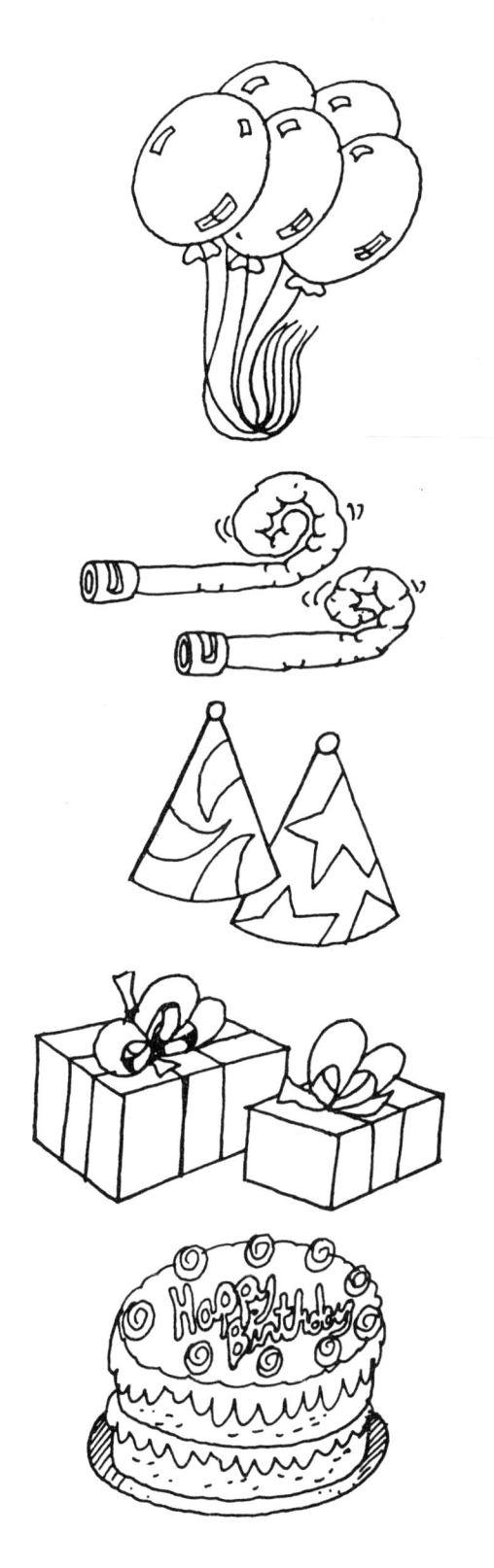

Skills: Association; Visual discrimination

197

READING READINESS

Look at the pictures on this page.
Draw lines to match the pictures that are the same.
Then color the pictures.

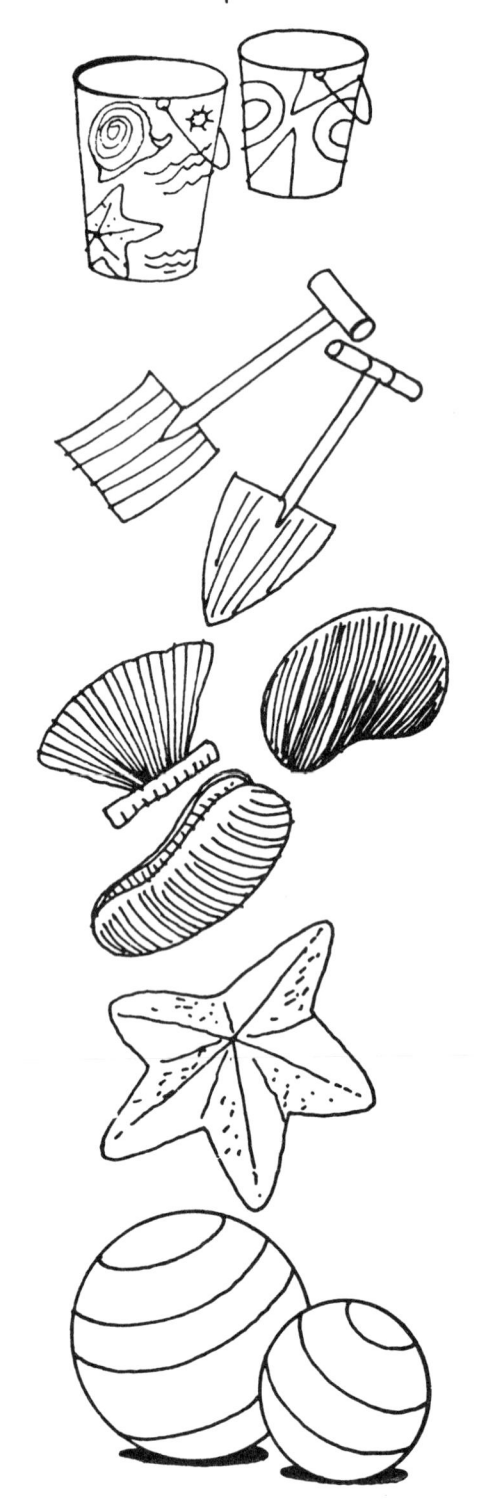

Skills: Association; Visual discrimination

198

READING READINESS

Look at the pictures in each row.
Cross out the one that is different.
Color the others.

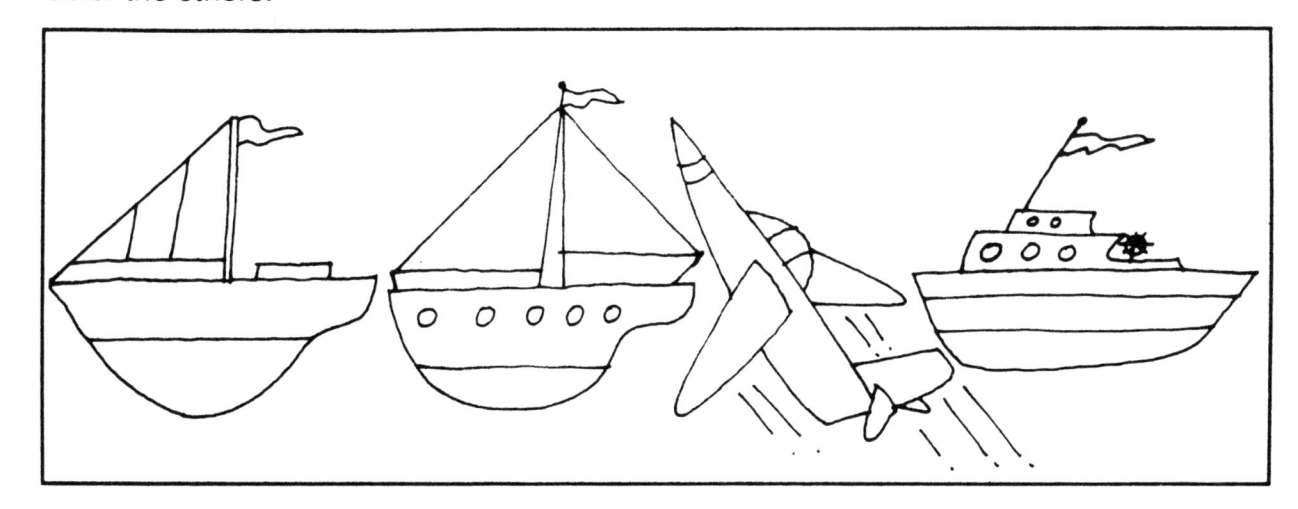

Skills: Understanding same and different

READING READINESS

Color the pictures in each row that belong together.

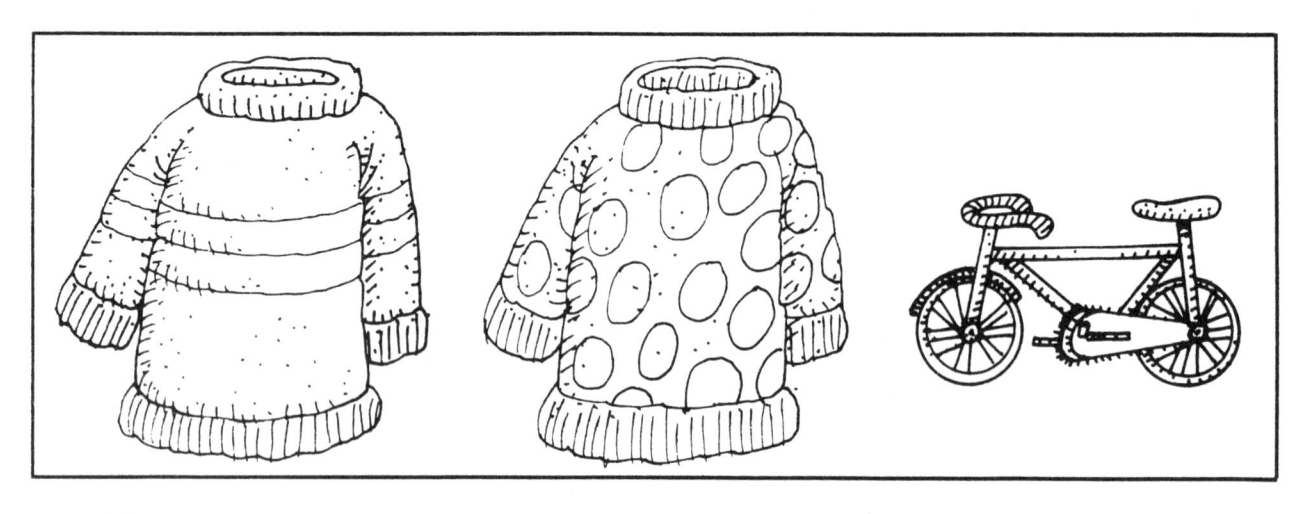

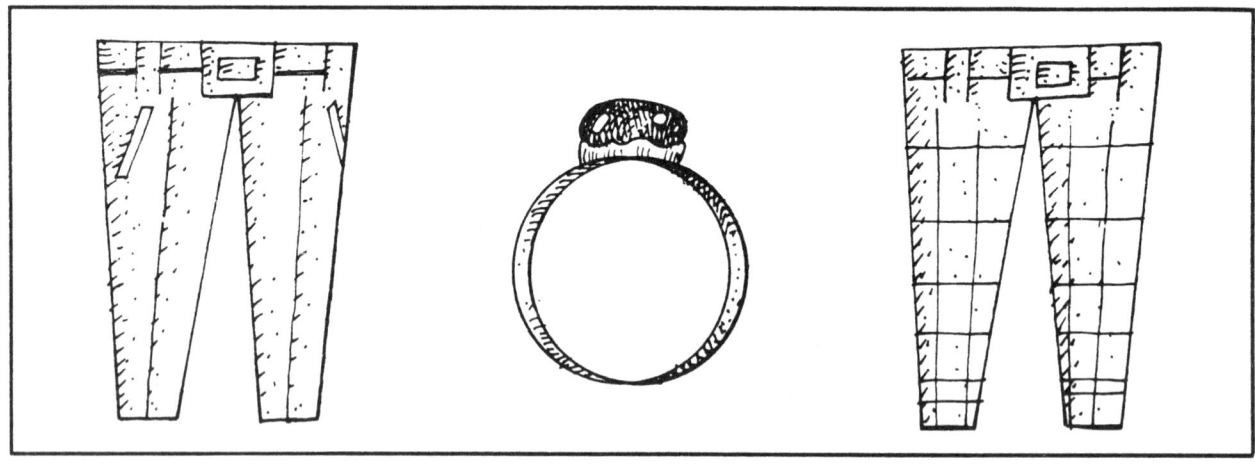

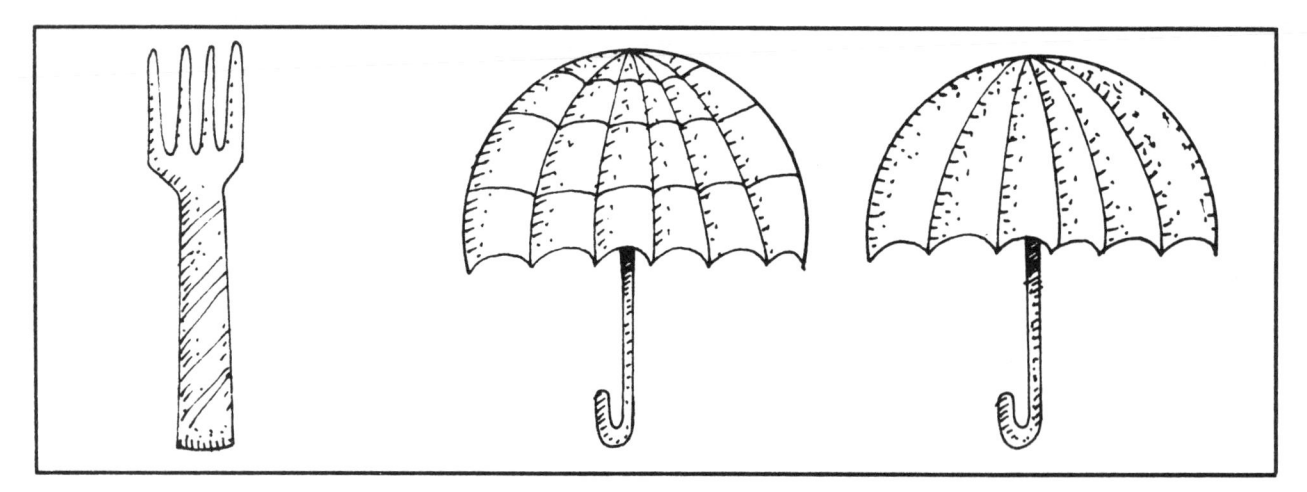

Skills: Association; Classification; Logical reasoning

READING READINESS

Color the pictures in each row that belong together.

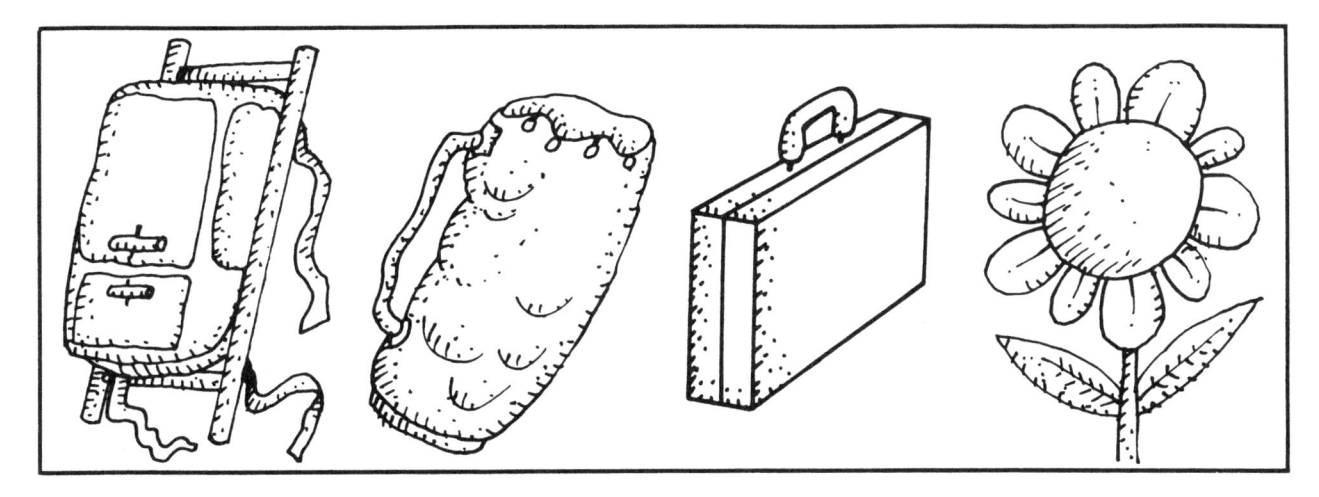

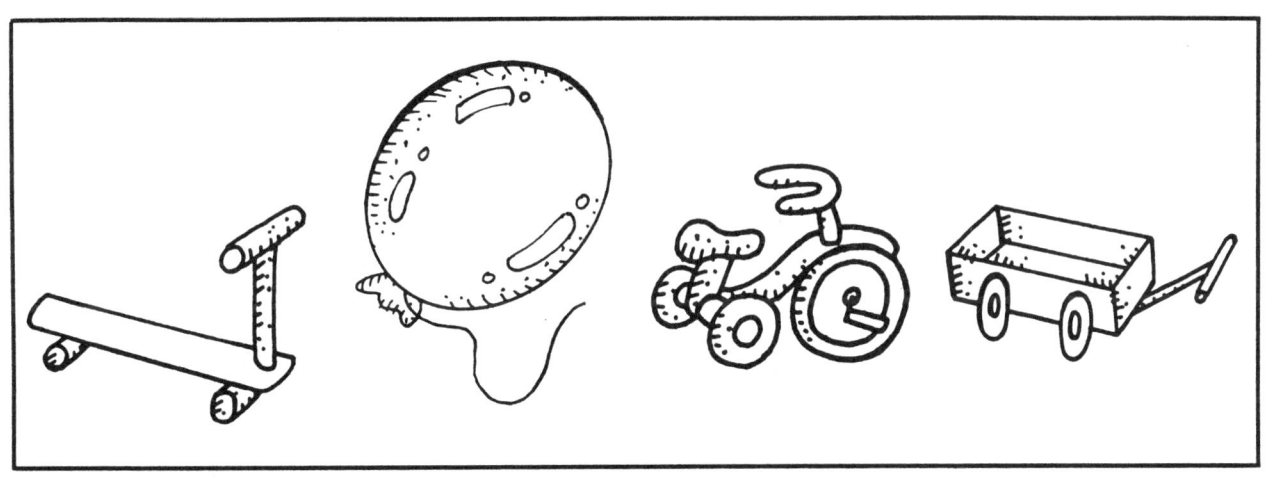

Skills: Association; Classification; Logical reasoning

READING READINESS

Look at the pictures in each box.
Draw lines to match the number of objects on top to the
number of objects on the bottom. Then color the pictures.

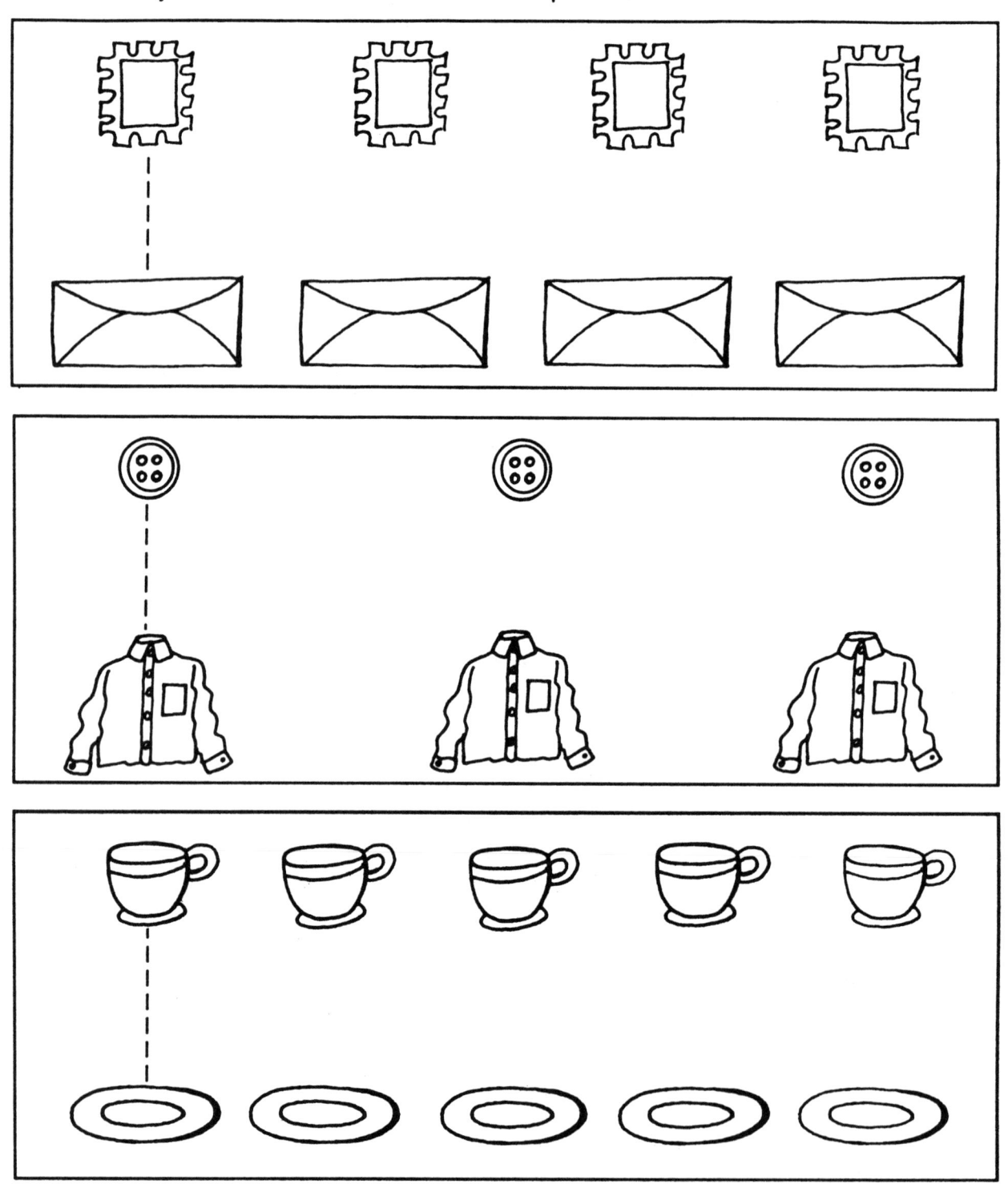

Skills: One-to-one correspondence

READING READINESS

Look at the pictures in each box.
Draw lines to match the number of objects on top
to the number of objects on the bottom. Then color the pictures.

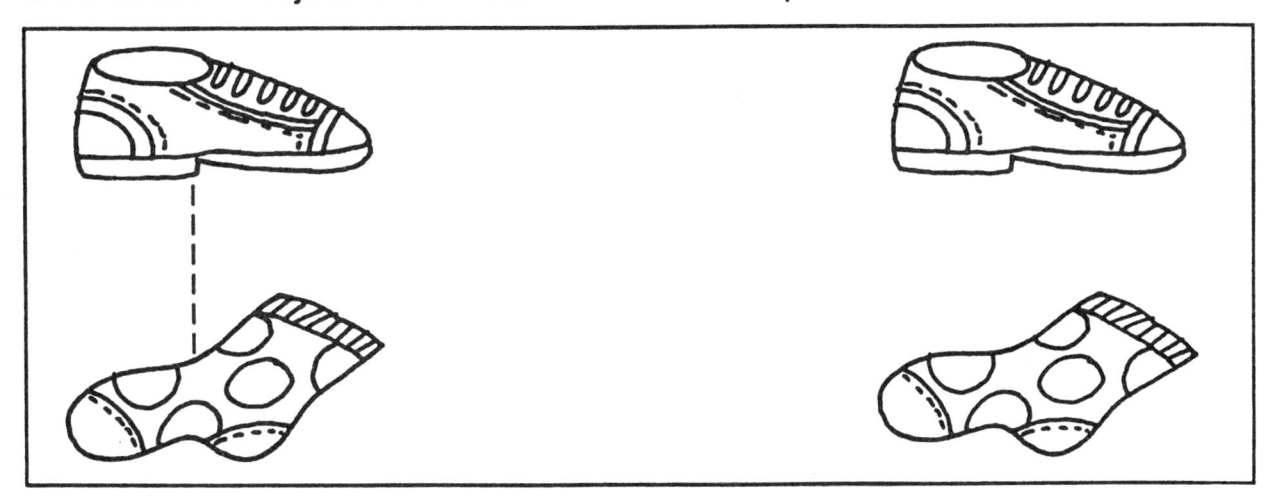

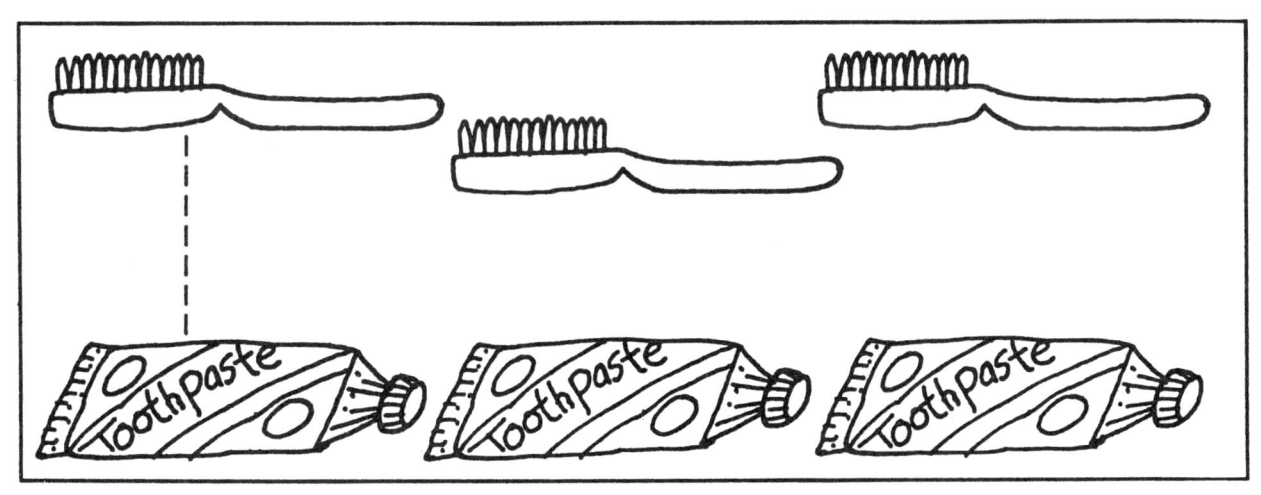

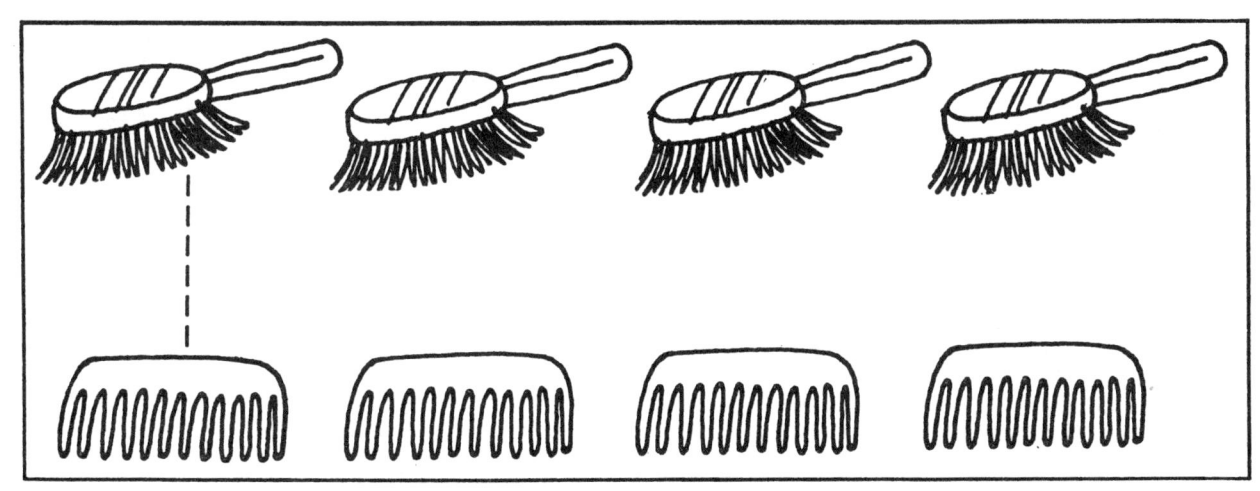

Skills: One-to-one correspondence

READING READINESS

Look at the pictures in each box.
Draw lines to match the number of objects on one
side to the number of objects on the other side. Then color the pictures.

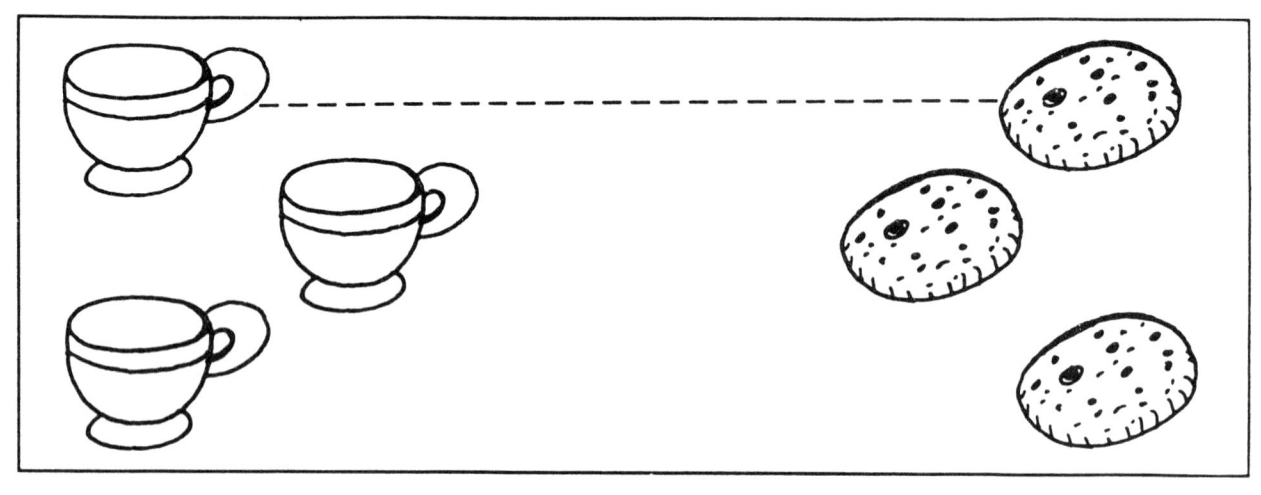

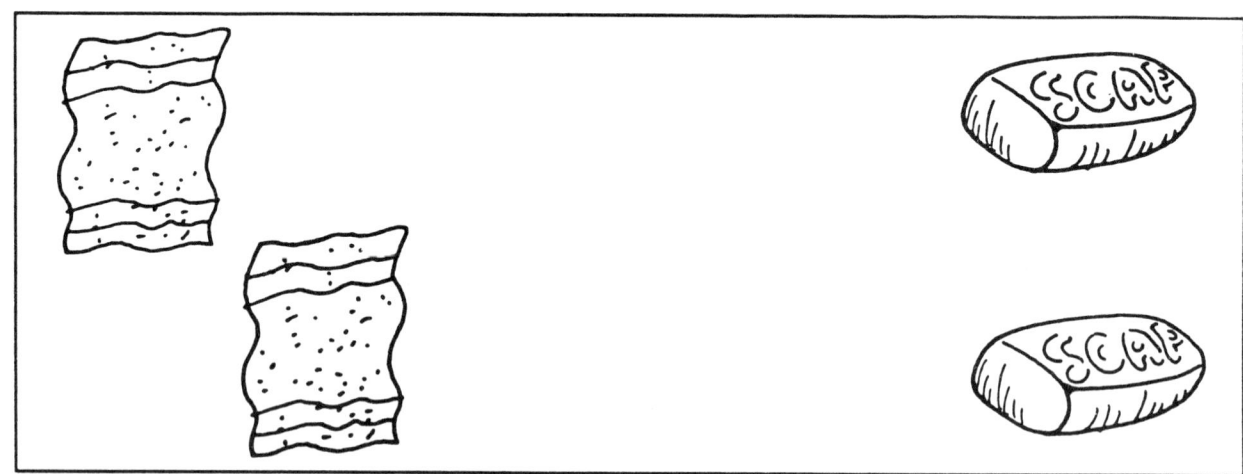

Skills: One-to-one correspondence

204

READING READINESS

Look at the pictures in each box.
Draw lines to match the number of objects on one
side to the number of objects on the other side. Then color the pictures.

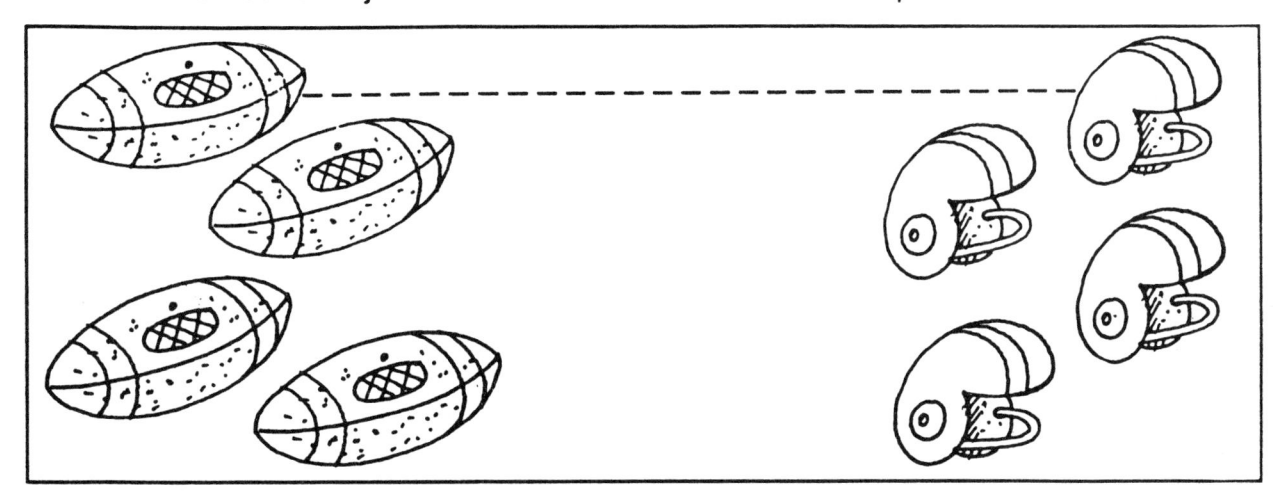

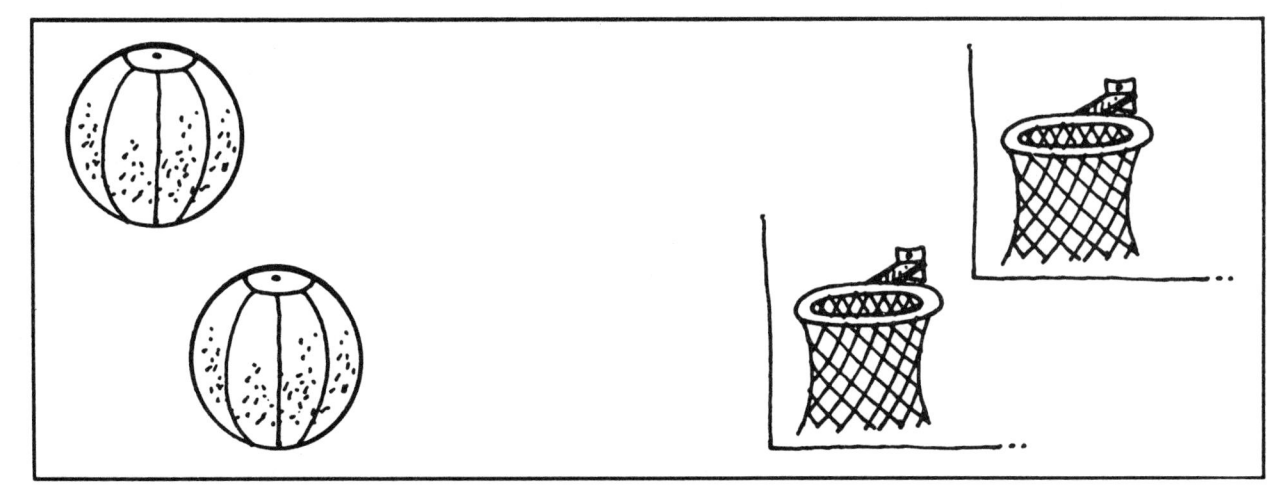

Skills: One-to-one correspondence

205

READING READINESS

Look at the pictures in each box.
Draw some food for each animal.
Then color the pictures.

Skills: One-to-one correspondence

READING READINESS

Look at the pictures in each box.
Circle the group that shows more.
Then color the pictures.

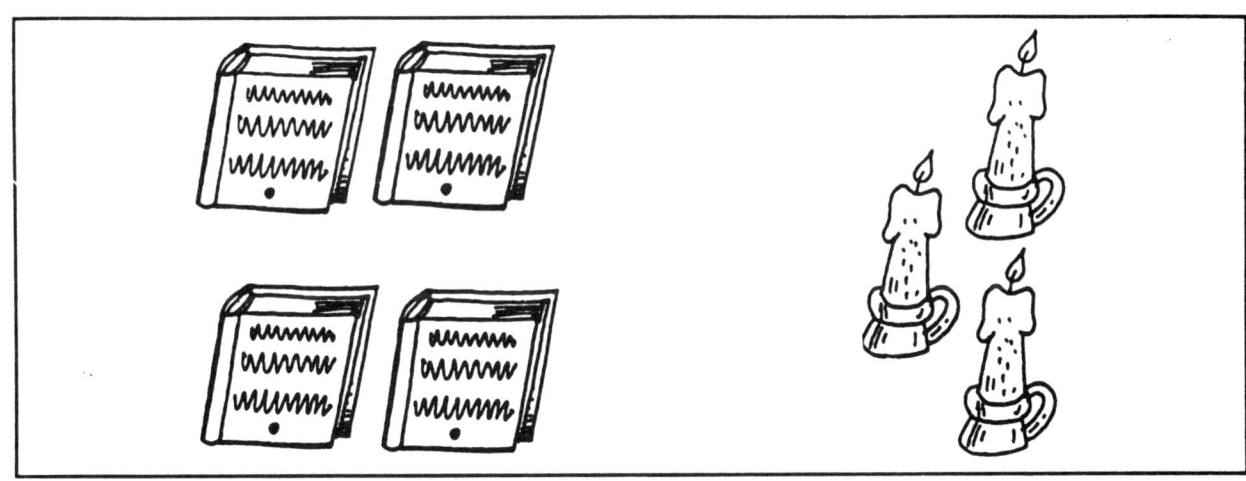

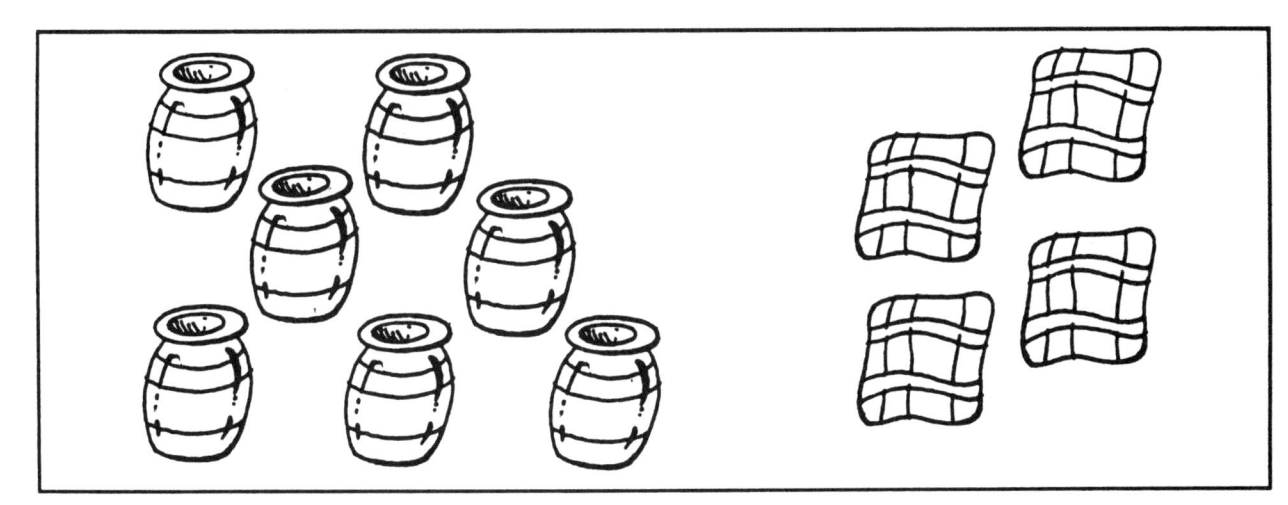

Skills: One-to-one correspondence; Understanding more and less

207

READING READINESS

Look at the pictures in each box.
Circle the group that shows more.
Then color the pictures.

Skills: One-to-one correspondence; Understanding more and less

READING READINESS

Look at the pictures in each box.
Circle the group that shows less.
Then color the pictures.

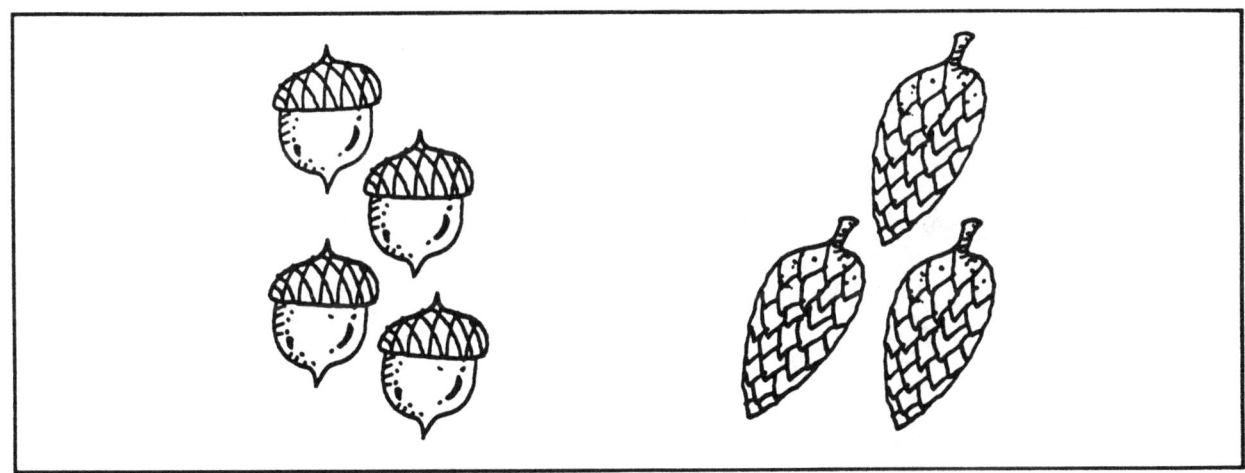

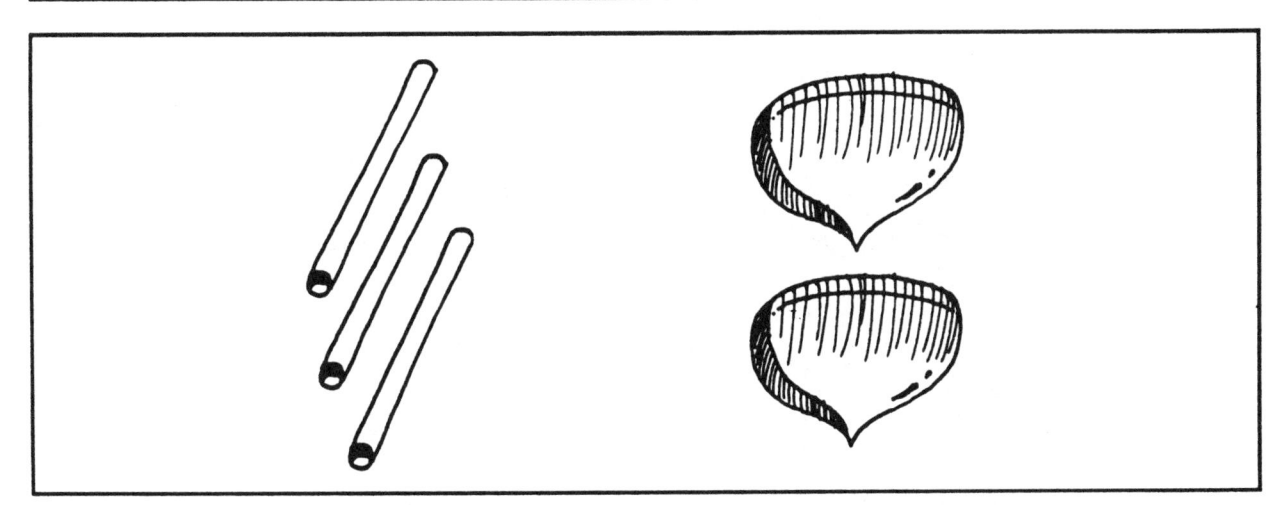

Skills: One-to-one correspondence; Understanding more and less

READING READINESS

Look at the pictures in each box.
Circle the group that shows less.
Then color the pictures.

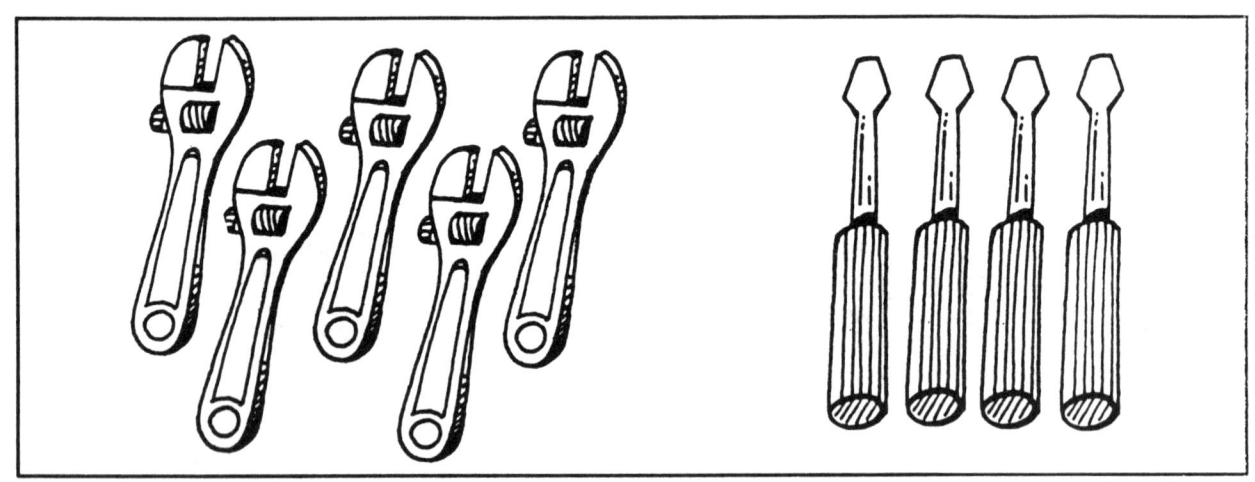

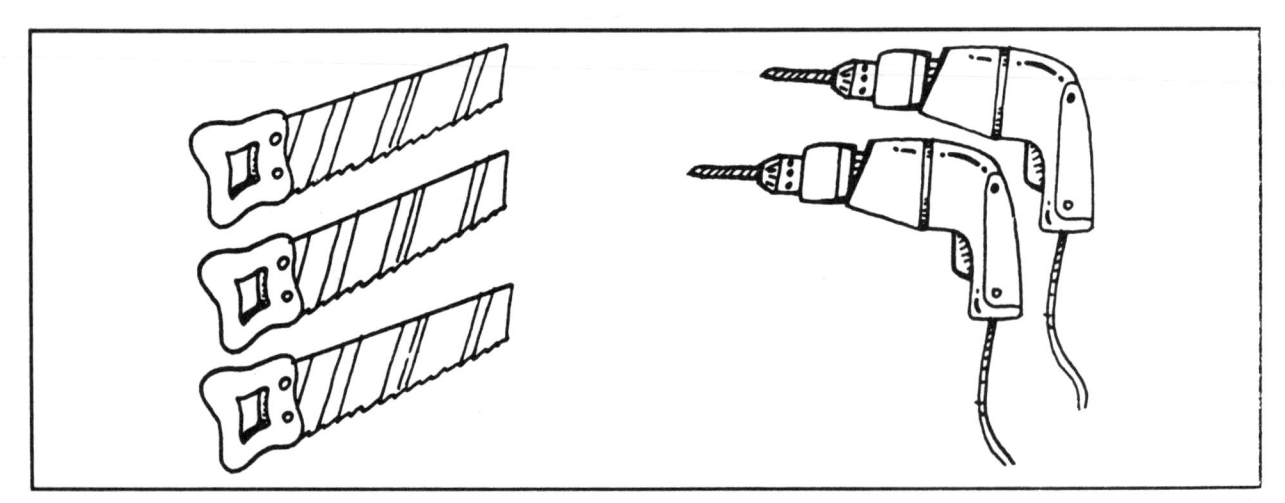

Skills: One-to-one correspondence; Understanding more and less

READING READINESS

Look at the pictures in each row.
Draw a line to the picture that continues each pattern.
Then color the pictures.

Skills: Observing and continuing patterns

211

READING READINESS

Look at the pattern in each row.
Draw the pictures that continue each pattern.
Then color the pictures.

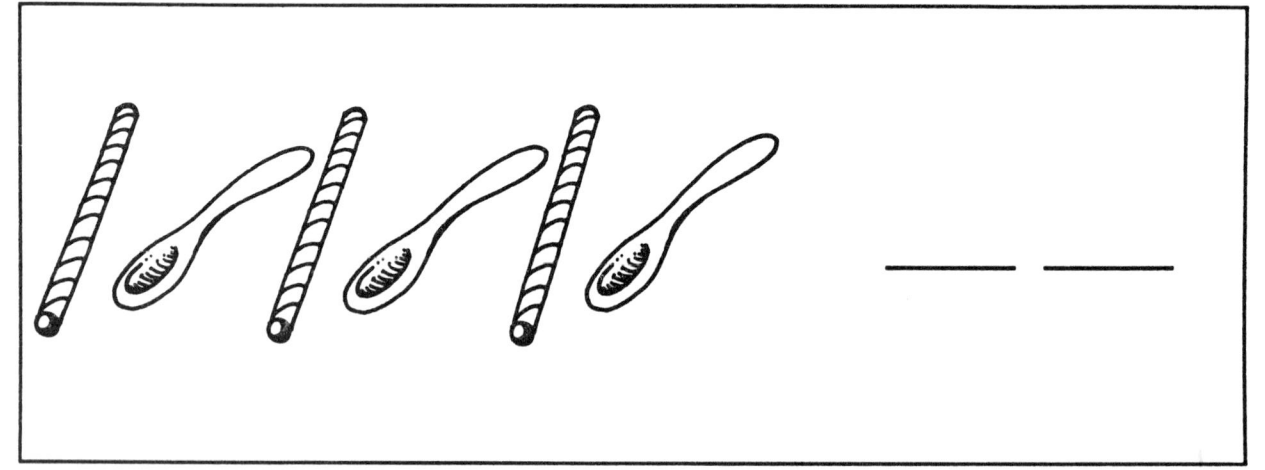

Skills: Observing and reproducing patterns

READING READINESS

Color the pictures in each box that belong together.

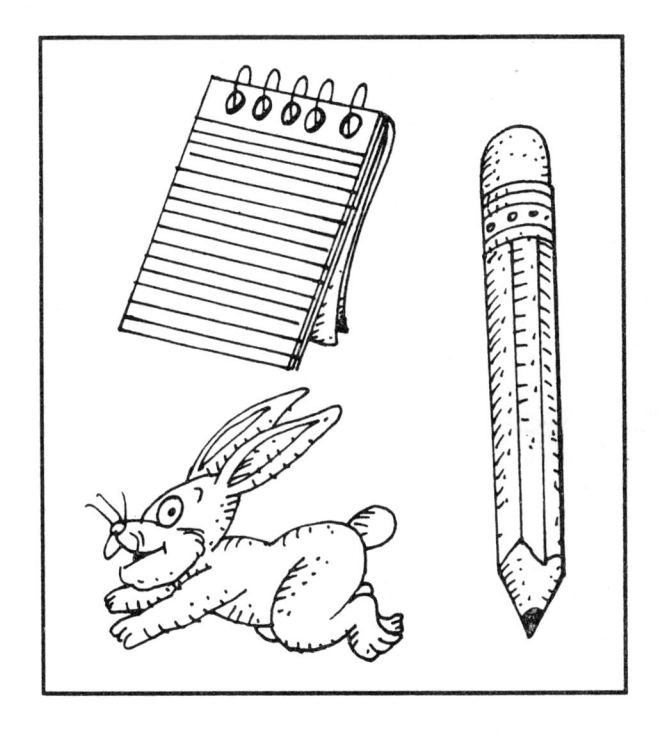

Skills: Association; Classification; Logical reasoning

READING READINESS

Look at the picture. Circle five things that do not belong.
Then color the picture.

Skills: Visual discrimination; Logical reasoning; Counting

READING READINESS

Cross out the picture in each box that does not go with the others.
Color the other pictures.

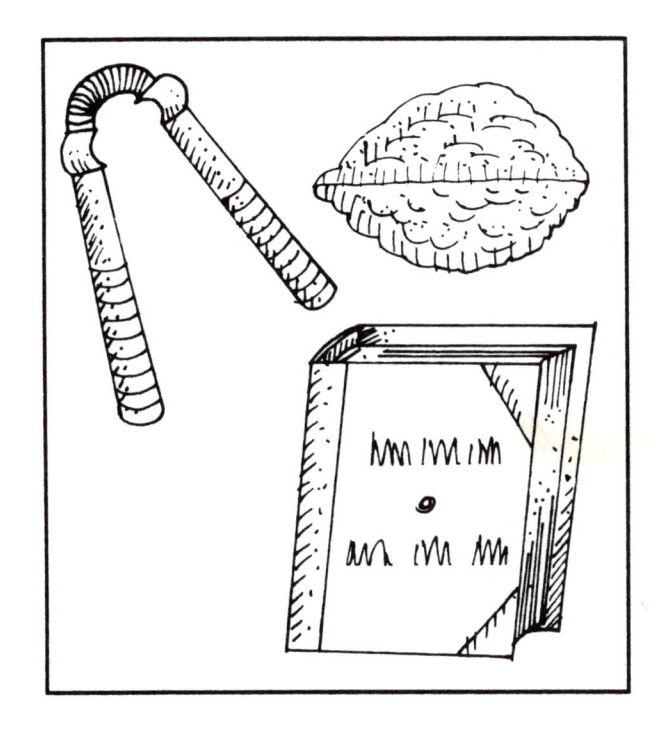

Skills: Association; Classification; Logical reasoning

READING READINESS

Look at each picture.
Something is missing.
Circle the picture that is different.

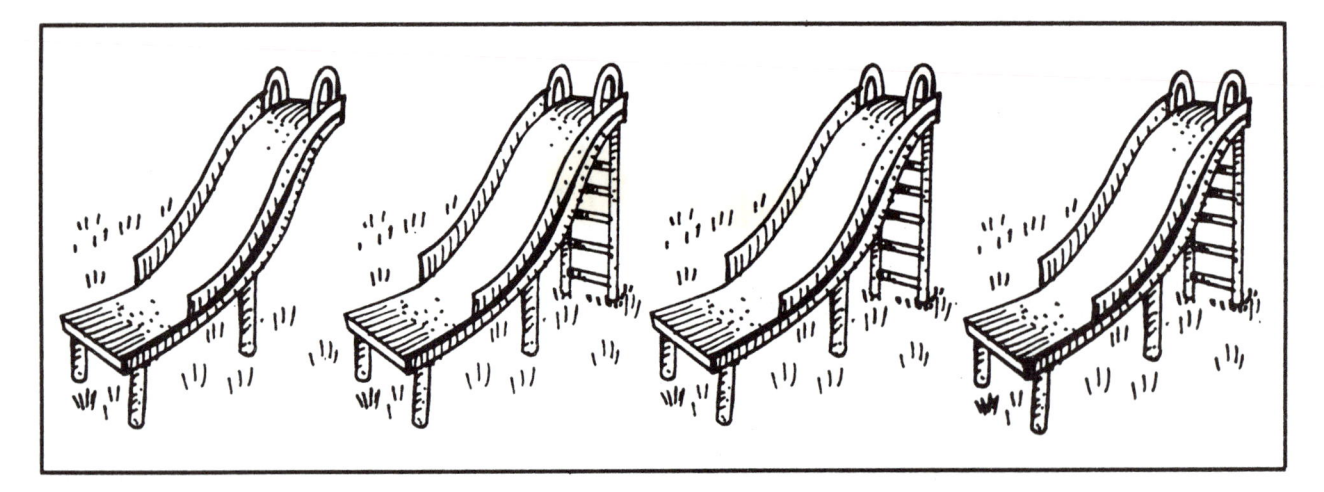

Skills: Visual discrimination; Noticing details; Following directions

READING READINESS

Look at the pictures in each row.
Cross out the one that is different.
Color the others.

Skills: Visual discrimination; Noticing details; Following directions

READING READINESS

Look closely at each row of pictures.
One of the objects is in a different position.
Cross it out and then color the other pictures.

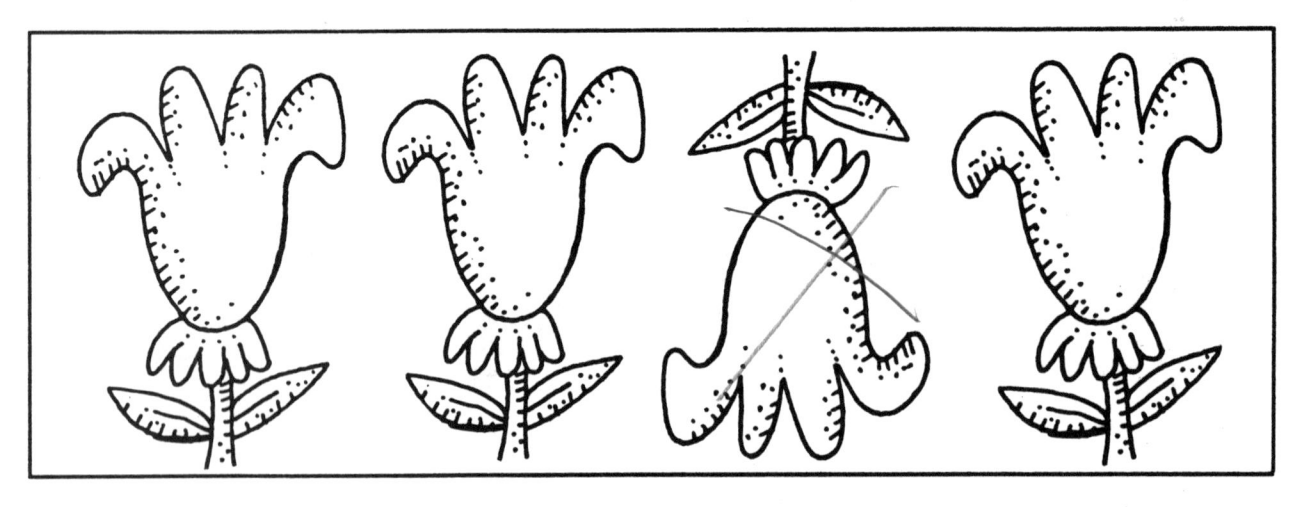

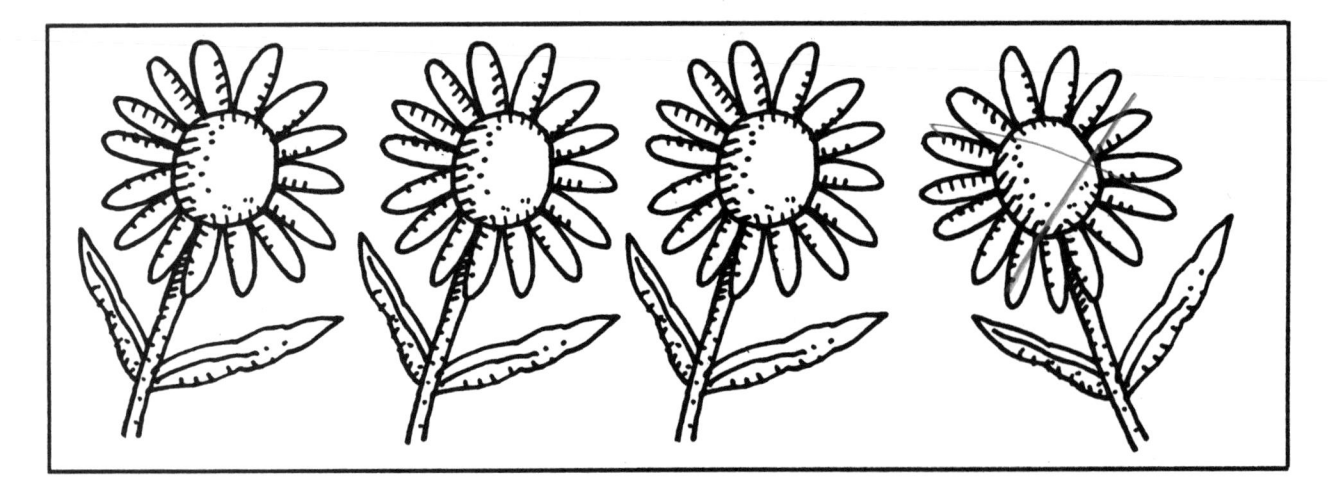

Skills: Visual discrimination; Noticing details; Following directions

READING READINESS

The car at the top of the page is heading right.
Look at the rest of the pictures.
Circle the pictures that show cars heading right.

right →

Skills: Recognizing directionality; Word recognition

READING READINESS

The bicycle at the top of the page is heading left.
Look at the rest of the pictures.
Circle the pictures that show bicycles heading left.

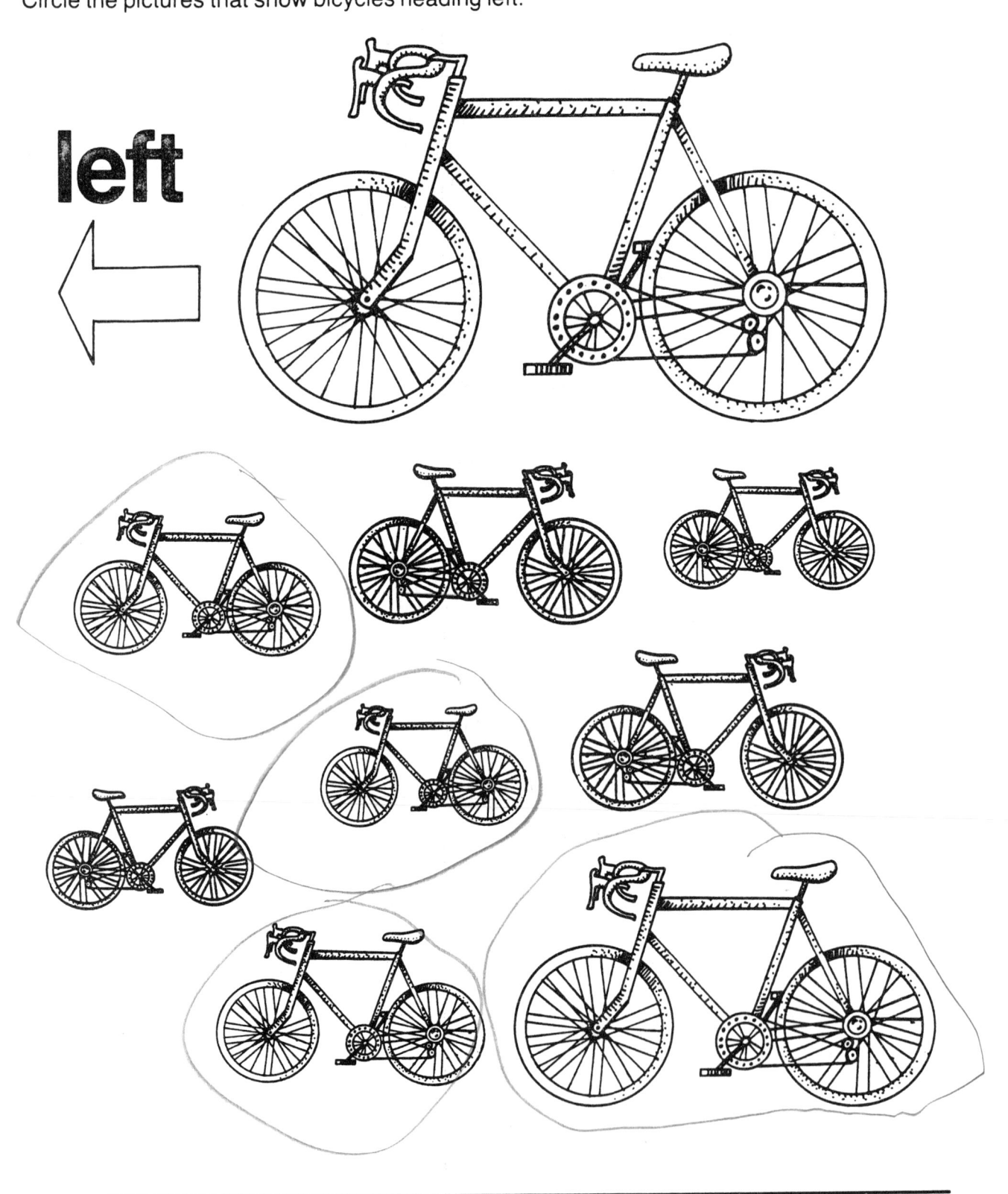

left

Skills: Recognizing directionality; Word recognition

READING READINESS

Look at the pictures at the top of this page.
One child is facing right. One child is facing left.
Then look at the rest of the pictures.
Circle the pictures that show children facing right.
Draw a line under the pictures that show children facing left.

left

right

Skills: Recognizing right and left; Word recognition

221

READING READINESS

Look at the uniform each person is wearing.
Draw a line to match the type of vehicle each person uses at work.

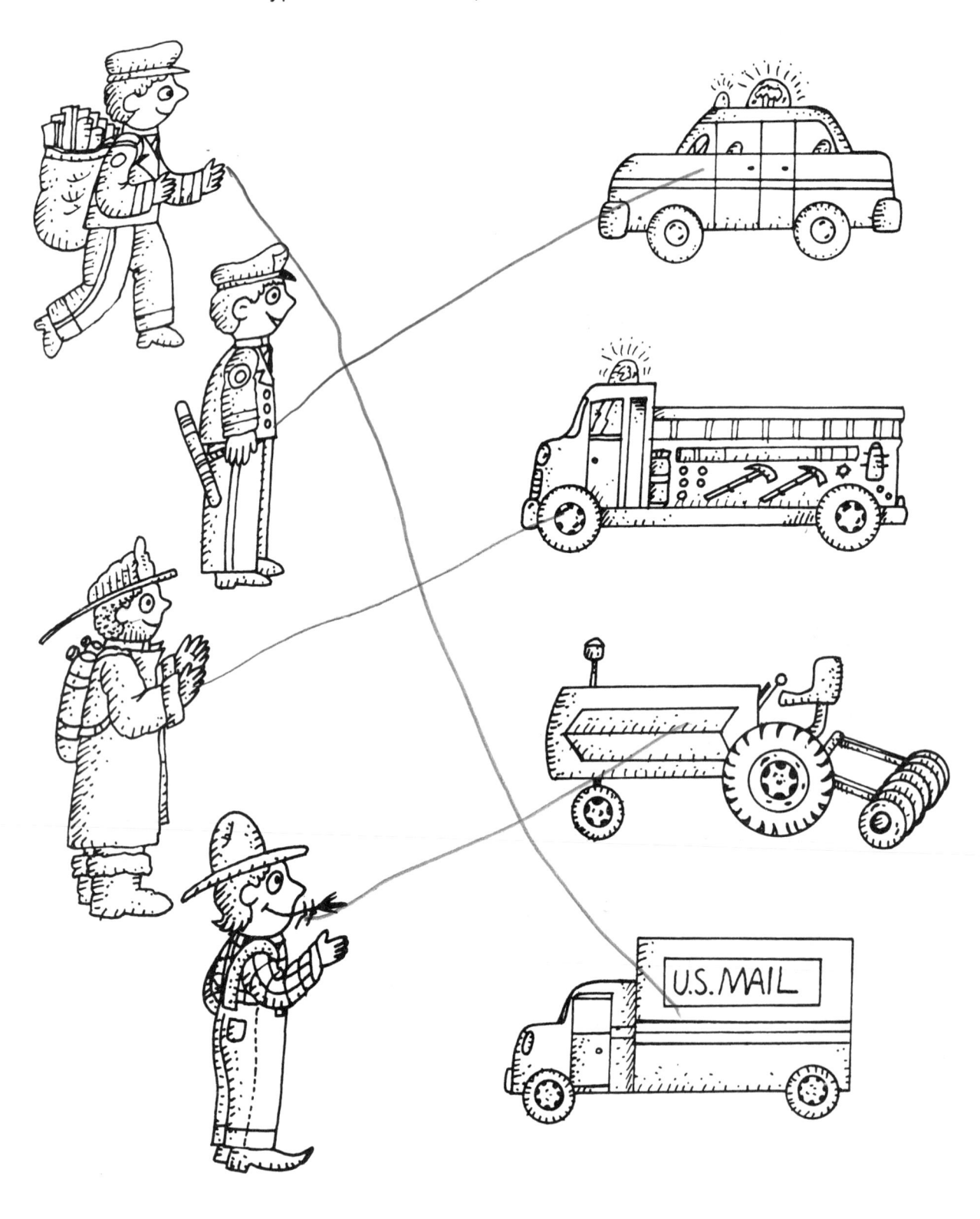

Skills: Association; Classification

READING READINESS

Look at the person at the beginning of each row.
Circle the picture that shows what each person uses at work.

Skills: Association; Classification

223

READING READINESS

Look at the pictures.
Draw a line between the pictures that are opposites.

Skills: Vocabulary; Opposites

READING READINESS

Look at the pictures.
Draw a line between the pictures that are opposites.

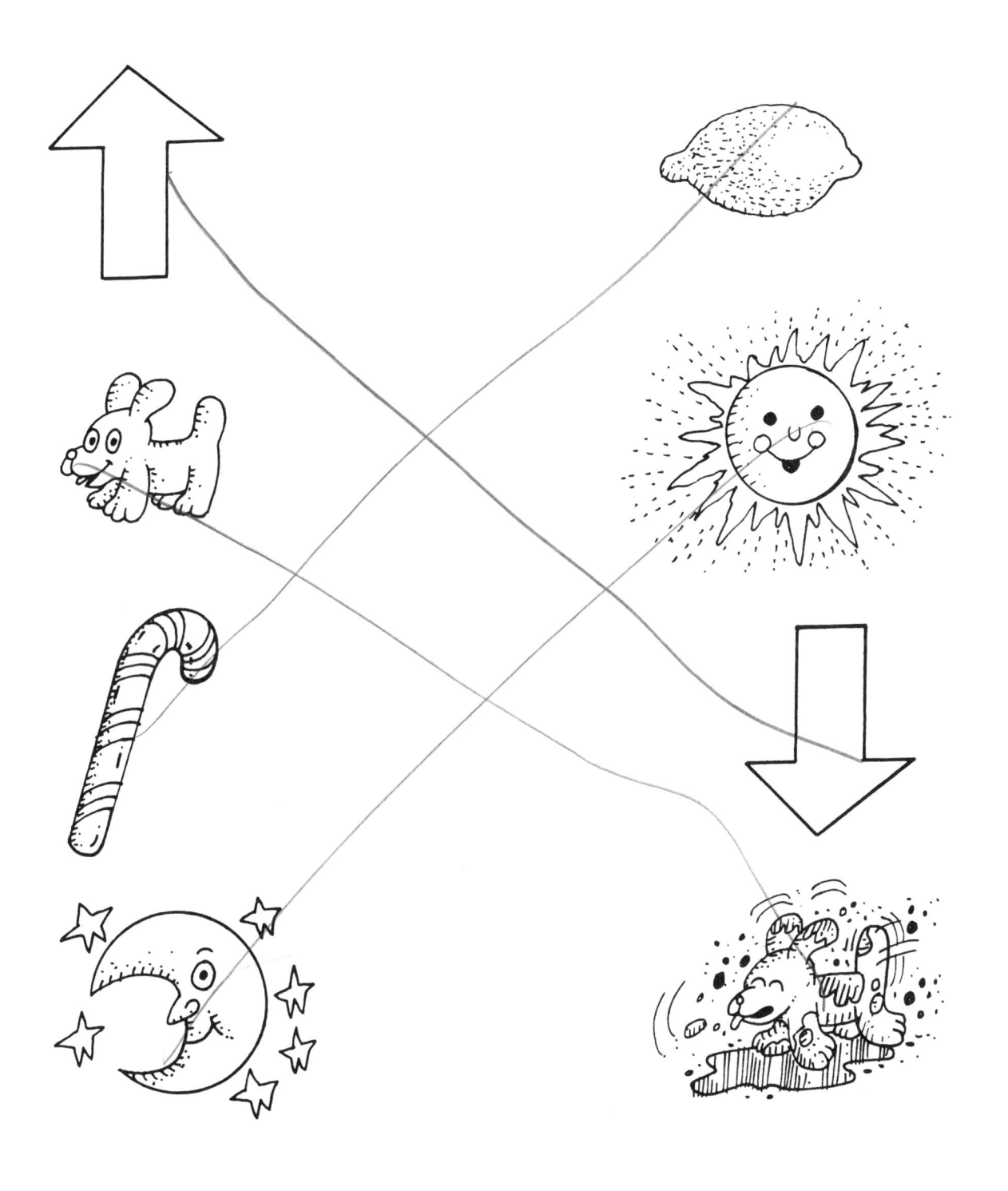

Skills: Vocabulary; Opposites

225

READING READINESS

The shoes in the shoe store got mixed up.
Draw lines between the shoes that belong together.

Skills: Understanding pairs; Vocabulary; Visual matching

226

READING READINESS

Look at the large pictures.
Then look at the detail in each small box.
Find the detail in each large picture and circle it.
Then color the page.

Skills: Visual discrimination; Noticing details; Following directions

227

READING READINESS

Look at the pictures at the top of the page.
Find and circle them in the larger picture below.

Skills: Association; Classification

228

READING READINESS

Look at the pattern in each row.
Draw a line to the picture that continues each pattern.
Then color the picture.

Skills: Observing and continuing patterns; Visual memory

READING READINESS

Look at the pattern in each row.
Draw a line to the picture that continues each pattern.
Then color the picture.

Skills: Observing and continuing patterns; Visual memory

READING READINESS

Look at the pattern in each row.
Draw a line to the picture that continues each pattern.
Then color the picture.

Skills: Observing and continuing patterns; Visual memory

READING READINESS

Look at the pattern in each row.
Draw the picture that continues each pattern.
Then color the picture.

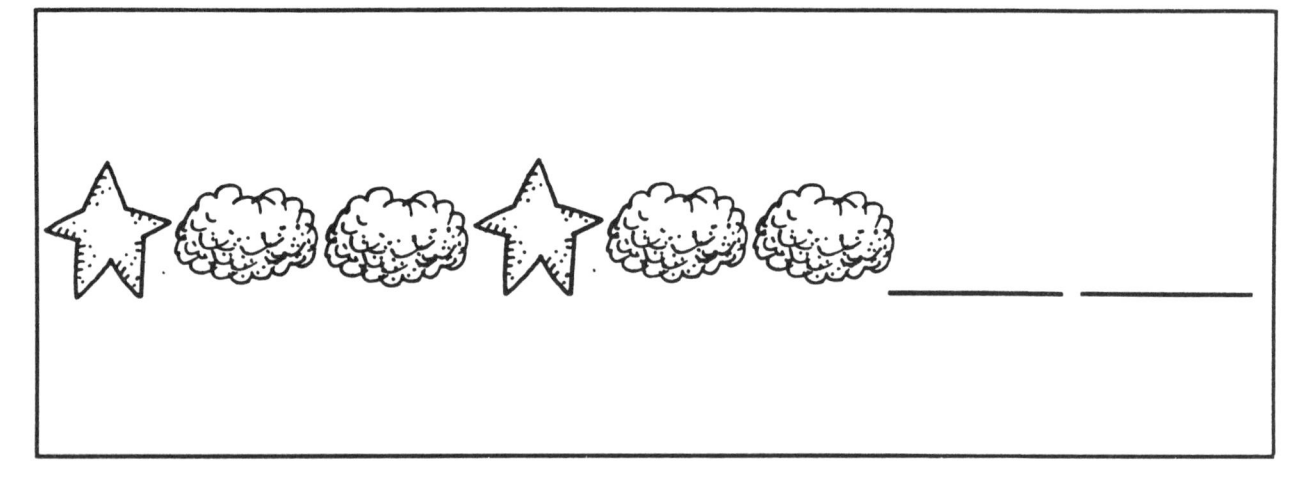

Skills: Observing and reproducing patterns; Visual memory; Fine motor skill development

READING READINESS

Look at the pictures.
Write a 1 in the picture that shows what happened first.
Write a 2 in the picture that shows what happened second.
Write a 3 in the picture that shows what happened third.
Then color the pictures.

Skills: Sequencing; Identifying parts of a story; Writing numerals

READING READINESS

Look at the pictures.
Think about the story they tell.
Write the numbers 1, 2, 3, and 4 in the boxes to put the story in the order.
Then color the picture.

Skills: Sequencing; Identifying parts of a story; Writing numerals

READING READINESS

Look at the pictures in each row.
Think about the story they tell.
Draw a circle around the small picture that shows what comes next.
Then color the picture.

Skills: Logical reasoning; Sequencing; Identifying part of a story

235

READING READINESS

Look at the picture of the cake.
Say the name of each picture.
Draw a line from the cake to each picture whose name rhymes with the word cake.

Skills: Auditory discrimination; Reproducing sounds

236

READING READINESS

Look at the first picture in each row and say its name.
Circle the picture whose name rhymes with it.

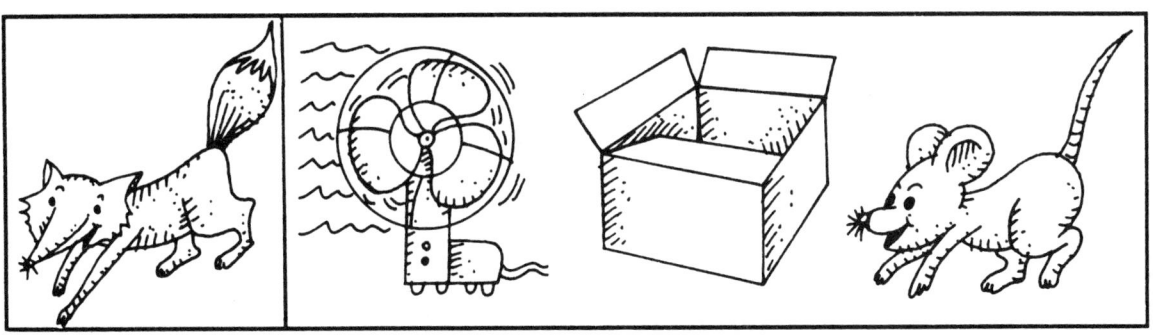

Skills: Auditory discrimination; Reproducing sounds

READING READINESS

Look at each picture and say its name.
Draw a line to match each rhyming picture.

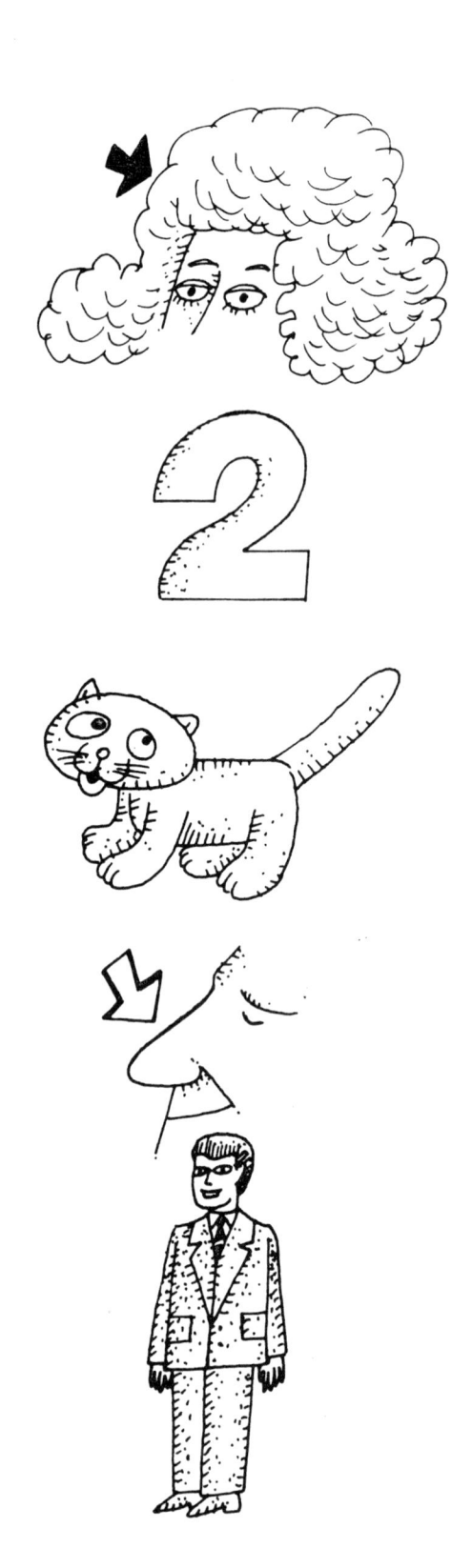

Skills: Auditory discrimination; Reproducing sounds

PHONICS SKILLS I

Initial consonant: **b**

Print the letters and words.

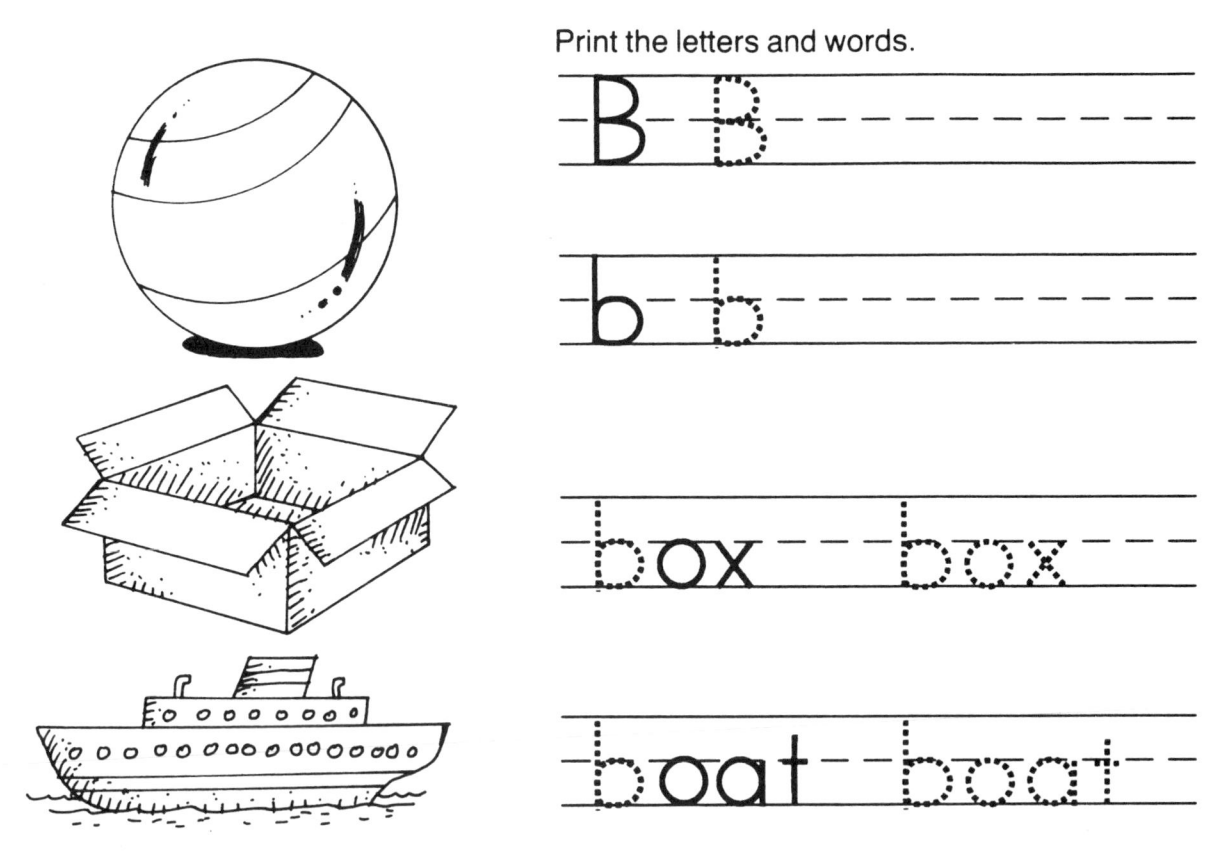

B B

b b

box   box

boat   boat

Finish the picture. Finish the word.

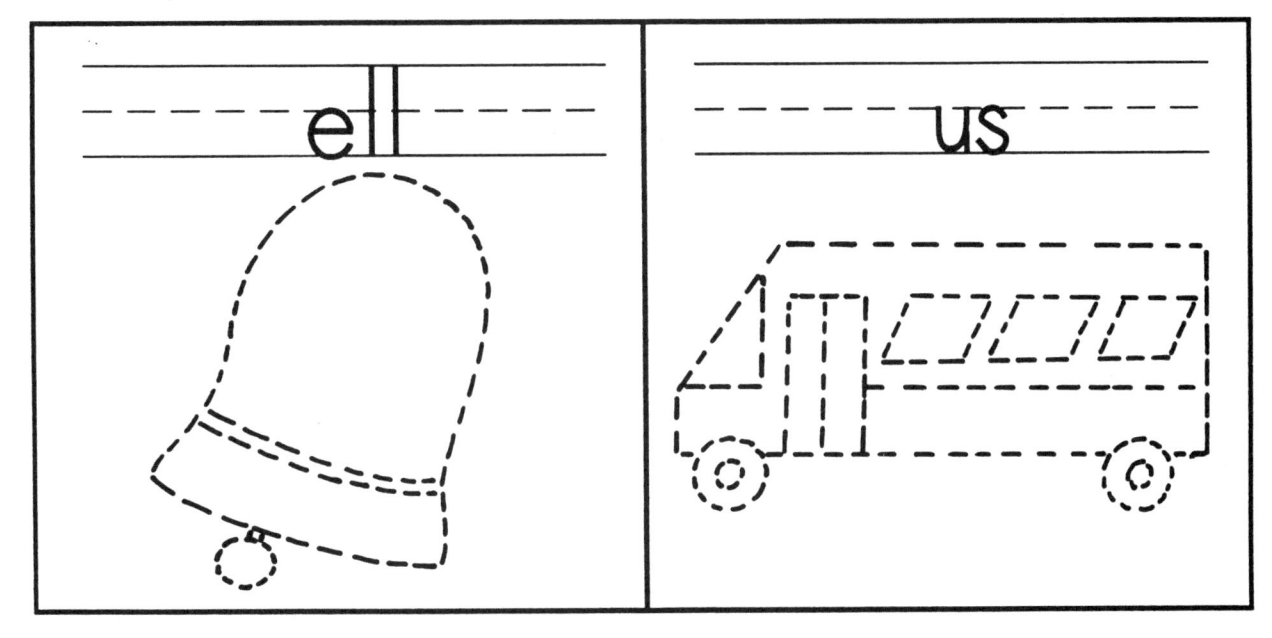

ell

us

Skills: Recognition of the initial consonant "b"; Writing letters and words; Association between sounds, symbols, and words

PHONICS SKILLS I

Initial consonant: **f**

Print the letters and words.

F F

f f

five five

fan fan

Finish the picture. Finish the word.

___ox

___ish

Skills: Recognition of the initial consonant "f"; Writing letters and words; Association between sounds, symbols, and words

PHONICS SKILLS I

Initial consonant: **g**

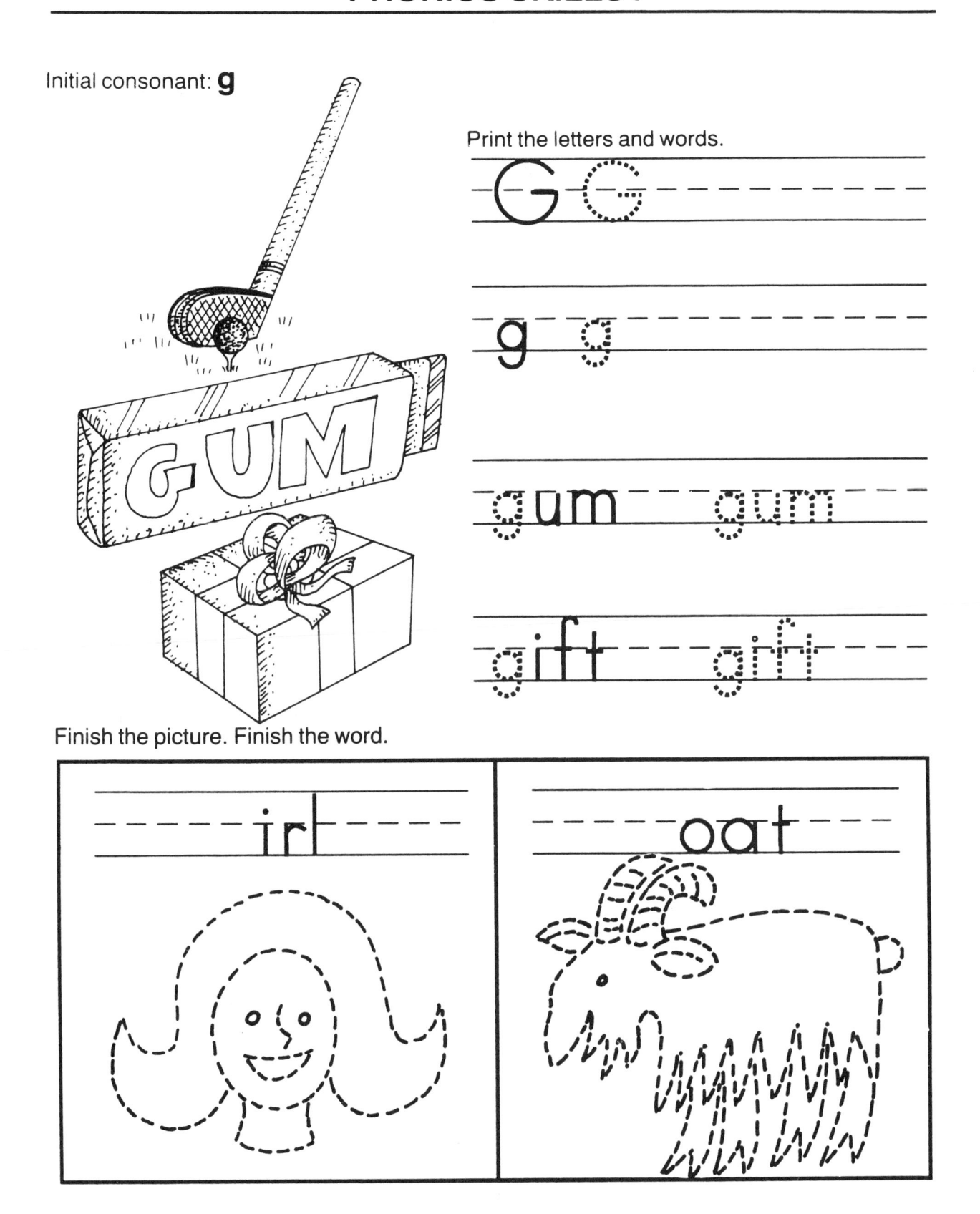

Print the letters and words.

G G

g g

gum gum

gift gift

Finish the picture. Finish the word.

girl

goat

Skills: Recognition of the initial consonant "g"; Writing letters and words; Association between sounds, symbols, and words

PHONICS SKILLS I

Initial consonant: **k**

Print the letters and words.

K K

k k

king king

kick kick

Finish the picture. Finish the word.

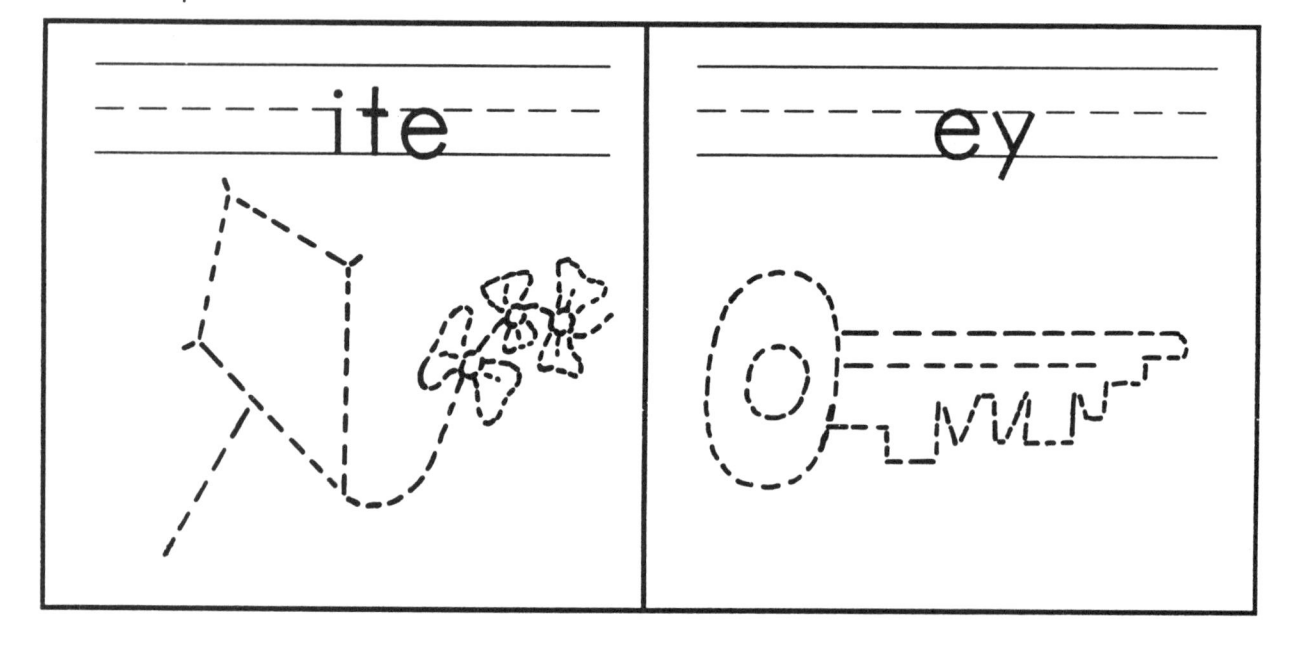

ite

ey

Skills: Recognition of the initial consonant "k"; Writing letters and words; Association between sounds, symbols, and words

PHONICS SKILLS I

Initial consonant: **V**

Print the letters and words.

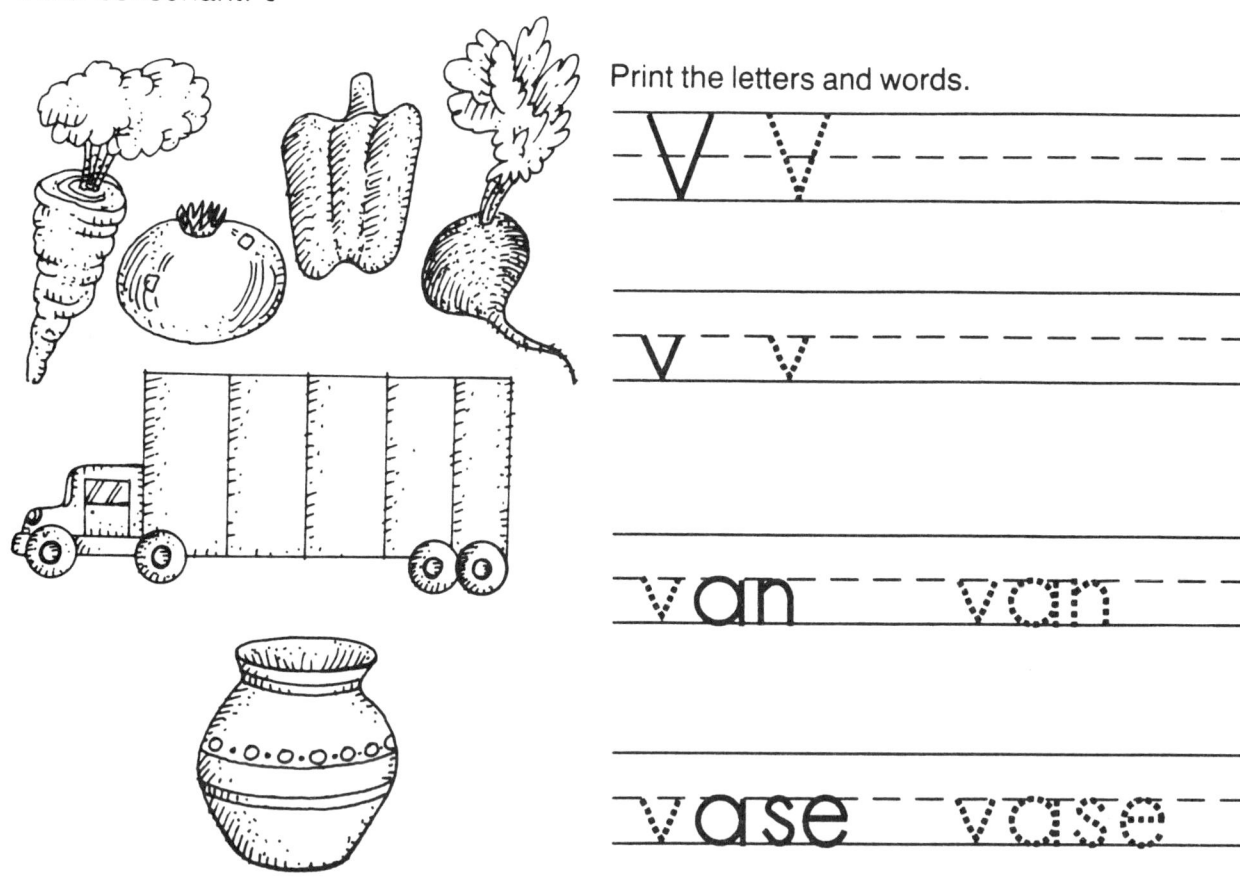

V v

v v

van van

vase vase

Finish the picture. Finish the word.

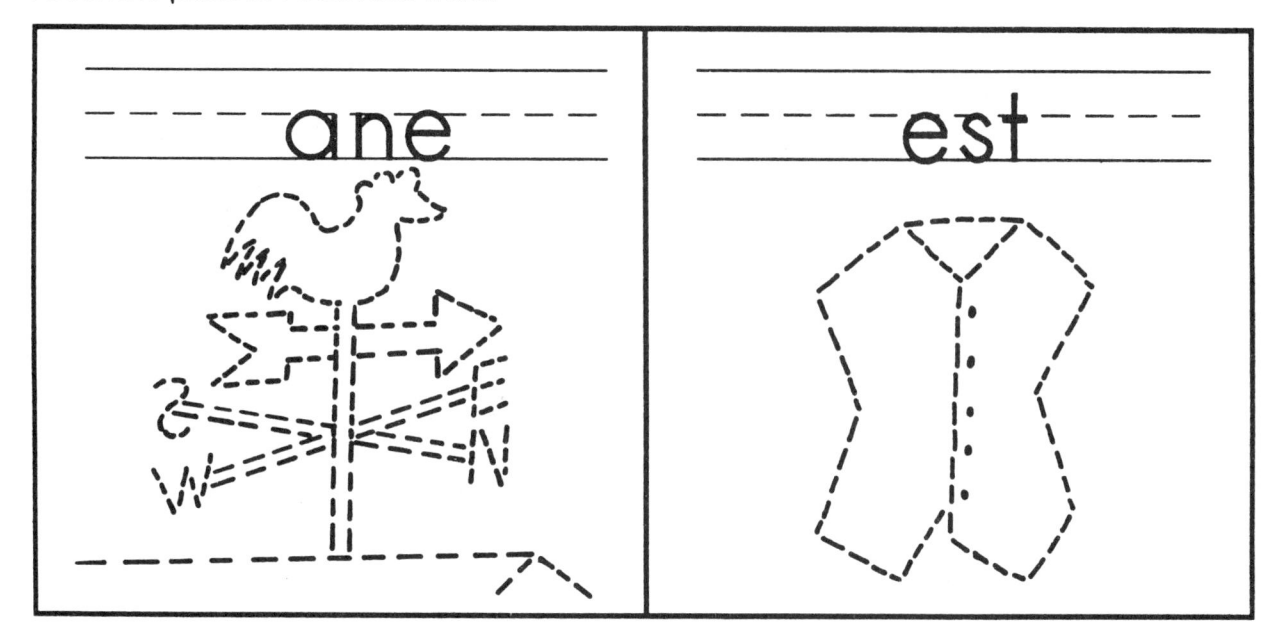

ane   est

Skills: Recognition of the initial consonant "v"; Writing letters and words; Association between sounds, symbols, and words

PHONICS SKILLS I

Initial consonant: **C**

Print the letters and words.

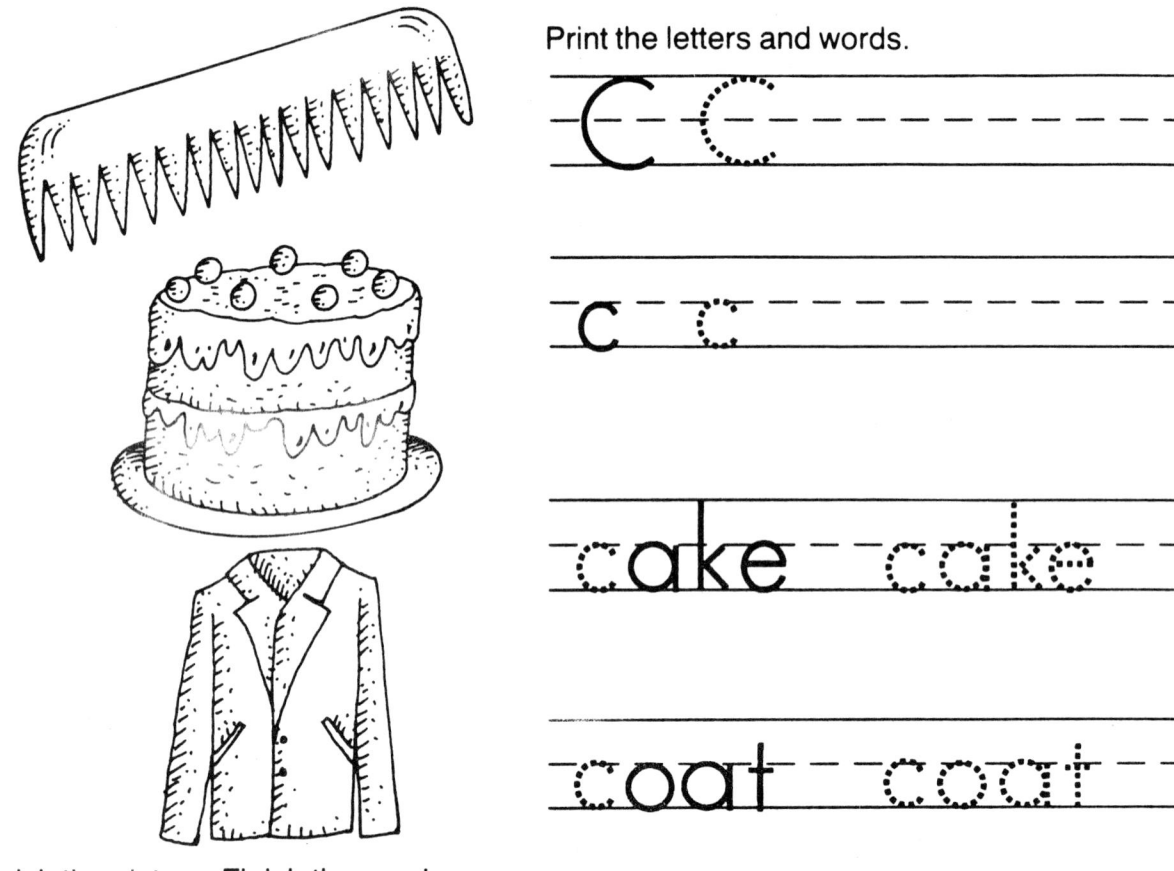

C C

c c

cake cake

coat coat

Finish the picture. Finish the word.

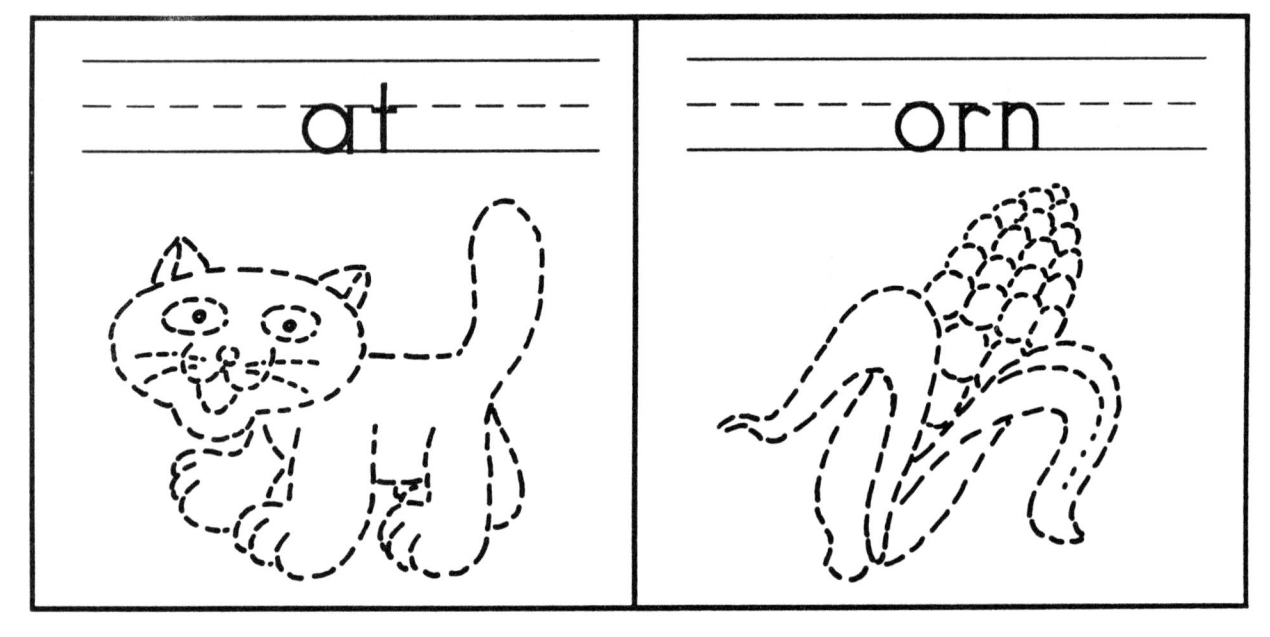

_at

_orn

Skills: Recognition of the initial consonant "c"; Writing letters and words; Association between sounds, symbols, and words

PHONICS SKILLS I

Initial consonant: **h**

Print the letters and words.

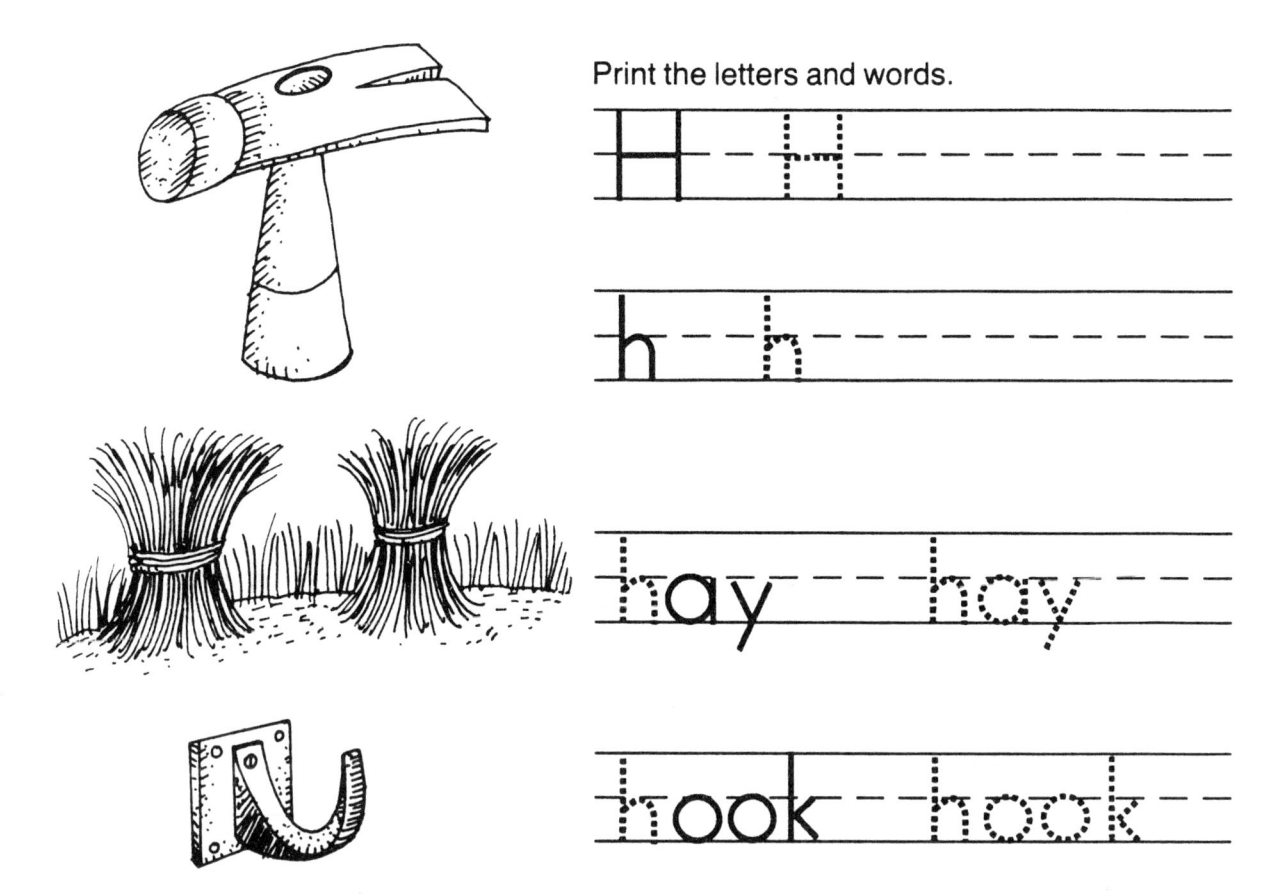

H H

h h

hay hay

hook hook

Finish the picture. Finish the word.

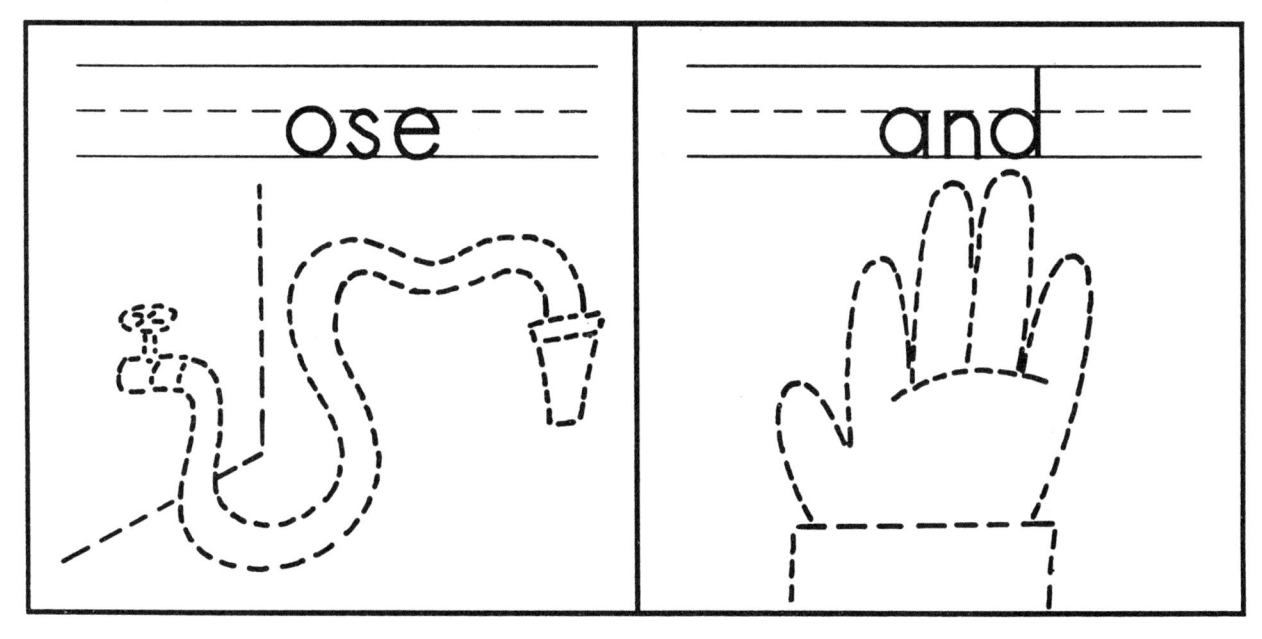

ose

and

Skills: Recognition of the initial consonant "h"; Writing letters and words; Association between sounds, symbols, and words

PHONICS SKILLS I

Initial consonant: **m**

Print the letters and words.

M M _____

m m _____

mask mask _____

man man _____

Finish the picture. Finish the word.

oon

at

Skills: Recognition of the initial consonant "m"; Writing letters and words; Association between sounds, symbols, and words

PHONICS SKILLS I

Initial consonant: **p**

Print the letters and words.

P P

p p

pan pan

pail pail

Finish the picture. Finish the word.

en

ot

Skills: Recognition of the initial consonant "p"; Writing letters and words; Association between sounds, symbols, and words

PHONICS SKILLS I

Initial consonant: **y**

Print the letters and words.

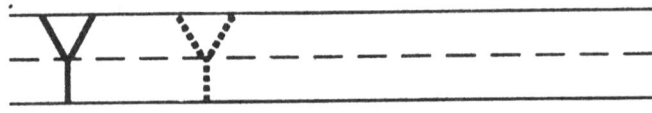

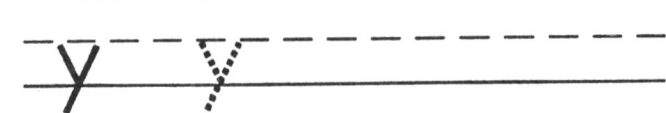

Y Y

y y

yo-yo yo-yo

yawn yawn

Finish the picture. Finish the word.

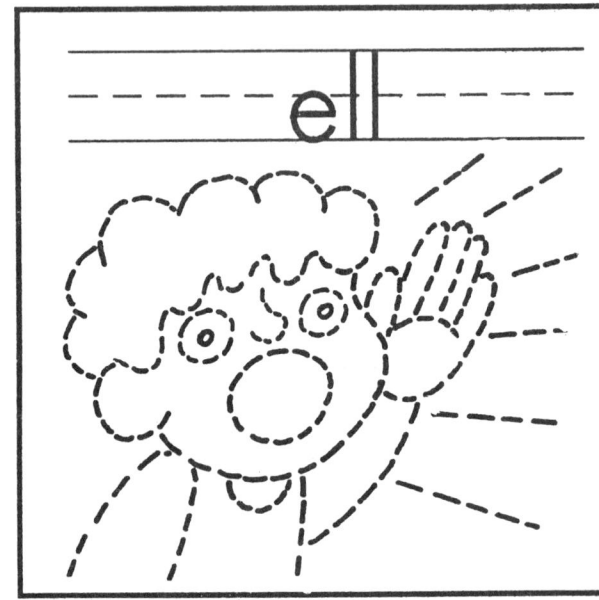

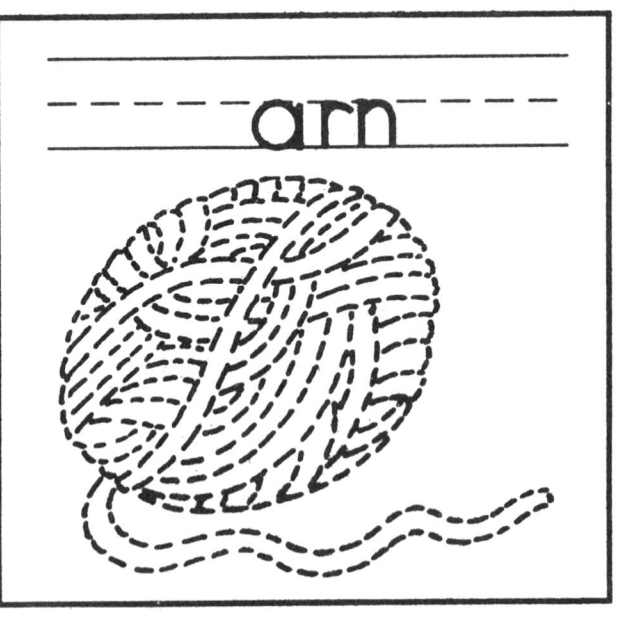

ell

arn

Skills: Recognition of the initial consonant "y"; Writing letters and words; Association between sounds, symbols, and words

PHONICS SKILLS I

Initial consonant: **d**

Print the letters and words.

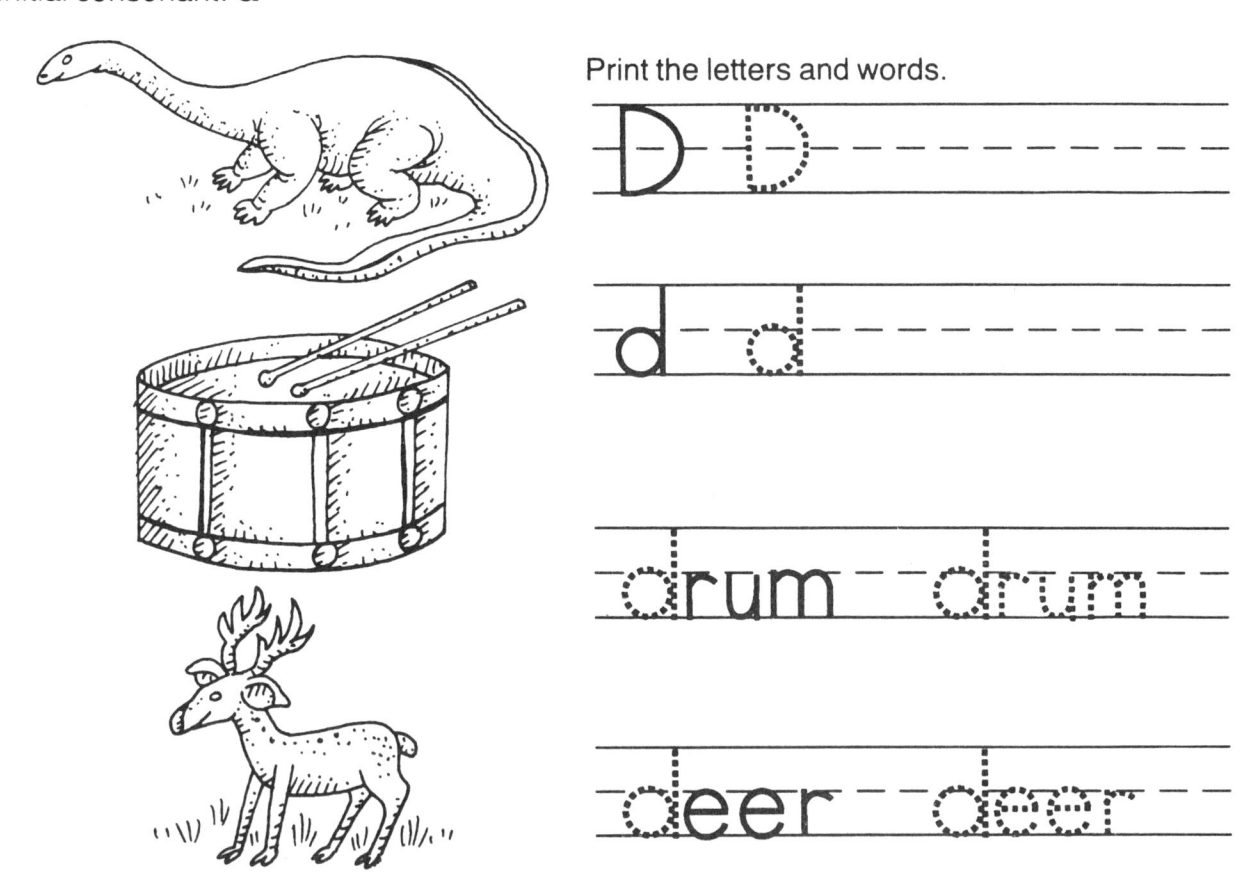

D D _____

d d _____

drum drum _____

deer deer _____

Finish the picture. Finish the word.

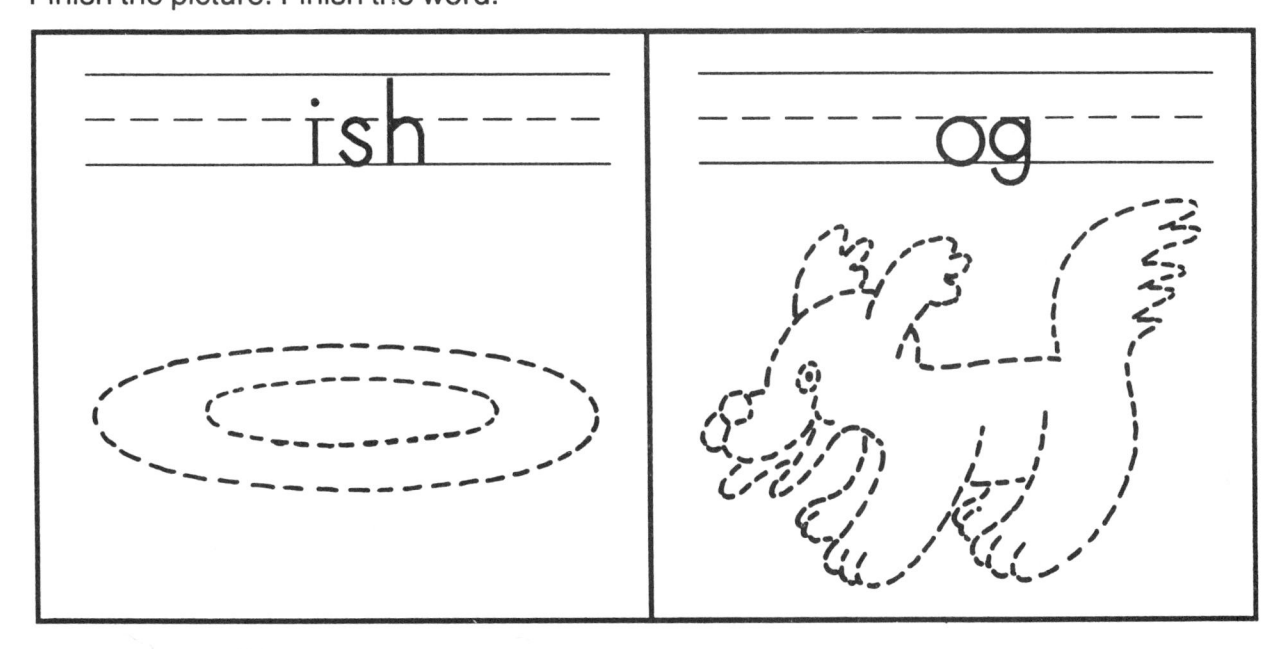

____ish____

____og____

Skills: Recognition of the initial consonant "d"; Writing letters and words; Association between sounds, symbols, and words

PHONICS SKILLS I

Initial consonant: **j**

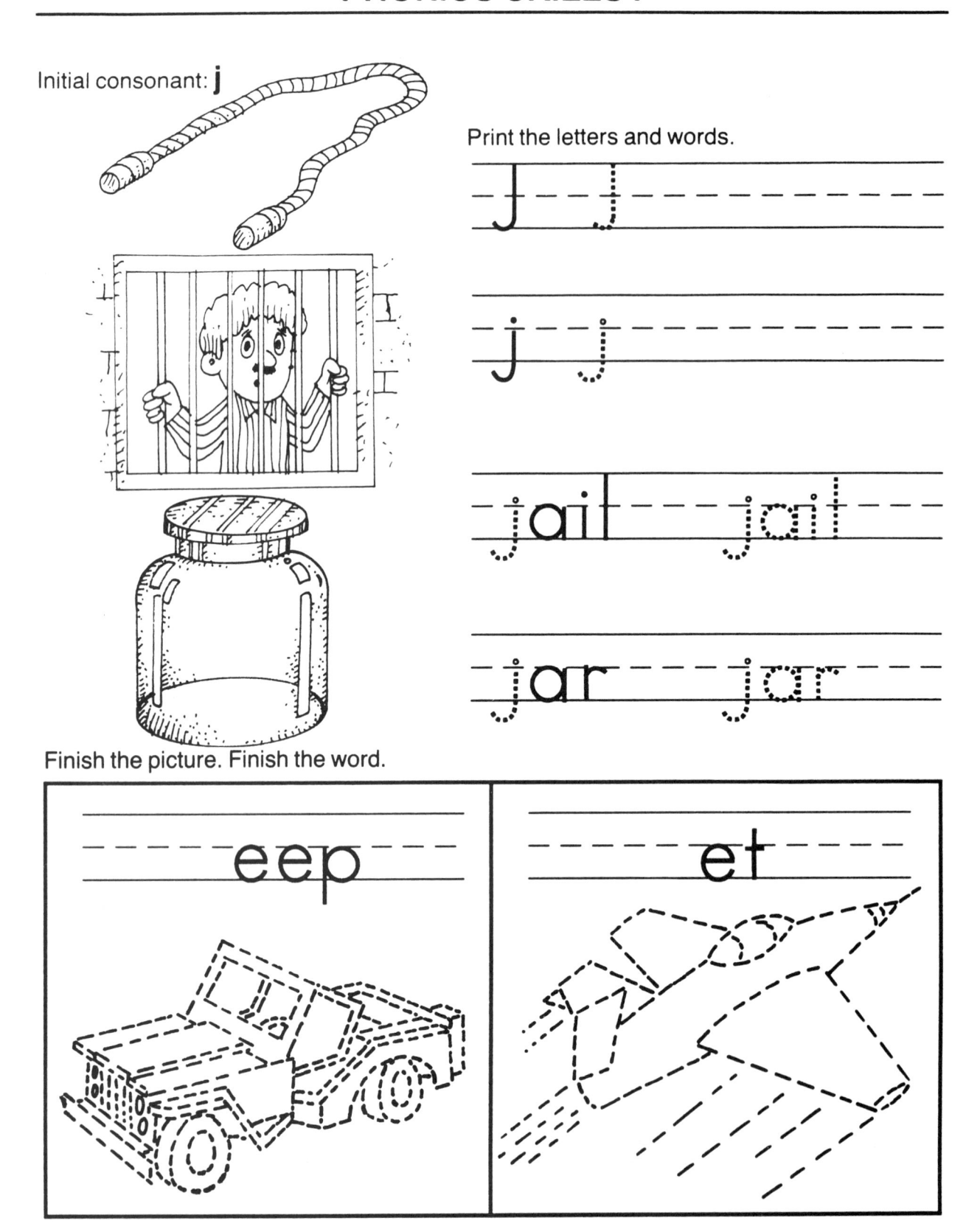

Print the letters and words.

J J

j j

jail jail

jar jar

Finish the picture. Finish the word.

eep

et

Skills: Recognition of the initial consonant "j"; Writing letters and words; Association between sounds, symbols, and words

PHONICS SKILLS l

Initial consonant: l

Print the letters and words.

L l

l

lamb lamb

leaf leaf

Finish the picture. Finish the word.

l ion

l ock

Skills: Recognition of the initial consonant "l"; Writing letters and words; Association between sounds, symbols, and words

251

PHONICS SKILLS I

Initial consonant: **W**

Print the letters and words.

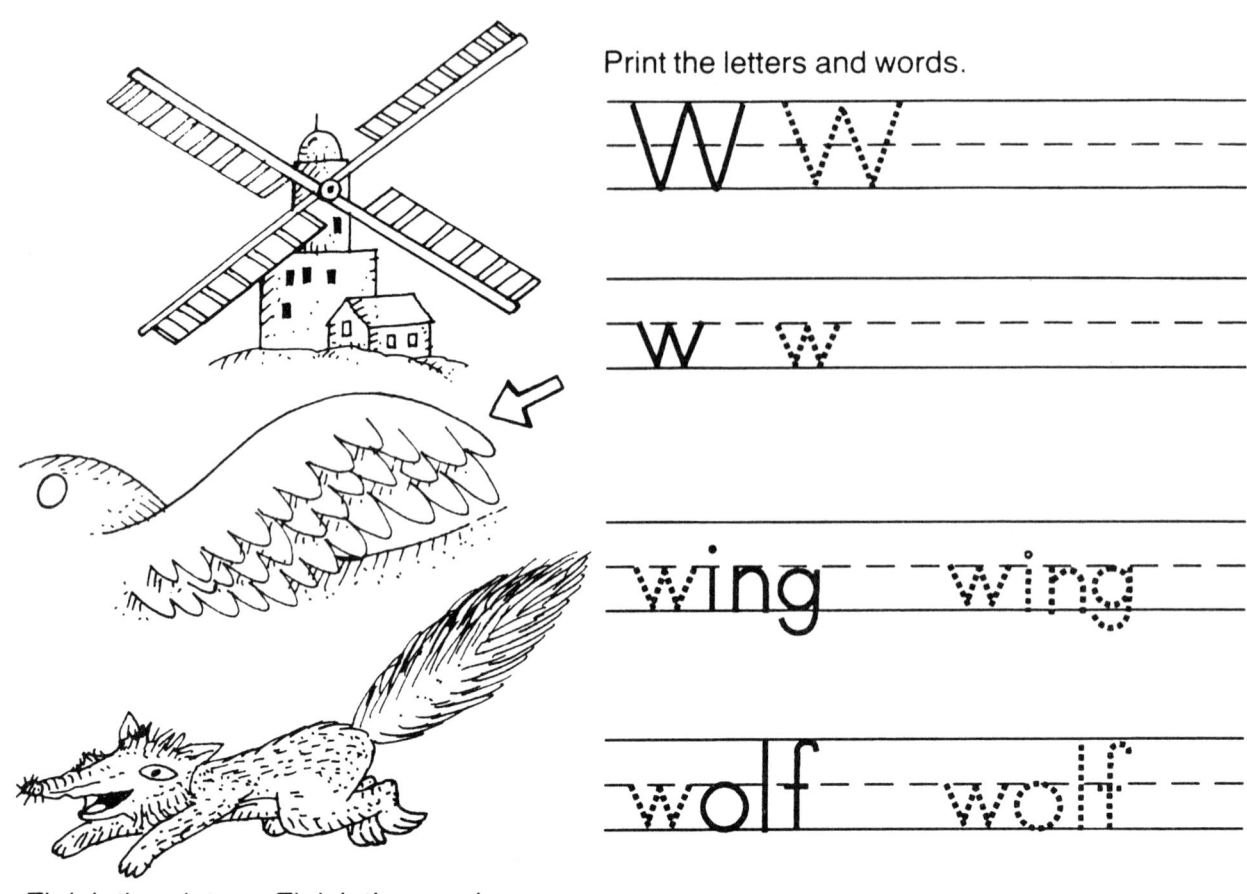

W w

W w

wing   wing

wolf   wolf

Finish the picture. Finish the word.

ell

agon

Skills: Recognition of the initial consonant "w"; Writing letters and words; Association between sounds, symbols, and words

PHONICS SKILLS I

Initial consonant: **Z**

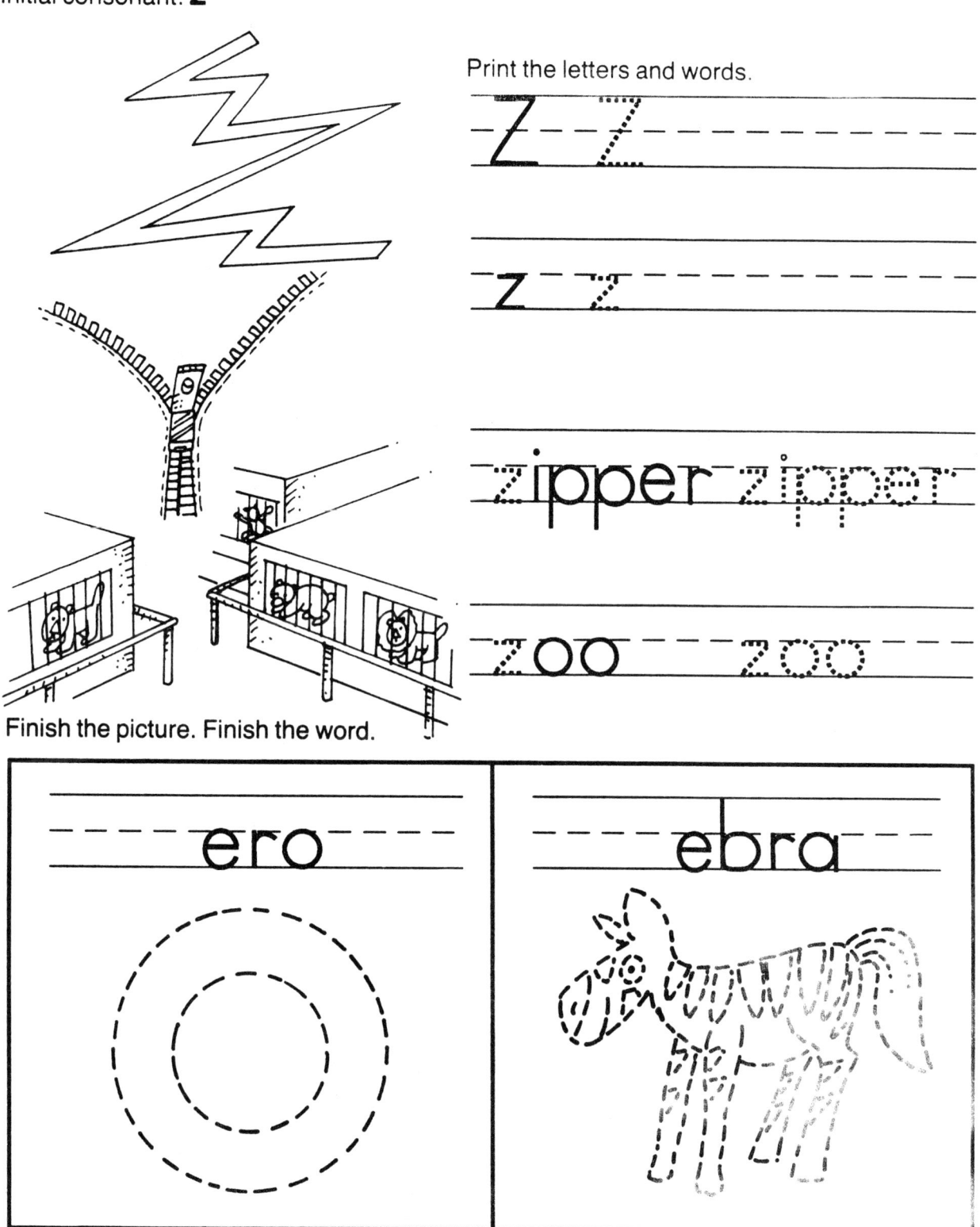

Print the letters and words.

Z Z

z z

zipper zipper

zoo zoo

Finish the picture. Finish the word.

ero

ebra

Skills: Recognition of the initial consonant "z"; Writing letters and words; Association between sounds, symbols, and words

PHONICS SKILLS I

Initial consonant: **n**

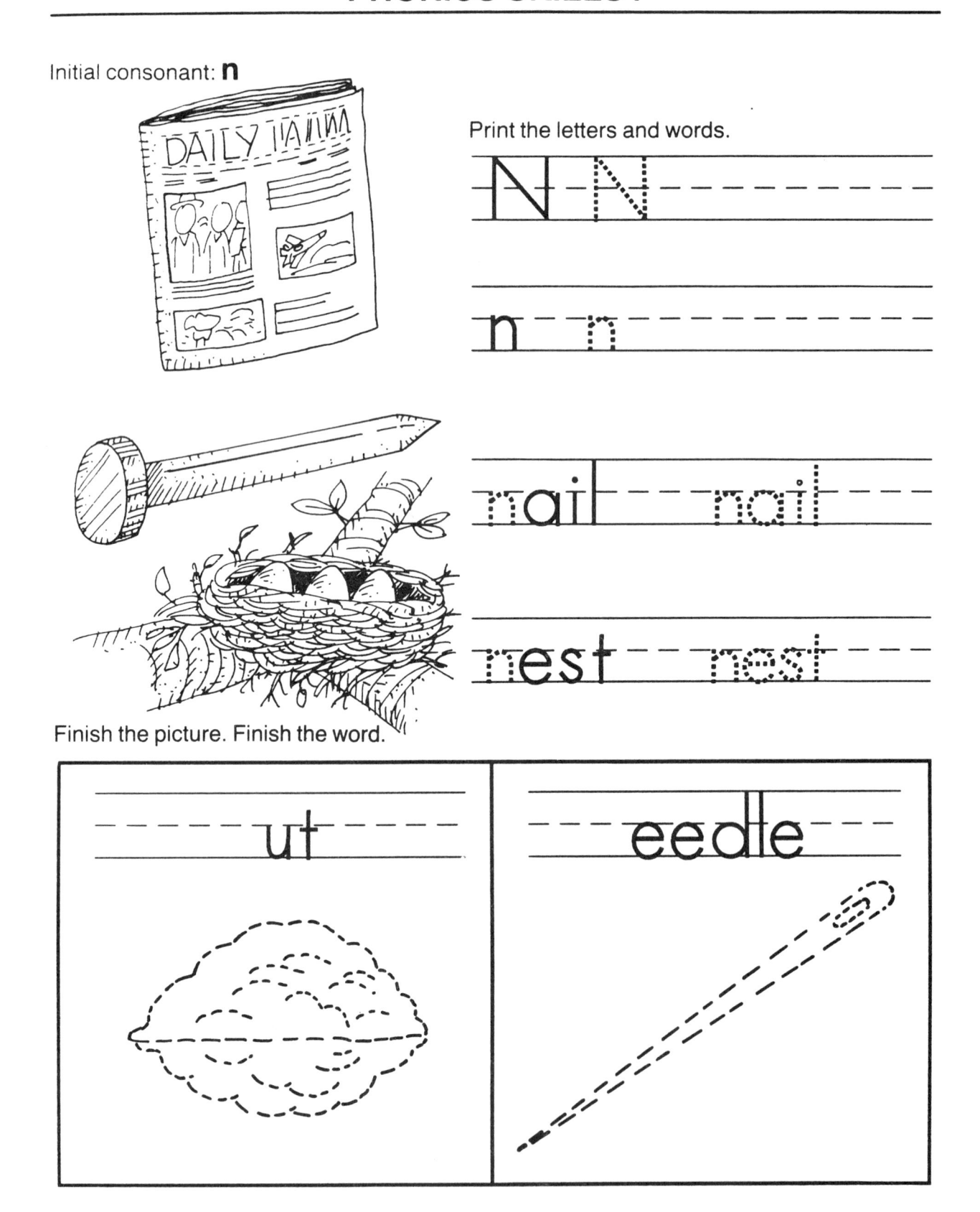

Print the letters and words.

N N

n n

nail nail

nest nest

Finish the picture. Finish the word.

_ut

_eedle

Skills: Recognition of the initial consonant "n"; Writing letters and words; Association between sounds, symbols, and words

PHONICS SKILLS I

Initial consonant: **q**

Print the letters and words.

Q Q

q q

quiet quiet

quilt quilt

Finish the picture. Finish the word.

_q_uarter

_q_uill

Skills: Recognition of the initial consonant "q"; Writing letters and words; Association between sounds, symbols, and words

255

PHONICS SKILLS I

Initial consonant: **r**

Print the letters and words.

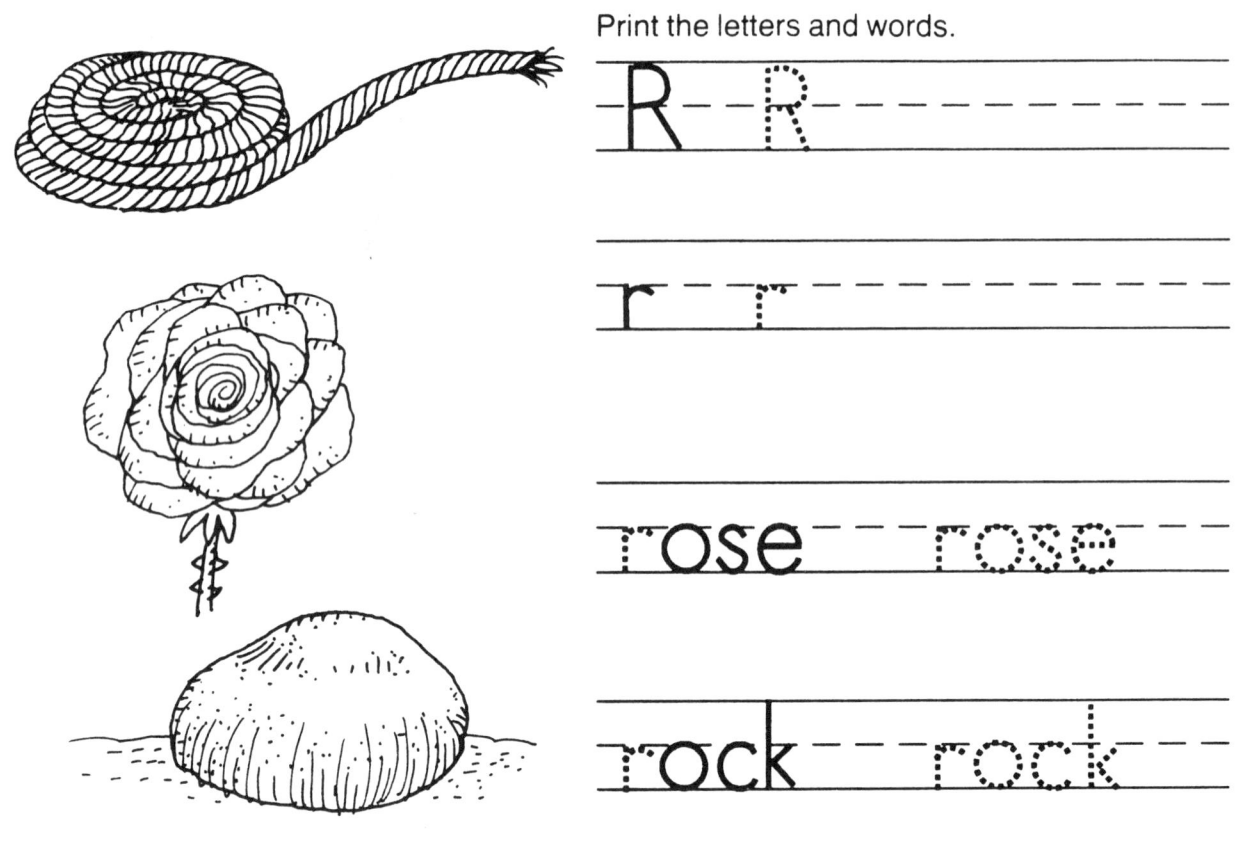

R R

r r

rose rose

rock rock

Finish the picture. Finish the word.

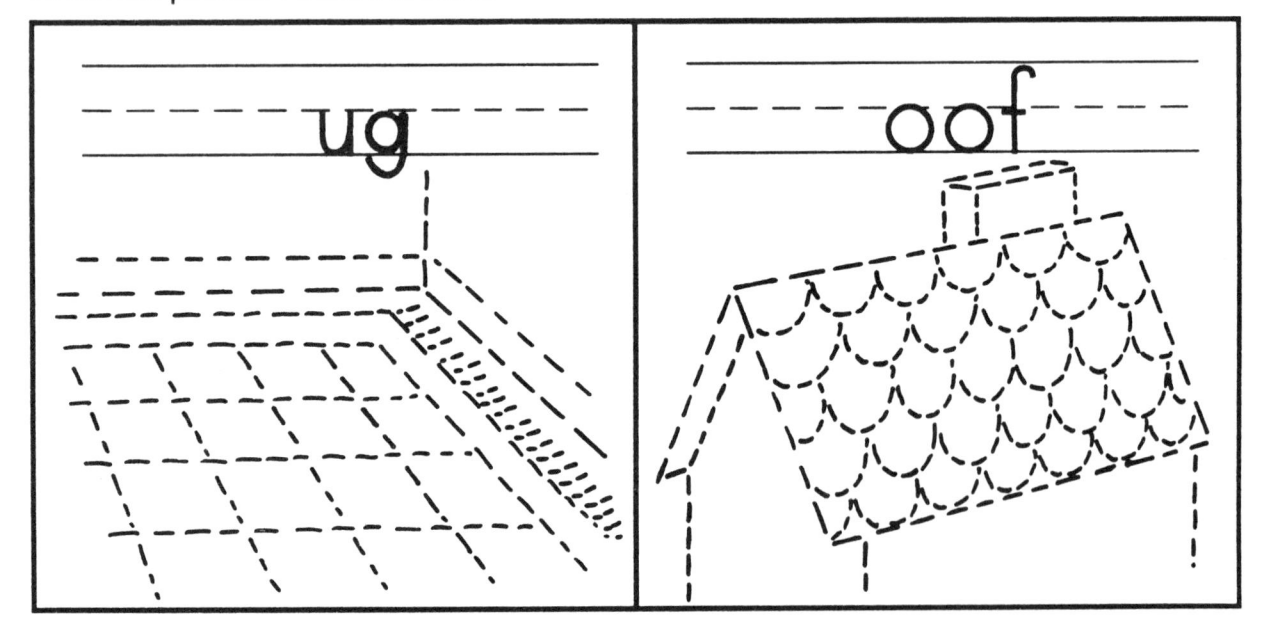

ug

oof

Skills: Recognition of the initial consonant "r"; Writing letters and words; Association between sounds, symbols, and words

PHONICS SKILLS I

Initial consonant: **s**

Print the letters and words.

S S

s s

soap soap

saw saw

Finish the picture. Finish the word.

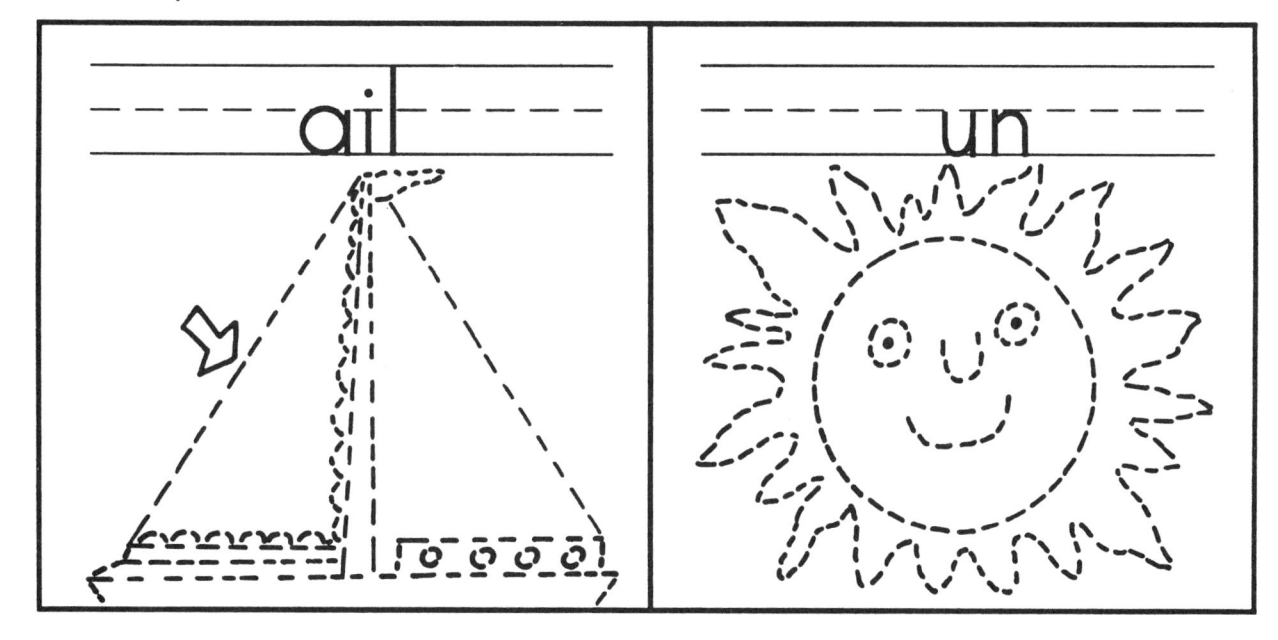

ail

un

Skills: Recognition of the initial consonant "s"; Writing letters and words; Association between sounds, symbols, and words

PHONICS SKILLS I

Initial consonant: **t**

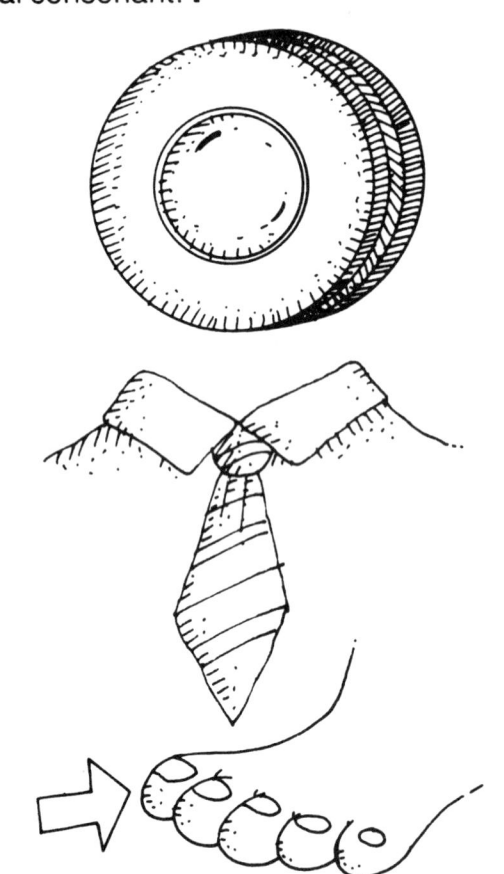

Print the letters and words.

T t

t t

tie   tie

toe   toe

Finish the picture. Finish the word.

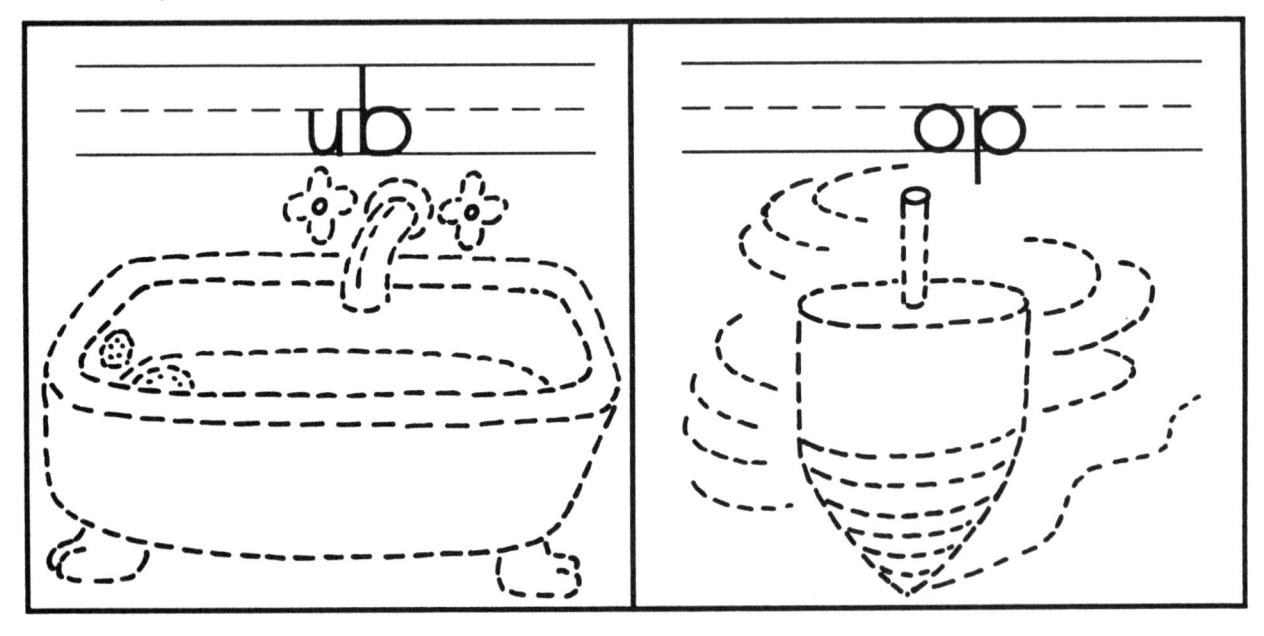

_ub

_op

Skills: Recognition of the initial consonant "t"; Writing letters and words; Association between sounds, symbols, and words

PHONICS SKILLS I

Final consonant: **b**

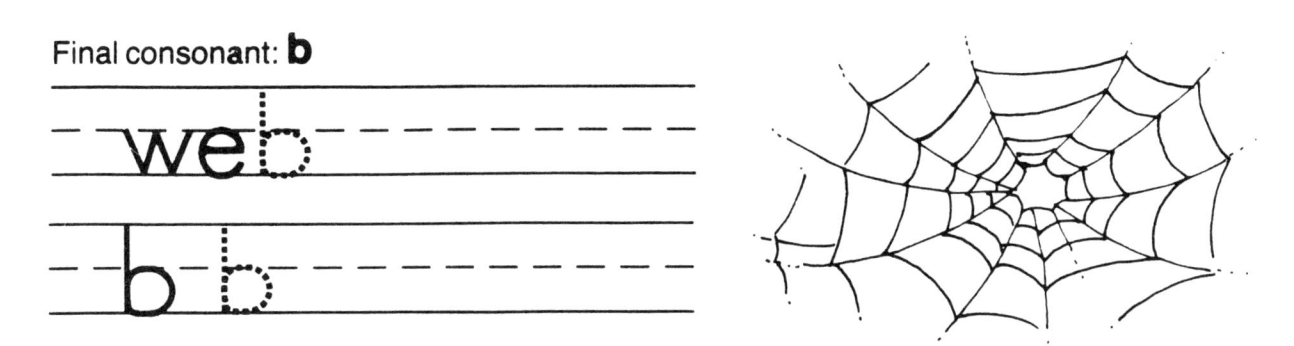

web

b b

Which ones end with **b**? Color them red. Color the other pictures blue.

Skills: Recognition of the final consonant "b"; Auditory discrimination; Writing the letter "b"; Sound/symbol association

PHONICS SKILLS I

Final consonant: **f**

hoof

f f

Which ones end with **f**? Color them green. Color the other pictures yellow.

Skills: Recognition of the final consonant "f"; Auditory discrimination; Writing the letter "f"; Sound/symbol association

PHONICS SKILLS I

Final consonant: **d**

b e d

d d

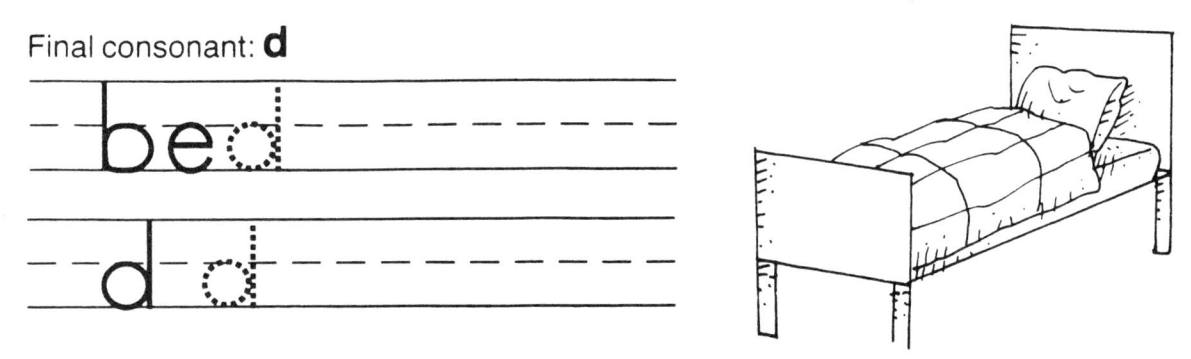

Which ones end with **d**? Color them purple. Color the other pictures orange.

Skills: Recognition of the final consonant "d"; Auditory discrimination; Writing the letter "d"; Sound/symbol association

PHONICS SKILLS I

Final consonant: **g**

bug

g g

Which ones end with **g**? Color them brown. Color the other pictures blue.

Skills: Recognition of the final consonant "g"; Auditory discrimination; Writing the letter "g"; Sound/symbol association

PHONICS SKILLS I

Final consonant: k

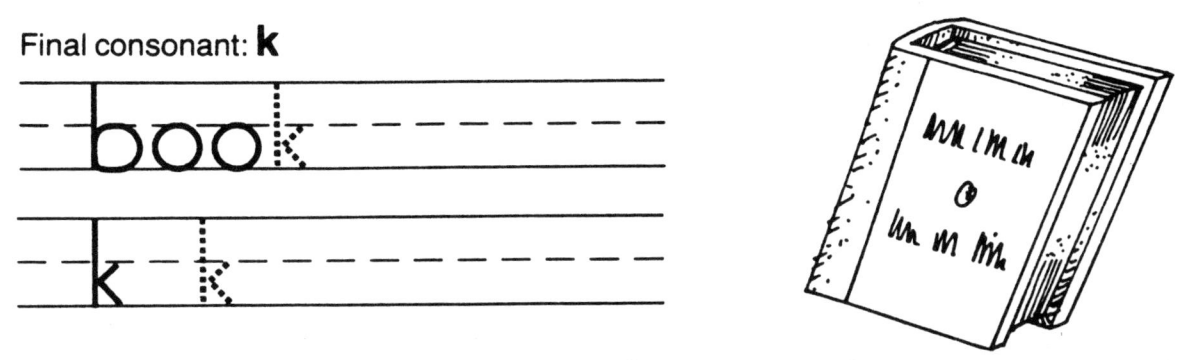

book

k

Which ones end with **k**? Color them red. Color the other pictures green.

Skills: Recognition of the final consonant "k"; Auditory discrimination; Writing the letter "k"; Sound/symbol association

PHONICS SKILLS I

Final consonant: **m**

plum

m m

Which ones end with **m**? Color them green. Color the other pictures yellow.

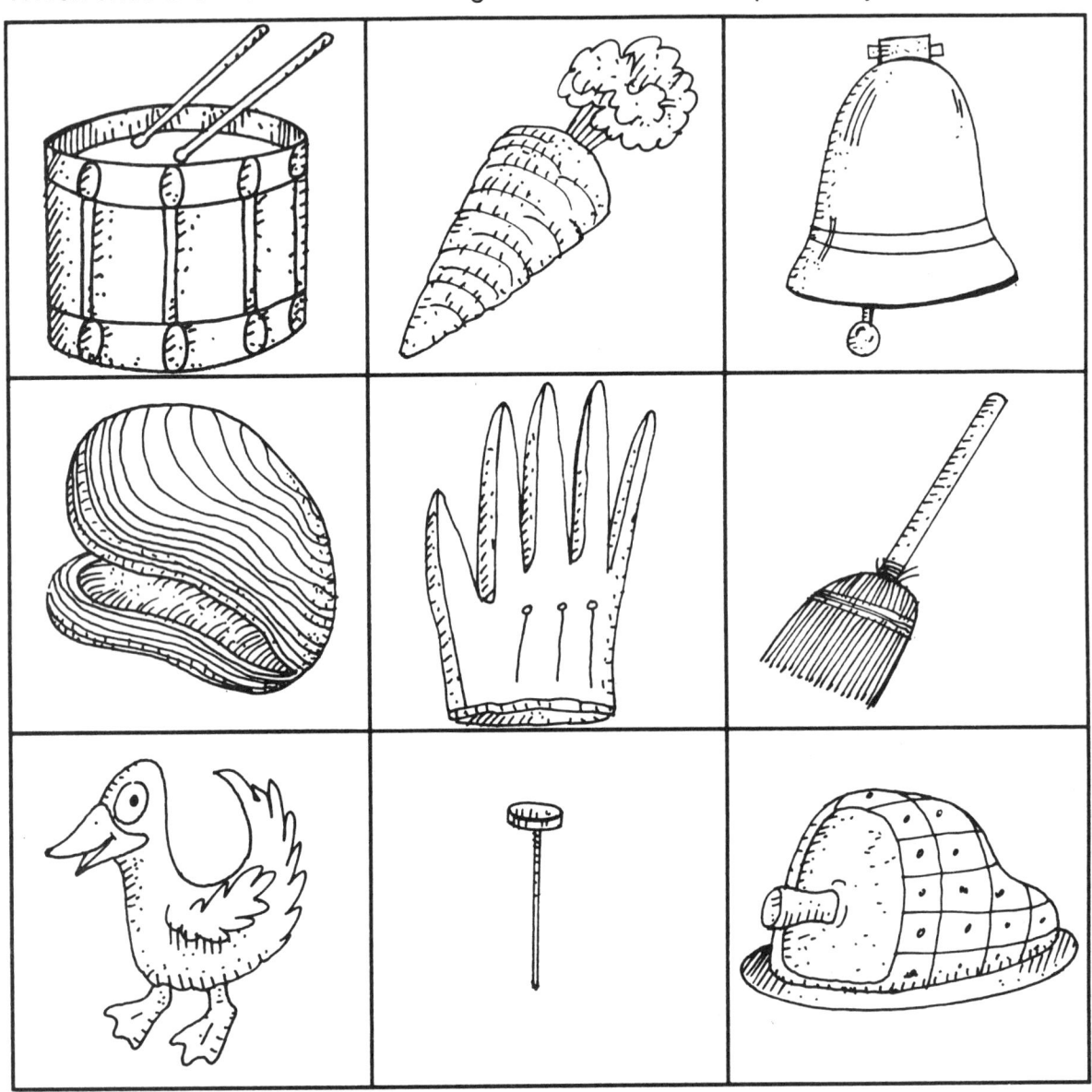

Skills: Recognition of the final consonant "m"; Auditory discrimination; Writing the letter "m"; Sound/symbol association

PHONICS SKILLS I

Final consonant: **l**

sea**l**

l

Which ones end with **l**? Color them orange. Color the other pictures purple.

Skills: Recognition of the final consonant "l"; Auditory discrimination; Writing the letter "l"; Sound/symbol association

PHONICS SKILLS I

Final consonant: **n**

moon

n

Which ones end with **n**? Color them brown. Color the other pictures blue.

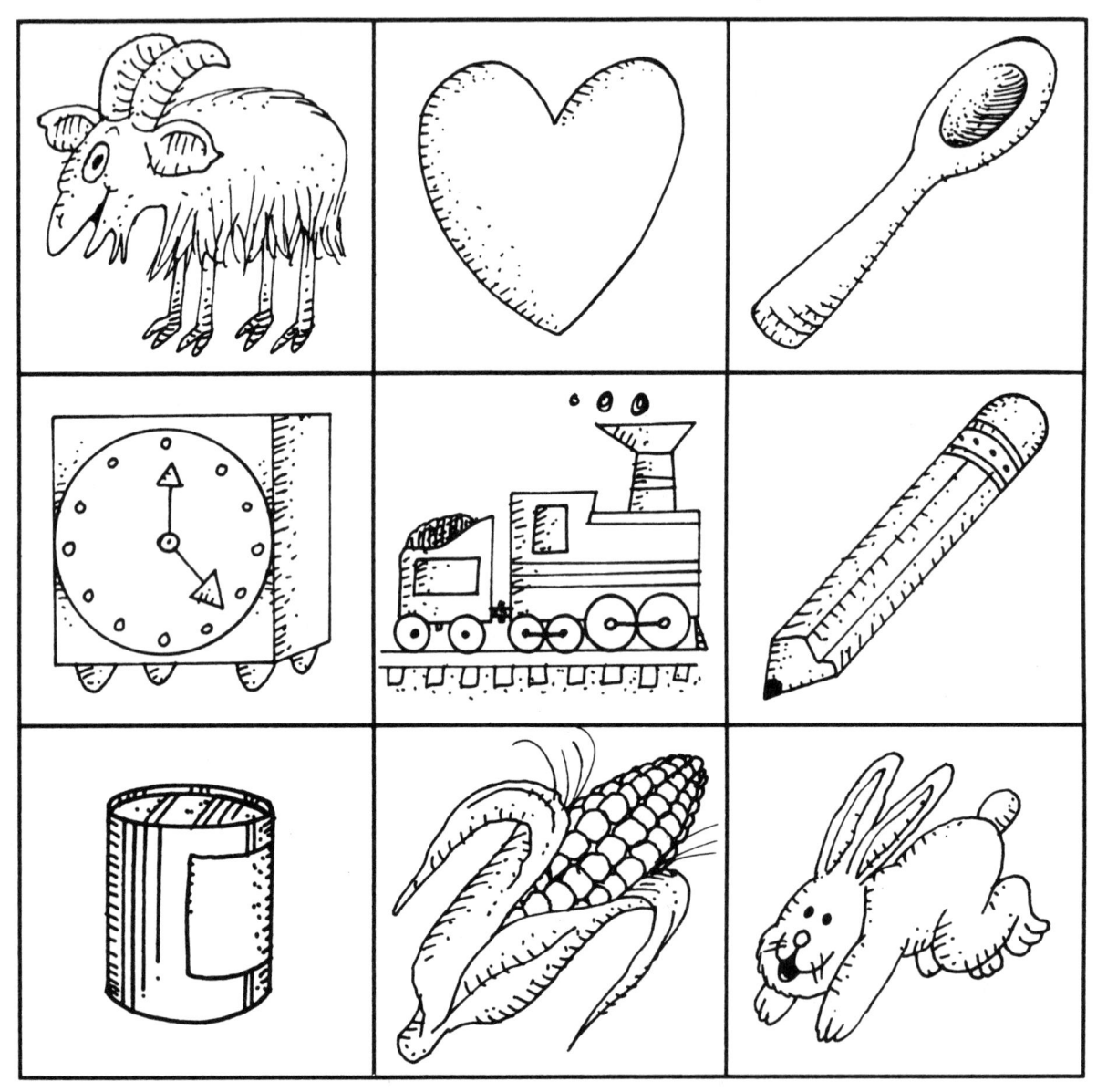

Skills: Recognition of the final consonant "n"; Auditory discrimination; Writing the letter "n"; Sound/symbol association

PHONICS SKILLS I

Final consonant: **p**

sheep

p p

Which ones end with **p**? Color them red. Color the other pictures blue.

Skills: Recognition of the final consonant "p"; Auditory discrimination; Writing the letter "p"; Sound/symbol association

PHONICS SKILLS I

Final consonant: **r**

car

r

Which ones end with **r**? Color them yellow. Color the other pictures green.

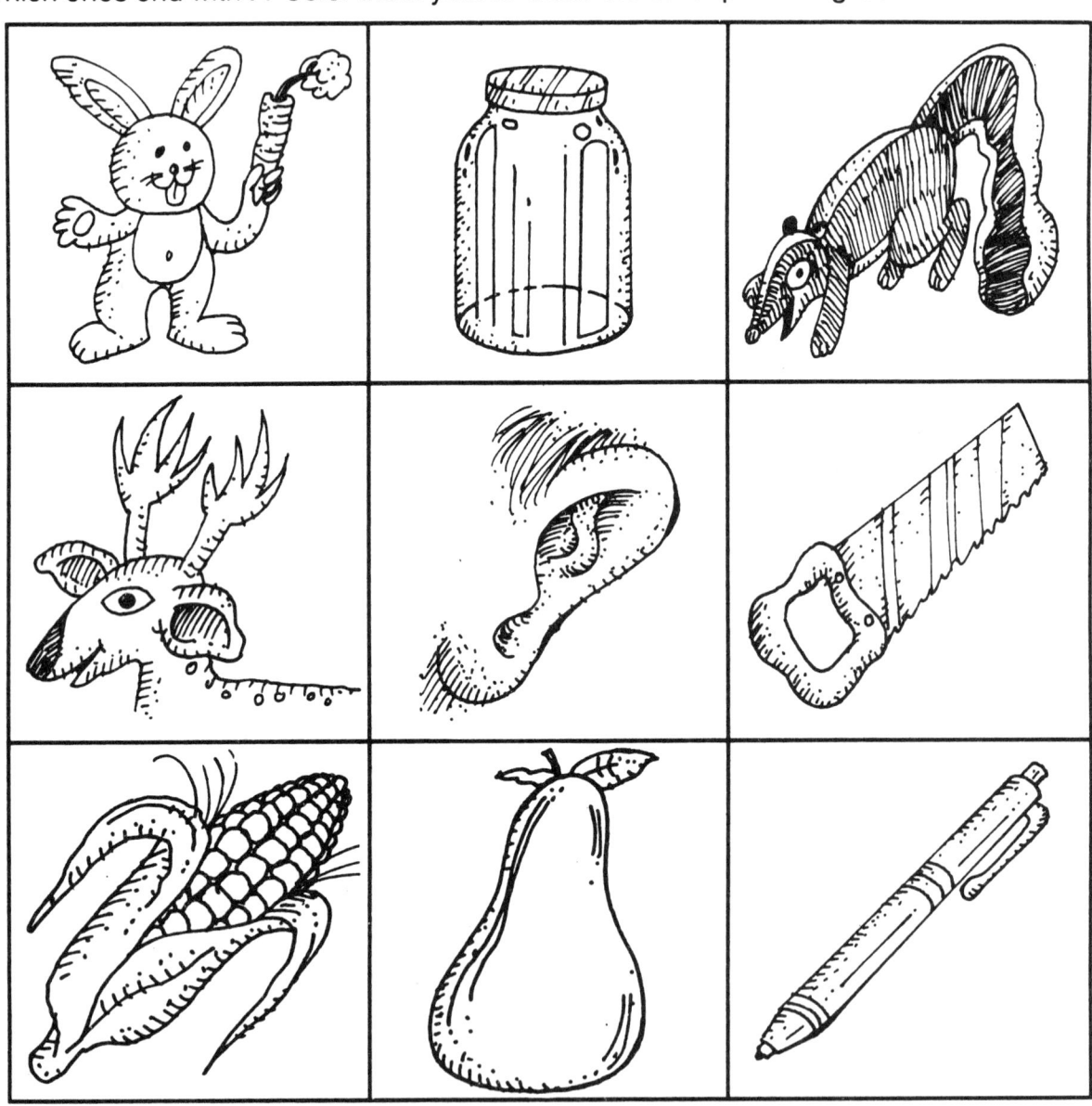

Skills: Recognition of the final consonant "r"; Auditory discrimination; Writing the letter "r"; Sound/symbol association

PHONICS SKILLS I

Final consonant: **t**

bat

t   t

Which ones end with **t**? Color them purple. Color the other pictures orange.

Skills: Recognition of the final consonant "t"; Auditory discrimination; Writing the letter "t"; Sound/symbol association

PHONICS SKILLS I

Final consonant: **X**

box

x x

Which ones end with **x**? Color them blue. Color the other pictures brown.

Skills: Recognition of the final consonant "x"; Auditory discrimination; Writing the letter "x"; Sound/symbol association

PHONICS SKILLS II

Short vowel: ă

Print the letters and words.

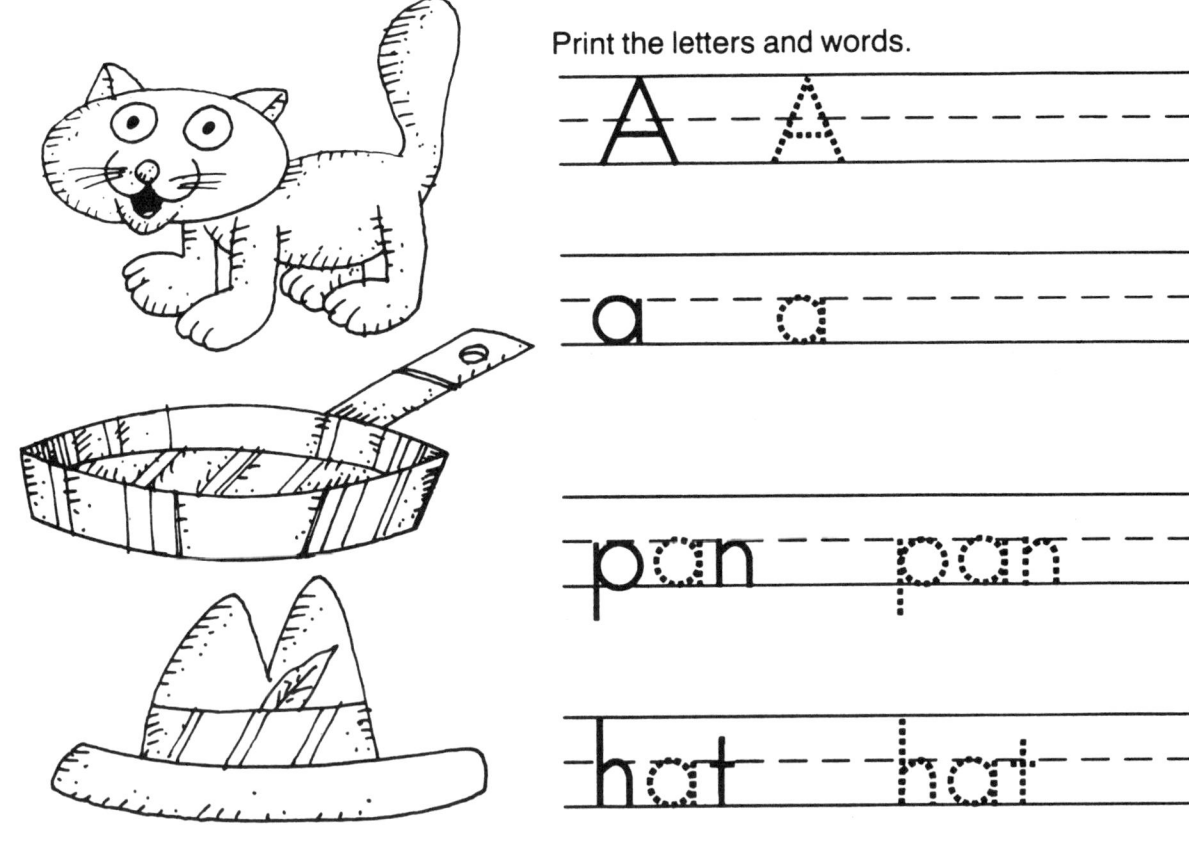

A   A

a   a

pan   pan

hat   hat

Finish the picture. Finish the word.

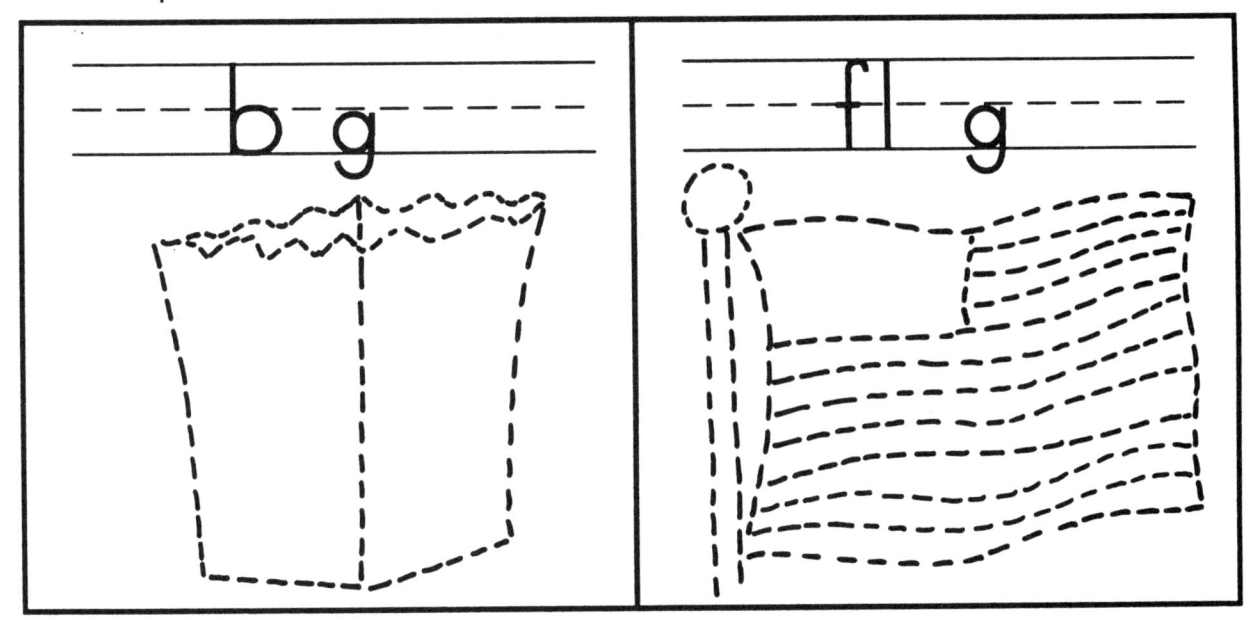

b_g

fl_g

Skills: Recognition of the short vowel "a"; Writing letters and words; Association between sounds, symbols, and words

PHONICS SKILLS II

Short vowel: ĕ

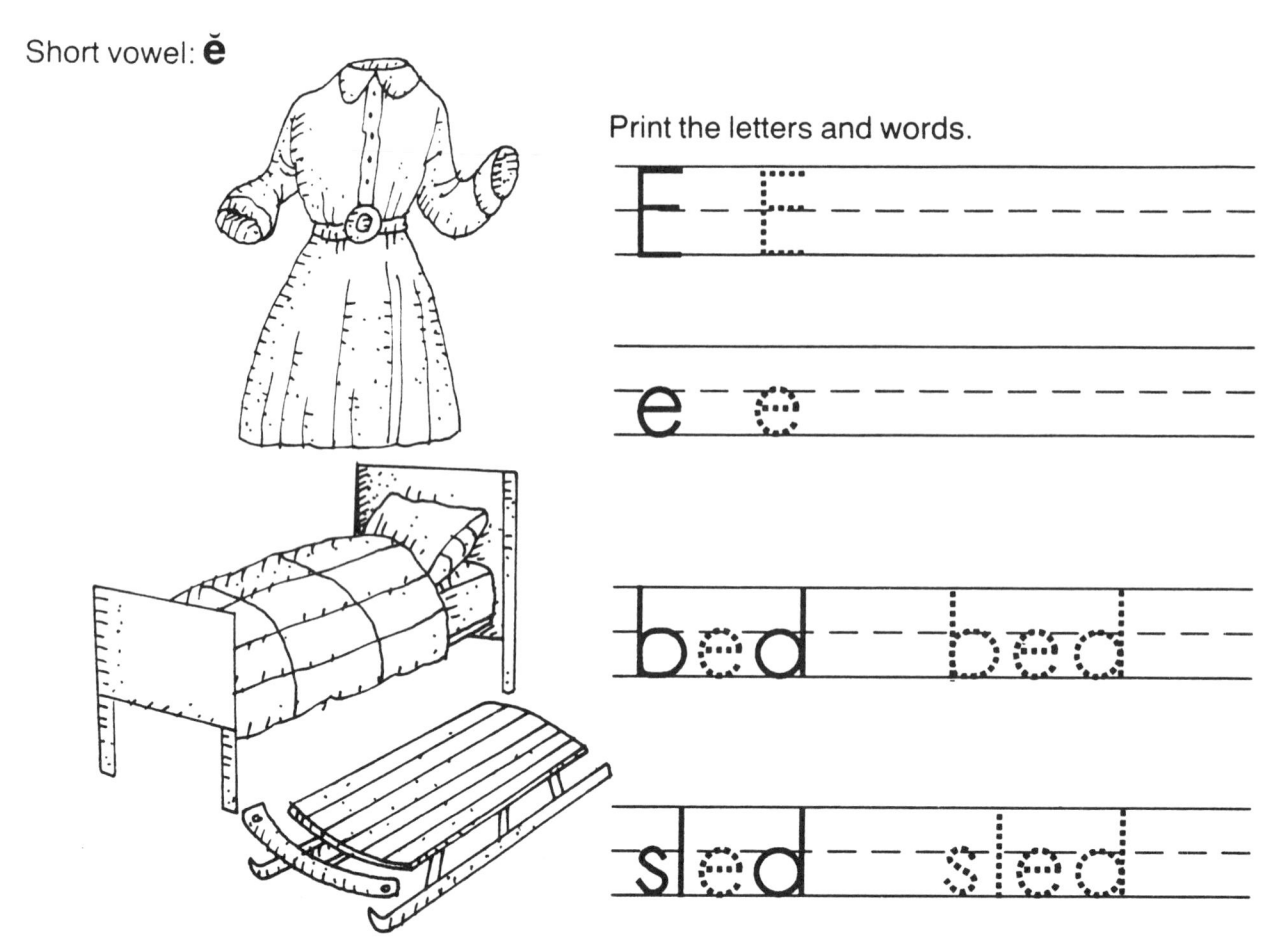

Print the letters and words.

E E

e e

bed bed

sled sled

Finish the picture. Finish the word.

w b

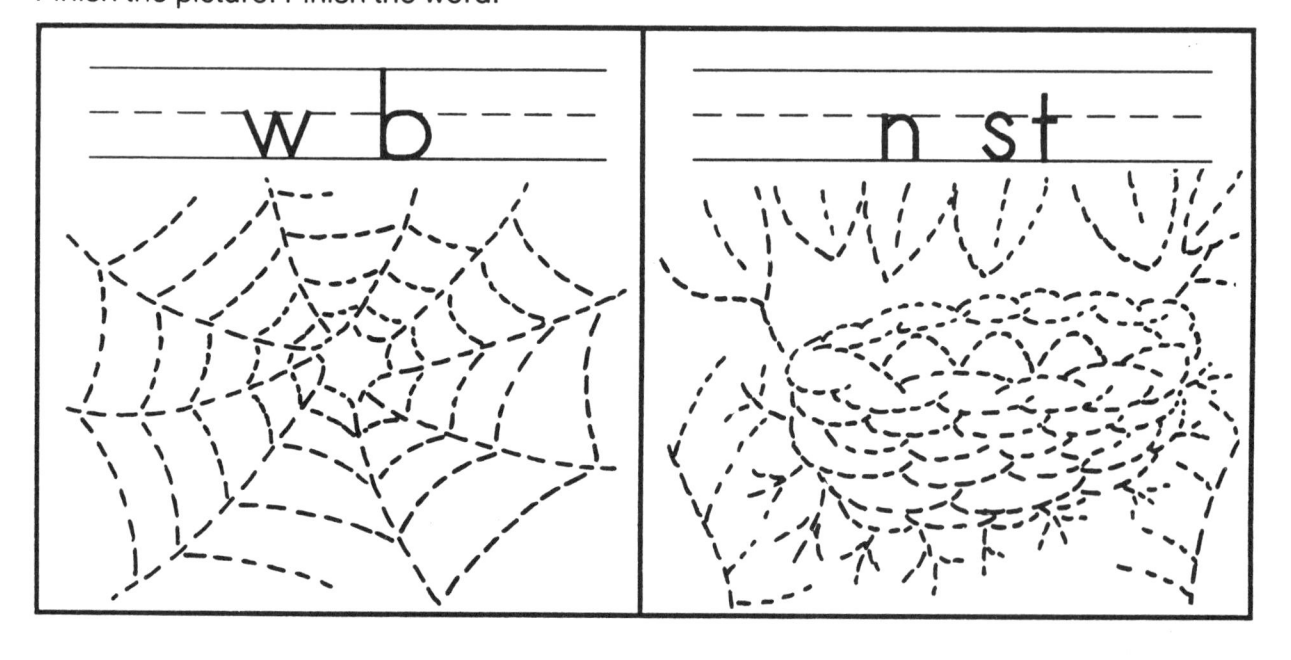

n st

Skills: Recognition of the short vowel "e"; Writing letters and words; Association between sounds, symbols, and words

PHONICS SKILLS II

Short vowel: ĭ

Print the letters and words.

I i

i i

pig pig

ship ship

Finish the picture. Finish the word.

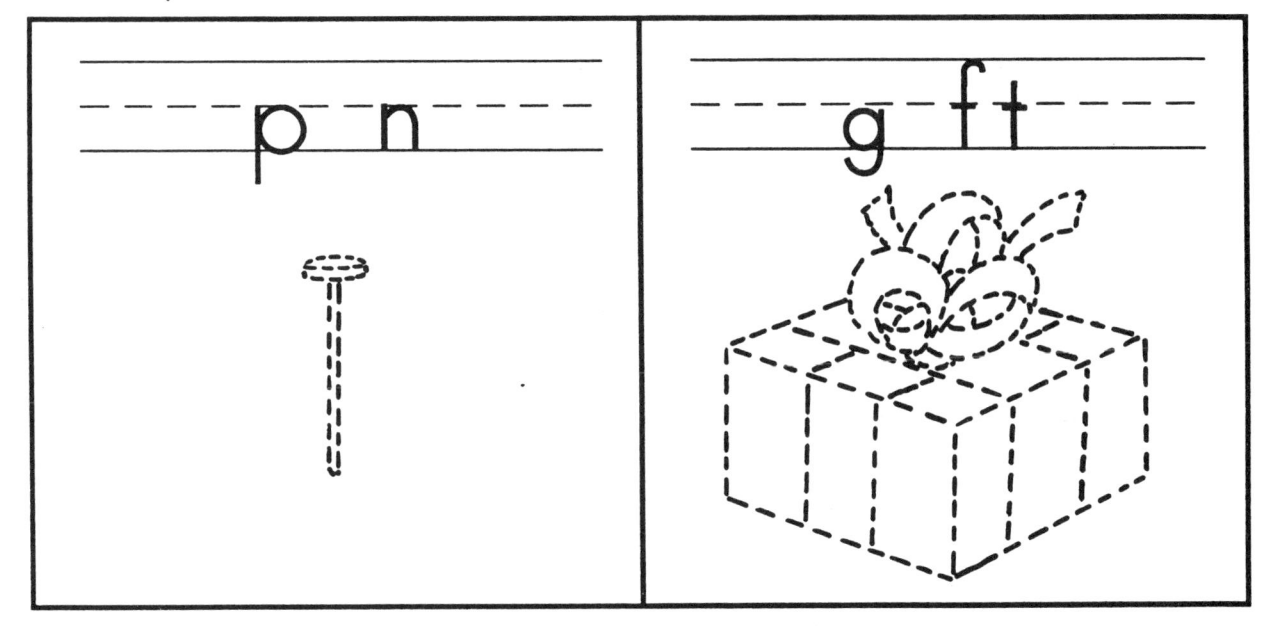

p _ n

g _ ft

Skills: Recognition of the short vowel "i"; Writing letters and words; Association between sounds, symbols, and words

PHONICS SKILLS II

Short vowel: **ŏ**

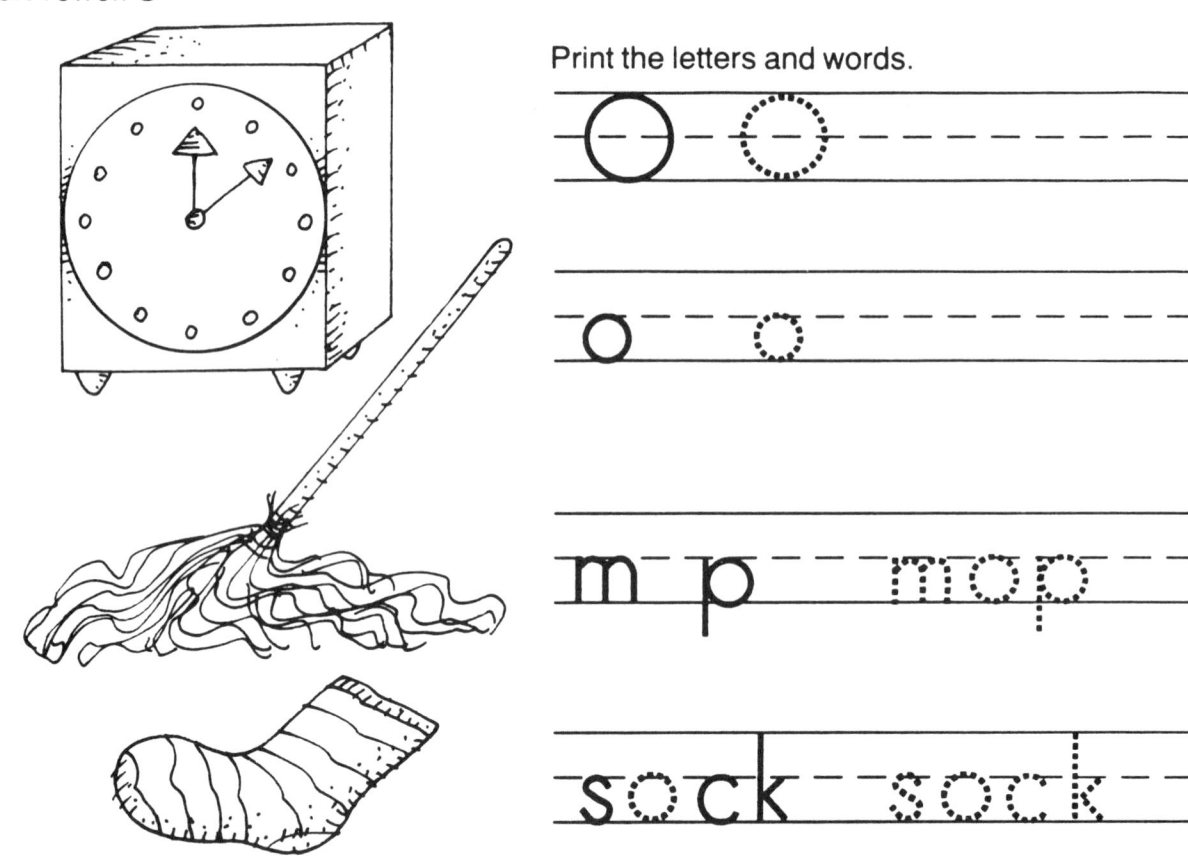

Print the letters and words.

O o

o o

m p   mop

sock   sock

Finish the picture. Finish the word.

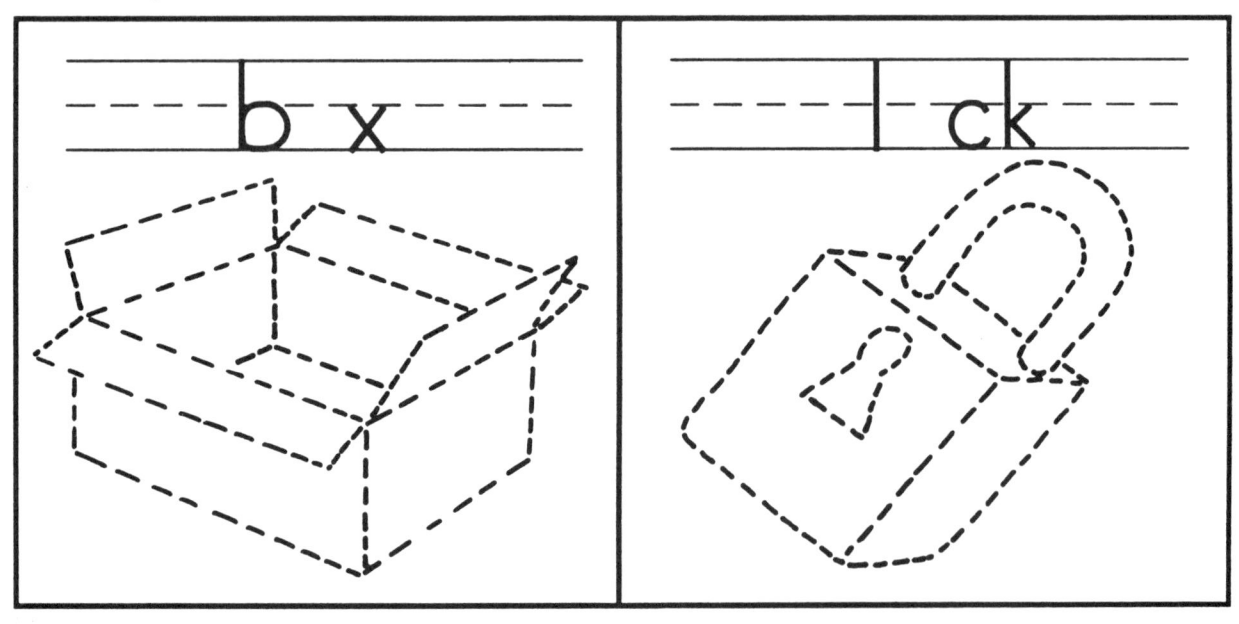

b x

l ck

Skills: Recognition of the short vowel "o"; Writing letters and words; Association between sounds, symbols, and words

PHONICS SKILLS II

Short vowel: ŭ

Print the letters and words.

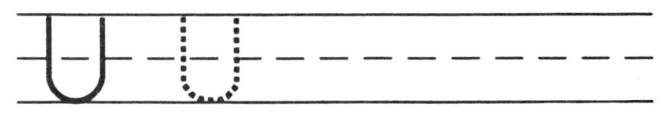

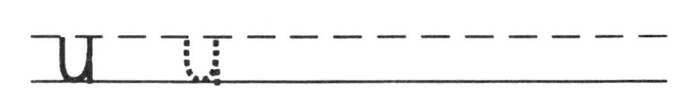

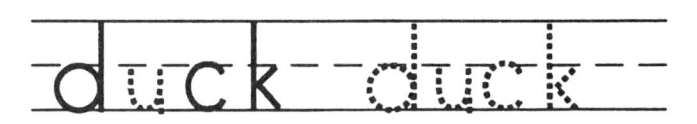

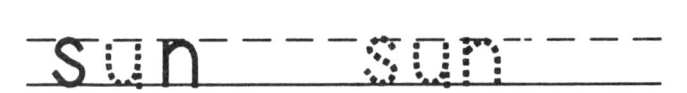

U U

u u

duck duck

sun sun

Finish the picture. Finish the word.

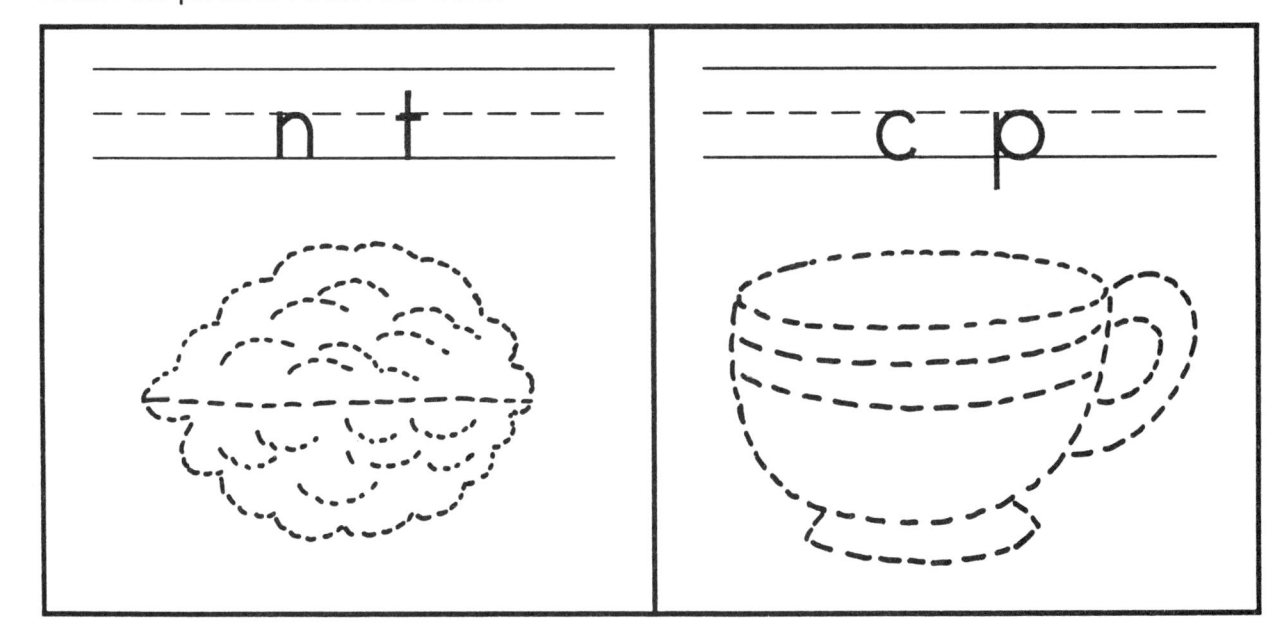

n t

c p

Skills: Recognition of the short vowel "u"; Writing letters and words; Association between sounds, symbols, and words

PHONICS SKILLS II

Long vowel: ā

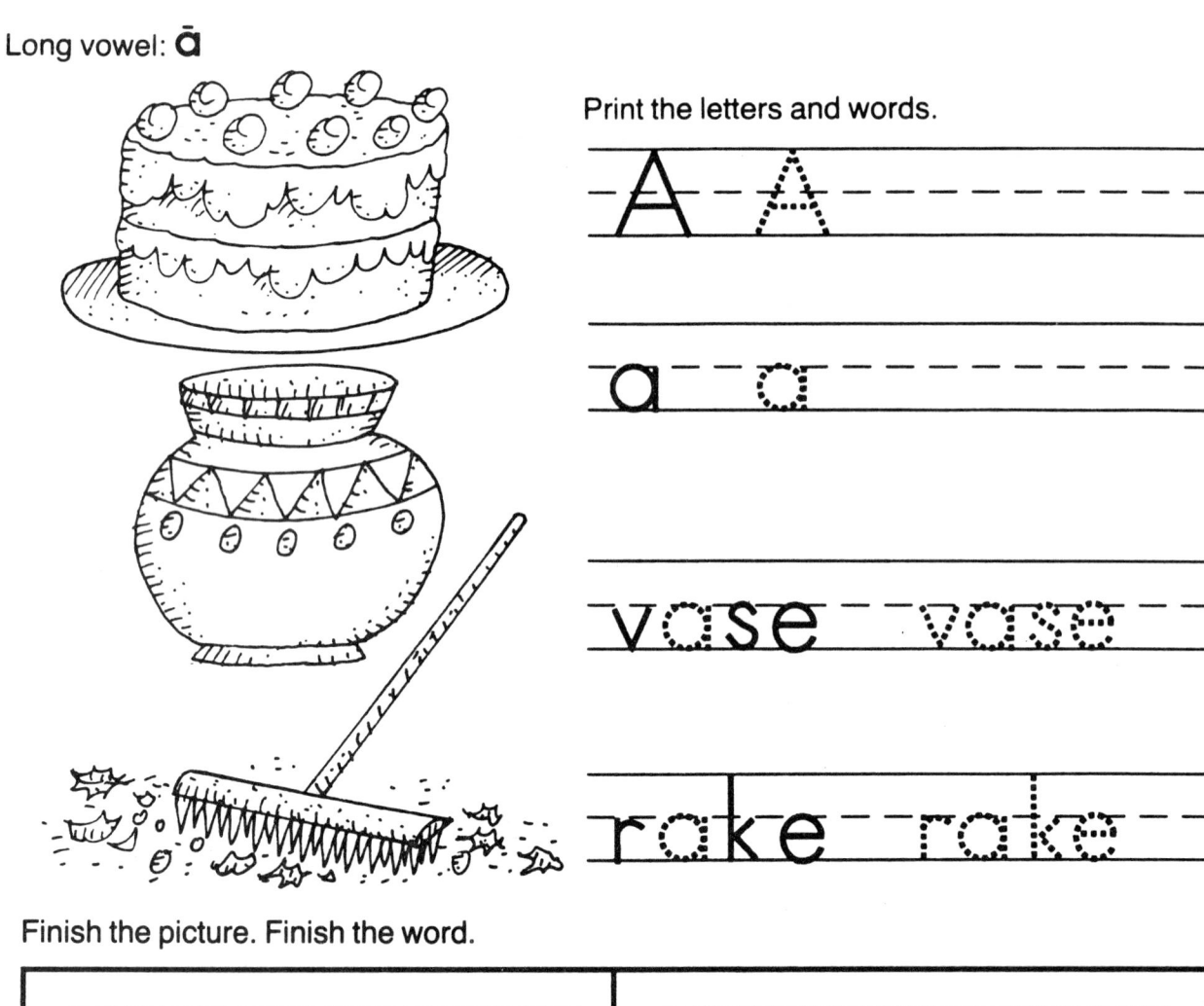

Print the letters and words.

A A

a a

vase vase

rake rake

Finish the picture. Finish the word.

sn_ke

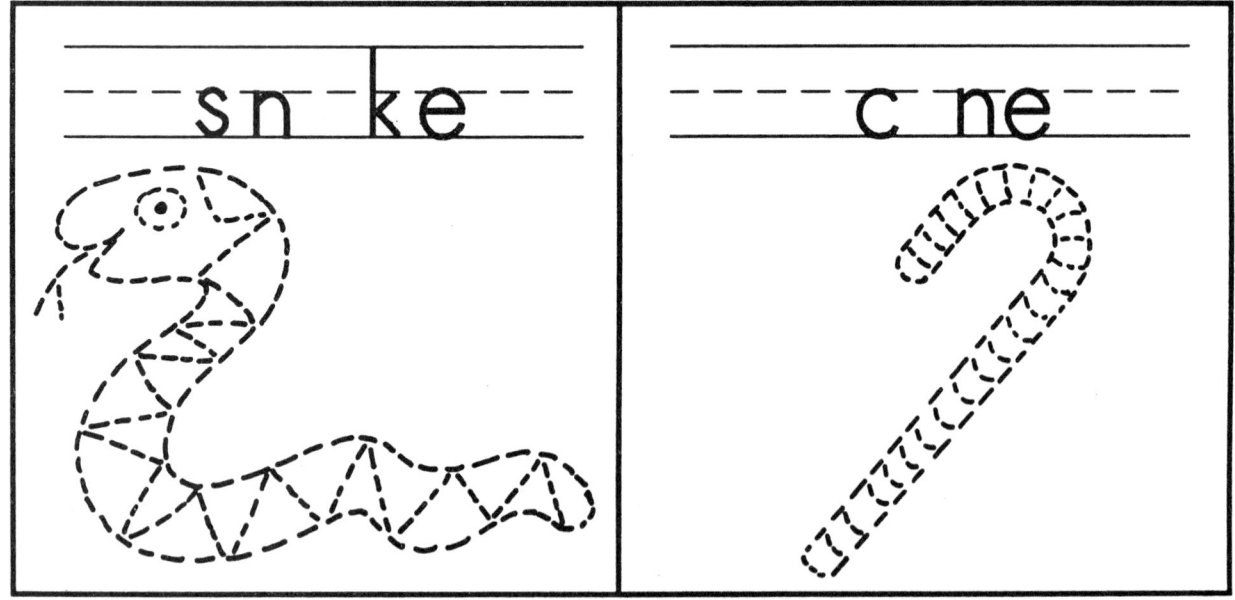

c_ne

Skills: Recognition of the long vowel "a"; Writing letters and words; Association between sounds, symbols, and words

PHONICS SKILLS II

Long vowel: **ē**

Print the letters and words.

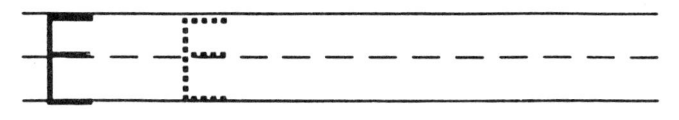

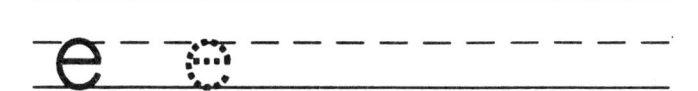

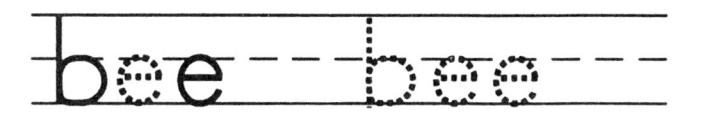

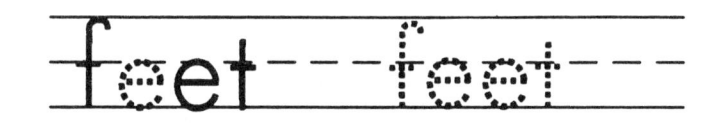

E E

e e

bee bee

feet feet

Finish the picture. Finish the word.

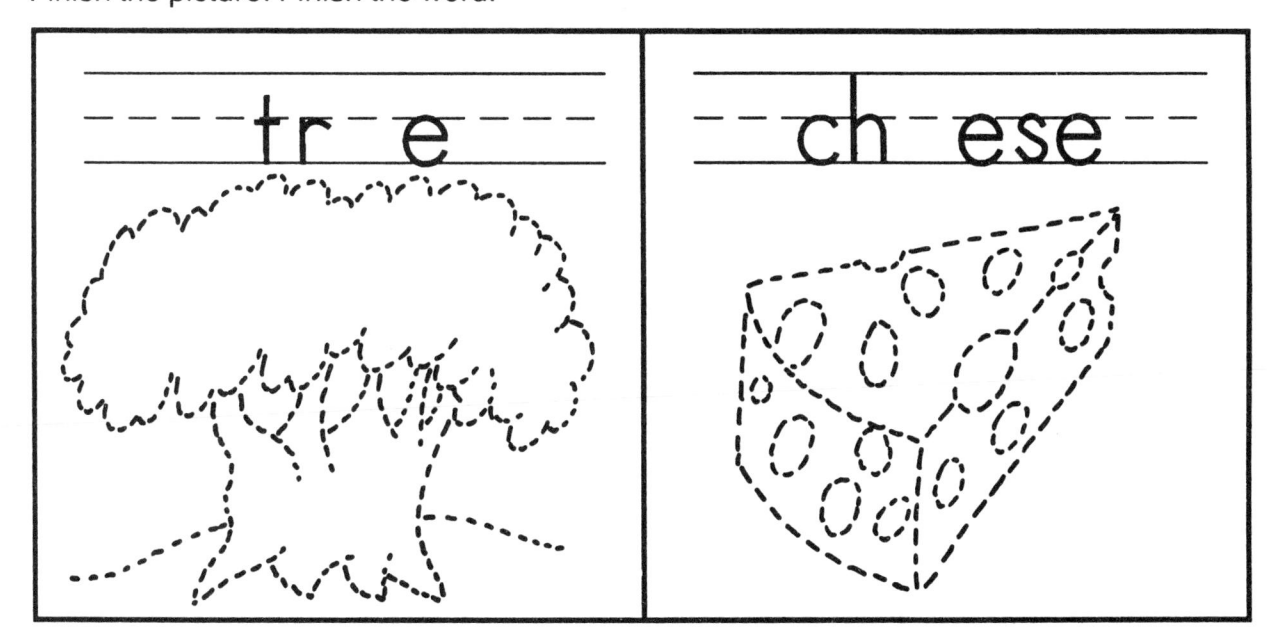

tr_e

ch_ese

Skills: Recognition of the long vowel "e"; Writing letters and words; Association between sounds, symbols, and words

PHONICS SKILLS II

Long vowel: ī

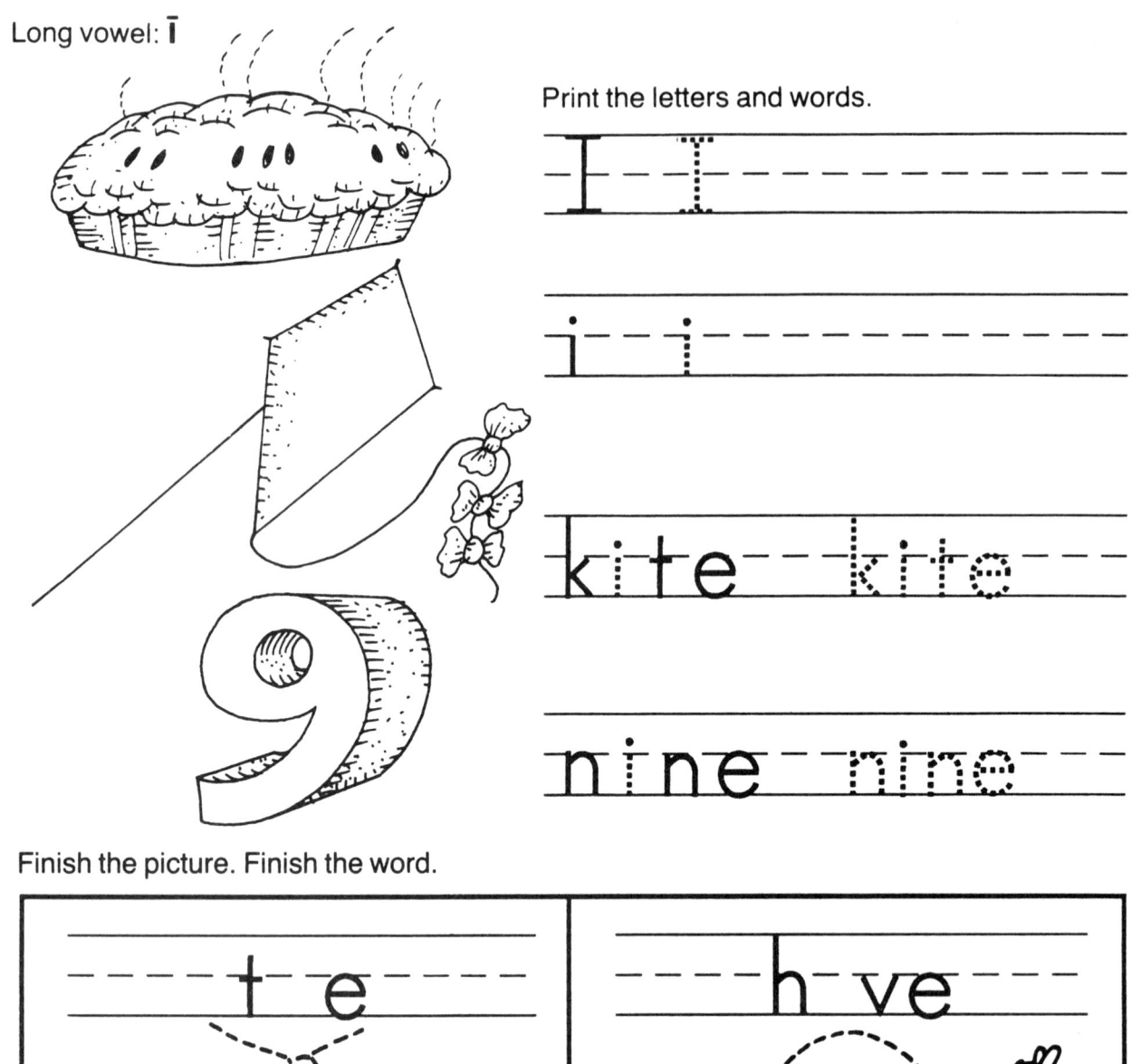

Print the letters and words.

I I

i i

kite kite

nine nine

Finish the picture. Finish the word.

t e

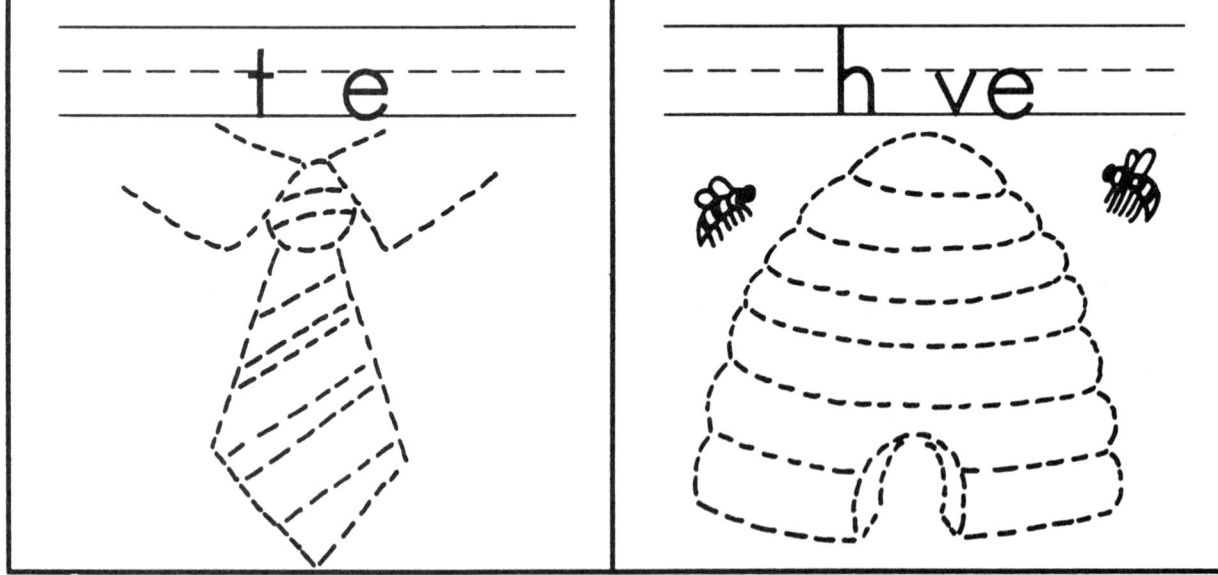

h ve

Skills: Recognition of the long vowel "i"; Writing letters and words; Association between sounds, symbols, and words

PHONICS SKILLS II

Long vowel: ō

Print the letters and words.

O   O

o   o

soap   soap

toe   toe

Finish the picture. Finish the word.

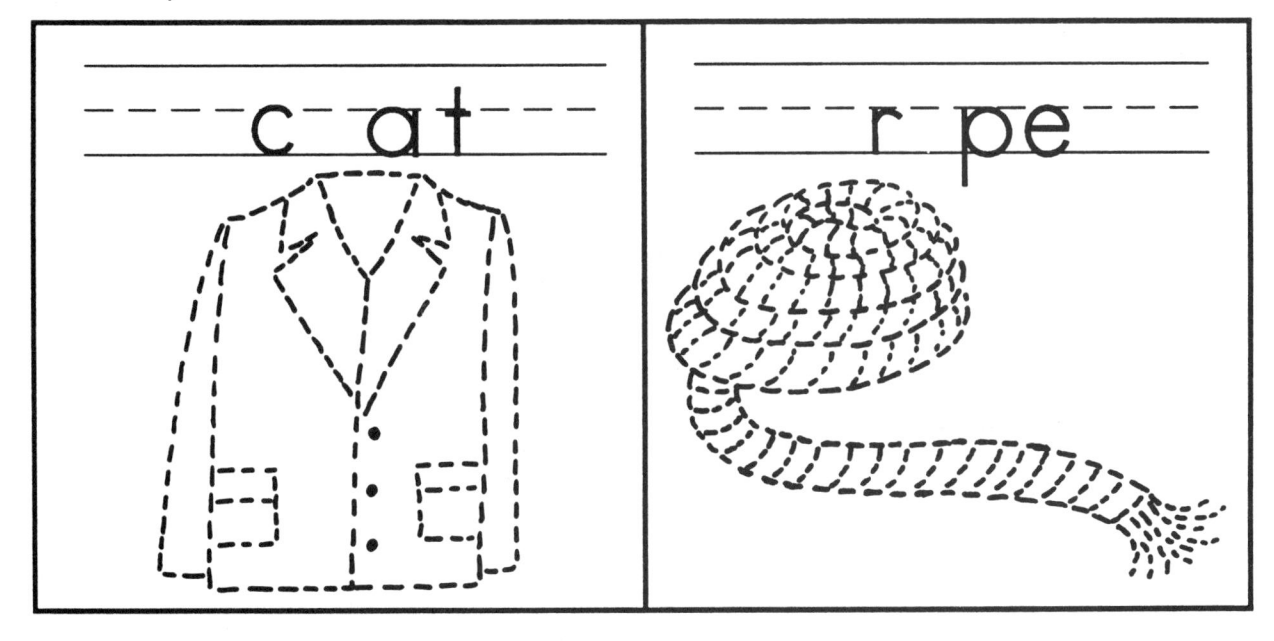

c at

r pe

Skills: Recognition of the long vowel "o"; Writing letters and words; Association between sounds, symbols, and words

PHONICS SKILLS II

Long vowel: ū

Print the letters and words.

U U

u u

ice cube ice cube

glue glue

Finish the picture. Finish the word.

m_le

fl_te

Skills: Recognition of the long vowel "u"; Writing letters and words; Association between sounds, symbols, and words

PHONICS SKILLS II

Initial consonant blends: **cl, cr**

c l ------------

c r ------------

Which ones begin with cl? Color them red. Which ones begin with cr? Color them blue.

Skills: Understanding that some consonants can be blended together; Sound/symbol association

PHONICS SKILLS II

Initial consonant blends: **bl, br**

bl

br

Which ones begin with bl? Color them red. Which ones begin with br? Color them blue.

Skills: Understanding that some consonants can be blended together; Sound/symbol association

PHONICS SKILLS II

Initial consonant blends: **dr**, **tr**

dr

tr

Which ones begin with dr? Color them red. Which ones begin with tr? Color them blue.

Skills: Understanding that some consonants can be blended together; Sound/symbol association

PHONICS SKILLS II

Initial consonant blends: **sk, sl**

Which ones begin with sk? Color them red. Which ones begin with sl? Color them blue.

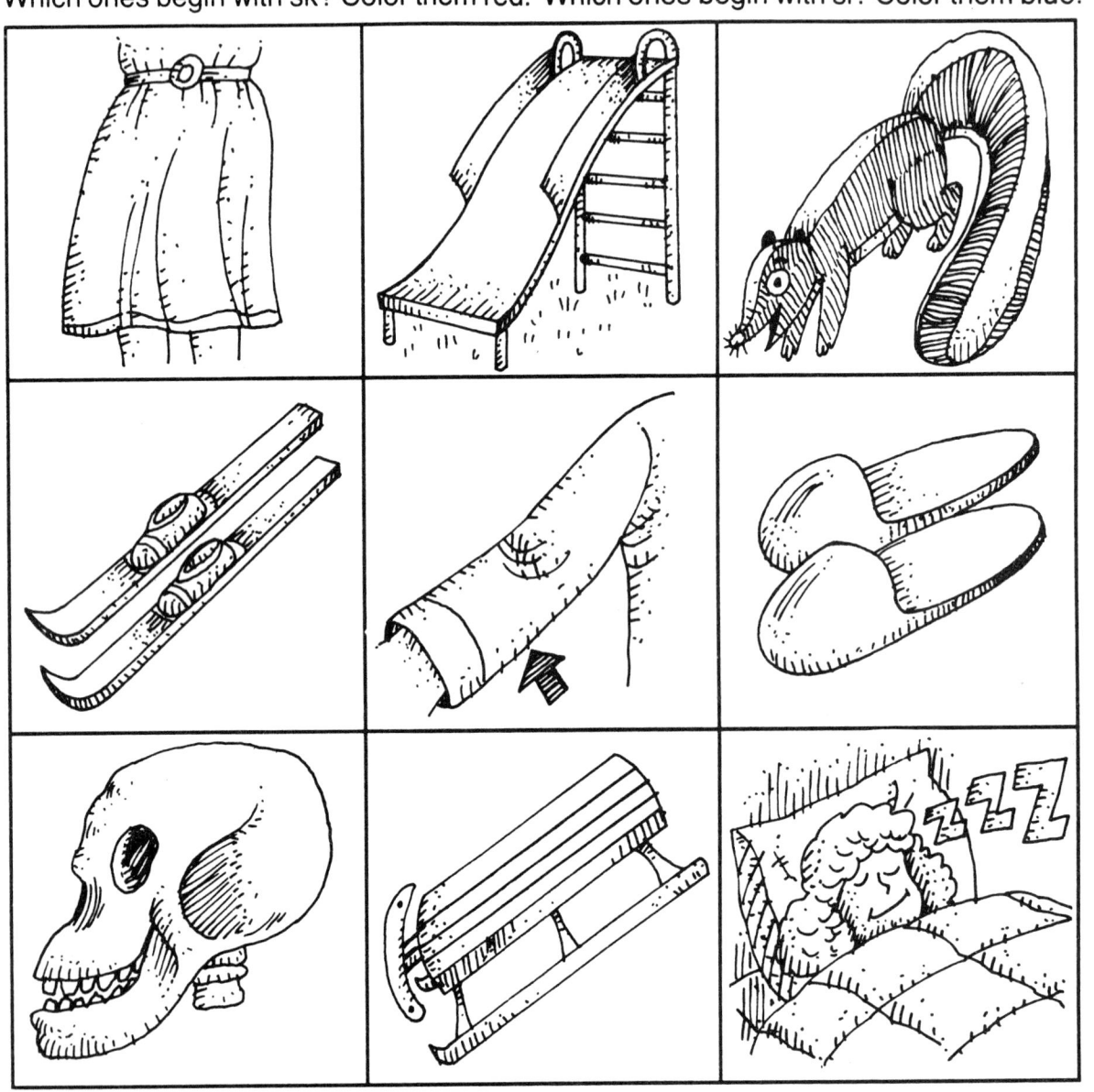

Skills: Understanding that some consonants can be blended together; Sound/symbol association

PHONICS SKILLS II

Initial consonant blends: **st**, **sp**

st

sp

Which ones begin with st? Color them red. Which ones begin with sp? Color them blue.

Skills: Understanding that some consonants can be blended together; Sound/symbol association

PHONICS SKILLS II

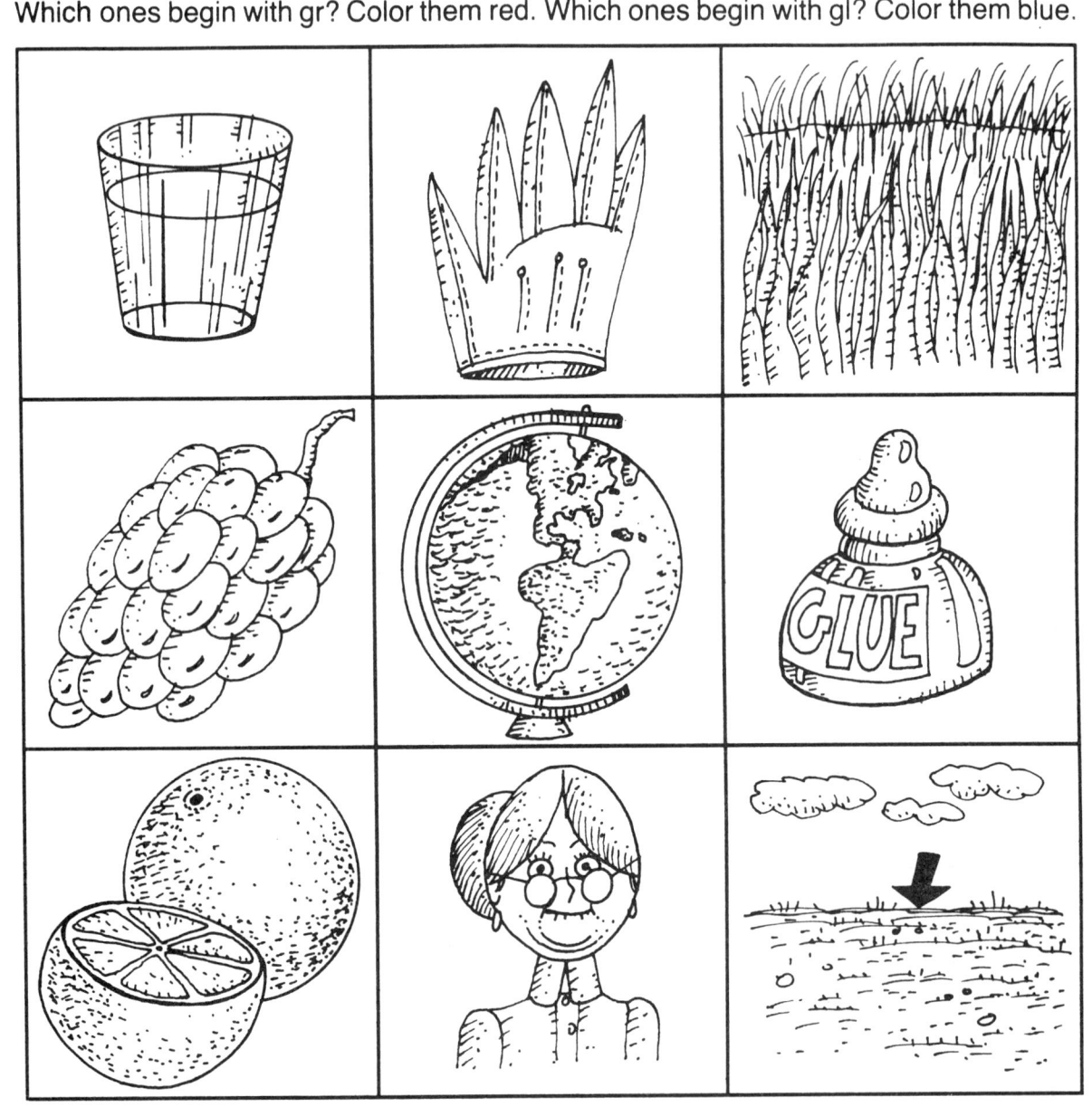

Initial consonant blends: **gr**, **gl**

gr

gl

Which ones begin with gr? Color them red. Which ones begin with gl? Color them blue.

Skills: Understanding that some consonants can be blended together; Sound/symbol association

PHONICS SKILLS II

Initial consonant blends: **pl**, **pr**

pl

pr

Which ones begin with pl? Color them red. Which ones begin with pr? Color them blue.

Skills: Understanding that some consonants can be blended together; Sound/symbol association

PHONICS SKILLS II

Initial consonant blends: **sn**, **sw**

sn

sw

Which ones begin with sn? Color them red. Which ones begin with sw? Color them blue.

Skills: Understanding that some consonants can be blended together; Sound/symbol association

PHONICS SKILLS II

Initial consonant blends: **fr, fl**

Which ones begin with fr? Color them red. Which ones begin with fl? Color them blue.

Skills: Understanding that some consonants can be blended together; Sound/symbol association

PHONICS SKILLS II

Consonant digraph: **sh**

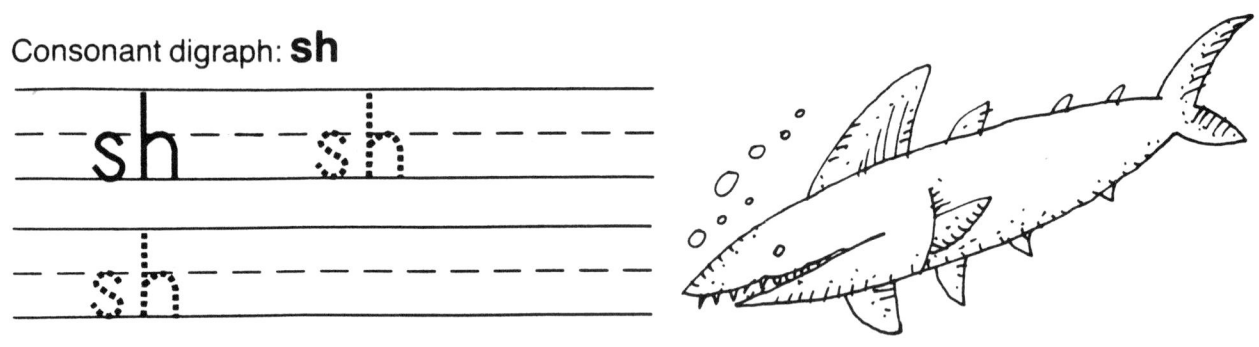

sh   sh

sh

Which ones begin with sh? Color them orange. Color the other pictures purple.

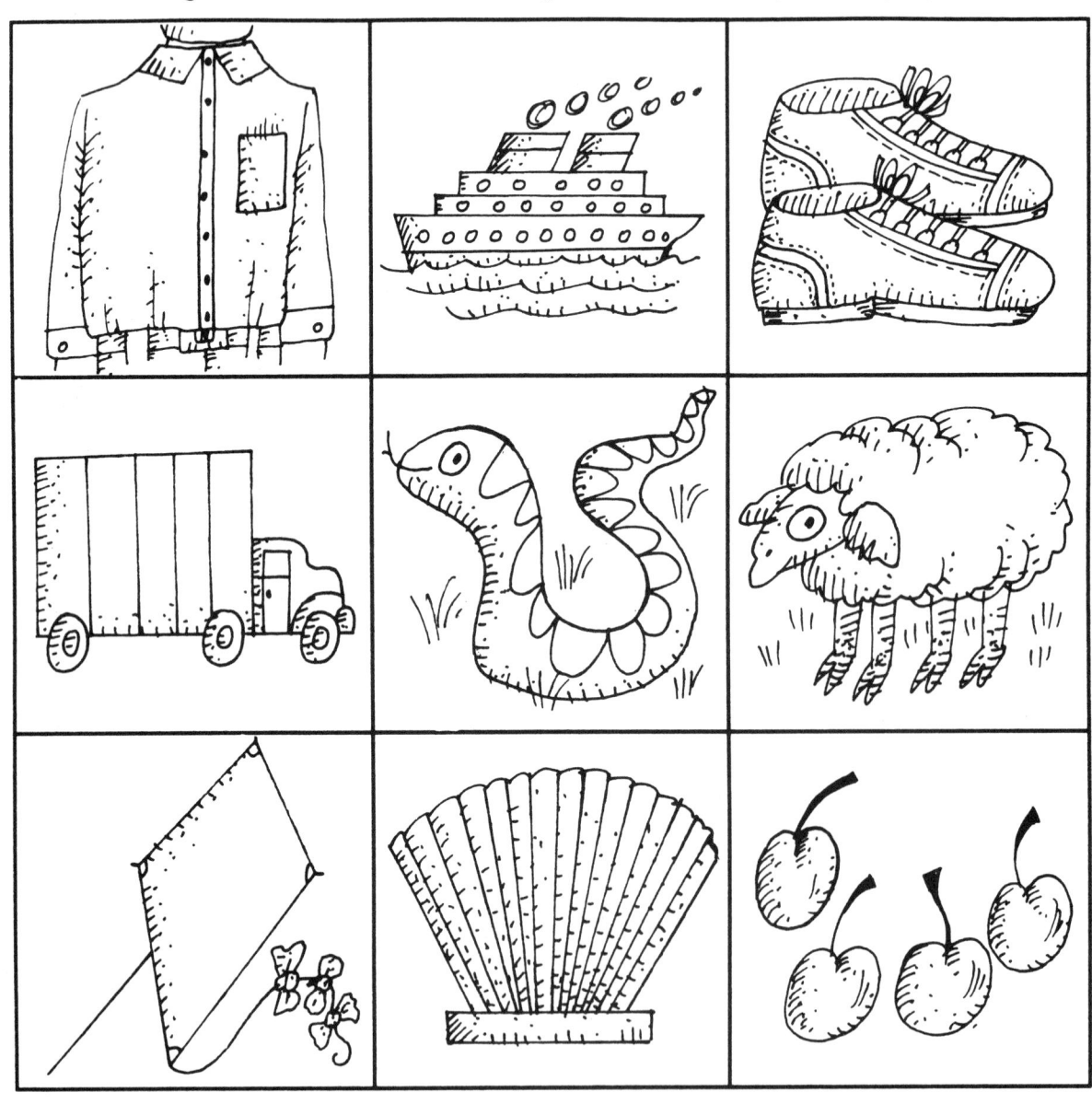

Skills: Recognizing and understanding consonant digraphs; Sound/symbol association

PHONICS SKILLS II

Consonant digraph: **th**

th th

th

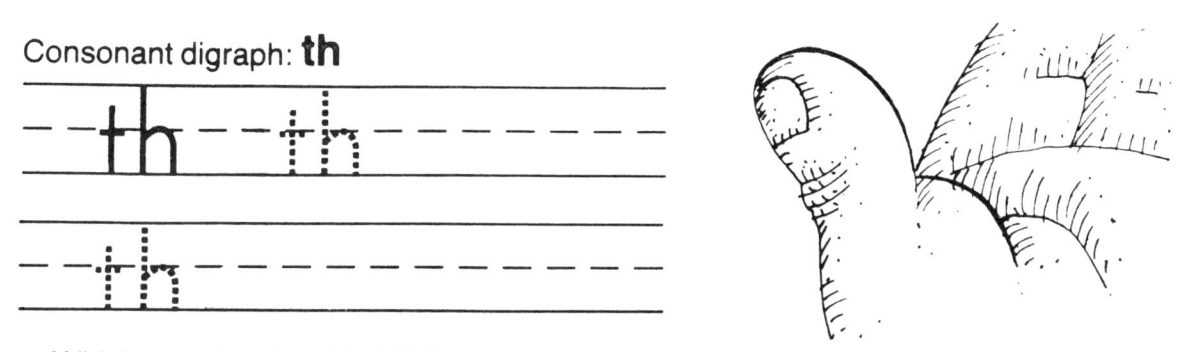

Which ones begin with th? Color them brown. Color the other pictures green.

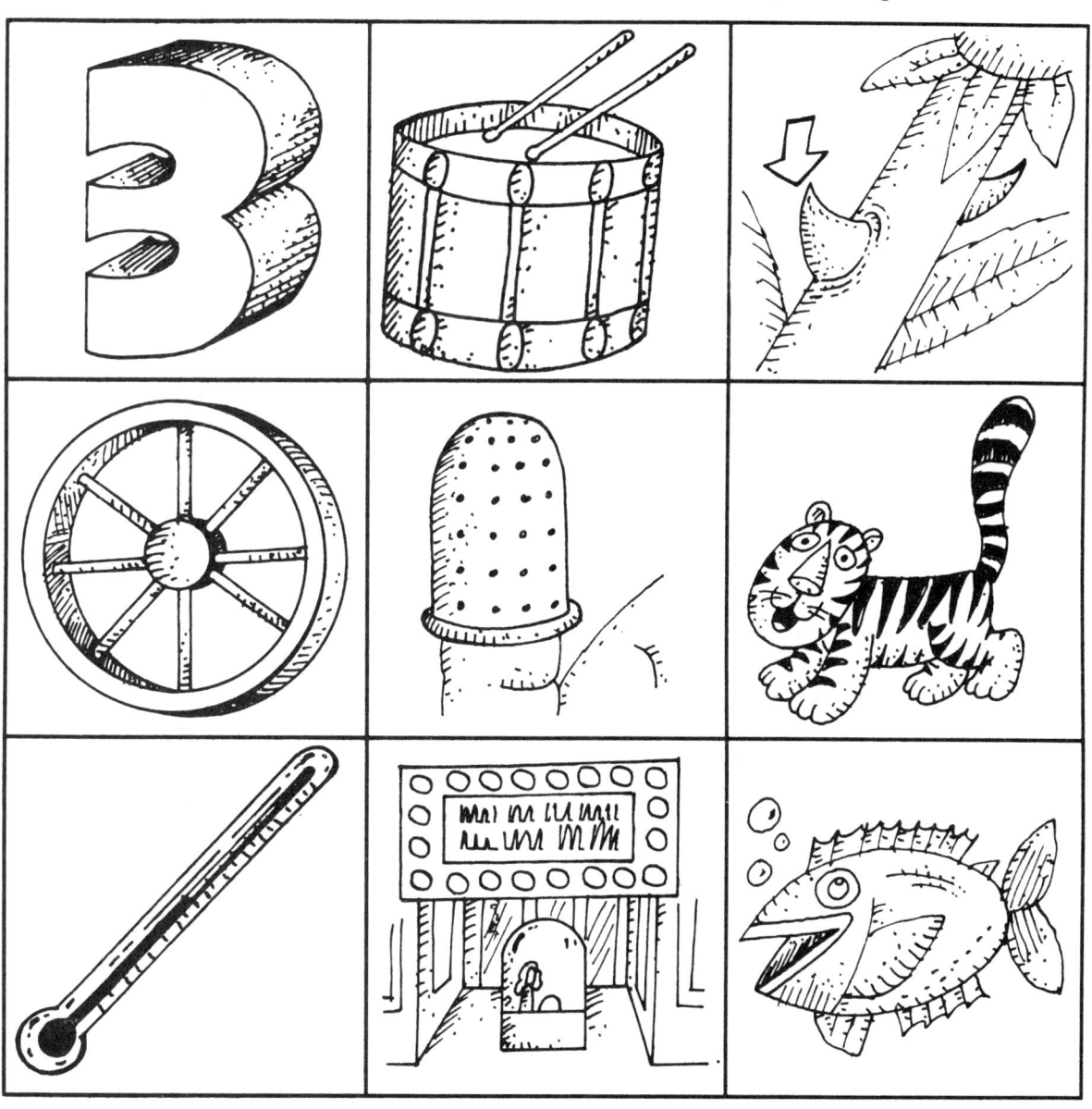

Skills: Recognizing and understanding consonant digraphs; Sound/symbol association

PHONICS SKILLS II

Consonant digraph: **wh**

wh wh

wh

Which ones begin with wh? Color them red. Color the other pictures blue.

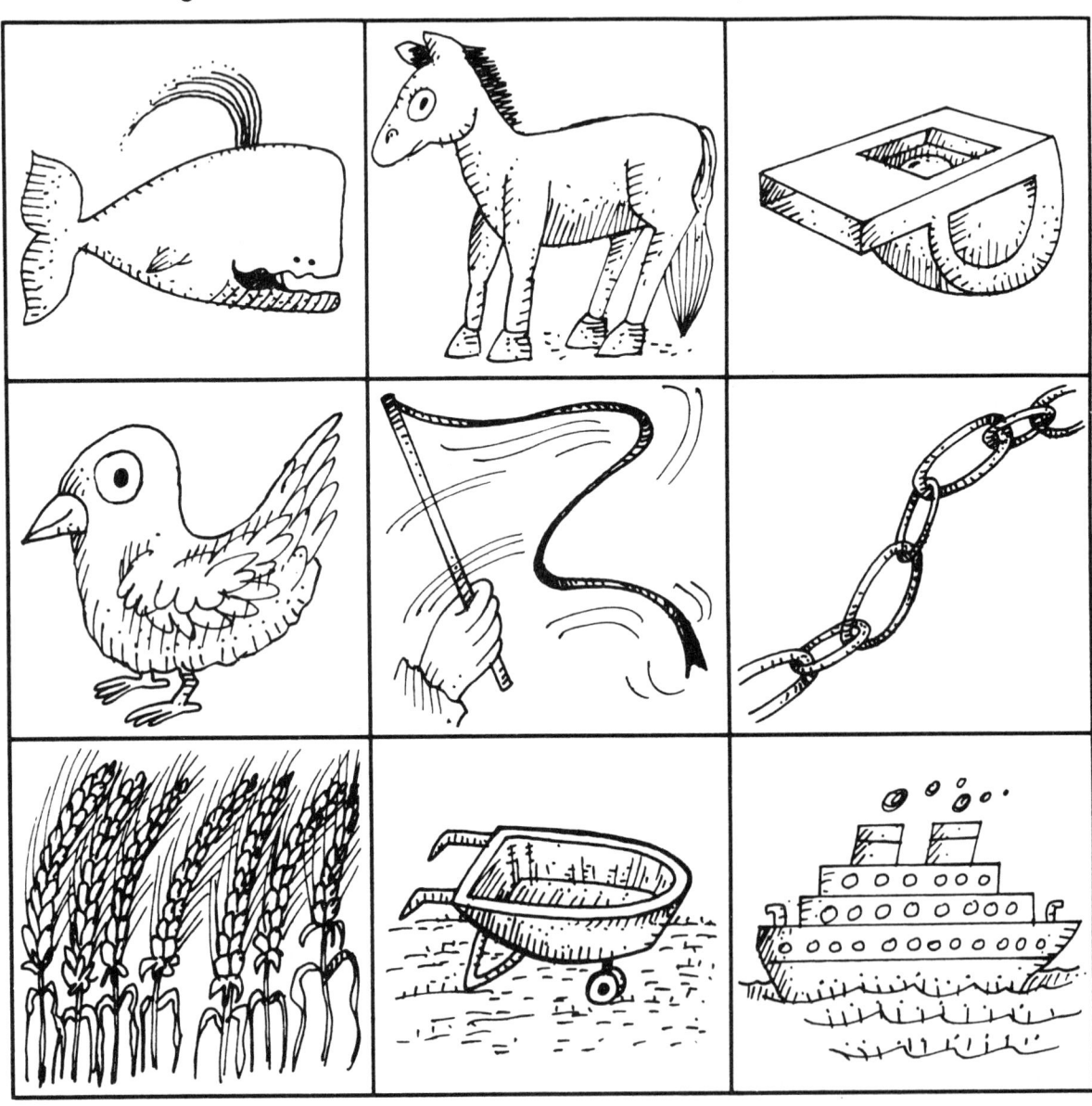

Skills: Recognizing and understanding consonant digraphs; Sound/symbol association

PHONICS SKILLS II

Consonant digraph: **ch**

ch   ch

ch

Which ones begins with ch? Color them brown. Color the other pictures red.

Skills: Recognizing and understanding consonant digraphs; Sound/symbol association

PUTTING WORDS TOGETHER

The word **and** helps things go together.

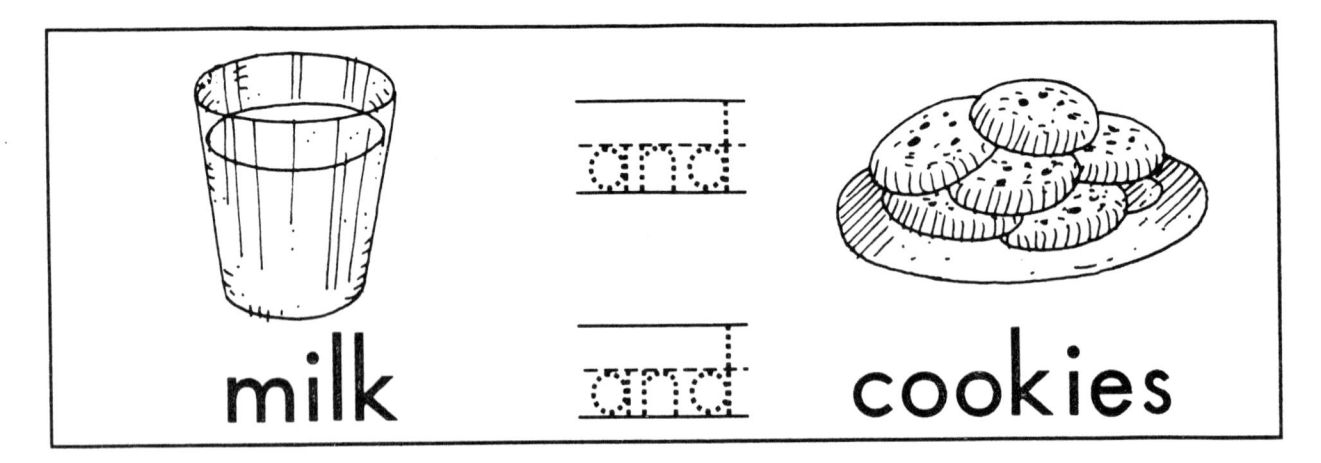

milk   and   cookies

Trace the word **and**. Then name the things that go together.

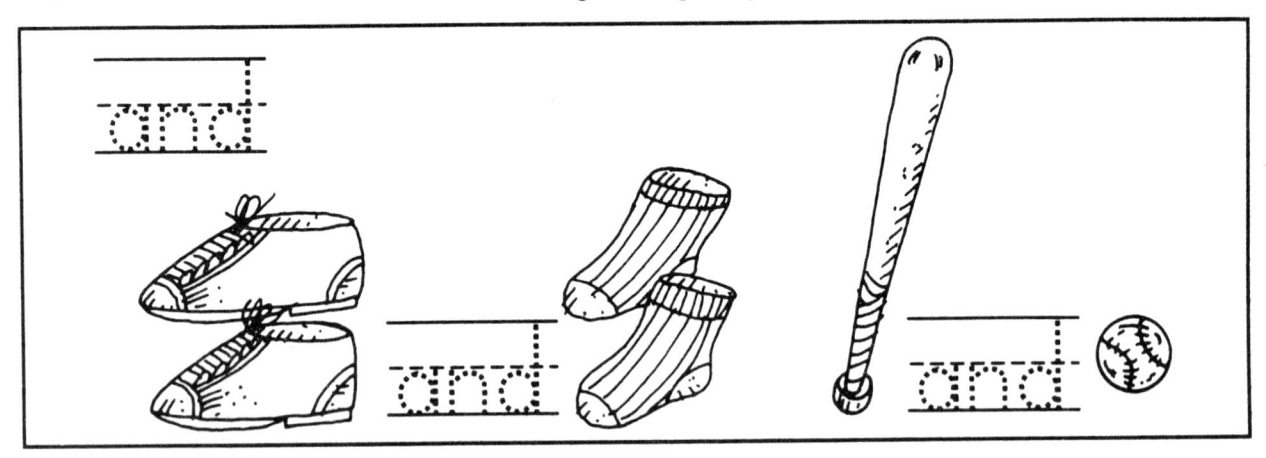

and

and

Draw two other things that go together. Then write the word **and**.

Skills: Spelling, writing and using sight vocabulary

294

PUTTING WORDS TOGETHER

Trace and read the words.

a giraffe   an elephant   the cage

Trace and write the words.

a

an

the

Skills: Spelling, writing and using sight vocabulary

PUTTING WORDS TOGETHER

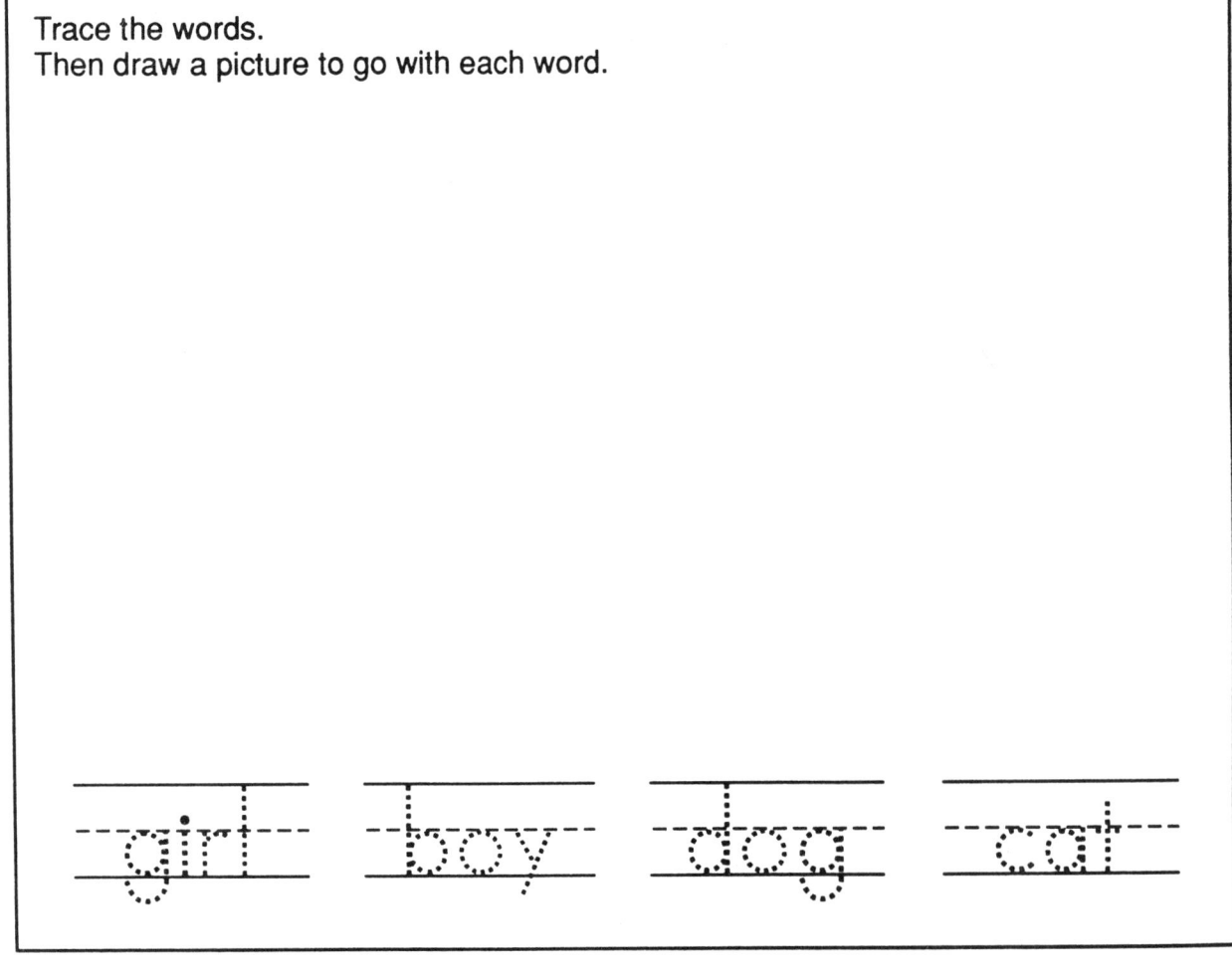

Read the words.

cat

dog

boy

girl

Trace the words.
Then draw a picture to go with each word.

girl boy dog cat

Skills: Spelling, writing and using sight vocabulary

PUTTING WORDS TOGETHER

Read the words.

mother   brother   father

Look at who won each medal.
Write the names of the winners.

mother

Skills: Spelling, writing and using sight vocabulary

PUTTING WORDS TOGETHER

Read the words.

pig

cow

duck

Connect the dots.
Write the name of each animal.

Skills: Spelling, writing and using sight vocabulary

PUTTING WORDS TOGETHER

Read the words.

car

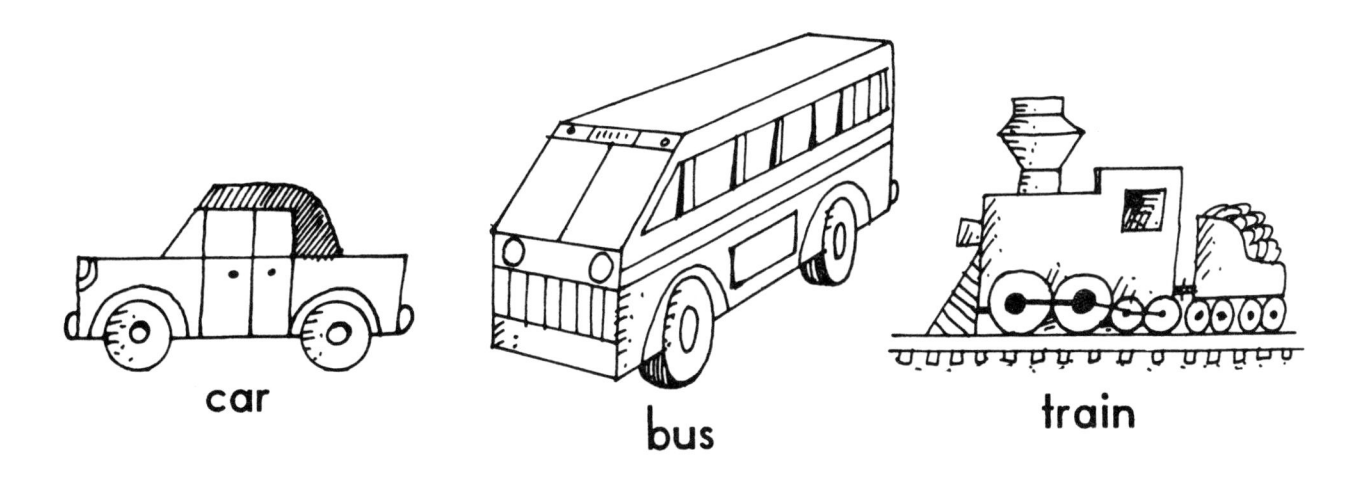

bus

train

Connect the dots.
Write the name of each vehicle.

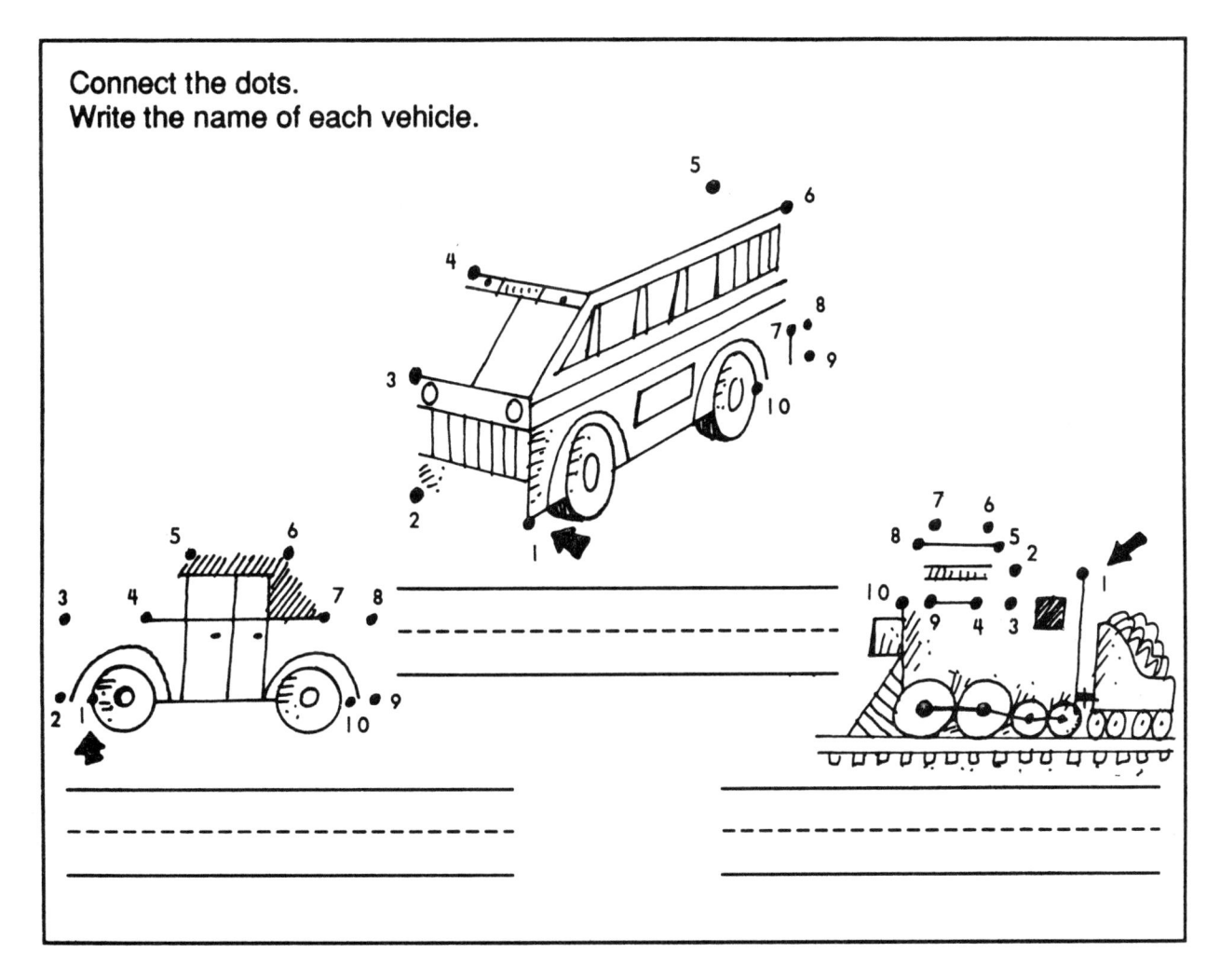

Skills: Spelling, writing and using sight vocabulary

PUTTING WORDS TOGETHER

Trace the words.

sit   go   play   read

Look at each picture and the list of words.
Then draw a line from each word to the matching picture.

sit

go

play

read

Skills: Spelling and using sight vocabulary

PUTTING WORDS TOGETHER

Trace the words.

sad   happy   old   young

Look at each picture and the list of words.
Then draw a line from each word to the matching picture.

sad
happy
old
young

Skills: Spelling and using sight vocabulary

PUTTING WORDS TOGETHER

Trace the words.

cold   hot   big   little

Look at each picture and the list of words.
Then draw a line from each word to the matching picture.

cold
hot
big
little

Skills: Spelling and using sight vocabulary

PUTTING WORDS TOGETHER

Read the words.

fly

jump

run

Trace each word. Look at each picture.
Then draw a line from each word to the matching picture.

run

jump

fly

Skills: Spelling, writing and using sight vocabulary

PUTTING WORDS TOGETHER

Trace the words.

will   can   is   not

Find and circle each word in this puzzle.

will
can
is
not

M F U W I L L E
D I S R X A K J
V T U C A N R S
Q Y T P N O T G

Skills: Spelling and using sight vocabulary

PUTTING WORDS TOGETHER

Trace the words.

have   come   are   am

Find and circle each word in this puzzle.

have   come   are   am

```
T B H A V E K R
A M S X W L O Y
D R E V C O M E
A R E G V X M G
```

Skills: Spelling and using sight vocabulary

PUTTING WORDS TOGETHER

Read the words.

on
off

in
out

Look at each picture.
Write the correct word in each blank.

_____   _____   _____   _____

Skills: Spelling, writing and using sight vocabulary

PUTTING WORDS TOGETHER

Read the words.

up
down
over
under

Look at each picture.
Write the correct word in each blank.

_____   _____   _____   _____

Skills: Spelling, writing and using sight vocabulary

PUTTING WORDS TOGETHER

Read the words.

they   it   he   she

Look at each picture.
Write the correct word in each blank.

_____ _____ _____ _____

Skills: Spelling, writing and using sight vocabulary

PUTTING WORDS TOGETHER

Look at the picture in each sentence.
Say the word. Spell the word. Write the word.
Then read the sentence.

pig   duck   cat   dog   bird

The _____ is in the mud.

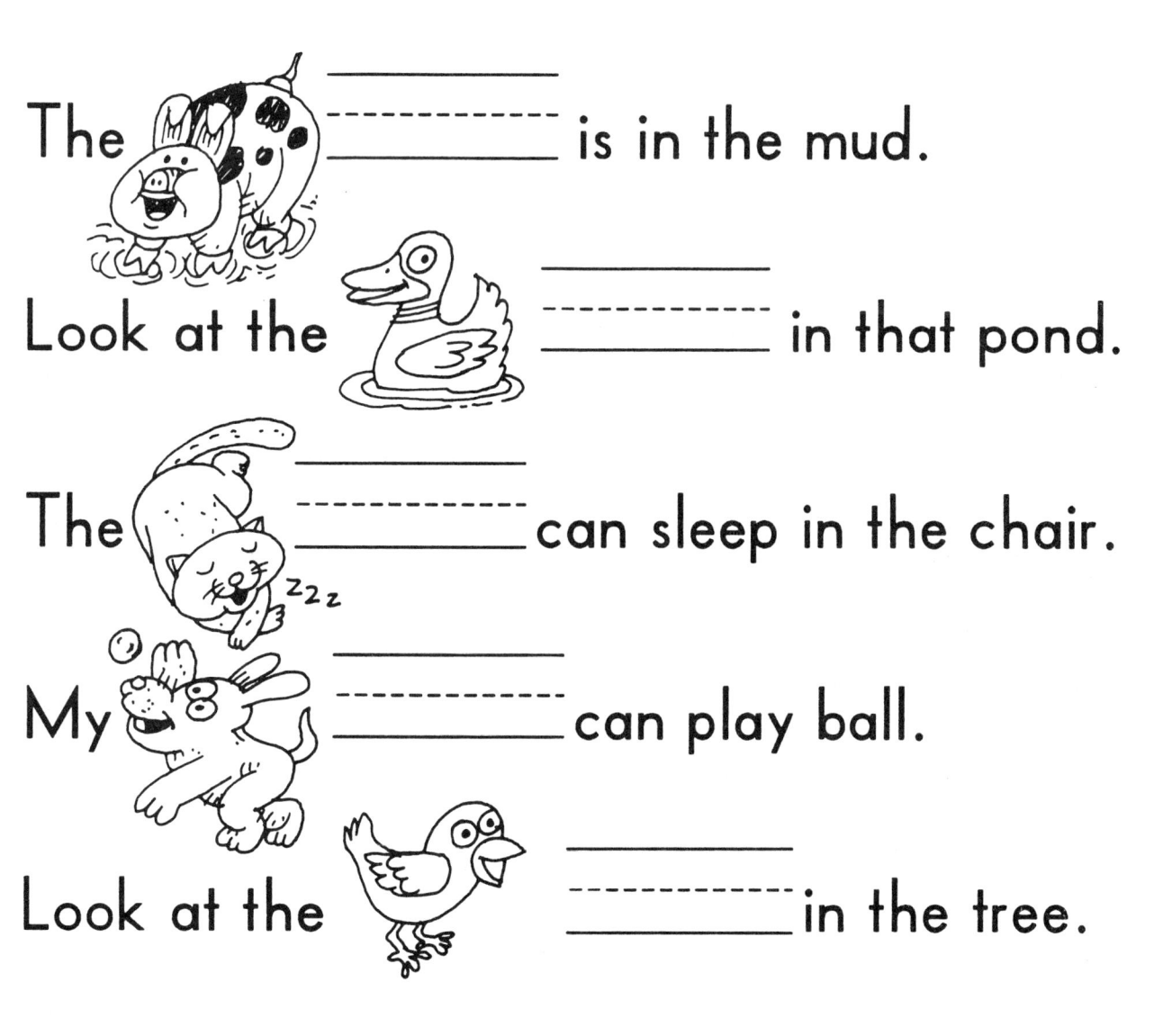

Look at the _____ in that pond.

The _____ can sleep in the chair.

My _____ can play ball.

Look at the _____ in the tree.

Skills: Spelling words in sentences

PUTTING WORDS TOGETHER

Look at the picture in each sentence.
Say the word. Spell the word. Write the word.
Then read the sentence.

car   dog   book   bus   cow

We go for a ride in the _____.

I like to play with my _____.

She reads a _____.

The _____ will come to my school.

My _____ is big.

Skills: Spelling words in sentences

PUTTING WORDS TOGETHER

Read the words.
Look at each picture.
Write the correct word in each blank.

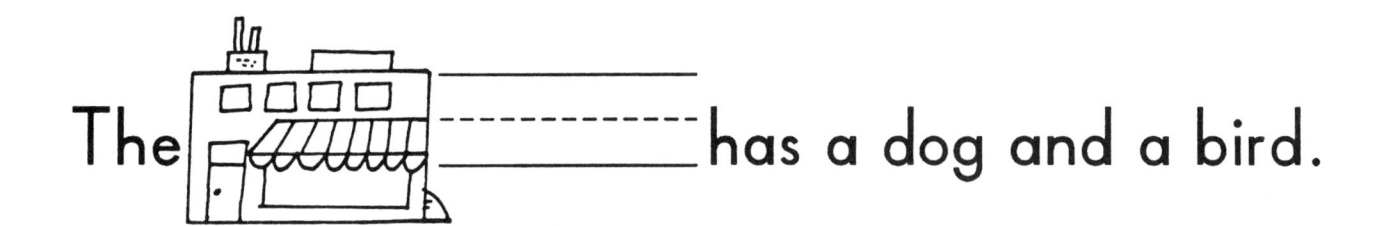

school   park   store

I play ball in the _____.

The _____ has a dog and a bird.

I can read my book at _____.

Skills: Spelling words in sentences

PUTTING WORDS TOGETHER

Use these words to complete each sentence.
Then read the sentences.

boy   happy   girl   train

The _____ has a car.

The _____ has a train.

Can I play with your _____?

The girl is _____.

Skills: Spelling words in sentences

PUTTING WORDS TOGETHER

Use these words to complete each sentence.
Then read the sentences.

cow   duck   pig   dog

The girl will feed the _____

My mother will feed the _____

Can I feed the _____ ?

The _____ will come and play.

Skills: Spelling words in sentences

PUTTING WORDS TOGETHER

Use these words to complete each sentence.
Then read the sentences.

fish
dish
bear
chair

My father and I look for _____.

We put the fish on a _____.

Do you want to sit in this _____?

Look at that big _____!

Skills: Spelling words in sentences

PUTTING WORDS TOGETHER

Use these words to complete each sentence.
Then read the sentences.

pail
sail
ball
small

The boy will put sand in the _____.

My mother will fix the _____.

Do you want to play _____ ?

We can use the ball that is _____.

Skills: Spelling words in sentences

PUTTING WORDS TOGETHER

Look at the picture.
Read the sentences.
Circle each sentence that is true.

The elephant is big.

The man has a little hat.

One clown is happy.

One clown is sad.

The dog can jump.

The girl will go up.

Skills: Using spelling words in sentences

PUTTING WORDS TOGETHER

Read each sentence.
Draw a line to match each sentence to the correct picture.

You can go in and out of this.

I can jump on this.

It can fly in the sky.

The duck can swim in it.

This is cold to eat.

Skills: Understanding sentences

PUTTING WORDS TOGETHER

Pat and Sam are getting ready for school.
Read the questions and the answers.
Circle the answer that is correct.

Can Pat take her dog to school?

Pat cannot take her dog to school.

Pat can take her dog to school.

Will Sam and Pat go on the bus?

Sam and Pat will go on the bus.

Sam and Pat will not go on the bus.

Can Sam take his book to school?

Sam can take his book to school.

Sam cannot take his book to school.

Skills: Understanding questions and answers

PUTTING WORDS TOGETHER

Read each riddle.
Write the answer beside each riddle.

duck   cow   dog

I like to eat hay.
I give milk.
Who am I? _____

I can wag my tail.
I can jump and run.
Who am I? _____

I can walk.
I can swim and fly.
Who am I? _____

Skills: Using context to answer questions; Spelling words

PUTTING WORDS TOGETHER

Read each riddle.
Write the answer beside each riddle.

bus   truck   train

I ride on tracks.
I go toot toot.
What am I?

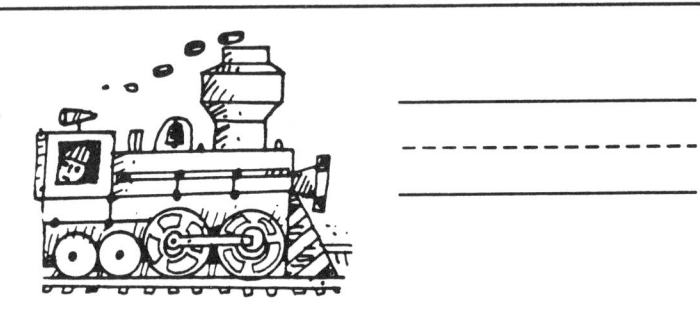

I take children to school.
I am yellow.
What am I?

I have wheels.
I carry food, toys,
and people.
What am I?

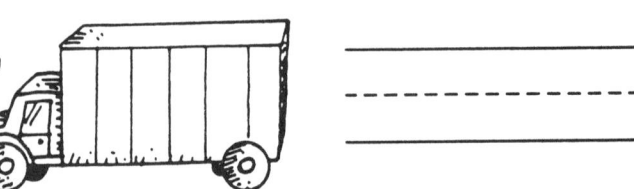

Skills: Using context to answer questions; Spelling words